Signs, Solidarities, and Sociology

Postmodern Social Futures
Edited by Stjepan Mestrovic

Ways of Escape, by Chris Rojek

Reluctant Modernity: The Institution of Art and Its Historical Forms, by Aleš
Debeljak

Feeling and Form in Social Life, by Lloyd E. Sandelands

Provocateur: Images of Women and Minorities in Advertising, by Anthony J.
Cortese

Forthcoming

Sociology after Bosnia and Kosovo, by Keith D. Doubt

*Science as Metaphor, Knowledge as Democracy: Interpreting John Dewey and
Emile Durkheim within Their Milieus,* by Donald R. LaMagdeleine

The Compassionate Temperament: Care and Cruelty in Modern Society, by
Natan Sznaider

New Forms of Consumption: Consumers, Culture, and Commodification, edited
by Mark Gottdiener

Civilization and the Human Subject, by John Mandalios

Signs, Solidarities, and Sociology

Charles S. Peirce and the Pragmatics of Globalization

Blasco José Sobrinho

ROWMAN & LITTLEFIELD PUBLISHERS, INC.
Lanham • Boulder • New York • Oxford

ROWMAN & LITTLEFIELD PUBLISHERS, INC.

Published in the United States of America
by Rowman & Littlefield Publishers, Inc.
4720 Boston Way, Lanham, Maryland 20706
www.rowmanlittlefield.com

12 Hid's Copse Road, Cumnor Hill, Oxford OX2 9JJ, England

British Library Cataloguing in Publication Information Available

Library of Congress Cataloging-in-Publication Data

Sobrinho, Blasco José, 1954–
    Signs, solidarities, and sociology : Charles S. Peirce and the pragmatics of
globalization / Blasco José Sobrinho.
        p. cm. — (Postmodern social futures)
    Includes bibliographical references and index.
    ISBN 0-8476-9178-0 (alk. paper) — ISBN 0-8476-9179-9 (pbk. : alk. paper)
        1. Peirce, Charles S. (Charles Sanders), 1839–1914. 2. Sociology—Philosophy. 3.
Globalization. 4. Pragmatism. I. Title. II. Series.

B945 .P44 S7 2001
301'.01—dc21

                                                                        2001020456

Printed in the United States of America

⊖™ The paper used in this publication meets the minimum requirements of American
National Standard for Information Sciences—Permanence of Paper for Printed Library
Materials, ANSI/NISO Z39.48-1992.

This one's for you,
Jivan Gilgamesh,
my absent eight-year-old son:
That you may appreciate the
global significance of your name,
"Gilgamesh alive!"
And that you may grow,
Insh-Allah—"God willing,"
to contribute your share
to the Universal Healing of
Tikkun Olam.

CONTENTS

ACKNOWLEDGMENTS

To the many who have in multiple ways contributed to my development of the theory of globalization presented here—a worldview that has been brewing in my mind almost all the way back to my childhood view of the then-Portuguese colony of Mozambique in East Africa—I can only offer a few words of thanks in a roughly chronological fashion.

So, beginning with Ramakant Sinari, the expert in comparative (Indian-Western) philosophy, who guided my first academic steps through my M.A. and Ph.D. degrees in philosophy in Bombay, India; to the theologian Rubem Alves, the educationalist Paulo Freire, the sociologists Francisco Weffort and Florestan Fernandes, and the philosopher of science Harvey Brown, who shaped my ideas at the Universities of São Paulo and Campinas in Brazil; to game-theorist Anatol Rapoport and computer scientist Niels Lobo at the University of Toronto; to cognitive psychologist Herbert Simon of Carnegie-Mellon University in Pittsburgh, Pennsylvania, who encouraged me to pursue my ideas about the social processes of human cognition from within the information-rich, inter-library-loan system of American universities, even if it meant pursuing a second Ph.D., I here say a heartfelt "thank you."

To globalization theorist Roland Robertson, chair, and the other members of my sociology doctoral dissertation committee—phenomenological sociologist Burkart Holzner, mathematical sociologist Patrick Doreian, and pragmatist philosopher Nicholas Rescher—at the University of Pittsburgh, who read and shaped the "first full draft" of the ideas presented here, in the form of my doctoral dissertation in sociology, titled *Agency and Power,* a doctoral dissertation that had itself reflected the influence of discussions with mathematical sociologist Harrison White, business historian Alfred Chandler, and global economists Robert Reich and Howard Raiffa at Harvard University, and sociologists Dietrich Rueschemeyer and Martin Martel at Brown University: to them and to my fellow graduate students at Pitt's sociology department, Phil Mabry, Pavarala Vinod, Joe Roidt, Jose Oviedo, and Lai-Lai-Li, who brought up the "rear guard" of informative (often late-night) discussions shaping my view of globalization, go my grateful thanks as well.

The many references to postmodern literary theorists in this book reflect my lengthy conversations with Terry Caesar, Eva Bueno, and Wayne Miller of Clarion University of Pennsylvania's Department of English, with those exchanges yielding ideas later reintegrated into the pragmatist philosophy-social science focus of this book, under the influence of philosopher Burton Porter and Maya-cultural anthropology specialist Richard Luxton of Western New England College, in Springfield, Massachusetts.

In my current position at the University of Cincinnati, my first debt of gratitude is to historians Janine Hartman, Mark Lause, Andy Villalon, Norman Murdoch, and Elisaveta Todorova, at whose monthly "faculty forum" I had first broached my unfamiliar idea about C. S. Peirce's three-step phenomenology of the cognitive act as holding the real key to the comprehension of global history, a strange idea that historian Hartman immediately referred to Durkheimian sociologist Stjepan Mestrovic, who is now my series editor at Rowman & Littlefield, the publisher of this book. To my immediate office-neighbor, philosopher Charles Seibert, goes my heartfelt thanks for nearly three years of his patient toleration of my constant interruptions to pick his brain for scholarly riches on the philosophies of Peirce and Heidegger. In this university's multidisciplinary system of committees in charge of reviewing my work, I thank sociologists Gerald Reid, Yolaine Armand, and Phillip (Neal) Ritchey, art historian Diane Mankin, psychologist Walt Griesinger, social worker Dorothy Napoli, and technical writing's Yvonne Brown, for having patiently plowed through whatever chapter section I happened to be then writing in order to submit peer-review reports on my progress to the administrative authorities here. To the pressures of these multidisciplinary peer-review committees, as well as the prompt responses of my department head, Catherine Strathern, and the college deans, John Bryan, Dan Humpert, and Terry Bullock, I owe the ready availability of resources, such as functioning printers and office computers, release time from teaching duties, and so forth, without which I could not have finished writing this book. For those more "intangible" resources of adequate time-protection from students' class-scheduling/grade record/change problems, book-order deadlines, and malfunctioning Xerox machines, I thank my fellow junior full-time sociologist, Roberta Campbell; my college's records officer, Susan Cogan; and student-advisors John (Ned) Donnelly and Molly Maher, as well as secretaries Linda Gosnell, Karen Weast, Denise Simpson-Turner, Nadine Horton-Garner, and Marjorie Pollitt. Thanks to the competent staffs of our library system's Dean David Kohl and of our computer system's Tom Wulf and Levan Skervin, I was assured ready access to the "global" pool of information that went into fashioning this comprehensive view of globalization: in those rare instances when needed texts had been delayed through the library/Internet channels, I thank Jonathan Alexander from our language arts and Joe Zins from our education college faculties, respectively, for their prompt substitution of the delayed materials with their own resources. Finally, my fellow faculty members at the University of Cincinnati, Sue Bourke and Chris Lottman, have, over the past three years, rendered indispensable indirect support to my writing efforts by helpfully rallying to preserve my precious time—especially in relation to those pressing phone-demands from my absent (heretofore) infant son regarding the latest Pokemon craze.

Which brings me to my family: my mother gave up her retirement haven in Portugal to "hold the home-fort" for me through my tough divorce and after. To her and to those members of my maternal family—my uncle Fernando, his wife Bernadette, his computer-savvy son Sanjay, and his wife Sneha, as well as to my cousin Jacinta at the University of New South Wales in Australia—I owe more thanks than words can express for the countless ways in which they helped me through my distracted days of writing.

To the editorial staff at Rowman & Littlefield—Chief Editor Dean Birkenkamp and his editorial staff of, first, Rebecca Hoogs, and then Renee Jardine, Matt Boullioun, Gretchen Hanisch, Chris Davis, and Christine Gatliffe—a million thanks for their patience and prompt responses to all my e-mailed and phoned questions of the last two years. To my series editor, Stjepan Mestrovic, I owe infinitely greater thanks beyond his editorial capacity: as I struggled to "situate" my love for the pragmatist formulations of Charles S. Peirce within sociology's traditions of classical theory, it was Stjepan's own extensive writing on Durkheim's philosophical background that encouraged my now sharp focus upon those 1913-14 lectures by Durkheim (on pragmatism and sociology) as it appears at the beginning of this book.

In the proverbial "last but not least" tradition, I can truthfully swear that but for the timely intervention of a couple of classics professors here at the University of Cincinnati, this book would surely never have been finished in a timely manner. Having first met Eric H. Cline and his wife, Diane Harris-Cline, in June 1999, I was surprised by this couple's kind, and unprecedented, offer to put aside time in their own busy professional careers and lives—even during the arrival of their second child and their impending move to another city—to informally edit and format the loose spread of my own writing into the tighter-knit book that my readers now see. While thanking all of the people mentioned in this acknowledgment, it is to Eric and Diane whom I especially say that, in dedicating this book to my own son, my hope that it may somehow contribute to a better global culture for his generation holds, most of all, for your two children as well. In a truly Biblical sentiment, I can only hope that the blessings due such generous parents as yourselves descend—multiplied a thousandfold—to your children and to your children's children.

Blasco José Sobrinho, Ph.D. (philosophy), Ph.D. (sociology)
University of Cincinnati

The completion of the soul . . . in which it takes the detour through the forma-tion of the intellectual-historical work of the species: the cultural path of the subjective spirit traverses science and the forms of life, art and state, vocation and knowledge of the world—the path on which it now returns to itself as higher and perfected spirit.

—Georg Simmel, "Die Krisis der Kultur" (1916), in
Das Individuelle Gesetz, ed. M. Landmann (Frankfurt:
Suhrkamp, 1968), 232 [quoted in Lawrence A. Scaff,
"Simmel's Theory of Culture," in *Georg Simmel and
Contemporary Sociology*, ed. M. Kaern, B.S. Phillips,
and R.S. Cohen (Boston: Kluwer Academic
Publishers, 1990): 288].

Generally, as soon as history stops being that of events, it tends to be struc-tural in that it brings out the deeper layers, which are thus more stable, slower phenomena. There is a slowing of the structures that, under the acceleration of events, provides, over time, an analogon of the synchronic. In sum, the more distance taken by the perspective, the more clearly stabilities appear. This is the lesson of long-term history, as has been demonstrated by F. Braudel, who saw the way kinship structures resist time, as shown by Levi-Strauss, a perfect example of observable phenomena recurring over centuries.

—Marcel Henaff, *Claude Levi-Strauss and
the Making of Structural Anthropology* (Minneapolis:
University of Minnesota Press, 1998), 229.

Just as many interpretations of Durkheim's development have left the earliest writings aside, so too the late works which appeared after his magnum opus on the theory of religion are often ignored. Of these, the lectures on "Pragmatism and Sociology" are worthy of mention. Regardless of precisely what motivated Durkheim to choose this theme—whether, as Robert Bellah thought, he wanted to avoid his work being confused with pragmatism, or whether, as is my con-tention, he recognized that pragmatism was the only competitor in the race to provide a theory of the social constitution of categories—these lectures . . . cannot be grasped in terms of such interpretive concepts as 'idealism' and 'positivism.'

—Hans Joas, "Durkheim's Intellectual Development:
The Problem of the Emergence of New Morality and
New Institutions as a Leitmotif in Durkheim's Oeuvre"
in *Emile Durkheim: Sociologist and Moralist*,
ed. Stephen P. Turner (London: Routledge, 1993), 242.

INTRODUCTION

Theory in a Time of Fragmentation: Toward the Fusion of Horizons

From Durkheim's Detour to Goffman's Gulch: The Need for Re-Framing Social Theory

In the winter of 1913-14—after the publication of his major work, *The Elementary Forms of the Religious Life,* and only a few years before his death— Emile Durkheim held lectures on "Pragmatism and Sociology." None of these lectures was published during his lifetime; indeed they did not appear until 1955, many decades after his death. They have been all but disregarded in the different strands which the reception of Durkheim's work has taken over the years. This is hardly surprising, considering that at the time these lectures were published pragmatism either was not highly regarded or was simply ignored, both in philosophy and in, particularly, sociology.[1]

Thus began the article by Hans Joas—originally published in French in 1984—titled "Durkheim and Pragmatism: The Psychology of Consciousness and the Social Constitution of Categories." The quotation from Joas helps frame the argument of this book in a most concise way: in order to effectively comprehend the onrushing processes of globalization in the twenty-first century, sociology has no choice but to "return to the beginning" (in the famous poetic statement of T. S. Eliot)—to that winter of 1913-14, when Durkheim wrestled with the issues of Pragmatism and sociology and misunderstood (as I will argue) the thought of Charles Sanders Peirce—so as to "know" Peirce's pragmati(ci)st methodology "for the first time."

Perhaps this book's rather strong thesis—that there can be no effective or complete sociology of globalization without incorporating the epistemological categories of Peirce's Pragmaticism[2]—can be better comprehended by introducing it here against the contrasting backdrop of the following three interrelated themes haunting the "received views" of current sociology.

Relativism: Fragmentation of the Global Picture

In the preface to his 1998 book *The Cultures of Globalization*, Fredric Jameson hails the sociologist Roland Robertson, whom he calls "one of the most ambitious theorists" of globalization for having provided "a valuable lead" in formulating "the dynamic of globalization" as "the twofold process of the particularization of the universal and the universalization of the particular." The most valuable lead I see in this formulation of the concept of globalization process by Robertson—highlighting as it does, the mutual contamination brought about by globalization, between those two hitherto sacrosanct pattern-variables of modernization theory, the subjectivistic particularism of traditional custom and the supposedly objectivistic universalism of modern legal-rationality—is its implicit problematization of the theme of relativism.[3]

The problem that relativism poses to sociological comprehension of the ongoing processes of globalization had already been very concisely stated by philosopher of anthropology Ian Charles Jarvie in the prologue to his 1984 book, *Rationality and Relativism*: whereas rationality, argued Jarvie, seemed to underlie the perceived "unity of mankind despite diverse appearances," it was relativism that seemed to "explain the *moral* unity of mankind despite diverse appearances" (italics added). The "central issue" then, as seen by Jarvie, was "how to reconcile rational and moral unity."[4]

What Jarvie saw as the "central issue" of late-twentieth-century anthropology—the reconciliation of rationality with relativism (with the latter admittedly, according to Jarvie, attempting to preserve a view of the "moral unity" of humanity)—appears also to be the central issue of any effective sociology of globalization, as is apparent in the anecdote recounted in 1999, in his polemic against the "extreme relativism" of American anthropology in the 1980s and 1990s, by the South Africa-born anthropologist Adam Kuper. Just before the release of Nelson Mandela from prison, says Kuper, Kuper had been consulted by "a distinguished American anthropologist" whose "first impulse" upon being invited by the University of Cape Town to deliver an "annual public lecture on the subject of academic freedom" had been to deliver a "classical Boasian discourse about culture." Following in the hallowed footsteps of Franz Boas, this American anthropologist had been planning to deliver at the University of Cape Town in South Africa the central message of Boasian cultural relativism: "that respect for cultural differences should be the basis of a just society." But, argues Kuper, such a relativist formulation, although a "benign argument in America, in South Africa . . . would come across as a last-ditch justification for apartheid."[5] What Canadians such as Jarvie or Kuper's "distinguished American anthropologist" see as relativism's "benign argument" on behalf of the "moral unity" of the human race, appears to South Africans as a "justification for apartheid"—a not-so-benign argument for the moral disunity of the human race! Can a sociology with a truly global vision continue to insist on pushing its ultimately provincial—i.e., Western—inheritance of relativism upon the rest of the world?

This situation of a "received view" of quasi-reflexive relativism in Western social science has been further complicated by the facile acceptance by academic sociologists in America of George Ritzer's 1975 argument that sociology is really "a multiple paradigm science." With most undergraduate textbooks in sociology now accepting Ritzer's defeatist attitude toward that unification of paradigms (not necessarily final, but tentative, as all scientific endeavor necessarily is) that any science needs for the growth and development of its research programs, we currently have sociology appearing to its next generation of practitioners as a shambles of "perspectives," thus encouraging that "perspectivism" that Steven Lukes defined in his 1982 essay, "Relativism in Its Place," as just another, more benign-sounding form of relativism.[6] That such an antithesis to the culturally unifying aim of education propounded by Emile Durkheim's *Moral Education* may be contributing to the epidemic of "personality disorders" among America's young people—by creating those very conditions of Durkheimian anomie that Durkheim expected modern education to control—is beside the point in this book on the sociology of globalization.[7] What is of cardinal importance here is to notice that in the present historical epoch when even religious fundamentalists—throughout the world—seek to legitimate their moral visions through scientific expertise,[8] this fragmentation of social theory may well defeat that goal of intercultural comprehension so important to the sociological comprehension of globalization.

Those among my readers who are familiar with the works of thinkers associated with that French intellectual movement collectively known as post-structuralism will perhaps see this book's attempt to repair this fragmentation of the global picture by contemporary Western sociology—through my excavation into the origins of sociological concepts all the way down to Durkheim's confrontation with the thought of Charles Sanders Peirce in his 1913-14 lectures—as an attempt on my part at an "archaeology of sociological knowledge" à la Michel Foucault. And such readers must surely be aware that the charge of *poststructuralist relativism* is leveled more against Foucault's later approach of genealogy than it is against his earlier method of an archaeology of knowledge.[9] It is to the attention of these readers that I offer the amazing statement from the *Collected Papers of C. S. Peirce*: "The meaning of a representation can be nothing but a representation."[10] Such a statement resembles nothing so much as it does the deconstructionist philosophy of Jacques Derrida, with its insistence on intertextuality and the pithy aphorism—*nothing outside the text*—associated with it.[11]

It is this, relatively recent, focus on the similarity between Peirce's Pragmaticism and Jacques Derrida's Deconstructionism that belies any attempt to use Peirce in any straightforwardly simplistic, antirelativistic stance. Thomas M. Olshewsky's

1994 essay "Realism and Antifoundationalism"—which brought to my attention that Derrida-like quotation from Peirce that I have just cited—goes on to argue that "this role for Peirce as the forerunner of poststructuralism gains increasing attention among literary critics at the same time that Richard Rorty rejects Peirce for his foundationalist character, and even refuses to accord to him the name that Peirce himself gave to America's most prominent philosophical movement."[12]

Rorty does not seem to say anything here that was not already said by Durkheim in ending the *First Lecture* on "The Origins of Pragmatism" in his 1913-14 course on pragmatism and sociology: "Peirce did not repudiate rationalism," argued Durkheim. "It would be more accurate to see William James as the true father of pragmatism."[13] I must nevertheless agree with Olshewsky's conclusion, "I think Peirce has been miscast in both roles," in either the role of extreme rationalist (realist) or of extreme relativist (antifoundationalist) that philosophers of anthropology such as Jarvie, or sociologists such as Martin Hollis and Steven Lukes, seem so fond of pitting against each other.[14]

The way to move, with Peirce, beyond these fruitless dichotomies is to notice the statement—which could have emerged from Talcott Parsons's functionalist sociology—made by that current expositor of the thought of Peirce, Nicholas Rescher: "All (or virtually all) human enterprises are at bottom teleological—conducted with some sort of end or objective in view." Therefore, argues Rescher, "The Achilles' heel of relativism lies in the fact that inquiry is a purposive enterprise and that some modes of *procedure* among the available possibilities will serve our *purpose better* than others"[15] (italics added).

Or, as illustrated in the beautiful example furnished by Christopher Norris of "aerodynamics as a test-case" for relativism, the end, or objective, that many self-professing academic relativists have in view these days of traveling across vast continents or oceans—on the way, possibly, to reading a paper denying the absolute nature of truth at a fashionably relativist academic conference—makes them (at least temporarily!) abandon their relativist mindsets, so as to ease their anxiety or fear of flying, by believing in the absolute truth of the laws of aerodynamics during their flight time within a modern airplane![16] But, by sliding into the antirelativist arguments of Rescher and Norris—both of whom are practicing philosophers of science—I have in fact already slid into my second overall theme, that of the impact of the philosophy of science upon contemporary sociology.

The Fragmenting Impact of the Philosophy of Science

The postpositivist (or postempiricist) revolution in the philosophy of science that followed upon the work of Karl Popper and Willard Van Orman Quine has so far, apparently, only added to the fragmentation of social theory. Joas lists contemporary social theorists—ranging from Jeffrey Alexander to Anthony Giddens, Jurgen Habermas, and Niklas Luhmann—who have delved into the maelstrom of current postpositivist philosophical debates to create more robust theoretical frameworks in social science. But I share with Joas the suspicion that all these hitherto attempted solutions to the fragmentation of social theory are at best only partial solutions, whose clashing visions have only exacerbated the existing fragmentation, because they have not sufficiently addressed that historical ghost that haunts all contemporary postpositivist or postempiricist philosophy, the philosophical tradition of Pragmatism.[17]

It is in fact the analysis of contemporary philosophy of science in this book's chapter 4, through a Peircean optic, that leads me to "epistemologize" Roland Robertson's theory of globalization—as "the twofold process of the particularization of the universal and the universalization of the particular"[18]—into its more cognitivist variant as "the ongoing double process of the subjectivization of objectivity and the objectification of subjectivity."

The Crisis of Pragmatism Itself

How could so many intelligent and well-informed readers—from William James in 1896 to Emile Durkheim in 1913, down to Richard Rorty in 1979—have "misunderstood" the writings of Charles Sanders Peirce?

According to our contemporary, the philosopher of science and Peirce scholar Nicholas Rescher, the philosophical movement known as Pragmatism has itself been "in crisis" since its beginning. This "crisis"—between the interpretations of its two early exponents, Peirce and James—which Rescher in 1997 saw haunting Pragmatism from its beginning, had already been clearly perceived by Durkheim in 1913. In the *First* and *Second Lectures* of his course "Pragmatism and Sociology," Durkheim had immediately pointed out how Peirce—whom he saluted as "the first thinker to use the word 'pragmatism'"—had by 1905 "sufficiently and explicitly dissociated himself from James's interpretations" by changing the name of his own thought from Pragmatism to Pragmaticism (the latter name being, according to Peirce—as reported by Durkheim—"ugly enough to be safe from kidnappers").What seemed to puzzle Durkheim was that, despite such a "sufficient and explicit" rebuff by Peirce as early as 1902, in Peirce's article in J. M. Baldwin's *Dictionary of Philosophy and Psychology*, James had continued to use Peirce's original term, Pragmatism, as was clear from the title that James had chosen for his 1907 book, and had continued to declare—in his 1909 book, which Durkheim cites—that he "shares Peirce's ideas." Of this seemingly unrequited loyalty of James for Peirce—despite the fact that by the 1909 publication of James's book *The Meaning of Truth*, it had been clear that James held to a relativist account of truth, whereas, as Durkheim pointed out, "Peirce did not repudiate rationalism"—Durkheim commented that it was "rather curious that James has continued to call himself his (Peirce's) disciple, has saluted him as the father of Pragmatism and has never pointed out these differences."[19]

The problem, according to Rescher, was that "for Peircean pragmatism's generalized concern with 'what works for anyone' (for humans in general) by impersonal standards they substituted a subjectivistic egocentrism of what 'works out' for us—those of some limited in-group—in our subjective evaluation." Rescher goes on to clearly identify "them"—those who had betrayed Peirce's aim of providing a "theoretical basis for cognitive objectivity"—as the "postmodern theorists from William James to Richard Rorty."[20]

The crucial question for the historian of sociological theory then becomes: Why did Durkheim not see in 1913 what Nicolas Rescher could see so clearly in 1997? Why did Durkheim so cavalierly brush aside the Pragmatist thinker closest to his own "generalized concern" for the larger human community—namely, Charles Sanders Peirce—to identify "Pragmatism" instead solely with the individualist/subjectivist/relativist thought of William James (which was, unlike Peirce's, clearly antithetical to his own)?

That Durkheim had, in his 1913-14 lectures, unambiguously chosen to identify what he called "Pragmatism" solely with the philosophy of James (apparently taking Peirce at his 1905 word, that despite having priority in coining the word he would henceforth label his own thought as Pragmaticism) seems crystal clear in even a cursory reading of the published version of those *Lectures*—as clear as the relativist disregard for truth that Durkheim then condemns in such (Jamesian) Pragmatism. Despite admitting in his *First Lecture* that "there is an essential difference" between the philosophy of Peirce and the "pragmatism" of William James in that "Peirce admits, following the classical theory, that truth imposes itself with a kind of 'inevitability' before which the mind can only bow" and that "consequently, when William James' works were later published, Peirce refused to ally himself with him, and insisted on pointing out the differences between them," Durkheim summarily dismissed such respect for truth, shown by Peirce, as a variant of "rationalism" and "the exact opposite of the pragmatist principle" and proceeded to proclaim, "It would be more accurate to see James as the true father of pragmatism."[21]

Although he specifically cited Peirce's article "What Pragmatism Is" in his *First Lecture*—in order to disclose his source for Peirce's decision to change the name of his philosophy from *Pragmatism* to *Pragmaticism*—Durkheim reinforced his decision to exclude Peirce's thought from his consideration of the meaning of Pragmatism in his *Second Lecture* by the surprising declaration that "Peirce used the word only in private talk," whereas James, according to Durkheim, had by 1907 used it as the title of his book and had by 1909 even obtained public recognition of his right to this term at "Oxford, the citadel of Hegelianism." Taking James at his word, when he supposedly declared in his 1909 book *The Meaning of Truth* that "he shares Peirce's ideas," that "Schiller recognizes James as his master," and that "Dewey, although he expresses some reservations, differs from James mainly on particular points," Durkheim had declared, in his *Second Lecture*, that there was "therefore, an identical orientation in all three" and that it was "not impossible to discover" Pragmatism's "basic theses and to find a common ground in them."[22]

That the "common ground" found by Durkheim, among the different exponents of "Pragmatism," turns out to be identical with that common ground—of a relativistic "subjectivistic egocentrism" so antithetical to Peirce's "cognitive objectivity"—found by Nicholas Rescher in the "postmodern theorists from William James to Richard Rorty," emerges with utmost clarity with those three "positive theses of pragmatism" enumerated by Durkheim in his Sixth Lecture:

1. Truth is human.
2. It is varied and variable.
3. It cannot be a copy of a given reality.[23]

This relativistic formulation about the nature of truth, which though pleasing to many "Pragmatists" such as James and Rorty[24] would have been seen as alien and false by Peirce—as Durkheim himself had recognized in his First Lecture and as his full course of twenty lectures on "Pragmatism and Sociology" delivered in the winter of 1913-14 attests—it was repugnant to Durkheim, too.

Now, at the end of the twentieth century, that leading philosopher of science and avowed Pragmatist, Rescher, calls for a return of Pragmatism to its "Peircian Roots" if it is to emerge from its "crisis" of post-James multiple definitions. And for social science to emerge from its current crisis of multiple paradigms, the present book would have it return to its roots in that central insight of the nonrelativistic social construction of meaning (not truth, as the relativistic interpretation of Pragmatism, from James to Rorty, would have it!) common to both Durkheim and Peirce. But for that Durkheim-Peirce commonality of vision to be clearly apparent, I must first further analyze both the reason for, and the consequences of, "Durkheim's detour"—from Peirce to James, in his study of Pragmatism—so as to attempt the completion of that project that Hans Joas sees Durkheim as having embarked upon "after the publication of his last major work, The Elementary Forms of the Religious Life, and only a few years before his death"—of providing social science with "a theory of the social constitution of categories" which "cannot be grasped in terms of such interpretive concepts as 'idealism' and 'positivism.'"[25]

Sociologist and Durkheim scholar Stjepan Mestrovic has consistently argued that the received view of Durkheim as an early positivist turned later idealist, put forward by American Functionalism and Neofunctionalism, is not only simplistic but false. He has been joined in this critique of Talcott Parsons's and Jeffrey Alexander's conception of Durkheim's methodological vision—as changing discontinuously from a supposed positivism in his 1893 writing of The Division of Labor in Society to the supposedly full-blown idealism of his 1912 The Elementary Forms of the Religious Life—by philosopher of science Warren Schmaus, whose analysis of Durkheim's intellectual development from his 1893 to his 1912 writings reveals—against the positivist-to-idealist metamorphosis proposed by Parsons and Alexander—an approach that developed John Stuart Mill's methods of elimination and Francis Bacon's notion of a crucial test "further," that is, beyond a positivistic empiricism which Durkheim considered anti-scientific "obscurantism . . . leading to irrationalism" to what is today called "scientific realism."[26] "Durkheim's beliefs about scientific method," argues Schmaus, "actually resemble Karl Popper's method of bold conjectures and severe tests more than the inductivist views of Popper's logical positivist opponents," with the method used in the 1897 study Suicide even resembling Peirce's method of abduction.[27]

This "narrowing down" of Durkheim's legacy is carried to even more absurd lengths in the average American textbook for introductory sociology, where Durkheim is pegged in the Functionalist corner with Karl Marx and Max Weber representing the "Conflict" perspective (and with Weber often sharing credit for the microperspective of Symbolic Interactionism with Charles Horton Cooley and George Herbert Mead). To claim that Durkheim ignored social conflict and change—even if only for a quick introductory synopsis of "The Classical Founding Fathers" for college freshmen—does violence to the vision of The Division of Labor section explaining professional specialization as a quasi-Darwinian product of conflict and competition among hitherto nonspecializing generalists.[28] In fact, all three books analyzed by Schmaus have Durkheim focusing on social conflict, with Suicide showing a pre-Freudian comprehension of the drastic consequences to the individual personality that stem from the internalization of unresolved social conflict (a comprehension of conflict internalization that today's "family therapists" would applaud).[29] In his last major book, The Elementary Forms of the Religious Life, Durkheim took this social mechanism of conflict-resolution to a wholly new level, as he saw the function of the Sacred time-and-place modulating and controlling the accumulated social conflicts of the Profane work a day week. It is this view of "Durkheim's paradigm" as being one of "conflict resolution" that perhaps best illustrates—for the non-philosophy-specialist—the conceptual kinship with Peirce.

Peirce's philosophy, as introduced to us by Christopher Hookway, begins with Peirce's 1868 list of "four denials." According to Peirce:

1. We have no power of introspection, but all knowledge of the internal world is derived by hypothetical reasoning from external facts.
2. We have no power of intuition, but every cognition is determined logically by previous cognitions.
3. We have no power of thinking without signs.
4. We have no conception of the absolutely incognizable.[30]

This list of Peirce's "four denials" is important to us here because it provides us with four points at which to compare Peirce's thought with that of Durkheim. Stjepan Mestrovic has criticized contemporary sociological theorists such as Anthony Giddens for propounding what Mestrovic calls the conception of "unlimited agency"—the delusion that human beings as subjective actors are privy to unlimited "knowledge" about all their motives for action and are therefore "competent" agents. This delusion of "unlimited agency," Mestrovic has argued, contradicts Durkheim's insistence that the structure of society is experienced by the individual as an external constraint.[31] Peirce's 1868 list of denials displays a convincing similarity—if not complete identity—with Durkheim's insistence upon society's manifestation to the individual consciousness as an external constraint, in that for Peirce, those "four denials" outlined four clear ways by which agency is limited. We may then address, in turn, each of the four ways—so as to compare each of the four with Durkheim's thinking—that Peirce outlined in 1868 by which each individual agent/knower lacks the power:

1. to introspect, except by hypothetical reasoning from external facts—a lack of introspective power that Durkheim showed his awareness of as early as 1895, when in chapter 3 of his *Rules of Sociological Method* he had argued that crime was "inevitable" in all societies, even in a "community of saints in an exemplary and perfect monastery," where "faults that appear venial to the ordinary person will arouse the same scandal as does normal crime in ordinary consciences" because such an "external" sanctioning of the "criminal" serves an essentially "internal" cognitive function of marking a moral boundary that is not to be trespassed.[32]
2. to intuit, except as determined logically by previous cognitions. It looks like a similar assumption about the limitation on the power of individual intuition could have prompted Durkheim toward the end of his working life, to take that step which has puzzled scholars: to seek comprehension of religion in its earliest, i.e., most "elementary" or "primitive," forms.
3. to think, except through signs. In defining his key concept of the *sign*, Peirce insisted that it could only exist in a triadic condition: to be a *sign* there necessarily had to exist "a genuine triadic relation" between itself, an object, and an *interpretant*, a "Peircean" insight apparent in Durkheim's emphasis on the "force" or "power" of collective representations on individual thought.[33]
4. to conceive the absolutely incognizable. Social scientists may be familiar on this point with Durkheim's identification of such metaphysical incognizables as the soul or God, with the felt, experienced religious force of the community itself, but may be unfamiliar with the very similar identification by Peirce of the conception of "the whole people" with the "Spirit of God."[34]

In the light of such an amazingly high—nay, almost total—convergence between Durkheim and Peirce, in their nonindividualistic, communal orientations in their respective theorizing about signs or collective representations, it is a disorienting experience to reread such a standard "American sociology text" discussing Durkheim and Pragmatism as Gregory Stone and Harvey Faberman's 1967 essay, "On the Edge of Rapprochement: Was Durkheim Moving toward the Perspective of Symbolic Interaction?" Starting with what we have seen is the totally false assumption of the identity between the Pragmatist philosophies of Charles Peirce and William James, Stone and Faberman proceed, through a study of the metaphors used by Durkheim in his writing, to develop another version of the *Division of Labor/Elementary Forms* split—different from the "positivist vs. idealist" dichotomies that Parsons and Alexander had imposed upon Durkheim—of Durkheim's intellectual development.[35]

Durkheim's earlier writing, *The Division of Labor*, first published in 1893, for example, is filled, according to Stone and Faberman, with metaphors from natural science—metaphors such as density, volume, and so forth—which suggest, argue Stone and Faberman, that Durkheim had, at that early phase of his career, conceived of society as a quasi-mechanical container of passive, quasi-inert human particles. But in his later writing, *The Elementary Forms of the Religious Life* first published in 1912, for example, "Durkheim begins," argue Stone and Faberman, "to see the contained as the creator of the container." One can hardly help but notice that such a turn of phrase—*creator of the container*—suggests that hubristic vision of "unlimited agency" which Mestrovic excoriates—from a Durkheimian point of view—in the writings of Anthony Giddens. Like Giddens, Stone and Faberman seem to have fallen victim to the hubris so characteristic of Western sociology in the second half of the twentieth century![36]

While, to their credit, recognizing that William James's "subjective pragmatism was unacceptable to Durkheim" and that G. H. Mead's "social, shared, and objective" Mind might have been more acceptable "had it been made explicit to him at the time," Stone and Faberman then expose the conceptual confusion underlying their own thinking—and that of the whole school of thought, begun by Herbert Blumer, known as "Symbolic Interactionism"—by attributing to Mead, and by implication to that philosophical movement known as "Pragmatism" within which they include the thought of Peirce, a conception of "pragmatic truth."[37]

But, as Durkheim was clearly aware in the 1913 *First Lecture* of his 1913-14 course on "Pragmatism and Sociology," for Charles Sanders Peirce, the founder of Pragmatism, there was absolutely no such thing as that "pragmatic truth" that Stone and Faberman impute to Mead! And it is against such a "crisis" of confusion in our current understanding of Pragmatism caused by James's misreading of Peirce's "Pragmatic Maxim"—which, as stated in Peirce's *Collected Papers* (5.467 and 5.9), was clearly intended by Peirce to be a theory of meaning (as the "sum total of its consequences") and not of truth (as James had mistakenly assumed, and then popularized, to the lasting damage of popular understanding of Pragmatism!)—as a Jamesian theory of truth as "what works" (which is apparently what Stone and Faberman mean by "pragmatic truth"), that the Peirce scholar Nicholas Rescher calls for a return of Pragmatism to its "Peircean roots." Rescher clearly identifies what he means when he speaks of the *Peircean roots of Pragmatism* by enumerating its "four key features":

- It adopts an objectivistic stance that averts the fragmentation of subjectivistic relativism.
- It is geared universalistically to the needs and interests of the human community at large and not just to some small-scale contingently constituted subgrouping (let alone the idiosyncratic preferences of individuals).
- Accordingly, it locates the crux for the quality control of our cognitive proceedings not in the sphere of diversified human wishes and desires but in the impersonal dealings of nature in their (often unwelcome) impact upon us. Pragmatic "success" here pivots on the impersonal issue of functional efficacy in the achievement of project-determined objectives, something that we clearly do not make up as we go along but that lies in the objective nature of things.
- Finally, it places an emphasis on impersonally normative rationality that enables it to implement the pursuit of objectivity.[38]

Durkheim himself, as is evident from his polemic against the relativistic subjectivism of the "Pragmatism" of William James in his lecture series "Pragmatism and Sociology," would have had no quarrel with this four-point "Peircean" program of objectivism presented by Rescher. Why then—given this convergence between his thought and that of Peirce, which I have demonstrated here by comparing Peirce's 1868 "four denials" with Durkheim's thinking—did Durkheim himself not recognize his philosophical kinship with Peirce? Why did he persist in identifying James as "the true father of Pragmatism" before lambasting the Jamesian version of "Pragmatism . . . as a theory of truth"?[39]

Hans Joas follows the lead provided by Durkheim himself—within the first three paragraphs of his *First Lecture* on the "origins of pragmatism"—by listing three possible reasons why Durkheim had approached "pragmatism as an armed struggle *against reason*."

- First—the most general reason of all—Durkheim viewed pragmatism as a source of danger because, more than any other doctrine, it was able to seek out the vulnerable points of rationalism, as it is commonly understood, and to make use of them for its own ends.
- Second, it was in the national interest to counteract an erosion of French culture, of which Cartesian thought was an essential component.
- Finally, an argument based on a philosophical interest in perpetuating the tradition that had persisted virtually throughout the history of philosophy—Pragmatism threatened the belief that true knowledge is possible. Durkheim saw it as a form of irrationalism that resembled Greek sophistry, its only benefit being the salutary pressure it brought to rouse philosophical thought from the "dogmatic slumber" into which it had relapsed after Immanuel Kant.[40]

Having already declared, in his *First Lecture* on "Pragmatism and Sociology," that "Peirce admits . . . that truth imposes itself with a kind of 'inevitability'
before which the mind can only bow" and that for Peirce "truth . . . possesses intrinsic rights, and all investigators are *obliged* to accept it," Durkheim could obviously not have meant to apply that third reason—what Joas describes as the suspicion "that pragmatism threatened the belief that true knowledge is
possible"—to the philosophy of Peirce. We can also be certain that—despite his
insistence that Peirce was *not* a Pragmatist because his nonrelativist respect for
objective truth "is the exact opposite of the pragmatist principle"—Durkheim's
understanding of Peirce's theory of knowledge was accurate because Durkheim
cited as his source the January 1879 translation into French—in the *Revue
Philosophique de la France et de l'Etranger* with the title "Comment rendre nos
idees claires"—of Peirce's article first published in January 1878 "in an American journal." The fact that the *Revue Philosophique* also carried an essay by
Peirce in the immediately preceding issue, December 1878 (on pp. 553-69), with
the title "Comment se fixe la croyance"—and that Durkheim also cited (in his
First Lecture) Peirce's 1902 article in Baldwin's *Dictionary* and also Peirce's
1905 article "What Pragmatism Is" in *The Monist*—certainly indicates
Durkheim's familiarity with some of Peirce's writings. It seems fair to assume,
however—in light of the fact that even a philosopher as erudite as Bertrand Russell had, in his 1910 essay on "William James' Conception of Truth," displayed
his apparent ignorance about Peirce having made the same objection to the relativism of James as he was then making, and that unearthing Peirce's voluminous
writings for publication is still an ongoing industry at the beginning of the
twenty-first century—that philosopher of science Warren Schmaus is probably
correct when he argues that "judging from Durkheim's lectures on pragmatism,
however, he seems to have been unfamiliar with Peirce's writings on scientific
method, identifying pragmatism largely with William James's theory of truth."[41]

The second reason cited by Joas for Durkheim's fixation on Jamesean Pragmatism—the defense of Cartesian rationalism on patriotic grounds—seems a bit
surprising, given his previous attacks on Cartesian rationalism, and can best be
understood only in the political climate of the time of the "Pragmatism and Sociology" lectures, the winter of 1913-14, when the mounting tensions with neighboring Germany, soon to break out into World War I, made it politically wise for
Durkheim to emphasize his very real preference for, but not total agreement with,
the "Cartesian" tradition of French rationality over the German penchant for irrationalism so evident at the time in Friedrich Nietzsche's writings and in German
romanticism. I will therefore focus—both in the larger body of this book, chapters
1-4, and in the second and third sections of this introductory chapter—on how
Peirce's version of Pragmatism, which Durkheim's *First Lecture* had accused of
"not repudiating rationalism," specifically stands up to the test of that first reason
cited by Joas, for Durkheim's ambivalent fascination with (and repulsion toward)
the ability of Pragmatism to "seek out the vulnerable points of rationalism."[42]

But before I proceed to this deeper exposition of Peirce's Pragmatism—to facilitate comprehension of my attempted cross-fertilization between the Durkheimian and Peircean theoretical projects, toward the development of a truly global sociology—our own historical epoch in the history of sociological theory might be better highlighted by a brief look beyond Durkheim's detour on his 1913-14 theoretical approach toward Peircean Pragmatism to the exitless gulch into which his more recent follower, Erving Goffman, plunged.

According to Randall Collins, "Goffman shifted the focus of Durkheimian theory from the macro to the micro level." Goffman's biographer, Philip Manning, considers Goffman's ideas to be "central to modern sociology," while asserting that "for his supporters it is the tension between his attempt to develop a theory of social interaction and his doubts that such a theory exists that makes his work so provoking." He traces Goffman's "Durkheimian" focus all the way back to the third section of his unpublished University of Chicago Ph.D. dissertation in 1953, "Communication Conduct in an Island Community," wherein Goffman alluded to Durkheim's *Elementary Forms of the Religious Life* in his statement that "an idol is to a person as a rite is to etiquette" and asserted that "etiquette is the islanders' right to expect unquestioned access to each other; it is a bond of allegiance, revealing one of the ways that the *conscience collective* limits game-theoretic approaches to social life."[43]

I found it particularly fascinating therefore—in my current role as excavator of the roots of sociological theory (so as to better expose the hidden assumptions that blight the prospects for a truly global sociology)—that Goffman's attempt to theorize the microsociology of interaction should have so closely paralleled the theoretical trajectory of Emile Durkheim at the macrosociological level. For, having begun in his dissertation with that critique of utilitarianism so similar to Durkheim's—for those "game-theoretic approaches to social life" whose "limits" Goffman plumbed are based on similar utilitarian assumptions as the theories of Herbert Spencer and those other economists that Durkheim had critiqued in 1893 in *The Division of Labor*—Goffman also ended his life, like Durkheim, with an interest in the tradition of Pragmatism, as shown by his posthumously published article, "Felicity's Condition," in the July 1983 issue of the *American Journal of Sociology* (Goffman died in 1982).[44]

Goffman's choice of title for this article—"Felicity's Condition"—was a play on the famous "felicity conditions" that the philosopher of language John Austin had specified as necessary for conversational interaction to occur. I will, in the next section of this introduction, analyze in greater detail how the *Pragmatic Maxim* of Charles Peirce led—via the acceptance by Rudolf Carnap and the Logical Positivists of Charles Morris's threefold split of Peirce's program of Semiotics into the separate disciplines of Syntax, Semantics, and Pragmatics—to the work in the Pragmatics of communicational meaning of Austin and H. Paul Grice. Suffice it for now to notice that it is to this work of Austin and Grice—in defining the conditions that facilitate human communication—that Goffman referred when, in the abstract of his July 1983 article, he declared his intention to "review the relevance and limitations of a scattering of near-recent work in sociolinguistics, pragmatics, and conversational analysis with respect to a central issue in the sociological interaction: the taken-for-granted and the inferences made therefrom." In an interesting (possibly unintended) echo of Durkheim's similar hope, expressed in the very first paragraph of his *First Lecture*—the hope for a mutual reinforcement and cross-fertilization between sociology and those other disciplines also studying the human construction of meaning—Goffman's abstract ended with "the hope" that "the line between micro sociological studies and sociolinguistics can be shown to be arbitrary, requiring those on each side of the division to address the concerns of those on the other side."[45]

But, just as Durkheim's hopes for a cross-fertilization between sociology and Pragmatist philosophy in comprehending the social construction of the categories of human knowledge beyond the received dichotomies of idealism and materialism had faded by 1913 into his critique of William James, so did Goffman's similar hopes of mutual interdisciplinary support between sociology and the Pragmatics of sociolinguistics also fade seventy years later, as Goffman declared, referring to the Pragmatics of Austin and Grice, that "the whole approach might strike the sociologist as somewhat optimistic, if not silly." After a brief examination of Austin's "felicity conditions," Goffman peremptorily offered his own "definition of the felicity condition behind all other felicity conditions, namely *Felicity's Condition*: to wit, any arrangement which leads us to judge the individual's acts to be not a manifestation of strangeness. Behind Felicity's Condition is our sense of what it is to be sane."[46]

Now, even a minimally alert reader familiar with Goffman's fellow micro-sociologist Thomas Scheff's definition of *insanity* as "residual rule breaking" should be able to recognize Goffman's "Felicity Condition" for the grand tautology—a logically circular definition—that it really is. For if, as Goffman's biographer Manning has it, Goffman's "Felicity's Condition is the requirement to demonstrate the sanity behind our actions," then what it really boils down to is the tautological statement that the *rules of interaction require us to demonstrate that we are not rule breakers*! The theoretical journey begun by "Durkheim's detour" from Peirce in 1913-14 ended with the "Durkheimian" Goffman stuck in a tautological gulch in 1983![47]

It is worth noting here—in order to comprehend just how abject the poverty of current Western sociological theory really is, and thereby to appreciate the pressing need for that marriage between the theoretical traditions of Durkheim and of Peirce that I am proposing—that what I have chosen to call "Goffman's gulch" here could also be termed "Giddens's gulch," for, in acknowledging that "Goffman offers an incomplete account of rule-following," Manning looks for salvation to that "one attempt to develop a general theory of 'the structure of social life'" which "thrusts Goffman to the center of contemporary debates about the relationship between structure and agency," the "structuration theory developed by Anthony Giddens." Referring to the "approach enshrined in Durkheim's

Rules of Sociological Method, where rules (called 'social facts') are thought to be independent constraints on the people who follow them," Manning argues that, though "for the most part, Goffman assumed that rules are primarily constraints," he also "emphasized the limitations of the Durkheimian idea that rules are constraints governing behavior." He therefore concludes that a completion of Goffman's incomplete theoretical project involves the recognition "that a Durkheimian view of rules and external constraints is misleading" and that "sophisticated analyses of social life have shown that rule-following is an activity that is achieved in interaction by participants who are knowledgeable about both the rules they should follow and their own ability to manipulate these rules." The theoretical recognition of such knowledgeability is found by Manning in the structuration theory of Giddens.[48]

Stjepan Mestrovic's critique of the thought of Anthony Giddens—which, according to Mestrovic propounds a theory of "unlimited agency"—hinges on just such a conception, by Giddens, of "knowledgeable" agents. If as insightful an observer of social life as Erving Goffman, whose whole career was dedicated to the observation and analysis of rule-following in everyday interactions, could not in his final statement of "the felicity condition behind all other felicity conditions" even sum up his life's work without falling into the meaningless tautology of asserting that rule-following consists—in the demonstration of sanity—in not breaking rules, then suffice it for me to say here that such claims by contemporary sociological theory about "knowledgeability" on the part of most agents in modern society—whose busy lives do not include the leisure time for reflection so conspicuously consumed by academic experts such as Goffman—appear to be only unwarranted assumptions.[49]

Pragmaticism: The Scientific Realist Completion of Durkheim's Project

If I am to accomplish my proposed marriage of Durkheim's and Peirce's intellectual projects, so as to achieve a more robust theoretical edifice which can comprehend globalization, I must now address the nature of Durkheim's method of inquiry. Against the received view propounded by Talcott Parsons in 1937 in *The Structure of Social Action* (and supported by Jeffrey Alexander in 1982-83 in his *Theoretical Logic in Sociology)*—that Durkheim had gradually moved from being a positivist in his 1893 *Division of Labor* writing to being an idealist in his 1912 *Elementary Forms of the Religious Life*—Warren Schmaus asserts in his recent book, *Durkheim's Philosophy of Science*, that "Durkheim's beliefs about scientific method actually resemble Karl Popper's method of bold conjectures and severe tests more than the inductivist views of Popper's logical positivist opponents."[50]

What Schmaus here calls "Karl Popper's method of bold conjectures and severe tests," a philosophy of science also referred to as *falsificationism* or *hypo-*

thetico-deductive methodology, had been crafted by Popper as a response to David Hume's famous analysis of the causal relationship. Hume had argued in the eighteenth century that if one held to the method of *empirical observation* propounded by John Locke (and supported by Isaac Newton), such a method could yield absolutely no knowledge of our idea of force—either externally, as had hitherto been assumed to have been the relationship between cause and effect, or even internally, as analogue to observation of our personal, individual wills. Since the force that empirical science assumed the cause to be exerting on the effect in every assertion of causation could not itself be empirically observed, Hume had argued, the method of reasoning by induction employed by science— by which the observed "conjunction" between two immediately succeeding events was generalized into a causal law—was of dubious logical validity. It fell to Popper, the philosopher of natural science, to respond to Hume's eighteenth-century challenge—in the second half of the twentieth century!—by accepting positivist methods of inductive verification to be invalid and proposing instead that science proceeded by "conjectures and refutations," with the scientific generalizations of causal law being only "conjectures" awaiting the "refutations," or falsification, of empirical observation.[51]

But, as Schmaus points out, in 1912—much earlier than Karl Popper—Emile Durkheim's *Elementary Forms of the Religious Life* had already provided a different kind of response to Hume's empiricist challenge. We do indeed experience force, argued Durkheim, but not through either external observation nor through internal experience of one's individual will—Hume was right on both those counts, said Durkheim—but through a third possibility ignored by Hume: the social force of religious ritual manifested in our internal experience. Without such understanding of the social origin of our knowledge of force, the whole philosophical tradition of *empiricism*—dating from Locke's famous assertion that all knowledge emerged from experience—could treat scientific laws of causation only as "purely artificial constructions." Empiricism, charged Durkheim, resulted in irrationalism.[52]

On the other hand, Schmaus confirms Stjepan Mestrovic's claim that Durkheim's method was a "renovated rationalism," in that, while Durkheim "accepted what he called the 'rationalist postulate' that 'there is nothing in reality that one may be justified in considering as radically refractory to human reason,'" he also "criticized what he called Cartesianism for overlooking the role of observation and experiment and attempting to reduce all of science to a universal mathematics."[53]

It is in the light of this double dissatisfaction with the two main philosophical approaches—positivistic empiricism and Cartesian rationalism—available to him in early twentieth-century France, that Durkheim seems to have approached what Karl-Otto Apel, our contemporary German philosopher and Peirce interpreter, has called the "constructivism" of Pragmatist philosophy. Apel traced this "constructivism" back to Immanuel Kant's equation of *knowing* with *making*, as in the formula "we can only understand what we could also have made if the material were given to us." Steven Lukes's biography of Durkheim identified him as a Kantian—

an identification apparently substantiated, if one is to believe the notes taken by one M. Marcel Tardy during his course on "Pragmatism and Sociology," by Durkheim's own words—and this identification has been accepted by Anthony Giddens and by many other English-speaking sociologists but has also been strongly denied by Mestrovic and by Schmaus, who cites Durkheim's 1909 statement in his essay "Sociologie religieuse et theorie de la connaissance" (Sociology of religion and the theory of knowledge) that for the Kantians "the categories preform the real, whereas for us, they recapitulate it. According to them, they are the natural law of thought; for us they are the product of human artifice."[54]

As the title of Durkheim's *Tenth Lecture* of his "Pragmatism and Sociology" course, "Constructing Reality and Constructing Truth," shows, Durkheim's attention had indeed been drawn to that element in the philosophy of Pragmatism that Apel has called "constructivism." But, of course, because the "Pragmatism" he was examining was the individualist version of William James—with the individual construction of reality leading to relativistic consequences for the concept of objective truth—we can still see, in the published version of that *Tenth Lecture*, Durkheim's doubt—despite his assertion that "our attitude toward the universe can no longer be the doctrinaire and authoritarian attitude of rationalism"—whether the "happy-go-lucky" attitude of that Jamesean pragmatism can really carry us "from individual to impersonal truth." The question arises, says Durkheim, "If the personal and affective factor plays such a major role, should we not conclude that truth is essentially individual and consequently incommunicable and untranslatable, since translating it means expressing it in concepts and thus impersonally?"[55]

Having thus raised—in the winter of 1913—the "translatability" issue later so prominent in the post-empiricist philosophy of W. V. O. Quine, Durkheim still lacked, according to Schmaus, the central insight of this later philosophy's "linguistic turn": that there is no thought—no separate realm of mental concepts or ideas—apart from language and its words. Citing a passage from *The Elementary Forms of the Religious Life* in its 1912 French original, which begins, according to Schmaus, "Now there is no doubt that language and, consequently, the system of concepts that it translates is the product of a collective collaboration," Schmaus argues:

> In this passage, Durkheim appears to have been suggesting that we operate with two "languages." On the one hand, we have a written and spoken language that consists of words. On the other hand, he seems to have believed, we have a language of thought that consists of collective representations. According to Durkheim "each word translates a concept" and the system of concepts with which we think is that expressed by our language.[56]

Such a lingering dualism of thought and language—a dualism completely absent, as we have already seen, in that third of Peirce's "four denials" of 1868: "We have no power of thinking without signs"—is traced by Schmaus to the blinding power of Durkheim's own education: "Educated in the philosophical tradition of ideas, he thought of a general concept as some sort of Lockean complex idea that is progressively compounded over time from simple ideas." But this "tradition of ideas" was borrowed by Locke—as Peirce saw so clearly in those of his 1868 papers in which Christopher Hookway sees him repudiating the "spirit of Cartesianism"—from the same sources as René Descartes. So, by refusing in his 1913-14 course on "Pragmatism and Sociology" to consider Peirce's arguments on their own merit (rather than see them as he did via William James), Durkheim also missed the boat of that 1868 Peircean insight—now so common in all philosophical writing, from Heidegger and Wittgenstein to Rorty and Lacan—of the total permeation of human thought by language. And, by missing such an important philosophical boat—a crucial turning point in the history of human self-consciousness because, as Michel Foucault saw so well, the denial of that "Cartesian" claim to the capacity to have ideas without the mediation of language is, in effect, also the "destruction" of the Cartesian ego-subject—Durkheim's legacy of sociological theory has risked backsliding, not only into Lockean empiricism but also into that "simplism," the metaphysical preference for simple ideas, that he had criticized in Descartes's rationalism.[57]

Furthermore, Durkheim's project of a scientifically rigorous sociological theory explaining human action remains perforce incomplete, as Schmaus explains:

> For something to count as an action, it must have some meaning for the agent. The meaning of the action also determines the type of action that it is. Thus, for example, Durkheim refused to accept self-imposed deaths as suicides if they were committed by insane people who did not understand what they were doing. . . . One way to explain the effects that meaning can have in the physical world without invoking magic is to appeal to the causal properties of the physical realizations of the way in which these meanings are represented in the mind. Durkheim appears to have been trying to do something like this by identifying meanings with mental representations and explaining the effects of society on the individual in terms of the power of collective over individual representations. . . . Ultimately, then, collective representations for him were real physical entities with causal properties.[58]

Such an attempt at sociological theorizing by positing the causation of individual representations by their collective counterparts may not be wrong, per se—although, as Schmaus saw, if Durkheim separated individual ideas from collective language, that dualism would fall afoul of that "linguistic turn" in modern philosophy which, pioneered by Peirce in 1868, has now won the day against all its Lockean "tradition of ideas" rival—but it is definitely incomplete. For though we may fully accept the point labored by Durkheim about the causal power, the "force" or "external constraint," exerted by society's collective representations upon our individual psyches, there will still remain that logically valid question: What, if anything—besides other collective representations, of course—causes, originates, or changes the collective representations themselves? Or, to put it in the terms of philosopher Arthur Schopenhauer so favored—as the primary philosophical influence on Durkheim's thought—by Mestrovic:[59] What is the nature, and what are the laws of motion, of the collective will that constructs those collective representations that Durkheim fixated upon as the ultimate causal forces over individual and collective action?[60]

By not addressing this ultimate causal question, Durkheim left his creation—the discipline of sociology—open to the strife of "multiple paradigms." The causal theory of a "material determinism in the last instance" (so dear to the exponents of that brand of thinking known as "vulgar Marxism"),[61] for example, rushes in to fill this theoretical vacuum left behind by Durkheim, and the "neofunctionalist" Jeffrey Alexander can thereby play off such "Marxist materialism" against the supposed "idealism" of Durkheim to argue for the superiority of Max Weber, and ultimately of Talcott Parsons, in the creation of sociological theory. The enormity of this theoretical vacuum left by Durkheim's unanswered question about the causal/constructivist influences over the collective representations seems to be recognized by philosopher of science Schmaus when he argues that

> Durkheim's mistake was first to distinguish different types of individual and collective representations as natural kinds and only second to seek the laws of sociology in the laws of "collective ideation" that govern collective representations. . . . What Durkheim should have done is first to have sought the laws governing social phenomena and then let these laws carve up the social world into natural kinds without concerning himself about the way in which these social facts are represented in the mind.[62]

But the question then becomes whether social science—dealing as it does with voluntaristic human actors anxious to defend the "freedom and dignity" of their agency to the point of willfully falsifying the predictions of social scientists—can aspire to those "law-regularities" of Newton's solar system and of natural science in general. At least one respected philosopher of science has gone on record to answer this question in the negative. In *The Poverty of Historicism*, Karl Popper excoriated those thinkers—especially Karl Marx and the Marxists—who attempted to derive long-term predictions based on the "laws" of human history; at one point Popper even asserted that, although the simple study of "social problems" was possible, no overall social *science*—in the sense that the word science has attained from its association with natural science—was possible, because of the difficulties in finding law-like regularities in social life.[63]

But it is at this point precisely that Peirce's philosophy can help us complete the project of forging a comprehensive science of society left incomplete by Durkheim. For, like Durkheim—who, according to Schmaus, maintained that "all of our basic categories of thought are but modifications of the ideas of our primitive forebears," and who, in his celebrated 1913 review of Lucien Levy-Bruhl's *Les Fonctions mentales dans les societes inferieures*, seemed to deny Levy-Bruhl's assertion of the existence of a "primitive mentality" different from ours because all humans, and all human mentality, "grew out of . . . the same process of evolution"—Peirce was an evolutionist. But unlike Durkheim, who never specifically addressed the question of evolution but seemed to be carried along in the generally accepted evolutionist assumptions of his era, Peirce, the professional philosopher, elaborated in great detail what Carl Hausman calls his "evolutionary philosophy."[64]

Of central importance to our question about law-like regularities in social science is the concept of *habit*—a concept that Stjepan Mestrovic claims underlies both the key Durkheimian concepts of "collective representations" and "social facts," and which was used rather extensively by Durkheim in his course on the educational institutions and practices, offered at the Sorbonne in 1902-03 and later published in book form under the title *Moral Education*.[65] This is the concept which Peirce's evolutionist focus sees—in all living organisms, including human beings—as in some sense incorporating the law-like regularities of nature. In the struggle for survival, biological habituation simply, by necessity, had to incorporate—as stored information or even genetic memory—the regular patterns of the physical environment. Those organisms that did not habituate to the regular, law-like patterns of their physical environment—the diurnal pattern of night and day, the yearly pattern of the seasons, the gravitational pattern that has shaped our sense of balance, and so on—simply would not survive. Their genetic extinction over the millions of years of evolution have ensured that we, the survivors, have the law-like regularities of the natural world built into all those "habits," not only of our physiological reflexes and "instincts" but also in our emotions, gestures, forms of social interaction—what Sigmund Freud and Claude Levi-Strauss would later call the "unconscious" aspects of our social interaction—and in our "habits of thought," or, as in the famous phrase borrowed by Robert Bellah from Alexis de Tocqueville, our "habits of the heart."[66]

One may straight away see that Peirce's concept of *habit* and *habituation* provides a more robust tool for understanding socialization and the formation of individual personality than does the weaker notion preferred by Talcott Parsons— and since then institutionalized in social science usage—of the "internalization of norms,"[67] which, with its implicit internal-external dualism, perpetuates that superfluous Giddens-like argument against Durkheim's perception of society as "external constraint" that we have already seen.[68] If our personal patterns of action are the result of years of unconsciously incorporated habits—as Peirce, G. H. Mead, and, as we shall see, Jacques Lacan would have it—rather than of the more shallow connotations that Parsons's normative internalization carry, then the Giddensian phantom of the "knowledgeable" agent gives way to a far more realistic "Durkheimian" appreciation of the massive power that the collective presence called "society"—itself the product of millennia of biological and cultural evolution—exerts on our "unconscious" habits of everyday behavior. Peirce's "habit," in its ontological continuity with the laws of physical nature, very presciently prefigured that helpful image associated with the writings of Theodor Adorno of the Frankfurt school of culture as "second nature" (Adorno had himself been influenced by Georg Simmel in this formulation).[69]

But, critics might object, did not William James, in his famous textbook *The Principles of Psychology*, call habit "the great flywheel" which conserves the stability of society by preventing the poor from acting out their envy of the rich? Am I then not, by my focus on Peirce's concept of habit, risking falling into the same trap that Functionalism supposedly fell into—of having such conservative assumptions built into my "theoretical perspective" as to blind me to the sources and processes of social change? My answer is no, because the concept of habit in Peirce's philosophy can hardly be separated from that other great concern of Peirce with the "pragmatics" of human communication: All social change—from the small incremental steps of fashion or technological change to those gigantic leaps known as revolutions or social movements—depend on the processes of communication. As sociologists from Neil Smelser to Charles Tilly have reminded us, social movements and revolutions require mobilization, which can only occur through effective communication. And all communication also requires physical resources—from the fax machines and printing presses which students of revolution emphasize to the very sensory structures of our human bodies which, in counteracting overstimulation, enforce that cooperative procedure in oral conversation, known as "turn taking"—which provide the quasi-physical, law-like regularities studied by Peircean Pragmaticism.[70]

It is to such contextual conditions and consequences of communication, such as the "turn taking" that is both condition and consequence of face-to-face conversation, that linguist Ellyn Lucas Arwood's book *Pragmaticism* refers when it defines Pragmaticism simply as the "methodology of pragmatics," which involves "the synergistics of cognition and socialization." Arwood hails Charles S. Peirce as "the father of pragmatics," but it is to the 1938 paper by Charles Morris, "Foundations of the Theory of Signs," that the credit goes for demarcating *pragmatics*, the science of the relationship between signs and their users, from *syntax*, which studies relationships between signs, and *semantics*, which studies the relationships between signs and their objects.[71]

Carl Hausman, while repeating the explanation that we have already seen Durkheim and Randall Collins give—that Peirce had changed the name of his own philosophy from Pragmatism to Pragmaticism to distinguish his own theory from that of William James—also chooses to emphasize that Peirce's philosophy is an "evolutionary realism," which adheres very strictly to "the so-called pragmatic criterion of meaning" (also known as "the so-called pragmatic maxim of meaning"). Hausman proceeds to quote from the very 1878 article by Peirce, "How to Make Our Ideas Clear," that Durkheim claimed to have seen "in translation in the *Revue Philosophique* of January 1879 under the title 'Comment rendre nos idees claires'":

> It appears, then, that the rule for attaining the third grade of clearness of apprehension is as follows: Consider what effects that might conceivably have practical bearings we conceive the object of our conception to have. Then, our conception of these effects is the whole of our conception of the object.[72]

Durkheim's *First Lecture* quoted most of the above passage from Peirce's 1878 article and then proceeded to use the "transubstantiation" example used by both Peirce and James to argue that—since the practical "effects" of the wine used in the Roman Catholic sacrament of communion are different from the practical "effects" of "blood"—Pragmatism must hold that truth is "human, varied, and variable" and that "it cannot be a copy of a given reality."[73]

It could be argued that, in using the Peirce-James example of transubstantiation, Durkheim had missed Peirce's word whole—as in "our conception of these effects is the whole of our conception of the object"—which would make all the difference between pre-transubstantiation "wine" and post-transubstantiation "blood" to a Roman Catholic such as novelist (and Peirce admirer) Walker Percy. However, it must be admitted that Peirce's wording in the above 1878 definition of his "Pragmatic Maxim" is not as sharply outlined as his later redefinition:

> In order to ascertain the meaning of an intellectual conception one should consider what practical consequences might conceivably result by necessity from the truth of that conception; and the sum of these consequences will constitute the entire meaning of the conception.[74]

This latter version of Peirce's "Pragmatic maxim" leaves one in no doubt that Peirce saw meaning, and not truth, as varying according to the consequences that necessarily result from the truth of a conception. Peirce's Pragmaticism—as Durkheim, to his credit, seemed to grasp—is a theory of the social construction of meaning and not, as William James apparently misunderstood it, and consequently misinterpreted it to the world, of truth. Also, as I point out in more detail in the next chapter, it is remarkable that—with *functionalism*, as defined by Robert Merton (and accepted by its critics, such as John Easter), as a method for determining the significance of an event or entity from its consequences—long before Niklas Luhmann's 1987 call for the *functionalization of meaning*, to save the functionalism of Talcott Parsons from its theoretical weaknesses, such a *functionalization* had already been carried by Charles Sanders Peirce more than a hundred years earlier![75]

What sociologists must comprehend to overcome the current fragmentation of social theory into "multiple paradigms" is the conceptual difference, introduced by Peirce and institutionalized by Morris in 1938 into the threefold division of the semiotic science of signs (syntax, semantics, and pragmatics), between *pragmatic* and *semantic* meaning. Jenny Thomas's informative 1995 book, *Meaning in Interaction: An Introduction to Pragmatics*, furnishes us with scores of examples where the pragmatic meaning—the effect the speaker intends, within particular socio-cultural conventions, to produce in the hearer—is different from a statement's semantic content. Thus, for example, the statement "Thank you for filling up my tank," uttered to a borrower of my car who has in reality neglected to fill it up, has a pragmatic meaning—i.e., a sarcastic reminder that he ought to have filled it up—opposite from its straight semantic, "dictionary" meaning. Or the statement "It is hot in here," which consultation with the dictionary would show to bear the semantic meaning of a simple proposition about temperature, could really carry a pragmatic meaning intended to influence the hearer's behavior, either to open the window or to engage in a sexual flirtation—neither of which is contained within the strict semantic content of the sentence.

It is with such "overflow" of meaning beyond its semantic banks that both sociology—from Durkheim's writings to those of the symbolic interactionists Gregory Stone and Harvey Faberman—and Peircean Pragmaticism are concerned. Thomas points out how the dominant philosophy of the earlier half of the twentieth century, Logical Positivism, attempted to arrest such meaning overflow by the simple expedient of conflating meaning with truth. Logical Positivist Bertrand Russell, for example, had declared the phrase "the king of France" to be meaningless because it is not true that France has a king. But such conflation of meaning and truth, a conflation apparent in that philosophy of James that Durkheim's course "Pragmatism and Sociology" so condemned—seems to have disappeared from the discipline of philosophy—but not yet, it seems, from sociology—in the Western world, since the 1944 publication of Alfred Tarski's article "The Semantic Conception of Truth and the Foundations of Semantics."

Just how important Tarski's "truth conditional semantics" is to Durkheimian sociology's rapprochement can be seen by analyzing Tarski's favorite example— the sentence "Snow is white"—through his "semantic theory of truth." No amount of manipulating what Stone and Faberman called "pragmatic truth" will change the truth—within our still-relatively unpolluted social environment—of snow really being white. But were our cities to become heavily polluted a hundred years from now, the term *snow* might be redefined, within such a polluted environment, to be gray rather than white. What would then have changed is not our criterion of truth—as representing facts accurately—but our construction of the meaning of our experience of snow. Or, as Jenny Thomas better states this same distinction between the concepts of *meaning* and of *truth* which I am trying to make, "According to this view, a sentence such as *The King of France is bald*, in a world in which there is no king of France, cannot be judged to be true or false, but merely meaningless."[76]

What Tarski's 1944 article—and later philosophical and linguistic explorations into that Peirce-inspired and Morris-executed separation of pragmatics, which studies how human communities construct (what the linguist, Jenny Thomas, calls) their "meaning in interaction," from *semantics*, which studies "truth-conditional" meaning—are attempting to define with ever-greater conceptual clarity had admittedly been intuitively understood by sociologists since at least that "theorem" supposedly uttered by University of Chicago sociologist W. I. Thomas (influenced, as almost every Chicago sociologist was, by Pragmatist philosophy): "What is believed to be true has real consequences." Perhaps I can do no better in my attempt to effect a latter-day meeting of the minds of Durkheim and Peirce than to state my Peirce-Morris distinction between the theoretical project of Peircean pragmatics, which I believe to be identical with, or co-extensive with, Durkheimian sociology, and *semantics*, which may belong more with linguistic or literary textual-analysis and may therefore be only an adjunct to sociology, in the terms (better known to sociologists) of W. I. Thomas: It is not the semantic content per se of cultural beliefs, but rather their pragmatic consequences, that Durkheimian sociology aims to study.[77]

Having begun my journey, in this introductory chapter, with Durkheim's encounter in 1913-14 with the founders of Pragmatism, I will retrace in chapter 1— which is an extended critique of those "received" themes in current sociological theory of *agency, rationality* and *meaning*—Erving Goffman's 1983 misadventure into the linguistic pragmatics of John Austin and H. Paul Grice, so as to appropriate for sociology that "Gricean" echo (from within linguistics) of Durkheim's concept of "solidarity": the cooperative principle underlying linguistic meaning. For now, in this introduction, suffice it to say that the Peirce-Morris-Grice tradition of pragmatics, with its conceptual separation of a deeper, explanatory level of "meaning in interaction" beyond that shallower level of observed semantics, recapitulates for the human (or social) sciences the methodological procedure of natural science. To take, for example, Jenny Thomas's example of the simple statement "It is hot in here," the observed semantics can only be comprehended through the pragmatics of shared meaning-conventions (i.e., that whether the particular "culture" in which this statement was uttered legitimates the listener's interpretation of the statement as a "hint" that he should conserve electricity or respond sexually is what the *pragmatics* of socially shared meanings is about). But such an epistemic move beyond the level of observation—to appeal to unobserved, theoretical entities to explain what has been observed—is known in natural science as *scientific realism*. The empirically observed bonding of one unit of carbon to four units of hydrogen in the chemistry of methane, for example, is explained by the theoretical entities (borrowed by chemistry from physics) of electron shells. The Peircean tradition thus converts a hermeneutic interpretation of meaning into a scientific realism that—pursued through the pragmatics of the (Gricean) cooperative principle from the semantics of agency in my book's chapter 1 to the social construction of community power and the socialized self in chapters 2 and 3, respectively—in a true "fusion of horizons" (à la Hans-Georg Gadamer) from within the current "strife of methods" (or multiple paradigms) of current sociological theory enables me to define in chapter 4 a new approach to the sociology of globalization.[78]

Global Cultural Process:
The Evolution of Interpretant Form

"The twentieth century," argues Randall Collins, "is the first in which comprehending world history has become possible. Previous generations of scholars knew too little about other parts of the world beyond their own." In order, then, to carry out his grand project of *The Sociology of Philosophies: A Global Theory of Intellectual Change*, Collins—this founding father of the "Conflict Tradition" in American sociology—has come to sound like the embodiment of that conceptual marriage between the theories of Durkheim and Peirce which I am proposing, as he defends what he calls "social constructivism" against precisely those charges—of undermining truth and lacking objectivity—that Emile Durkheim had, in his 1913-14 course of lectures on "Pragmatism and Sociology," feared would accrue to his sociology if it approached the (Jamesean) philosophy of Pragmatism. "It is often supposed," says Collins, "that social constructivism undermines truth. If reality is socially constructed, there is no objectivity and no reality. I deny the conclusion. Social constructivism is sociological realism; and sociological realism carries with it a wide range of realist consequences."[79]

Far from the Weberian themes of *methodological individualism* or *social nominalism*—themes central to the "conflict perspective" of current American sociology, of which Collins had been an early pioneer—this new "sociological realism" of Collins's writing in 1998 echoes the external "constraint" theme of Durkheim as well as that "denial" of the power of the individual to think without (linguistic) signs in Charles Sanders Peirce's *Collected Papers* (5.265). "Language," now argues Collins,

> takes place in words which carry meaning, and follows a grammar which is to a large degree inescapable if statements are to make any sense. I do not invent my own language; my thinking depends on *forms* which have come to me ready-made, from beyond the present moment of consciousness. The constraints of language use, along with its capability for conveying meaning, imply the existence of communicative beings beyond myself. To deny that other people exist—in this specific sense—is to deny the communicability and objectivity, indeed the meaningfulness, of one's own sentences.[80]

Collins's use of the word "forms" here seems to echo the statement by Georg Simmel that "the richness of form lies in the fact that it can absorb an infinite number of contents," and such a formal approach—a strategy dictated by what could otherwise be the incomprehensibly "infinite" multiplicity of the world's cultures—is indeed what I will outline here, in my theorizing of the global cultural process. Meanwhile, we should note that while it is an erstwhile opponent of "Durkheim's functionalism," Collins, who now appreciates the nature of "the constraints" (of language use) on human agency, it is a self-proclaimed admirer and follower of Durkheim, Jean Piaget, who criticizes Durkheim for having "stretched" and overgeneralized his concept of "constraint." "The tendency of Durkheim's later works," argues Piaget, is

> to fuse into a single explanation the analyses he gave of the different aspects of morality . . . In the case of constraint, Durkheim has stretched his definition of the word to cover all social phenomena whatsoever. Whether he is talking of the inner attraction felt by the individual for universal human ideals, or of the coercion exercised by public opinion or police, it is all constraint. The "externality" of the social phenomena gives rise to the same generalizations.[81]

Such a critique by Piaget of Durkheim's sole focus on the "external constraint" exerted on the individual by society—a critique of Durkheim, which, as we have seen, is of central importance to the structuration theory of Anthony Giddens—stems from Piaget's low estimate of "Durkheim's later works" when compared to "his book on the division of labor, *La Division du Travail Social*, the least dogmatic and, theoretically, the most suggestive of his works," where, says Piaget, "Durkheim has shown greater caution than he did later on with regard to the unity of social facts and consequently the identity of moral facts with each other." Of the "two great types of society" analyzed by Durkheim in that earlier work, argues Piaget—the "conformist communities" of mechanical solidarity versus the "differentiated communities" of organic solidarity—"the first are exclusive of inner freedom and of personality, the second mark the growth and expansion of individual dignity."[82]

How then, asks Piaget, can Durkheim's "later works"—especially his *Moral Education*—propose "external constraint" as the central principle of morality for both the traditional as well as the modern types of society? It seems to me that the question Piaget asks—a question unfortunately ignored by Giddens in his structuration theory, as Stjepan Mestrovic points out—is that of the under-theorized relationship between modern and premodern society.[83] Durkheim's earlier work, in *The Division of Labor in Society*, at least attempted to outline the process by which a modern type of society could evolve from its premodern ancestor. As late as 1913 Durkheim still suggested, as is apparent in his review of Lucien Levy-Bruhl's work on "primitive mentality," his belief in some underlying process by which modern society, or at least its "mentality," "evolved" from its premodern ancestor:

> We consider these two types of human mentality, however different they may seem, are mistakenly thought to have originated from different sources: they grew out of each other and represent two stages in the same process of evolution. . . . If then human mentality has varied over the centuries and with societies—if it has evolved—the different types of mentality it has successfully produced have each given rise to the other.[84]

The problem left us by Durkheim, as E. E. Evans-Pritchard has emphasized in several of his writings since his 1934 article on Levy-Bruhl,[85] is the precise relationship between the two mentalities—between the Azande theory of witchcraft, which leaves no room for "natural death" but imputes all Azande deaths to human witchcraft, and, say, the medical theories used in any modern hospital or coroner's office, which impute many such "deaths from natural causes" to microorganismic infection,—between the modern and the premodern mentalities, which Durkheim had asserted in 1913, just a few years before his death "grew out of each other and represent two stages in the same process of evolution."[86]

What could this "same process of evolution" that Durkheim referred to—encompassing all human societies and their "mentalities" across the globe—be?

Dominique Merllie ends her recent essay, titled "Did Lucien Levy-Bruhl Answer the Objections Made in *Les Formes Elementaires*?" by appealing to the 1965 work of French anthropologist Roger Bastide, which, devoted to a "confrontation between Leenhardt and Levi-Strauss," begins by attributing to this more recent "confrontation" in social science "the same nature as of the comparison between Durkheim and Levy-Bruhl"—with Claude Levi-Strauss echoing Durkheim in the same way that Maurice Leenhardt echoed Levy-Bruhl. "Durkheim only wants to see the unity of reason," Bastide argued, "because reason is of social origin and all men belong to society—whereas Levy-Bruhl wants to see only the multiplicity of reasons, because human intelligence is always fashioned by the culture of the surrounding environment, and there is a multiplicity of cultures."[87]

While this problem—of reconciling the supposed universality of human rationality with the multiplicity of (cultural) perspectives—has already been posed at the beginning of this introductory chapter and will be again examined, in greater depth, in chapter 1, suffice it here to note that this theoretical quarrel between Durkheim and Levy-Bruhl, or between Evans-Pritchard's "Levy-Bruhlian" critique of Durkheim and Levi-Strauss's "Durkheimian" critique of Levy-Bruhl[88]—in short, the "big question" about the unity of human reason versus the relativism of perspectives that seems to haunt not only social science but the wider civic culture in the current culture wars of today's globalizing, multicultural America—can be addressed, and effectively tackled, via the following steps into the thought process of Charles Sanders Peirce:

Understanding Peirce's Concept of the "Interpretant"

This concept of the interpretant, first introduced by Peirce in his 1868 paper "Some Consequences of Four Incapacities"—a paper also containing Peirce's "four denials," which had earlier been used to introduce Peirce's philosophy in juxtaposition against Durkheim's—is explained by Christopher Hookway through an apposite illustration:

> The fundamental thought Peirce uses here is that when clouds signify rain, or an utterance signifies that snow is white, there is more involved than a simple dyadic relation between the clouds and the rain, the utterance and the color of snow. The fact that we can ask, "To whom do the clouds signify rain?" brings out the fact that our idea of one thing signifying another incorporates the first thing being understood as or interpreted as a sign of the second.[89]

The beauty of Hookway's simple example of clouds and rain is that I can—without resorting to the needless exoticism of standard textbook illustrations of the Sapir-Whorf hypothesis (which use Hopi tense-grammar or West African color-terminology—illustrate the utility of Peirce's concept of the interpretant from within Western culture by a simple comparison of "subcultures." Thus, while gathering storm clouds on a Friday afternoon in any American city would signify

to most tired office workers a rained-out, destroyed weekend, they might also signify to a community of artists a welcome opportunity to paint a storm scene. The
contrasting emotions of these two subcultures—gloom on the part of the office
workers who had been planning a weekend outing but joy on the part of the artists
who had awaited just such an opportunity to paint a storm scene—would be explained in Peircean semiotics through the difference in interpretants that the two
subcultures employed. Peirce's concept of the interpretant can then also be used to
explain the difference in the reactions to a sudden death, between the Azande
witchcraft culture of Evans-Pritchard—without appeal to any pejorative connotation of a "primitive mentality" à la Levy-Bruhl—and a modern medical culture.

The "cooperative principle" of H. Paul Grice's linguistic *pragmatics* (which
I will adapt in chapter 1 to a sociological usage)—in that "synergistics of cognition and socialization" which Arwood defines as the subject of study of pragmatics—has structured the interpretants of Azande culture in such a way as to fix
their habits of attention on human persons as the "cause" of death, without in any
way making them seem less "rational" in their other dealings with Western social
scientists such as Evans-Pritchard, Levy-Bruhl, Durkheim, or Levi-Strauss.
Peirce's interpretant functions much as the key to a code—and keys to codes in
espionage, war, the stock market, or football games would indeed be fine examples of Peircean interpretants—a Pragmatic Code structuring a culture, that is explained in more detail in chapter 4. Inasmuch as Peirce's concept of the interpretant highlights the multiplicity of interpretations possible in any cognitive
situation—without assigning any hierarchy of valuations (of "rationality") to
such multifarious interpretations—it is a conceptual bow in the direction of the
relativistic proponents of hermeneutical "perspectivism."[90]

*Peirce Also Bows, in a Three-Stage Hierarchy, to the Unity of Human Reason, in
His "Phenomenology"*

Carl Hausman introduces us to Peirce's phenomenology with the statement
that "Peirce's phenomenological analysis is opposed to atomism found in British
empiricism." This anti-Positivist sentiment is echoed in H. P. Rickman's position-
ing of Dilthey's hermeneutics in opposition to "British Empiricism and Positivism
from Locke to J. S. Mill," in that "experience is not just taking in colored dots or
simple sounds; it is seeing my friend cutting the grass, hearing birds singing in the
trees, observing a family friend setting out for a picnic, and the like." Indeed it is
this commonality between the emphases by both Diltheyan Hermeneutics and
Peircean Pragmatism on being true to experience in its presentation of whole objects and events—against the analytical breakdown of perceptual wholeness into
atomistic sensations favored by positivism and by the Lockean tradition of British
Empiricism—that leads Rickman to note "the striking parallels between Dilthey's
thought and American Pragmatism." This emphasis on the *wholeness of experience was also the inspiration behind Edmund Husserl's* anti-Positivist founding,
programmatic statement for his Phenomenology—"Back to the things them-

selves"—and was, according to Schmaus, in no small measure behind Durkheim's opposition to Positivistic Empiricism. Careful as he was to answer possible objections from the Positivists that without their program of analytical atomism the wholeness of experience could lead to error in perception and judgement—as in the straight rod immersed in water that appears, to holistic experience, to be bent, unless the Positivism's atomistic analysis of sensations (by opposing the sensation of touch to that of sight) reveals the phenomenon of refraction making a straight rod *appear* bent—Peirce had replied that his phenomenology of knowledge by experience revealed not one but three phases of such accurate knowledge, the "categories" of *Firstness, Secondness,* and *Thirdness*.[91]

While I would encourage my readers to suit their individual tastes in introducing themselves to Peirce's famous trio of signs—*icon, index,* and *symbol*—through any of the current cornucopia of books on the subject, ranging from Peirce's own terse nineteenth-century language as presented in *Lecture Three: The Categories Defended* of Peirce's recently published 1903 Harvard "Lectures on Pragmatism" to the simplicity of John Fitzgerald's *Peirce's Theory of Signs as Foundation for Pragmatism* or the scattered references to these three categories in the Hookway and Hausman texts that I have, so far, been leaning upon in my own presentation of Peirce's philosophy here, I prefer to follow Peirce's (and Durkheim's) examples by attempting my own concise explication of these three categories by one relatively clear anecdote from quotidian experience:

A friend (I'll call him Charles, in honor of Peirce) and I are walking uphill at dusk on a steep road at the top of which is a construction site, near which I had earlier seen some children playing. A round object suddenly rolls downhill toward us. I think that it is a rubber ball left behind by the children, while my friend Charles believes it to be a metallic wrecker's ball left behind by the construction crew. So convinced am I that it is the rubber ball that I had earlier seen the children kicking around, that—to prove my point to Charles—I gleefully kick it as it rolls downhill toward us. To my surprise, my foot explodes in a spasm of pain that brings me to my knees and sends Charles running for medical help: It was indeed a metallic wrecker's ball, as he had suspected.

In this simple life-world narrative, we may see all three of Peirce's categories illustrated.

Firstness (a category that Peirce describes by the words "quality" or "feeling"). With neither Charles nor I able to judge decisively, on the basis of our initially none-too-comprehensive evidence, the nature of the round object rolling downhill toward us, we were left to individually reach, on the basis of that image of "rolling roundness," the *icon* of a "ball" which we had perceived, a preliminary belief about the nature of the object we were experiencing. Each of us had arrived at a belief based on our intuitive feelings or qualities perceived as "similar" to our (respective) past experiences: I, who had earlier seen a rubber ball of the same visual appearance being kicked around by some children but had seen *no* wrecker's ball, had believed it to be a rubber ball; Charles, on the other hand, having seen a wrecking crew around a few days earlier but *not* having seen the children playing, had immediately feared it (i.e., experienced the feeling of fear about it) to be a wrecker's ball. At this first of three stages in our decision process, we have a cognitive situation of relativistic, as yet incommensurable, perspectives.

Secondness. I decide to test my hypothesis by kicking the ball. Peirce describes this second stage by the words "existence," "quantity," and "brute force," all of which featured in my painful experience. The ball's *existence*—as a metallic wrecking-ball—erupted by *brute force* into my experience with the *quantity* of the impact, clearly having had "more" of an impact on my foot than would a rubber ball, producing the indexical sign (pain in my foot being my index, bodily posture and howl of pain being the indices) and literally indicating the true nature of existential reality to both Charles and myself.

Thirdness (which Peirce describes most often by the word "generality" and its symbolic sign). After that second stage of my kicking the ball, it had become clear to both of us that this ball was indeed a wrecker's ball. The *icon*, which had been, at the first stage, merely a "round, rolling object," similar to other such "round, rolling objects" each of us had previously experienced, had, at this third stage, assumed the clear delineation of the symbol, "metallic wrecker's ball," with its clear mentalized position at the intersection of generalized classes of such objects, having the generalized, abstract associations of "metal" (hard and painful to kick, unlike "rubber") and "wrecker's ball" (used for the "serious business" of demolishing buildings, unlike "rubber balls" used in children's play).

It is worth noting here how Peirce's *triadic phenomenology*—as I have just illustrated from a simple example, well within the range of normal human experience—shows not only how we humans all daily move, within our quotidian lives as human knowers, from appearance to reality, i.e. to the "truth," but also how this "truth" is intersubjective, as we move from individual perspectives to that communal consensus which Gadamer's Hermeneutics idealizes as "the Fusion of Horizons."[92]

Formal-Pragmatics as the Method of Study of Global Cultural Process

Pragmatics, the study of how the communicative cooperation of any linguistic community constructs and structures its cultural, semantic signs, involves—in its received methodology handed down from the philosophical epistemology of Charles S. Peirce to the linguistic philosophy of H. Paul Grice—what the linguistic pragmaticist Ellyn Lucas Arwood calls "the synergistics of cognition and socialization." When two separate communities appear to interpret differently what seems to us to be the same class of event—such as that event of sudden death which Evans-Pritchard's Azande tribe and the subculture of modern Western medical hospitals would interpret, as we have seen, in two distinct ways—the question to be asked is how have their different "interpretants" been structured by the socialization patterns of each culture? In other words, how does *socialization*, in each case, construct the cognitive habits of each culture?[93]

It may appear fulsomely novel or original on my part here when I propose that the third of the three Peircean steps which should resolve the "rationality vs. relativism" dispute that, according to Dominique Merllie, has haunted French social science from Durkheim to Levi-Strauss (and, as we have seen earlier, haunts Anglophone social science, too) entails the adaptive generalization of Peirce's phenomenology of three categories—of that *Iconic Firstness, Indexical Secondness*, and *Symbolic Thirdness* that we have just seen—from the level of the cognizing individual, which is the level that most philosophical students of Peirce should recognize as legitimately Peircean, to the grand-historical level of the cognizing cultural community. It is precisely such a conceptual leap, from Peirce's individual thinker to the communal thought processes of whole societies over the *longue durees* of historical time, that I take in chapter 4, where I use Peirce's three categories to inform my three pragmatic codes whose interpretants function— through the differences in geography and historical eventualities—to construct and structure sequentially formal similarities between human cultural semantics.

But the point for my attentive reader to note is that the apparent novelty of my conceptual leap—from the phenomenology of knowledge of Peirce's individual inquirer to the socio-historical processes of cognition of whole communities—is just that, more apparent than real, for that leap had already been accomplished by Charles Sanders Peirce himself. Consider, for example, the import of the following words from his oration "The Place of Our Age in the History of Civilization," delivered by Peirce at the reunion of the Cambridge High School Association on the evening of Thursday, November 12, 1863: "First there was the *egotistical* stage when man arbitrarily imagined perfection, now is the *idistical* stage when he observes it. Hereafter must be the more glorious *tuistical* stage when he shall be in communion with her."[94]

These words—which bring to mind the Piaget-inspired view of modernity by Jurgen Habermas as the de-centering of traditional egocentrism—were from a period in Peirce's life, lasting from 1857 to 1867, when Peirce had been explicitly attempting to define his categories of knowledge within the social dynamics of I, It/He, and Thou. According to Max Fisch, the editor of these early writings of Peirce, "though by 1867 Peirce had abandoned I, IT and THOU as *names* for his categories," he never really abandoned these social bases for his three categories for, says Fisch, as late as "1891 Peirce defines *tuism* for the *Century Dictionary* as 'The doctrine that all thought is addressed to a second person, or to one's future self as to a second person.'" In fact, adds Fisch—in a statement that would deny the claim of novelty or originality to not only my own threefold division of human cultural evolution in chapter 4 but also to Peirce's similar threefold division of human thought-stages—"the *Oxford English Dictionary* later quotes this definition in its own entry. There and in its *illetism* entry, it is recorded that Coleridge had used the terms *egotism, illetism*, and *tuism*, but not in any systematic or technical way."[95]

But, given that in today's overspecialized academic scene—where sociologists accustomed to those dual, dichotomized categories of modernization theory's "traditional vs. modern," or Immanuel Wallerstein's "capitalist world-system vs. anti-systemic movements," might puzzle over my novel or antiquarian interest in the philosopher Peirce's triadic system of categories—it behooves me to justify my turn to the "young Peirce" in more than antiquarian terms, I should here emphasize most of all that my "creative adaptation" of Peirce's phenomenology was occasioned by my effort at attaining a sociological understanding of an empirical situation, one which—in containing global or macro components within a situation of microsociological interactions—may yet be rare, but should soon become increasingly common as the globalization of the economic marketplace brings actors from radically different cultures increasingly into face-to-face interaction. At the university where I completed my Ph.D. in sociology between 1986 and 1990, there happened to be a sizable component of graduate students from the People's Republic of China, with most of these Mainland Chinese students having originated not from the more "cosmopolitan" Chinese cities such as Shanghai but from smaller towns in the Chinese interior. With the notable exception of that brief, shining moment in 1989 when the display of that very "American" symbol of the "goddess of liberty" in Tiananmen Square brought Chinese and American graduate students into a brief phase of Durkheimian effervescence and mutual communion, the relations between the Chinese and American students were most often punctuated by an atmosphere of underlying tension and mutual hostility, with the Americans usually venting their hostile sentiments in my office, which I shared with an older American student—a middle-aged lady, mother of four, who was treated by the other American students as their unofficial matriarch. The xenophobic outbursts of "damned foreigner" sentiments usually tended to occur on Mondays, as the anxious American students, returning from their usual leisure-activity-filled weekends to rush completion of due assignments before 2 P.M. graduate seminars, would usually find themselves frustrated in their expectation of a quick typing stint at an office computer by some Chinese student who had been logged on at that computer all weekend!

What was particularly noticeable was that such American frustration with the computer-hogging habits of hard-working foreigners did not extend to the sizable contingent of students from India, who, despite sharing the Chinese fondness for "working weekends" at the office computers, were usually found by the Americans to be amenable to some negotiated time-sharing accommodation. I might, as most American observers would, have attributed such a blatant difference in the way Chinese and Indians were treated to "language problems"—the Indians already spoke fluent English upon their arrival, unlike the Chinese, whose usage of English as their primary language tended to coincide with the period of their American stay—had I not noticed that the odd Chilean or Brazilian student, whose use of the English language was often as "stilted" as that of the Chinese students, was usually considered by the Americans as "cooperative," i.e., as amenable to computer time-sharing negotiations as the Indians were. Also of great relevance to my "microsociological" curiosity was the fact that when I finally dared to (playfully) protest these Monday outbursts of xenophobia, on the grounds that I, too—an immigrant, born in Africa of Indian parentage, and not yet an American citizen—was a "damned foreigner," I was greeted by the collective laughter of the American students assembled in my office and the collective assertion that I was "as American" as they were!

My microsociological investigations into this fascinating topic of the "shared understandings" behind these multicultural interactions in one group of sociology graduate students at a large Midwestern research university might have stopped there—at the very salient fact that my marriage to a fellow graduate student of Midwestern (American) origin was responsible for this easy granting of "fellow American" status to me by the American students—had an additional anomaly not stared me in the face: that although, with a few relevant exceptions to which I will return, the Indian students shared the American presumption of my Americanness, the Chinese stubbornly refused to treat me as anything but a fellow foreigner! In fact, because of my predilection for working late in my office, I grew accustomed to the daily routine of having American students trooping into my office to treat me as a fellow American until 5 P.M., and then, after the Americans had departed, having an average of about three Chinese students wander in to interact with me as a fellow foreigner, with the favored topic of conversation usually being those personal topics—such as "What led you to marry your American wife"—that, as these Chinese students were well aware, tended to stop their attempts at conversation with the Americans. After some reflexive observation, I noticed to my surprise that this switch from the impersonal—such as the usual "means-ends" American conversations about courses to register for, or committee members to choose toward rapid degree completion, or gasoline prices and quantity of time available for weekend outings—to the personal, such as questions of loyalty to significant others, which in American circles was usually signaled by the drop in interacting numbers to dyadic or, at most, triadic interactions, and in Indian circles was triggered by my willingness to join the usual "family" talk usually indulged in by Indian students at "Indians-only" weekend dinners, was, in my interaction with Chinese students, triggered by my own obsessive questions about their political history. What, I wondered, could all my conversational "cues"—those cues in my own speech that triggered the switch in my listeners from impersonal to personal topics of conversation—have in common? After all, on the surface, my conversations with the non-Chinese graduate students would seem different from my conversations with their Chinese counterparts: my personal conversations with Americans (usually in dyadic or triadic conversations only) and with Indians (in larger groups than the Americans, but only on special occasions) were purely about family or childhood experiences; but in my conversations with the Chinese even a supposedly nonpersonal "political question" such as "Did you say that when you were younger you were exiled to the countryside during the Cultural Revolution?" could elicit, in the process of conversation, the personal counterquestion, "Do you and your American wife plan to have children?"

The answer I finally developed to this microsociological problem of the "shared understandings" in the small-group interactions of sociology graduate students, which perforce also involved macrosociological questions of inter-cultural understanding within the contemporary process of globalization, is contained in chapter 4. This is the transition between two *Pragmatic Codes* or (Peircean) interpretants, which I had originally called "familism" and "exchange," respectively, but which I now, aware as I am that these particular terms have already accumulated other connotations within the social sciences, choose to call the signification codes of "*filiation*" and "*calibration*," respectively. ·

At first, being sharply aware of what Georg Simmel's sociological tradition (as developed by the urban sociology of the Chicago School's Robert Park and Louis Wirth) would have called my "marginal status"—indeed, as a native of East Africa of Indian parentage, speaking Portuguese at home, brought up as a Roman Catholic, and married to a Midwestern American of German origin, I was obviously perceived as just so very "marginal," as compared to all the recognized cultural groups within the Sociology Department's graduate student body at my university, that Roland Robertson, the sociological theorist of globalization who taught there, delighted in referring to me as "Mr. Global"!—I attempted to understand my microsociological situation within the terms expressed in Simmel's 1905 essay, "The Metropolis and Mental Life." "Money economy and the dominance of the intellect are intrinsically connected," Simmel had argued, and the blasé attitude—the American cool—of the urbanized American graduate students appeared indeed to contrast very sharply with the more "emotional" speech of the Chinese students, who were not only just emerging into the global "money economy" after Deng-Xiao Ping's 1979 normalization of relations with capitalist America but were also recent migrants into an urban setting from their Chinese villages and small towns. (As an undergraduate at the University of Bombay in India, it had been the plaintive self-directive that I had often heard from college freshmen recently emerged from rural areas of India to be "less emotional" that had first attracted me to the Primary vs. Secondary Group conception of that other Chicago School sociologist in the "Pragmatist" tradition, C. H. Cooley.)[96]

But it was the striking difference in the themes of conversation, with the Chinese students preferring what Peirce would have called *iconic* sign-themes—with their conversation not only veering almost automatically to topics of similarity and difference between persons, but also being peppered with references to *icons* in the literal, non-Peircean sense, of both the family-photographs scattered on both my American office mate's and my own desk and the icons of their late "Great Helmsman" Chairman Mao Zedong, whose overwhelming "fatherly" presence they seemed so keen to "outgrow"—in glaring contrast to what Peirce would have called the indexical sign-themes of means-ends *calibration* that the American students favored, that led me to examine the capacity of Peirce's *Iconic Firstness* and *Indexical Secondness* phenomenological categories to serve as containing concepts for those various received sociological dualistic imageries—

ranging from the Gemeinschaft-to-Gesellschaft historical direction of Ferdinand Toennies to Durkheim's "Mechanical-to-Organic Solidarities" to Marx/Simmel's "Emotional-to-Cash Nexus bonds" to Max Weber's "Personal-to-Impersonal Power-and-Legitimation"—of the transition to modernity, which the "blasé" Americans took for granted, while the Chinese "late modernizers" were still approaching it with the intense emotional excitement and great trepidation of late modernizers.

This successful "fit" of the transition-to-modernity themes of the classical founders of sociology within the first two of three categories of Peirce's phenomenology is demonstrated—in the historical detail that such a theoretical demonstration merits—in chapter 4. After duly addressing the theme of the Durkheim-Mauss 1903 essay on "Primitive Classification"—that the categories of "primitive" cosmologies echo the classification patterns of society itself—chapter 4 follows, in narrative form, the cultural trajectory of that structural journey outlined by Gerard Lenski: from the relative equality of hunter-gatherer tribes to the steep inequalities of agrarian societies. Taking our cue from the suggestion put forward in Barry Schwartz's 1981 book on "structuralism and the sociology of knowledge," *Vertical Classification*, that the cultural legitimation of historically increasing inequality in premodern societies seems to utilize the metaphorical similarity of such "vertical classification" in society to the child's perception of vertically bigger adults[97]—we duly integrate such thinking-by-similarity into its rightful Peircean matrix of phenomenological "Firstness" at the end of chapter 4. Beginning with the iconic similarity perceived by "primitives" between rocks and human beings, noted by Durkheim, all human societies utilize the same cognitive form of legitimating the increasingly steep "vertical" inequalities of later (agrarian) societies in the "familistic," or filiative, terms all humans understand from their experience as infants vis-à-vis powerful adult protectors—from Western popes (from *papa*—father) and kings (from the Germanic root of "*kin*-ship") to the Chinese Imperial "Son of Heaven," to the "Big Brother" of supposedly modernizing Stalinism. Such family-iconic imagery is then also projected onto the cosmos, with increasingly "upwards" cognitive abstraction as the geographical and population size of the sociocultural (political) unit increases, from the totemic animal representing the "primitive" clan of Durkheim (which Freud's *Totem and Taboo* had seen as representing the "resemblance" of the collective to parental will) to the "family" of gods on Mount Olympus of the Greek city states to "Our Father in Heaven" of medieval Christendom.

Modernity, by contrast, projects no parental icon on either its social or natural cosmos.[98] Its total cosmology is instead cognized through Peirce's category of Secondness. Its pragmatic-code—its dominant interpretant—is the sign of the index, that "measure" of all things, which is, as Simmel had seen so well when he had asserted at the beginning of the twentieth century that "money economy and the dominance of the intellect are intrinsically connected," either money, or the measuring indices of the skeptical Cartesian intellect. Weber's description (at the end of *The Protestant Ethic*) of modern "specialists without spirit"—where face-less bureaucrats "follow procedure" in calibrating the means to unquestioned ends—echoes, most of all, Descartes's geometrical *Res Extensae*, where abstract points (humans "disenchanted" of all their premodern *filiation* contents) are con-nected to each other by calibrated lines (the measurable merit and qualifications of bureaucratic hiring and promotion or of monetary worth in the economic mar-ket place). This concept of modernity as the cognitive dominion of the measur-ing—calibrating—index has been confirmed recently in historian Alfred W. Crosby's 1997 book, *The Measure of Reality: Quantification and Western Society, 1250-1600*, where, after decades of researching into that very Weberian question about the reason for modernity's emergence in the West (rather than in China or India), Crosby concluded that it had been the West's increasing focus on the measurement of all reality (a quantitative focus seen by Crosby to have exponen-tially increased in the West between 1250 and 1600) that is the principal factor.[99]

While not denying the thesis of Weber's *Protestant Ethic*, that the emer-gence of the modern "spirit of capitalism" can be historically located in the theol-ogy of Protestant reformer John Calvin—a thesis now given a quasi-Peircean cognitive form by the contemporary historian William Bouwsma's writings on the "Augustinian Humanism" of John Calvin, which split reality into the two Au-gustinian realms of the theological "heavenly city" of Biblical hermeneutics and the scientifically quantifiable "earthly city" including nontheological sciences ranging from physics to economics—in chapter 4 we put Weber's thesis into broader perspective by placing it within the larger historical picture suggested by the cultural equivalent of Joseph Needham's 1969 geographical hypothesis (pos-tulating the large coastline-to-landmass ratio of the European continent, as con-trasted to the small coastline-to-landmass ratio of the Chinese mainland, as being responsible for the emergence of navigation-driven modern science in Europe). Given the historical fact that Archimedes' Law of the Flotation of Bodies is the earliest known historical instance of a "scientific law," I postulate the rise of a so-cial equivalent of Jean Piaget's concept of "object permanence"—the social cog-nition of an objectively lawful reality independent of human (or godly) will—in the culture of waterborne navigation that was transmitted from the navigation-oriented culture of ancient Ionian and Athenian Greece, via the Aristotelian and Platonic philosophical medium of Christianity, to the Italian Renaissance naviga-tional culture that bred Galileo, through the "Augustinian Humanism" of Calvin—whose theological notion of "predestination" prefigured the "determin-ism" of Lockean and Newtonian science (also bred in the navigational ethos of Britain's Royal Society)—all the way to Laplace's Napoleonic assertion of a per-fectly deterministic universe where God was "an unnecessary hypothesis," to James Madison's "social mechanics" of "checks and balances" and a "govern-ment of laws and not of men."[100] Without such cognitive "object permanence"—the sufficient condition for the transition to modernity—European culture, like Indian, Chinese, Arab or African Agrarian High Cultures, would have stagnated in centuries-long cycles of orthodoxy (the centralizing force of abstract dogma promulgated by the religious and political leaders of imperial centers) and hetero-doxy (local responses to the human need for concrete imagery).

Once the object permanence of the mechanistic world-picture had been at-tained by a society, the mechanical advances of the accompanying technology— such as Gutenberg's printing press, which converted thinking itself into a textual "object" and made the attitude of cognitive "objectivity" socially widespread[101]— we have the answer to that question posed by Durkheim and Mauss in 1903 (in their study of "Primitive Classification") and still haunting the sociology of knowledge, of how truth-conditional semantics could attain textual autonomy from the pragmatics of social organization. In a modern world of widely dissemi-nated textual information, as Karl Popper pointed out in his famous three-world theory, our knowledge of the objective world achieves an autonomous existence, relatively independent of the social stratification pattern of the subjective know-ers; or, as Popper's sociological follower, Margaret Archer, points out in her 1988 book, *Culture and Agency*, it is in the modern world that culture is relatively au-tonomous, not dependent, as it had been in premodern historical time, upon the patterns of social structure.[102]

But the ultimate advantage of my sociological adaptation of Peirce's triadic phenomenology over the received dualistic imagery (of modernity's Gesellschaft vs. premodernity's Gemeinschaft) inherited from sociology's classical founders is demonstrated in chapter 4, in the conceptual capacity of my third pragmatic code—of *globalization* (or "global identity" as I had originally called it)—based as it is on Peirce's phenomenological category of *Thirdness*, to elucidate the prob-lem of "postmodernity" posed by contemporary debates about postmodernism. While keeping in mind the phenomenon pointed out by Niklas Luhmann and Juliet Flower MacCannell that observers living through a major historical transi-tion tend to mistakenly comprehend—or misread—the transition in the terms of the old cognitive code rather than of the new, my Peirce-based formal theory en-ables the skirting of such postmodernist *meconnaissance* by the sufficiently ab-stract level, called for by Luhmann, of its deductive logic.[103]

The deductive-logical elegance of a Peirce-based sociological formal prag-matics is outlined in chapter 4, by first outlining those formal conditions which could bring modernity's objective code of *calibration* into its self-referential cri-sis—thus causing the widespread perceptions of "fragmentation" so endemic to postmodernist writing. Just as the premodern pragmatic code of *filiation* (or familism) had been brought into crisis by perceptions of "too many people"—as in the late Roman Empire, when the mutual jostling of Greek Olympian religios-ity and Jewish Sinaitic Yahwism in the Eastern Mediterranean tended to delegiti-mate each other's belief systems, and such a crisis of belief and legitimacy could then only be "stabilized" by Constantine's imperial forcing of more abstract for-mulations about a Christian Trinity containing both Greek and Judaic elements, or as the European voyages of discovery, by bringing "too many people" and their

beliefs into the pre-existing European cognitive system ruptured it in the skeptical questioning of the French Encyclopaedists—so modernity's code of measurable objectivity is now threatening to rupture in the Western world's increasing
perception of the "incommensurabilities" of "too many objects." The nausea
caused by this phenomenological perception of the superfluity of too many objects—so well comprehended in the literary works of Jean-Paul Sartre or Thomas
Pynchon, for example—is not only in that supermarket realm of too many objects
of consumerism (though the superfluity of consumer choice itself occasions
"crises of identity," as the question "What should I buy?" reflects back as the
"lifestyle" question of identity, "Who am I?" that modernity had long forgotten in
its rush to measurable objectivity) but also the realm of all the possible "objects
of cognition" texts and other information packages that now proliferate wildly in
a "knowledge explosion" of unmanageable (Baudrillardian) hyper-reality. Where
the cognitive beginning of modernity can be traced back to the measurable geometry of René Descartes's *Res Extensae*, the cognitive limit to modernity can be
glimpsed in the incommensurability broached by Kurt Godel's mathematics.

It is precisely in this crisis of Cartesian modernity that Peirce's radically
anti-Cartesian epistemology is a beacon of lucid comprehension. The possibilities of a postmodern "cognitive order" beyond the perceptions of fragmentation
that currently accompany the panicked apprehension modernity's impending
breakdown—"impending" still, because the majority of the world's people are
still undergoing a transition *to* modernity's code of objective measurability—are
explored in the final section of chapter 4. The temptations of local solutions to
the suddenly reappearing questions about subjective identity, the "identity politics" that now suddenly replaces modernity's emphasis on cognitive objectivity,
are shown to be illusory, as the environmental crisis created by too many human
artifacts—"too many objects"!—is of planetary proportions demanding only
global solutions. The articulation of such a postmodern globalization's pragmatic
code of symbols (to replace modernity's *calibration* by index) is explored in this
last section of chapter 4. The possibilities of achieving "symbolic coherence"—
the postmodern stabilizing equivalent to modernity's "object permanence"—are
explored in several cultural trends, as the subjective question of value suddenly
looms larger at modernity's end than does its earlier emphasis on objective questions of truth.

Let me briefly sum up, then, the threefold advantage of my Peircean comprehension—for an emerging global social arena—of that academic project of
sociology begun by Emile Durkheim:

First, it ends the current fragmentation of social science into "multiple paradigms." Peircean Pragmaticism would be in full agreement with Luhmann's assertion that "social systems . . . consist of communications and nothing but communications." As the differing responses by Roosevelt's New Deal in America
and Hitler's Nazi program of rearmament in the 1930s showed, the same economic factor—the Great Depression—occasioned very different responses in the

two nations. Those differing responses cannot be explained by "economic factors" nor by a hazy concept of "multidimensionality," but can be effectively studied by a Pragmaticist focus on the *semantic content*—and the *pragmatic* structuring of that semantic content by such Gricean "cooperative principles" as underlie the U.S. Constitution.

That "synergistics of cognition and socialization" which Arwood defines in *pragmatics* underlies all the possible cohesion and value-consensus that sociology's current "functionalist paradigm" looks for, all the cleavages and conflicts between groups and coalitions that the "conflict paradigm" hopes to study, and, of course, the processes of cognition and socialization which the microsociological "paradigm of symbolic interactionism" takes for its domain. Further, in a deductively rigorous "ironing out" of the "multidimensional" wrinkles left by Alexander's "theoretical logic in sociology," this *Pragmaticist* sociology is truly "postempiricist" in that it takes us beyond the empiricist logic of David Hume, for whom, as the logician and philosopher Anthony Kenny shows, an empirical "actuality" could only have as its "cause" another empirical "actuality."

In contrast to the empiricist confusions of current sociological theory, Peirce's *Pragmati(ci)sm*—as Kenny demonstrates—followed Aristotle in arguing that behind every empirically observed actus (action or actuality) lay an unobserved potentia (potentiality, potency, or power). In the Formal-*Pragmatic* social theory outlined in detail in the subsequent chapters of this book, where observed individual action inevitably implies a form of collective power, Kenny's "two-way" modal logic rigorously applies: whereas observed agency logically implies a corresponding social power, and conversely the absence of any social power— as, for example, the power (capacity) of literacy in any society—necessarily implies the corresponding absence of certain possibilities of agency, the *presence* of that social power—as, for example again, the literacy that comes from legally compulsory universal schooling—does not automatically imply the presence of its corresponding agency, but only its *possibility*.

Thus, such Aristotelian-*Pragmaticist* theory enables what Kenny calls the "two way" modal logic, which the Humean empiricism of sociology's current statistical correlations of empirical actualities is unable to comprehend. For example, in the situation where (1) the observed phenomenon of agency—of John "writing" to Mary—necessarily implies the existence of some form of that social power called "elementary education" in John and Mary's culture, and (2) the known absence of all literacy and elementary education in !Kung hunter-gatherer society would also necessarily imply the impossibility of the !Kung equivalent of "John" writing to the !Kung equivalent of "Mary," Aristotelian-Pragmaticist "theoretical logic" emphasizes the third logical path: that the existence of the social institutional power of literacy and education does not necessarily imply—as is indeed the case in contemporary America's cases of "functional illiteracy"—that the agency, the act, of John writing to Mary actually takes place. Such a modal logic—the logic of possibility—is beyond what Jeffrey Alexander would consider "theoretical logic" in sociology. But in an age of global interactions, when computerization enables a far more complex modeling of human agency involving "many-valued" and "fuzzy" logics, Pragmaticism would carry social science safely to that global shore.[104]

Second, my Peircean comprehension restores the unity of the history of the human species across time and space. Mestrovic has recently accused the structuration theory of Giddens of conceptually sundering the connection of modern society from its premodern ancestor(s). As both Durkheim and the "New Institutionalism in Sociology" school of thought insist, the elements of modern contractual obligations—the cognitive *calibration* code of modernity—are "embedded" in the "precontractual elements of contract," the relations of mutual trust between contractual exchangers, whether in economic deals or the contract of marriage, established through the centuries of tradition and custom: the *filiation* code(s) of premodernity.

Not only does Pragmaticism enable the global comparisons of how hitherto separate and different societies, ranging from Anglo-America to Japan to Islamic Iran, all build their modern contractual expectations (in their *calibration* codes) upon their prior (premodern) cultural identities (their *filiation* codes), but—as is clear from the writings of both Charles S. Peirce and George Herbert Mead—such pan-human unity is premised upon a common evolutionary heritage, a nature-culture continuum. In a recent commentary on the concept of "effervescence" in Durkheim's *Elementary Forms of the Religious Life*, a social anthropologist, N. J. Allen, has compared that state of "emotional effervescence" first discussed by Durkheim in the "primitive" societies at the hunter-gatherer stage of social organization to the "chimp carnivals" observed by the primatologist V. Reynolds, in that both human and chimpanzee populations display great "social excitement" in such group meetings and "vocalize loudly and sometimes rhythmically or in chorus."

While the science of primatology is still (even more than sociology) in a state of infancy, its studies of nonhuman patterns of socialization have, since at least 1959—when Harry Harlow first published his studies of maternal deprivation among rhesus monkeys—helped suggest the possible human areas of attachment to significant others and emotional bonding that the modernizing ideology of the European Enlightenment in the eighteenth century had ignored in its rush to create a model of the "rational" human individual. Such suggestions concerning the possibilities of the "hard wiring" of human emotionality could enhance intercultural understanding in our emerging global arena of human interaction.[105]

Finally, in being strictly based on the *phenomenology* of human experience, Peirce's Pragmaticism eliminates the "reification" of theoretical constructs. I have, throughout this introduction, emphasized how Peirce's phenomenology cuts through the polemics between subjective "hermeneutics" and objective science that needlessly dogs current debate in the social sciences. In my critique of existing sociology's master concepts of agency (rationality), domination (power), and the knowledgeable, individual self in chapters 1-3, the reader will have a chance to comprehend, in the detail that such a sweeping deconstruction of sociology's received hubris deserves, the unnecessary baggage which contemporary social theory still carries—in this post-Wittgensteinian era of the awareness of the impossibility of a "private language"—from those nineteenth-century formulations about "subjective meaning."

In what seems to me to be a last gasp of such nineteenth-century visions of the individual as "captain of his fate and master of his soul," Anthony Giddens has recently rushed in to defend the last bastions of the individualist personality by declaring himself "concerned to criticize the idea of society-personality homology as an analytical postulate of social theory." What Giddens seemingly fails to realize is that for the "shared meanings" necessary for the occurrence of all human communication to exist, there *must*, at some basic or minimal level, exist a continuity between what individuals *qua* individuals cognize and what the social group *qua* group socially cognizes. It is in this basic sense of individual-social continuity of cognition that Levi-Strauss had declared in *The Savage Mind* that "ethnology is first of all psychology" and further, in his *Introduction to the Work of Marcel Mauss*, that "the unconscious is thus the mediating term between self and others . . . because, without requiring us to move outside ourselves, it enables us to coincide with forms of activity which are both at once ours and other: which are the condition of all men at all times."[106] It is in this quest for the elimination of such artificial barriers between psychology and sociology—between the phenomenology of individual and of intersubjective experience—that I recently became aware of the reason for that seemingly intense need felt by contemporary "modern" individuals for that collective "effervescence" of religious ritual.

In an attempt to theoretically comprehend the epidemic of "Dissociative Identity Disorder" (or at the very least, states of amnesic dissociation)—the fragmentation of identity—currently being experienced in all the economically developed societies of the West, psychologists John and Helen Watkins reach out (in their 1997 book) to the deviant "Freudian" theory put forward by Freud's disciple, Paul Federn (in 1952), that the individual personality consists of not one, unified ego but a *multiplicity* of mostly dormant "ego states." While this does seem a belated recognition by Freudian psychoanalysis of that "un-Cartesian pluralism" of "various . . . possible selves" which Talcott Parsons had recognized as a "particular important" contribution of the American philosophical tradition of Pragmatism, it does cement a crucial insight that is currently in danger of being completely ignored by both sociology and psychology. If, as Durkheim's *Rules of Sociological Method* had implied and Peirce had explicitly stated in the first of his four denials of 1868, "we have no power of introspection, but all knowledge of the internal world is derived . . . from external facts," then it is only in the experience of "collective effervescence" that the individual can ever hope to know—in experiencing the movements of the multiplicity of other bodies—all those possible "ego states" lying dormant within herself. Collective effervescence thus provides not only social but *personal* integration as well. A fragmented society without the unifying power of collective ritual is necessarily a "society" of fragmented personalities, and a global society that remains undertheorized can only further such disintegration at the personal level.[107]

Notes

1. Hans Joas, *Pragmatism and Social Theory* (Chicago: University of Chicago Press, 1993; originally published in *Revue Francaise de Sociologie* 25), 55. The 1913-14 course of lectures on "Pragmatism and Sociology" by Emile Durkheim was originally published in French as *Pragmatisme et sociologie* (Paris: Librarie Philosophique J. Vrin, 1955), with its English translation titled *Pragmatism and Sociology* (Cambridge: Cambridge University Press, 1983). It is to this 1983 English translation that I will be referring throughout this book, when I refer to—or quote—Durkheim's opinions about Peirce, James, or Pragmatist philosophy.

2. Randall Collins, *Four Sociological Traditions* (Oxford: Oxford University Press, 1994), 248. Sociologists puzzled by my sudden change from the word *Pragmatism*, which Durkheim had used in the title of his 1913-14 course of lectures on "Pragmatism and Sociology," to *Pragmaticism*, the word currently preferred by linguists and Peirce scholars when referring specifically to Peirce's philosophy, will there see Collins's explanation for Peirce's own sudden change of terminology: "when he objected to the way [William] James had developed pragmatism and announced that he would use the word 'pragmaticism' for his own doctrine because it was 'ugly enough to be safe from kidnappers.'" Alternatively, sociological readers could refer to Durkheim's own explanation for this change in Peirce's terminology in his *Pragmatism and Sociology*, 6, which contains not only that explanation we have just seen in Collins's 1994 book but also the article by Charles Sanders Peirce, "What Pragmatism Is," *The Monist* (1905) explaining this change, which Durkheim had read.

3. Frederic Jameson, "Preface," in *The Cultures of Globalization*, ed. Fredric Jameson and Masao Miyoshi (Durham: Duke University Press, 1998), xi. Jameson quotes from Roland Robertson, *Globalization: Social Theory and Global Culture* (London: Sage, 1992), 177-78.

4. Ian Charles Jarvie, *Rationality and Relativism: In Search of a Philosophy and History of Anthropology* (London: Routledge & Kegan Paul, 1984), 7.

5. Adam Kuper, *Culture: The Anthropologists' Account* (Cambridge, Mass.: Harvard University Press, 1999), xii. For Kuper's polemic against the post-Clifford Geertz "turn in American anthropology . . . toward an extreme relativism," see p. 206. In attempting to explain this turn to "extreme relativism," Kuper on p. 220 quotes from a satirical essay by Ernest Gellner, *Postmodernism, Reason, and Religion* (London: Routledge, 1992), 6: "Colonialism went with positivism, decolonization with hermeneutics, and it eventually culminates in postmodernism. Positivism is a form of imperialism, or perhaps the other way round, or both. Lucidly presented and (putatively) independent facts were the tools and expression of colonial domination."

6. George Ritzer, *Sociology: A Multiple Paradigm Science* (Boston: Allyn and Bacon, 1975). Steven Lukes, "Relativism in Its Place," in *Rationality and Relativism*, ed. Martin

Hollis and Steven Lukes (Cambridge, Mass.: MIT Press, 1982), 301-5. By defining *perspective* as a "set of . . . assumptions that specify how social reality is to be understood" and then arguing that "in applying them, one may explain from some perspective what could not be explained from no perspective," Lukes had, in 1982, accurately portrayed the situation which still exists in sociology textbooks today, with their presentation of almost any and all sociological knowledge from within each of at least three "paradigms or perspectives" (usually named *functionalism, conflict theory,* and *symbolic interactionism*).

7. Emile Durkheim, *Moral Education: A Study in the Theory and Application of the Sociology of Education* (Paris: Libraire Felix Alcan, 1925; English translation, New York: Free Press of Glencoe, 1961). For an informative global-comparative application of Durkheim's *Moral Education,* see Roger Goodman, "Japanese Education: A Durkheimian Ideal Type?" in *Durkheim and Modern Education,* ed. Geoffrey Walford and W. S. F. Pickering (London: Routledge, 1998), 95-107.

8. In the West, the attempts of Creation Science to substantiate the Biblical accounts of Creation in Genesis through scientific data—at the very least by pointing to loopholes in existing scientific or evolutionist accounts of the origins of life—are by now well known. What may be less known is that Hindu as well as Muslim fundamentalisms also lean heavily on the research findings of "secular" science. For a comprehensive study of the rise of the new religious movements of Hindu "fundamentalism," see Chetan Bhatt, *Liberation and Purity: Race, New Religious Movements, and the Ethics of Postmodernity* (London: University College London Press, 1997), and Thomas Blom Hansen, *The Saffron Wave: Democracy and Hindu Nationalism in Modern India* (Princeton, N.J.: Princeton University Press), 5-12. For an enlightening, superbly documented account of how Iran's Khomeini-led Islamic revolution depended for its mass mobilization of the Iranian people on the prior creative adaptations of Western scientific (including social-scientific) concepts by Islamic ideologues such as Ali Shariati, see Hamid Dabashi's *Theology of Discontent: The Ideological Foundations of the Islamic Revolution in Iran* (New York: New York University Press, 1993).

9. Philip Barker, *Michel Foucault: An Introduction* (Edinburgh: Edinburgh University Press, 1998), 91-112. Barker (pp. 96-97) mentions "Foucault's anger" at those readers who had read his book, *The Order of Things: An Archaeology of the Human Sciences* (London: Tavistock Publications, 1970), first published in French in 1966, as a structuralist, arguing that "it is Foucault's insistence on the historical dimension of knowledge . . . that distinguishes his project in the *Order of Things* from both classical structuralism and the conjunction of psychoanalysis and structuralism in the work of Jacques Lacan." I must emphasize here that (difficult as I find Foucault's writing style, having myself been trained within the Anglo-American tradition of philosophy of science and sociology), by depending on the Pragmatist philosophy of Peirce and Mead, my book not only encompasses Foucault's concern with such a "historical dimension of knowledge" but also such other Foucaulian themes as the *episteme* (see Barker, 96-98)—in my definition of pragmatic codes in chapter 4—the "long periods that lie . . . below the surface of political events" (Barker, 99) and the "disappearance of the subject" (Barker, 102-10)—which in fact is carried through by the end of chapter 3 in this book—by the relatively simple reading of Lacan's theory as a continuation of the theoretical tradition of Peirce and Mead. Barker's assertion that "in contrast to the negative, repressive account of power, Foucault develops his 'productive' model" (25) is, in a way, echoed throughout my chapter 1, which looks for such a "productive" model of power not in Foucault but in Talcott Parsons! While in no way min-

imizing either the depth of Foucault's empirical vision—such as for example in *The Birth of the Clinic: An Archaeology of Medical Perception* (London: Tavistock, 1973)—or his observation that "in the Victorian age when we typically imagine maximum repression was in operation . . . sex was constantly spoken of" (Barker, 25), I would deny that such Foucaulian insights necessarily require Foucault's theoretical edifice. As proof of this assertion I offer this interesting coincidence, that the three "pragmatic codes" I define in chapter 4—based as they are, not on Foucault but on Peirce's famous triad of categories, and first defended as a doctoral dissertation in April 1990—coincide with the three-fold periodization of history, based on Foucault's concepts, of Mark Poster in *The Mode of Information* (Chicago, University of Chicago, 1990), which I first read only in James D. Marshall's "The Mode of Information and Education: Insights on Critical Theory from Michel Foucault," in *Critical Theories in Education: Changing Terrains of Knowledge and Politics*, ed. Thomas S. Popkewitz and Lynn Fendler (New York: Routledge, 1999).

10. Charles Sanders Peirce, *Collected Papers of Charles Sanders Peirce*, 6 vols., ed. Charles Hartshone and Paul Weiss (Cambridge, Mass.: Harvard University Press, 1931-35), 1.339.

11. To be fair to Derrida, Christopher Norris, in his *Against Relativism: Philosophy of Science, Deconstruction, and Critical Theory* (Oxford: Blackwell Publishers, 1997), 7, argues that the slogan "nothing outside the text" is "so blatant a misreading of Derrida's texts as to place the burden of proof very squarely where it belongs, on the side of those who would regard history . . . as a wholly textual or rhetorical construct." For the reasons why French structuralist and poststructuralist texts—such as Claude Levi-Strauss's *The Savage Mind* (Chicago: University of Chicago, 1968), Jacques Derrida's *Of Grammatology* (Baltimore: Johns Hopkins University Press, 1978), or Jean Baudrillard's *For a Critique of the Political Economy of the Sign* (St. Louis: Telos Press, 1981)—often bear an uncanny resemblance to the writings of Peirce but cannot really be subsumed within the tradition of Peirce's philosophy, see James Jakob Liszka, *A General Introduction to the Semeiotic of Charles Sanders Peirce* (Indianapolis: Indiana University Press, 1996), 15-17, 110 n. 9. These French thinkers have all been influenced by Ferdinand de Saussure, who is, like Peirce, "considered to be an independent founder of the study of signs"; says Liszka (p. 15). The difference between the semiology of Saussure and the semeiotic of Peirce, says Liszka (p. 15-17), is that Saussure designed his semiology to be a purely empirical science and is therefore guilty of that relativistic psychologism which empirically studies how people do think (in contrast to Peirce's emphasis on logic's function in elucidating how they ought to think). Of Derrida's *Of Grammatology*, Liszka says that although he "allies himself with a Peirce of his own invention, still grammatology is built out of a reflection of Saussure" (110 n. 9). Ino Rossi, *From the Sociology of Symbols to the Sociology of Signs: Toward a Dialectical Sociology* (New York: Columbia University Press, 1983), 132-34, traces the influence of two nonlinguists on the linguistic theory of Ferdinand de Saussure's *Course in General Linguistics, 1916* (New York: McGraw-Hill, 1966), 13: John Locke's use of the term *semiotiche* to "designate the study of signs used by the mind to understand things and convey knowledge," and Emile Durkheim's concept of a "social fact," which Saussure understood to include his own concept of *langue*. Rossi sees Peirce's semiotics and Saussure's semiology to be in agreement in shifting the study of subjective symbols to objective signs: "The shift from an intrinsic and subjective notion of meaning to a relational and objective notion of meaning marks the advent of semiotics, or the science of signs."

12. Thomas M. Olshewsky, "Realism and Antifoundationalism," in *Living Doubt: Essays Concerning the Epistemology of Charles Sanders Peirce*, ed. Guy Debrock and Menno Hulswit (London: Kluwer Academic Publishers, 1999), 25. Olshewsky is here referring to Richard Rorty, *Philosophy and the Mirror of Nature* (Princeton, N.J.: Princeton University Press, 1979). For a Peirce-based critique of Rorty's relativism, see Susan Haack, "Vulgar Pragmatism: An Unedifying Prospect," in her *Evidence and Inquiry: Towards Reconstruction in Epistemology* (Oxford: Blackwell Publishers, 1993), 182-202, and "'We Pragmatists . . . ': Peirce and Rorty in Conversation" and "Reflections on Relativism: From Momentous Tautology to Seductive Contradiction," in her *Manifesto of a Passionate Moderate: Unfashionable Essays* (Chicago: University of Chicago Press, 1998), 31-47 and 149-66.

13. Durkheim, *Pragmatism and Sociology*, 6-7. Interestingly, Martin Kusch's *Psychologism: A Case Study in the Sociology of Philosophical Knowledge* (London: Routledge, 1995), while acknowledging the fact (p. 15) that the arch-relativist David Bloor—of the "strong program in the sociology of knowledge" fame—had actually credited Durkheim with the "classic denunciation of psychologism," nevertheless ends up citing phenomenologist Max Scheler's accusation against Durkheim of "sociologism (which is a counterpart of psychologism)" because of Durkheim's "claim . . . that reasoning and perception could be shaped by social position" (Kusch, 257). Kusch (p. 10) also cites Peirce scholar Susan Haack's *Philosophy of Logics* (Cambridge: Cambridge University Press, 1978) as arguing (Haack, 238-42) for three possible positions with regard to *psychologism*: the *antipsychologism* of logicians Gottlob Frege and Karl Popper that holds that "logic has nothing to do with mental processes"; the *strong psychologism* of Rorty and the Saussurean semiology of French post-structuralists, which, in holding that "logic is descriptive of how humans in fact think," lapses into extreme relativism; and what Haack labels weak *psychologism*—which she attributes to Charles Sanders Peirce—which holds that "logic is *prescriptive* of how we should think" (italics added). Kusch's argument (pp. 10-257) places my own argument in this book in relief: whereas Durkheim's own formulations often lead to mutually contradictory epistemological interpretations (and Peirce's do, too, as I will show later), Durkheim and Peirce shared this common focus on the normative or prescriptive pressure of science, as a collective enterprise exerted upon individual tendencies to deviant or relativistic interpretation. Sociological theory can therefore be reinforced—and better applied to the current social phenomenon of *globalization*—if this shared focus is utilized to reformulate it in Peirce's terminology.

14. Olshewsky, "Realism and Antifoundationalism," 25; Hollis and Lukes, eds., *Rationality and Relativism; Jarvie, Rationality and Relativism*. While I may seem, within the immediacy of this chapter, to be conducting a one-sided campaign against *relativism* only, in chapter 1 I will proceed to deconstruct the concept of rationality, too, as used by social science. While I felt it strategically important here, in this introductory chapter, to immediately disentangle Peirce from that "pragmatism = relativism" equation popularized by Richard Rorty, it is also important for the reader to remember that what Kusch (in *Psychologism*, 10, following Haack, *Philosophy of Logics*, 238-42) called the *weak psychologism* of Peirce really positions Peirce neither with the "rationalism" of *antipsychologism* nor with the "relativism" of what Kusch and Haack call *strong psychologism*. As we will see later, Peirce's triadic phenomenology of knowledge has each act of inquiry beginning in "relativistic" *firstness* and ending in "rationalistic" *thirdness*. Since every actor in society engages continually in such acts or processes of inquiry, the attitudes that sociologists like Hollis and Lukes

dichotomize into these seemingly pure ideal types of "rationality" and "relativism" really constantly intermingle and interpenetrate in Peirce's evolution of inquiry.

15. Nicholas Rescher, *Objectivity: The Obligations of Impersonal Reason* (Notre Dame, Ind.: University of Notre Dame Press, 1997), 73. The same point—that the pragmatic success attained in reaching our goals guarantees not the truth of any statement but specifically that *adequatio ad re* or "truth" of the means or "methods" employed—was made by Rescher earlier, in his *Methodological Pragmatism: A Systems-Theoretic Approach to the Theory of Knowledge* (New York: New York University Press, 1977).

16. Christopher Norris, "But Will It Fly? Aerodynamics as a Test Case for Anti-Realism," in Norris, *Against Relativism*, 249-64.

17. Hans Joas, "Introduction: Steps toward a Pragmatist Theory of Action," in Joas, *Pragmatism and Social Theory*, 1-13. Richard Rorty, in his *Philosophy and the Mirror of Nature*, has successfully popularized an *anti-representationalist* view of Pragmatism, as eschewing a passive "mirror of nature" view of knowledge—an epistemological view which Rorty traces to the empiricist epistemology of John Locke—and thereby combined such a version of "Pragmatism" with the philosophies of Martin Heidegger and the later Ludwig Wittgenstein in a social constructionist, postmodern epistemology. Susan Haack, in "'We Pragmatists . . . ,'" 35, responds to Rorty's identification of Pragmatism with anti-representationalism with Peirce's definition of his key-term sign, with *representamen*—that which represents—to show that Rorty distorts Peirce's philosophy. Despite such a misrepresentation of the thought of Peirce—the founder of Pragmatism—Rorty's popularization of that very word, *Pragmatism*, came at a time when the ubiquity of its influence was being recognized. For example, Karl Popper, in *Objective Knowledge: An Evolutionary Approach* (Oxford: Clarendon Press, 1972), 296, and W. V. O. Quine, in *Word and Object* (Cambridge, Mass.: Harvard University Press, 1960), 23 had both by 1972 identified aspects of their own philosophies with that of Peirce. We have already seen Thomas Olshewsky's pointing to the image of Peirce "as the forerunner of post-structuralism" "Realism and Antifoundationalism," 25). H. P. Rickman, in *Dilthey Today: A Critical Appraisal of the Contemporary Relevance of His Work* (New York: Greenwood Press, 1988), xii, 172, assimilates Wilhelm Dilthey's *hermeneutics* to Peirce's formulation of *interpretant* signs.

18. Robertson, *Globalization*, 177-78.

19. Nicholas Rescher, "Pragmatism in Crisis," in *Profitable Speculations: Essays on Current Philosophical Themes* (Lanham, Md.: Rowman & Littlefield, 1997), 27-48; Durkheim, *Pragmatism and Sociology*, 5-10. The works cited by Durkheim (which I have mentioned) are, in their chronological order of publication, J. M. Baldwin, ed., *Dictionary of Philosophy and Psychology* (New York: Macmillan & Co., 1901-05), 2:321-22; Charles S. Peirce, "What Pragmatism Is"; William James, *Pragmatism: A New Name for Some Old Ways of Thinking, Popular Lectures in Philosophy* (London: Longmans, Green & Co., 1907), 46-47; and William James, *The Meaning of Truth* (London: Longmans, Green & Co., 1909), 51-52. Acknowledging James's 1909 belief in the commonality of his own thinking with Peirce's, Durkheim (*Pragmatism and Sociology*, 10) says: "In *The Meaning of Truth*, James declares that he shares Peirce's ideas." Randall Collins (*Four Sociological Traditions*, 248) declares that "James was a rather lightweight philosopher . . . not really interested in questions of epistemology, but in using philosophy to defend religion."

20. Rescher, "Pragmatism in Crisis," 31.

21. Durkheim, *Pragmatism and Sociology*, 6-7.

22. Durkheim, *Pragmatism and Sociology*, 6-10. Karl-Otto Apel, in his *Charles S. Peirce: From Pragmatism to Pragmaticism* (Amherst: University of Massachusetts Press, 1981), 54-55, 213 n. 4, mentions that James had called Peirce's writings of 1877-78—one of which is that very article, "How to Make Our Ideas Clear" that Durkheim cites in his *First Lecture* on "Pragmatism and Sociology"—the "birth certificates of Pragmatism." I do not know if the talk, mentioned by Apel, that Peirce gave in 1871 before the Metaphysical Club, during which he unveiled the name—derived from Kant—*Pragmatism* for his own philosophy, is what Durkheim refers to, in his *Second Lecture*, as "private talk." But Apel also quotes a 1908 article from Peirce's *Collected Papers* (6.482) saying: "In 1871, in a Metaphysical Club in Cambridge, Massachusetts, I used to preach this principle as a sort of logical gospel, representing the unformulated method followed by Berkeley, and in conversation about it I called it 'Pragmatism.'"

23. Durkheim, *Pragmatism and Sociology*, 36-37; Rescher, "Pragmatism in Crisis," 31.

24. For a scathing critique of Richard Rorty's version of Pragmatism—written from the perspective of Peirce's thought—see Susan Haack, "Vulgar Pragmatism." See also Haack, "'We Pragmatists . . . ,'" 31-47.

25. Rescher, "Pragmatism in Crisis," 36-39; Joas, "Durkheim and Pragmatism: Psychology of Consciousness and the Social Constitution of Categories," 55, and Joas, "Durkheim's Intellectual Development," 242, both in Joas, *Pragmatism and Social Theory*.

26. For an informative presentation of the scientific epistemology of different "levels"—a deeper level of unobserved but real theoretical entities underlying and explaining a surface level of phenomena open to empirical observation—see Mario Bunge, *Metascientific Queries* (Springfield, Ill.: Charles C. Thomas, 1959), or his "Phenomenological Theories," in the Festschrift that he edited in honor of Karl Popper, *The Critical Approach to Science and Philosophy* (London: Collier-MacMillan, 1964). An interesting metaphor differentiating his own hypothetico-deductive scientific realism from positivism was provided by Karl Popper in his *Conjectures and Refutations: The Growth of Scientific Knowledge* (London: Routledge & Kegan Paul, 1963) and *Objective Knowledge*, 341-61, in his positivism-as-"bucket" vs. realism-as-"flashlight" analogy: whereas the method of positivism was to passively append empirical observations onto each other to produce theory—like a bucket passively collecting drops of rainwater—realism is like a flashlight, actively searching out and selecting facts in its theory-construction. Popper's metaphor holds relevance in understanding not only Durkheim's *Tenth Lecture* on reality-construction (*Pragmatism and Sociology*, 54-58) but also the emphasis on cultural "selectivity" of Niklas Luhmann, "The Evolutionary Differentiation between Society and Interaction," in *The Micro-Macro Link*, ed. Jeffrey Alexander et al. (Berkeley: University of California Press, 1987), 112-31. Luhmann's suggestion of "epistemic levels" to differentiate the concepts of "society" and "interaction" makes him a scientific realist, *malgre lui*.

27. Stjepan G. Mestrovic, *Emile Durkheim and the Reformation of Sociology* (Totowa, N.J.: Rowman & Littlefield, 1988); Stjepan G. Mestrovic, *The Coming Fin de Siecle: An Application of Durkheim's Sociology to Modernity and Postmodernism* (London: Routledge, 1991); Stjepan G. Mestrovic, *Durkheim and Postmodern Culture* (New York: Aldine de Gruyter, 1992); Talcott Parsons, *The Structure of Social Action* (Glencoe, Ill.: Free Press, 1937 [1949]); Jeffrey Alexander, *Theoretical Logic in Sociology* (Berkeley: University of California Press, 1982); Warren Schmaus, *Durkheim's Philosophy of Science and the Soci-*

ology of Knowledge (Chicago: University of Chicago Press, 1994), 7, 12-18, 62-68, 90-91, 121. See also Schmaus, *Durkheim's Philosophy*, 161-62, for a useful explanation designed for nonspecialists in philosophy of Peirce's method of abductive or retroductive inference.

28. Emile Durkheim, *De la division du travail social: Etude sur l'organization des societes superieures* (Paris: Alcan, 1893), English translation, *The Division of Labor in Society* (New York: Free Press, 1933); Schmaus, *Durkheim's Philosophy*, 22-23.

29. Emile Durkheim, *Le Suicide: Etude de sociologie* (Paris: Alcan, 1897); English translation, *Suicide: A Study in Sociology* (Glencoe, Ill.: Free Press, 1951). Theodore Millon, "The Borderline Personality: A Psychosocial Epidemic," in *Borderline Personality Disorder: Etiology and Academe*, ed. Joel Paris (London: American Psychiatric Press, 1993), 206-9, specifically credits Durkheim for having provided the best explanation for the current "epidemic" of borderline personality disorders, with his concept of "social anomie." Dr. Millon, a clinical psychologist, is the creator of the well-known Millon scales for measuring the severity of personality disorders.

30. Christopher Hookway, *Peirce* (London: Routledge & Kegan Paul, 1985), 23; 5.265. Peirce's complete 1868 paper, "Some Consequences of Four Incapacities"—originally published in the *Journal of Speculative Philosophy* 2 (1868): 140-57—can also be found in its entirety in Charles S. Pierce, *Writings of Charles S. Peirce*, vol. 2: 1867-1871, ed. Edward C. Moore et al. (Bloomington: Indiana University Press, 1984), 211-42 (the "four denials" are listed on p. 213).

31. Stjepan G. Mestrovic, *Anthony Giddens: The Last Modernist* (London: Routledge, 1998), 179-206.

32. Emile Durkheim, *The Rules of Sociological Method* (New York: Free Press, 1982), 98-100.

33. Peirce, *Collected Papers*, 2.274; Liszka, *General Introduction to the Semeiotic*, 19; Hans Joas, "Durkheim's Intellectual Development," 239, remarks about psychologist Jean Piaget's criticism of Durkheim's *Moral Education*, "Piaget's theory must be seen as a correction of deficiencies inherent" in Durkheim's thought, despite "the extent to which Piaget based his moral theory on Durkheim" (see Jean Piaget, *The Moral Judgement of the Child*, New York: Free Press, 1997: 341-71). A similar point must be noted here: like Piaget's, Peirce's theory, I am arguing, must also be "seen as a correction of deficiencies inherent" in Durkheim's thought, and one of those "deficiencies" occurs, according to Warren Schmaus (*Durkheim's Philosophy*, 253) at this point. Unlike Peirce, whose third of his four denials would completely rule out all possibility of an individual being able to think without those "collective representations" which he calls *signs*—i.e., the words in a language—Durkheim, according to Schmaus, seems to have hesitated on this point. In one passage from Durkheim's 1912 book, *The Elementary Forms of the Religious Life* (New York: Free Press, 1915), Schmaus finds Durkheim implying that thought is separate from language, in that thought operates by "ideas"—which term Schmaus traces back to its definition by John Locke (who himself believed that Rene Descartes had so defined *ideas*) as "mental images"—whereas *language* consists of words. Peirce, on the other hand—as Carl R. Hausman's *Charles S. Peirce's Evolutionary Philosophy* (New York: Cambridge University Press, 1993), 194-225, points out—pioneered the "linguistic turn" of contemporary philosophy by his 1868 insight that we have no power of thought without linguistic signs. This inconsistency in the later Durkheim's thought—his incomplete acceptance of the collective-linguistic structuring of individual thought—is what calls for that completion of the Durkheimian project of sociology by Peircean Pragmaticism advocated in this book.

34. Durkheim, *Elementary Forms of the Religious Life*. Peirce, Collected Works, 5.402 nn. 2-3, says, "What is it, then, that the whole people is about, what is this civilization that is the outcome of history, but is never completed? We cannot expect to attain a complete conception of it. . . . We may say that it is the process whereby man . . . becomes more and more gradually imbued with the Spirit of God." While Peirce's community seems here to extend—in both space and time—beyond the tribal community of Durkheim's *Elementary Forms of the Religious Life*, I thought—in the light of Hausman's own astonished remark that "Peirce even introduces a religious element" into his otherwise straightforwardly theory-of-knowledge discussion—that I ought to mention this more-than-coincidental resemblance between the thinking of Peirce and Durkheim even in their respective conceptions of religious phenomena. *Charles S. Peirce, Writings of Charles S. Peirce*, vol. 1: *1857-1866* (Bloomington: Indiana University Press, 1982), 37-44, has four essays written by Peirce on infinity and God between 1859 and 1860.

35. Gregory P. Stone and Harvey A. Faberman, "On the Edge of Rapprochement: Was Durkheim Moving toward the Perspective of Symbolic Interaction?" in *Social Psychology through Symbolic Interaction*, ed. Gregory P. Stone and Harvey A. Faberman (Waltham, Mass.: Xerox College Publishing, 1970), 100-112. This article by Stone and Faberman had been originally published in the *Sociological Quarterly* 8 (Spring 1967): 45-53. See also Parsons, *The Structure of Social Action*; Alexander, *Theoretical Logic in Sociology*.

36. Stone and Faberman, "On the Edge," 104; Mestrovic, *Anthony Giddens*, 179-206.

37. Stone and Faberman, "On the Edge," 110. It is worth noting that Stone and Faberman dedicated their 1970 edited collection of articles, *Social Psychology through Symbolic Interaction*, "to Herbert Blumer, teacher and scholar, who has kept the perspective of symbolic interactionism alive and lively."

38. Durkheim, *Pragmatism and Sociology*, 6; Peirce, Collected Papers, vols. 1-6; Rescher, "Pragmatism in Crisis," 36.

39. Durkheim, *Pragmatism and Sociology*, 7-10, 36-98; Peirce, *Collected Papers*, 5.265; Hookway, Peirce, 23. Max Fisch, in his introduction to the *Writings of Charles S. Peirce*, vol. 1, xxviii, points out that Peirce's famous three categories of knowledge, which Peirce himself associated after 1867 with *scientific epistemology*, had been actually derived from his early awareness of the process of *intersubjective communication*. As evidence of such a quasi-sociological interest by the early Peirce and its influence on his later scientific theory, Fisch points to Peirce's Spring 1861 article—on pp. 45-46 of the same vol. 1 of the *Writings of Charles S. Peirce*—titled "I, It, and Thou: A Book Giving Instruction in Some Elements of Thought."

40. Joas, "Durkheim and Pragmatism," 55-56; Durkheim, *Pragmatism and Sociology*, 1. Randall Collins (*Four Sociological Traditions*, 248) says: "James was rather a lightweight philosopher, and the lack of objectivity in his system left him an easy target for his professional colleagues." Stjepan Mestrovic—in a personal communication—would seem to agree: "William James," writes Mestrovic, "made a better 'straw man' argument for what Durkheim feared and despised."

41. Durkheim, *Pragmatism and Sociology*, 5-6, 114 n. 10. The editor of the published version of Durkheim's lectures on "Pragmatism and Sociology" mentions in his note 10 to the *First Lecture* that "the general title of the series of papers by Peirce is 'La logique de la science'" and that "the first article appeared in Dec. 1878, pp. 553-69." Because he believes

that Durkheim was unfamiliar with Peirce's writings on scientific method, Schmaus (*Durkheim's Philosophy*, 161-62) denies the possibility raised by Toby Huff that in his 1897 book on Suicide Durkheim was using Peirce's abductive method of hypothesis formation. Rescher ("Pragmatism in Crisis," 30) asserts that in 1910 Bertrand Russell "knew pragmatism only in its Jamesean version." I am indebted to my University of Cincinnati office-neighbor—philosopher and Peirce scholar Dr. Charles Seibert—for having shown me the French translations, in the December 1878 (pp. 553-69) and January 1879 (pp. 39-57) issues of the *Revue Philosophique de la France et de L'Etranger*, of Peirce's seminal 1878 essays, "The Fixation of Belief" and "How to Make Our Ideas Clear," respectively, now (both) reprinted—in both the English and French versions—in *Writings of Charles S. Peirce*, vol. 3: 1872-1878 (Bloomington: Indiana University Press, 1986), 242-76, 338-74. The director of Indiana University's Peirce Edition Project, which has published several volumes of these *Writings of Charles S. Peirce*, states in his preface (in volume 1, xi): "The writings Peirce himself published run to approximately twelve thousand printed pages. At five hundred pages to the volume, these would make 24 volumes. The known manuscripts that he left unpublished run to approximately eighty thousand handwritten pages. If, on the average, two manuscript pages yield one book page, it would take eighty additional volumes for the unpublished papers and a total of 104 volumes for his complete works."

42. Durkheim, *Pragmatism and Sociology*, 5-6, dedicates a section each to Nietzsche and to Romanticism before introducing Peirce and the other Pragmatists in his *First Lecture*. Joas, "Durkheim and Pragmatism," 55-56, in calling attention to that second of three reasons that Durkheim, *Pragmatism and Sociology*, 1, cites for Durkheim's choice of the philosophy of Pragmatism for his 1913-14 lectures—Durkheim's nationalistic interest in defending the Cartesian rationalism of French culture—reminded me that Durkheim had not been the only prominent intellectual on the Allied side around World War I to focus on the *irrationalism* of prominent German thinkers (such as Nietzsche). George Santayana, *Egotism in German Philosophy* (New York: C. Scribner's Sons, 1916) should remind one that the suspicion of German philosophy around and during World War I reached all the way to Harvard University, across the Atlantic. Schmaus, *Durkheim's Philosophy*, 62-64, points out that although Durkheim accepted what he called the "rationalist postulate" that "there is nothing in reality that one may be justified in considering as radically refractory to human reason," he nevertheless questioned Cartesian rationalism's a priori belief that "the logic of things is identical to that of mind," declaring it to be a "simplism" that overlooked the role of observation and of experiment.

43. Collins, *Four Sociological Traditions*, 203; Philip Manning, *Erving Goffman and Modern Sociology* (Stanford, Calif.: Stanford University Press, 1992), 1-2, 34-35.

44. Erving Goffman, "Felicity's Condition," *American Journal of Sociology* 89, no.1 (July 1983).

45. Goffman, "Felicity's Condition" 1; Durkheim, *Pragmatism and Sociology*, 1. For a superb, brief introduction to the Pragmatics of John Austin and H. Paul Grice for the nonspecialist in linguistics, see Jenny Thomas, *Meaning in Interaction: An Introduction to Pragmatics* (London: Longman, 1995).

46. Goffman, "Felicity's Condition," 25-27. For a brief analysis of Austin's "felicity conditions" tailored for the quick understanding of the non-linguistic specialist, see Thomas, *Meaning in Interaction*, 37-40.

47. Thomas Scheff, *Being Mentally Ill: A Sociological Theory* (Chicago: Aldine, 1966).

48. Manning, *Erving Goffman*, 2, 158, 175-83; Anthony Giddens, *The Constitution of Society* (Cambridge, England: Polity, 1984).

49. Mestrovic, *Anthony Giddens*, 179-207. Anthony Giddens, *Politics, Sociology, and Social Theory: Encounters with Classical and Contemporary Social Thought* (Stanford, Calif.: Stanford University Press, 1995), 258, insists that any adequate theory of social reproduction should "recognize the skillful and knowledgeable character of the everyday participation of actors in social practices." The conceptual polar opposite of Giddens's "knowledgeable" actors seems to me to be what Henaff, *Claude Levi-Strauss*, 104, calls the "Objective Intersubjectivity" concept of the interpersonal role played by *unconscious* phenomena, such as, for example, in Claude Levi-Strauss, *Structural Anthropology* (New York: Basic Books, 1963), 21—"the unconscious activity of the mind consists in imposing form upon content"—or Claude Levi-Strauss, *Introduction to the Work of Marcel Mauss* (London: Routledge, 1987), 35: "The unconscious would thus be the mediating term between self and others." Ino Rossi, ed., *The Unconscious in Culture: The Structuralism of Claude Levi-Strauss in Perspective* (New York: E. P. Dutton, 1974) contains a number of interesting perspectives within the debate among anthropologists about Levi-Strauss's use of this concept of the "unconscious." My book's chapter 3 follows Jacques Lacan's similar positions: both Levi-Strauss and Lacan—with their emphasis on the important role played by unconscious factors—would appear to be closer to Durkheim's original view of society as a source of *constraint external* to subjective voluntarism than would Giddens's countersuggestion of that unlimited agency of "knowledgeable" actors.

50. Schmaus, *Durkheim's Philosophy*, 12-18, 90-91.

51. John Locke, *An Essay Concerning Human Understanding* (London: Dent, 1961 [originally published 1690]); David Hume, *A Treatise of Human Nature*, 1739 (Oxford: Clarendon Press, 1888 [originally published 1739]); David Hume, *An Enquiry Concerning Human Understanding* (Indianapolis: Hackett, 1977 [originally published 1748]); Popper, *Conjectures and Refutations*.

52. Emile Durkheim, *Elementary Forms of the Religious Life*, 20, 26 n. 2, 519-27 n. 1; Locke, Essay; Schmaus, *Durkheim's Philosophy*, 63, 216-22.

53. Shmaus, *Durkheim's Philosophy*, 62-64; Stjepan G. Mestrovic, "Durkheim's Renovated Rationalism and the Idea That 'Collective Life Is Only Made of Representations,'" *Current Perspectives in Social Theory* 6 (1985), 199-218. See also Mestrovic, *Emile Durkheim and the Reformation of Sociology*, 40-53.

54. Karl-Otto Apel, *Understanding and Explanation: A Transcendental-Pragmatic Perspective* (Cambridge, Mass.: MIT Press, 1984), 59; Anthony Giddens, *Durkheim* (Hassocks: Harvester, 1978), 111; Steven Lukes, *Emile Durkheim: His Life and Work* (Stanford, Calif.: Stanford University Press, 1985), 54-57, 356. Lukes provides no evidence whatsoever for his assertion that Durkheim was a Kantian, beyond the fact that Durkheim admired the Kantian Charles Renouvier, that he had declared it to be the German philosophy best reconcilable to science, and that Paul Nizan, his Marxist critic, had labeled it so! On the other hand, Durkheim, *Pragmatism and Sociology*, 102, 131 n. 1, has Durkheim declaring himself "firmly in the Kantian tradition"—but this appendix to Durkheim's published "Pragmatism" lectures was "based upon notes provided by M. Marcel Tardy" and not by Durkheim himself. See also Mestrovic, *Emile Durkheim and the Reformation of Sociology*, 19-39, 54-75; Schmaus, *Durkheim's Philosophy*, 190. Perhaps nothing illustrates better what Durkheim would have called an "anomic division of labor" existing among academics today than that the sociologist Mestrovic—notorious among sociologists as a pro-

ponent of Durkheim's roots in Arthur Schopenhauer's (not Kant's) philosophy—should suddenly find himself labeled by philosopher Warren Schmaus—in Schmaus's "Durkheim on the Causes and Functions of the Categories," in *On Durkheim's Elementary Forms of the Religious Life*, ed. N. J. Allen et al. (London: Routledge, 1998), 177—as one of "many of Durkheim's critics . . . who assume that he (Durkheim) meant the categories in Immanuel Kant's sense."

55. Durkheim, *Pragmatism and Sociology*, 54-57.

56. Shmaus, *Durkheim's Philosophy*, 253.

57. Schmaus, *Durkheim's Philosophy*, 64, 253; Emile Durkheim, *Les Formes elementaires de la vie religieuse* (Paris: Alcan, 1912), 620; Hookway, *Peirce*, 19-23.

58. Schmaus, *Durkheim's Philosophy*, 250.

59. Mestrovic, *Emile Durkheim and the Reformation of Sociology*, 1, cites from Andre Lalande, "Allocution," in *Centenaire de la naissance d'Emile Durkheim* (Paris: Annales de l'Universite de Paris, 1960), 23, a remark made on the occasion of the 100th anniversary of Durkheim's birth, that Durkheim was "so enamored of Schopenhauer" that he earned the nickname "Schopen" from his students. Hans Joas, "Durkheim's Intellectual Development," 232, citing this same information about Durkheim's "Schopen" nickname from the same source, gives credit to Mestrovic for ensuring that "this enthusiasm" of Durkheim for Schopenhauer, which "has long been known," is now "considered seriously." Joas argues that Schopenhauer's influence on Durkheim "must be seen not only as the source of specific assumptions in, for example, the study of suicide, on the dangers of the anarchy of the individual's instinctual life, but also for the presuppositions of Durkheim's 'rationalism' which from the outset was never a simple rationalism." According to Joas, neither the assumption by Talcott Parsons—"who had a rather limited background in nineteenth-century continental philosophy"—that Thomas Hobbes was "the source of specific assumptions" made by Durkheim nor "the frequent description of Durkheim as a Kantian" is "very helpful." Mestrovic has, over several writings between 1988 and 1992, made a plausible case for Schopenhauer, rather than Kant, being the dominant philosophical influence on Durkheim: Schopenhauerian pessimism, argues Mestrovic, reigned supreme over the high culture of the approaching 1900 *fin de siecle*, and that pessimism is apparent in Durkheim's passages on happiness in *The Division of Labor in Society*, 170-96. Schmaus, *Durkheim's Philosophy*, 190, as we have already seen, cites Durkheim's 1909 article on the "The Sociology of Religion and the Theory of Knowledge," for the crucial difference he (Durkheim himself) saw between how the Kantians treated the "categories" as "the natural law of thought" and how "for us they are the product of human artifice." Bryan Magee, *The Philosophy of Schopenhauer* (Oxford: Clarendon Press, 1997), 162, 205, not only clearly demarcates for us the difference in epistemology between Kant and Schopenhauer—for Schopenhauer, argues Magee, "the constitution of phenomena in space and time . . . can never occur except as activities involving a subject" (an epistemological position identical with Durkheim's: Durkheim had simply used the words "human artifice" in 1909, where Schopenhauer had said "activities involving a human subject")—but also furnishes us with the possible reason for that negative reaction of some self-proclaimed Durkheimians to Mestrovic's championing of Schopenhauer as Durkheim's philosophical muse, in the statement he quotes from Schopenhauer *The World as Will and Representation*: "Nations are in reality mere abstractions; only individuals actually exist" (2:591). Having grown accustomed to contrasting Durkheim's ontological *collectivism* with Max Weber's methodological *individualism*, the current generation of sociologists cannot then

be expected to easily stomach Mestrovic's seemingly sudden linkage of the names of the *collectivist* Durkheim and the *individualist* Schopenhauer!

60. Kusch, *Psychologism*, 15, cites David Bloor's crediting of Durkheim's strategy in having "the determining cause of a social fact . . . be sought among the social facts preceding it and not among the states of the individual consciousness" as the *avoidance* of *psychologism*, but Kusch responds by citing the phenomenologist Max Scheler's charge against Durkheim of "sociologism (which is a counterpart of psychologism)" (257). In fact, by refusing to go outside the text of *collective representations* to seek the cause of their meaningfulness, I believe that Durkheim prepared the way—via his admirer, the linguist Saussure—for Jacques Derrida's "Intertextual" *Grammatology*.

61. Eric Hobsbawm, *On History* (New York: Free Press, 1997), 145-46, gives the term *vulgar Marxism* a precise definition in seven numbered points.

62. Alexander, *Theoretical Logic in Sociology*; Schmaus, *Durkheim's Philosophy*, 251.

63. Karl Popper, *The Poverty of Historicism* (London: Routledge and Kegan Paul, 1957), 65, 147-52; Popper, *Objective Knowledge*, 290-95. Popper's argument—also put forward by Friedrich A. von Hayek in "The Results of Human Action but Not of Human Design," in his *Studies in Philosophy, Politics, and Economics* (London: 1961), 96-105—is that because almost all social institutions are unintended and unforeseen products of human action, social sciences can only study the "laws" of unintended consequences. Frederick A. Olafson, *The Dialectic of Action: A Philosophical Interpretation of History and the Humanities* (Chicago: University of Chicago Press, 1979), 280 n. 44, criticizes Popper for having left an "unresolved problem concerning the relationship of situational logic (which Popper advocates for social science) stands to his equally emphatic sponsorship of the covering-law theory of explanation (which Popper advocates for the scientific study of the objective world)." It is this "unresolved problem" of Popper's that Peirce had—as I will show—in fact already resolved.

64. Hausman (*Charles S. Peirce's Evolutionary Philosophy*, 168-206) seems to be in total agreement with the view put forth by Apel (*Charles S. Peirce*, 134-90) that it was specifically the *evolutionism* that Peirce elaborated between 1885 and 1898 which led Peirce to break away—with, what he later called his Pragmaticism—from the general Pragmatism of James (and later, Rorty). It then becomes clear that it was specifically Peirce's 1885-98 writings on evolution that Durkheim had failed to comprehend in his attempt to understand how Peirce's "rationalism" fitted in with William James's Pragmatism. Dominique Merllie, "Did Lucien Levy-Bruhl Answer the Objections Made in *Les Formes elementaires*?" in *On Durkheim's Elementary Forms of Religious Life*, ed. Allen et al., 33, quotes that response by Durkheim to Levy-Bruhl—that Levy-Bruhl was wrong in positing the existence of a special "primitive mentality" because all humans "grew out of . . . the same process of evolution"—that I quoted in my text. David R. Olson, *The World on Paper: The Conceptual and Cognitive Implications of Writing and Reading* (Cambridge: Cambridge University Press, 1994), 29, says that, in defending what he thought were the implicitly evolutionist connotations of his concepts of *primitive mentality, affective thinking,* and *participation mystique,* "Levy-Bruhl explained such thoughts by appeal to Durkheim's notion of collective representations." A. Rivaud, "Notice sur la vie et l'oeuvre de L. Levy-Bruhl" (Paris: Institut des Sciences morales et politiques, 1950), is cited by Merllie as having been "grieved and disturbed" when he discovered "by the attacks . . . of orthodox Durkheimians" that not all readers of Durkheim shared his own belief that his own *cultural evolutionism* had been shared by Durkheim.

65. Durkheim, *Moral Education*, 27, 46, 216, 225, 271. Mestrovic, *Emile Durkheim and the Reformation of Sociology*, 44, 48, 86, 115, traces this central usage of the concept of "habit" from Durkheim's *Rules of Sociological Method*—where Mestrovic, in fact, sees Durkheim defining his central concept of "social facts" as habits—to Marcel Mauss's *Sociology and Psychology* (London: Routledge and Kegan Paul, 1950), 12, defining "collective representations" as "habitual actions and ideas," to the Durkheimians Georges Davy's and Robert Hertz's research-concerns with "habits" such as the use of the right hand. See also Piaget, *Moral Judgement of the Child*, 344. In quoting from Durkheim, *Moral Education* (in the original 1925 French version edited by Paul Fauconnet), Piaget renders what the 1961 English language translation has as the word custom as *habit*, thus: "The affinity between *habit* and moral practice is even such that any collective *habit* almost inevitably presents a certain moral character. Once a form of behavior has become habitual in a group, any departure from it provokes an impulse of disapproval very closely akin to that called forth by moral faults properly so called. Such *habits* command, in a measure, the special respect that is paid to moral practices. While all collective habits are not moral, all moral practices are undoubtedly collective habits" (italics added). When the same passage appears in the 1961 English translation (pp. 27-28), there is a substitution of the English word *custom* for what Piaget seems to have understood as *habit* and the words *social custom* for the more powerful connotation in Piaget's reading of *collective habit*; Durkheim's words seem to lose their Peircean ring!

66. Hausman, *Charles S. Peirce's Evolutionary Philosophy*, 5-45, sees this congruence between habits—including habits of belief—and natural laws, as the corner-stone of Peirce's Pragmaticism, as well as the source of that doubt (expressed for example by Hookway, *Peirce*, 262) that Peirce's evolutionism was not *realist* but *idealist*, in that, for Peirce, matter was a sort of "effete mind" whose habits had grown too rigid, too inflexibly ossified, into the "laws of nature." Sociologists—mindful of that positivist/idealist dichotomy charged against Durkheim by Talcott Parsons and Jeffrey Alexander—interested in this debate among philosophers about whether Peirce was a realist or an idealist, would do well to first read Nicholas Rescher, *A System of Pragmatic Idealism*, vol. 1 (Princeton, NJ: Princeton University Press, 1992), 310: "There is, however, yet another version of epistemic idealism—distinctive from cognitive idealism and far more tenable than it—that might be called conceptual idealism. This position holds that whatever is real is in principle knowable, and that knowledge involves conceptualization." It is in this strictly limited sense of what Rescher—a respected Peirce scholar—calls *conceptual idealism*, that Peirce—as well as Durkheim—could be considered *idealists*. On p. 305, Rescher lists eight varieties of idealism, so it is important for sociologists who choose to follow Parsons and Alexander in blithely using this philosophical term to be held accountable in defining which of these eight varieties of idealism they really mean to apply (to Durkheim, Peirce, or any other thinker).

67. Parsons, *The Structure of Social Action*. As I will demonstrate in greater detail in chapter 3, Parsons's formulation of the concept of the "internalization" is not wrong per se, but just weak, if it does not include habituation—the formation of all those habits of thought, feeling and action—that encompass the whole process of socialization. Thus if Parsons's concept of the "internalization of norms" can be restated so as to explicitly comprehend the full concept of socialization—"normative internalization as habit formation"—then it coincides with the subject-matter of pragmatics, defined by Ellyn Lucas Arwood, in her *Pragmaticism: Theory and Application* (Rockville, Md.: Aspen, 1983), 11, as

that "synergistics of cognition and socialization." Giddens, *Politics, Sociology, and Social Theory*, 258, makes it clear that his distaste for Parsons's concept of internalization comes from its implicit opposition to his own favored notion of "the skillful and knowledgeable character of the everyday participation of actors in social practices"—a notion that Mestrovic (*Anthony Giddens*, 179-206) has criticized and that I have shown to be contrary to the reality of those largely "unconscious" processes that govern social interaction.

68. Manning, *Erving Goffman*, 158, 175-83. Schmaus, *Durkheim's Philosophy*, 12-13, traces that perception of a supposed split between an earlier "positivist" phase in Durkheim from a later "idealist" phase, by Talcott Parsons and Jeffrey Alexander, to Parsons's misguided attempt to read his own problem of the "internalization of norms" back into Durkheim.

69. Susan Buck-Morss, *The Origin of Negative Dialectics: Theodor W. Adorno, Walter Benjamin, and the Frankfurt Institute* (New York: Free Press, 1977), 57, 229 n. 114, 242 n. 87. Buck-Morss says that "Adorno recognized his debt to Simmel in a lecture delivered in New York April 19, 1940," and that Adorno probably inherited this idea of the "double character of concepts" from Simmel "through his early mentor, Siegfried Kracauer."

70. William James, *The Principles of Psychology* (London: Encyclopaedia Brittanica, 1993); Neil Smelser, *Theory of Collective Behavior* (New York: Free Press, 1963); Charles Tilly, *From Mobilization to Revolution* (Reading, Mass.: Addison-Wesley, 1978). Emanuel A. Schegloff, "Between Micro and Macro: Contexts and Other Connections," in The Micro-Macro Link, ed. Jeffrey C. Alexander et al. (Berkeley: University of California Press, 1987), 207-234, is a sociological study of the pragmatics of cooperative turn-taking in conversation.

71. Arwood (*Pragmaticism*, 9-12) bases her claim to *filiation* from Peirce on those same "four denials" cited by Hookway (*Peirce*, 23) from Peirce's 1868 writings. See also Charles Morris, *Foundations of the Theory of Signs* (Chicago: University of Chicago Press, 1938).

72. Peirce, *Collected Papers*, 5.402; Hausman, *Charles S. Peirce's Evolutionary Philosophy*, 2-6; Durkheim, *Pragmatism and Sociology*, 5-6, 114-15 nn. 8-14.

73. Durkheim, *Pragmatism and Sociology*, 5-37, 115 n. 14.

74. Peirce, *Collected Papers*, 5.9; Kenneth Laine Kettner, *A Thief of Peirce: The Letters of Kenneth Laine Kettner and Walker Percy* (Jackson: University of Mississippi Press, 1995).

75. Robert Merton, "Latent and Manifest Functions," in *Social Theory and Social Structure* (New York: Free Press, 1957); Jon Easter, *Logic and Society* (Chichester, England: Wiley, 1978); Luhmann, "The Evolutionary Differentiation between Society and Interaction," 178.

76. Thomas, *Meaning in Interaction*, 30; Stone and Faberman, "On the Edge," 110; Alfred Tarski, "The Semantic Conception of Truth and the Foundations of Semantics (1944)," in *The Philosophy of Language*, ed. A. P. Martinich (New York: Oxford University Press, 1996). For an informative review—for the nonspecialist in philosophy—of current philosophical debates about *truth*, including a discussion of Tarski's semantic theory, see Frederick F. Schmitt, *Truth: A Primer* (Boulder, Colo.: Westview Press, 1995). W. V. O. Quine, *Quiddities: An Intermittently Philosophical Dictionary* (Cambridge, Mass.: Belknap Press of Harvard University Press, 1987), asserts that "the separation between semantics and pragmatics" carried out by Peirce and Charles Morris "is a pernicious error." I will

point out in greater detail in chapter 1 why Quine is wrong, from the perspective of social science's ethnography of meaning.

77. Apel (*Charles S. Peirce*, 129-30, 230 n. 116) while having no quarrel with the threefold distinction—into *syntax, semantics*, and *pragmatics*—made by Charles Morris in 1938, nevertheless protests the "behaviorist" or "positivist" interpretations Morris had made of Peirce's "Pragmatic Maxim" because the rules and consequences of signs cannot be discerned "simply by external observation and a statistical summary of the characteristics we observe," and therefore Morris-influenced behaviorists end up breaking the triadic relationship—of "A gives B to C"—into two dyadic relationships: "A separates from B," and "C takes possession of B." Because of Apel's belief (which I share) that the complexity of triadic relationships often defy observation—in chapter 2, for example, I argue that most social power is unobservable—he has, in *Understanding and Explanation*, called for a "transcendental" pragmatics. The formal pragmatics I define in chapter 4 are indeed "transcendental" in that sense that Apel borrows from Kant.

78. Thomas, *Meaning in Interaction*, 1: "If a single group of words such as *It's hot in here*! could mean so many things at different times . . . these and many other issues, are addressed within the area of linguistics known as pragmatics." Rickman, Dilthey Today, 57, 133: this thinker—who as we have already seen (in *Dilthey Today*, xii, 172) compared Dilthey's hermeneutics to Peirce's Pragmati(ci)sm—actually takes the current followers of Gadamer's hermeneutics to task for not appreciating Dilthey's "concern with external criteria of truth." I have already pointed my non-philosophy-specialist readers in the direction of Mario Bunge's *Metascientific Queries* and his article "Phenomenological Theories" in his edited Festschrift to Karl Popper, *The Critical Approach to Science and Philosophy*, for informative introductions to the philosophical issues of scientific realism and its methodology of two epistemic levels. Nicholas Rescher, *Scientific Realism: a Critical Reappraisal* (Boston: Reidel, 1987), xii, and Roy Bhaskar, "Philosophy and Scientific Realism," in *Critical Realism: Essential Readings*, ed. Margaret Archer et al. (London: Routledge, 1998), 16, also contain pithy definitions of what Bhaskar calls the "two sides of 'knowledge'" methodology of scientific realism. Hans-Georg Gadamer, *Truth and Method* (New York: Continuum, 1993), 245, 306, 374-75, uses the term "horizon" in the sense of Edmund Husserl's phenomenology of time-consciousness, and the "fusion of horizons" to mean, specifically, the fusion of present and past historical consciousness; but so also—in its attempt to maintain *predictive stability over time*, as Bunge, in his "Phenomenological Theories," points out—does *scientific realism*. Claude Levi-Strauss, *Tristes Tropiques* (New York: Atheneum, 1974), 58, in comparing his two "different levels of reality" to the methodological procedure of Marx, Freud, and geology, also aims implicitly at the two-epistemic-level procedure of *scientific realism*, with the same purpose: of maintaining a stable knowledge of deep structure over long periods of historical time.

79. Randall Collins, *The Sociology of Philosophies: A Global Theory of Intellectual Change* (Cambridge, Mass.: Belknap Press, 1998), xvii, 858. On p. 1, Collins presents his book's subject matter as being "the dynamics of conflict and alliance in the intellectual networks which have existed longest in world history." By the end of chapter 2, the reader will see that my Peircean Pragmaticism will have generalized such "dynamics of conflict and alliance" beyond the "intellectual networks" of Collins, to the bigger stage of all human communication in global history. See also Durkheim, *Pragmatism and Sociology*, 1-58.

80. Collins, *The Sociology of Philosophies*, 858-59 (italics added). See also Hookway, *Peirce*, 23.

81. Georg Simmel, *Fragmente und Aufsatze* (Munich: Drei Masken, 1967), 3, cited in Michael Kaern, "The World as Human Construction," in *Georg Simmel and Contemporary Sociology*, ed. Michael Kaern et al. (Boston: Kluwer Academic, 1990), 85. See also Piaget, *The Moral Judgement of the Child*, 342-43.

82. Piaget, *The Moral Judgement of the Child*, 341-71.

83. Joas, "Durkheim's Intellectual Development," 239, citing this same argument made by Piaget on the basis of "Durkheim's distinction between two types of 'solidarity'" that I have just cited, calls Piaget "the most vociferous critic of this deficiency in Durkheim's work." But, argues Joas, "this criticism has often concealed the extent to which Piaget based his moral theory on Durkheim and to which Piaget's theory must be seen as a correction of deficiencies inherent in Durkheim's attempt to implement his own program." About these "inherent deficiencies" in Durkheim's theory, toward which Joas sees Piaget's own theory as "a correction," Joas reminds us that "Durkheim lacked the means in terms of a developmental psychology and a theory of socialization that would have actually enabled him to describe the genesis of a morality of cooperation." Interestingly, that more recent attempt cited by Joas—Jurgen Habermas, *A Theory of Communicative Action* (Boston: Beacon, 1987)—to utilize just such "a developmental psychology and a theory of socialization"—that of Jean Piaget himself—"to describe the genesis of a morality of cooperation," has attracted criticism from Anthony Giddens (*Politics, Sociology and Social Theory* 258) for its "society-personality homology." While I will be defending the legitimacy and logical validity of just such "society-personality homology" later in this introduction—and in chapter 3 as well—we should not forget here that the Piaget-based theory of "communicative action" put forward by Habermas is an explicitly evolutionist theory of social development—as is my own Peirce-based theory in this book (Habermas has also used the Peircean term *formal pragmatics* which I use here)—and Giddens has gone on the record before, criticizing evolutionism.

84. Merllie, "Did Lucien Levy-Bruhl," 32-33.

85. Dominique Merllie ("Did Lucien Levy-Bruhl," 12) quotes from "the detailed letter" written by Levy-Bruhl on November 14, 1934, to Evans-Pritchard, "expressing his pleasure at the interest shown in him by the British field anthropologist": "Your article renders my theory the most invaluable of services." Merllie (p. 33) also cites the 1950 statement by Rivaud as "the evidence of a former student which shows that he (Levy-Bruhl) was wounded by the manner in which Durkheim's criticisms were expressed": "Levy-Bruhl, grieved and disturbed by the attacks whose violence and injustice took him unawares, did not, as it were, defend himself. He suffered in silence, but I am sure that his views, much more nuanced and subtle than those of orthodox Durkheimians, did not give ground." Merllie (p. 33) suggests as a possible "additional explanation of why Levy-Bruhl did not reply explicitly" to Durkheim "the fact that Durkheim was dead in 1917."

86. Merllie, "Did Lucien Levy-Bruhl," 33.

87. Merllie, "Did Lucien Levy-Bruhl," 37. Interestingly, this debate—or rather, incompatibility—between Levy-Bruhl's approach to culture and that of Durkheim continues within the field of French history of mentalites. Roger Chartier, *Cultural History: Between Practices and Representations* (Cambridge: Polity, 1988), 24-25, 95, quotes the criticism that Robert Darnton leveled against his concept of *outillages mentaux*—"mental tools or

mental equipment"—which Chartier had borrowed from Levy-Bruhl, via Lucien Febvre: "The French have not developed," argued Darnton, "a coherent conception of *mentalites* as a field of study. They tend to load the term with notions of *representations collectives* derived from Durkheim and the *outillage mental* that Lucien Febvre picked up from the psychology of his day. Whether *mentalite* will bear the load remains to be seen."

88. In his book *Claude Levi-Strauss and the Making of Structural Anthropology*, Marcel Henaff (p. 234) characterizes the position of Levi-Strauss on the supposed existence of a "primitive mentality" by saying, "Abilities are the same everywhere. This situation is compared by Levi-Strauss to the 'possibles' that are in a seed and that only a certain number of external factors—thus events—will allow to develop, to emerge from their 'dormancy.'" Henaff then proceeds to quote from Levi-Stauss's book *From Honey to Ashes*: "The same is true of civilizations. Those which we term primitive do not differ from the others in their mental equipment but only by virtue of the fact that nothing in any mental equipment ordains that it should display its resources at a given time or utilize them in a certain direction" (Claude Levi-Strauss, *From Honey to Ashes: Introduction to a Science of Mythology* [New York: Harper and Row, 1973], 474, cited in Henaff, p. 234). I found it particularly interesting that Henaff's (p. 234) language in describing Levi-Strauss's position reflects accurately Peirce's distinction between phenomenological *Firstness*—the stage of "potentiality," those "possibles" in seed form—from *Secondness*, the stage of "actuality," of "existence" (note Henaff's "external factors—thus events" phrasing!) which develops the "dormancy" of *Firstness*. I will explain these "categories" of Peirce's phenomenology later in this chapter.

89. Hookway, *Peirce*, 15, 23, 32 (italics in original); Peirce, *Collected Papers*, 5.265; Arwood, *Pragmaticism*, 9-10.

90. Arwood, *Pragmaticism*, 11.

91. Hausman, *Charles S. Peirce's Evolutionary Philosophy*, 10; Rickman, *Dilthey Today*, xii, 172-73; Schmaus, *Durkheim's Philosophy*, 62-64.

92. Hans-Georg Gadamer, *Truth and Method*, 576, says: "The universal hermeneutic process of horizon-formation and fusion, which I have made conceptually explicit, applies to such eminent texts as well." While Gadamer is here applying the concept of "horizon"—which he has borrowed from Husserl's *phenomenology of time consciousness*—to the process of interpretation which goes on in reading, it seems clear that his concepts of "horizon formation" and the "fusion of horizons" correspond rather accurately with the *First* and *Third* categories of Peirce's triadic phenomenology of the process (over time) of inquiry. Mary Hesse, *The Structure of Scientific Inference* (Berkeley: University of California Press, 1974), had utilized the linguistic philosophy of W. V. O. Quine to outline a three-step process—similar to Peirce's triadic phenomenology—of analogical or metaphorical reasoning in science. For example, a scientific process such as Albert Einstein's theorizing about the nature of light involved, first, a pre-Einstein analogy of light as a wave, similar to sound and water "waves;" second, Einstein's "negative analogy" of postulating that light waves, unlike sound or water waves, lacked a medium (ether); and third, the general acceptance by the scientific community of Einstein's new definition of mediumless "waves" in the case of light. Interestingly, without the helpful grounding that Peirce's evolutionary epistemology would have given her, Hesse, in *Revolutions and Reconstructions in the Philosophy of Science* (Bloomington: Indiana University Press, 1980), later drifted toward the relativism in the strong program in the sociology of knowledge of Barnes and Bloor (discussed later in chapter 1) before finding solid ground again—in

Hesse, "Socializing Epistemology," in *Construction and Constraint: The Shaping of Scientific Rationality,* ed. *Ernan McMullin* (Notre Dame, Ind.: University of Notre Dame, 1988)—in Emile Durkheim's social realism.

93. Arwood, *Pragmaticism,* 9-12.

94. Peirce, *Writings of Charles Sanders Peirce,* 1: 113 (italics added).

95. Max H. Fisch, "Introduction," in Pierce, *Writings of Charles S. Peirce* 1: xxvii-xxx; Jurgen Habermas, *Communication and the Evolution of Society* (Boston: Beacon, 1979); Habermas, *The Theory of Communicative Action.*

96. Georg Simmel, "The Metropolis and Mental Life" (1905), in *The Sociology of Georg Simmel,* ed. Kurt H. Wolff (New York: Free Press, 1950), 409-24. This contrasting imagery here between a "modern/urban/monetary/rational" mentality and a more "traditional/rural/nonmonetary/emotional" mentality has been presented in the terms of Georg Simmel and Charles Horton Cooley. But hovering in the background—as I press toward my main argument that the received dualities-in-imagery from sociology's classical founders can all be encompassed by, and reformulated with, the greater logical elegance in, Peirce's triadic phenomenology—is Lucien Levy-Bruhl's attempt to distinguish between a generalized modern mentality and its "primitive" forebear. In chapter 4, this "transition-to-modernity" is explicated in greater detail by appeal to Benjamin Nelson's—*The Idea of Usury: From Tribal Brotherhood to Universal Otherhood* (Princeton, N.J.: Princeton University Press, 1949)—"Weberian" rephrasing of John Calvin's legitimation of banking "usury" as a move "from tribal brotherhood to universal otherhood," i.e., from a premodern mentality of Peircian "firstness"—with the whole universe cognized by *iconic* similarity to the "family" in which one experiences one's early *filiation*—to the modern mentality of Peircian "secondness"—the domain of objective *calibration* where even family affection (as Shakespeare pointed out in King Lear's demand on his daughter, Cordelia) can now be objectively quantified and *indexed.*

97. What Barry Schwartz, in his *Vertical Classification: A Study in Structuralism and the Sociology of Knowledge* (Chicago: University of Chicago Press, 1981), misses is that other perceptual similarity: that the emotional "effervescence" noted by Durkheim in the "primitive forms" of religious ritual is similar to the emotional effervescence displayed by the infant—as described by Freud and the "object relations" followers of Melanie Klein to the "presence" of the caretaking parent, traditionally the mother. It is this emotional similarity between the infant's experience of "joyful awe" in the presence of the mother—the "metaphysics of presence" so execrated by Derrida's writing-centered deconstructionist philosophy—that underlies the religious nature of the semantics of legitimation of premodern society's forceful integration of possibly disgruntled serfs and peasants at the bottom of its stratification system into the social "matrix" (from "mother" in Latin!).

98. Zygmunt Bauman, *Life in Fragments: Essays in Postmodern Morality* (Oxford: Blackwell, 1995), 56, 59-60, 64-68, 74, 148, 269, credits the insight of philosopher Emmanuel Levinas—that the mistake of modernity was to base morality on universalistic rules and laws enforced by the state, instead of the particularistic empathy evoked by the human face—for the intellectual transition from modernity to postmodernity. It should be noted here that in my insistence that the power legitimations of all premodern societies evoke the experience of dependence on powerful care-giving adults, such a Levinasian morality of the face belongs as much to pre- as to post-modernity in that, as neo-natal psychology has demonstrated, the very first object which the newborn human child seems genetically programmed to recognize is the human face. The cultural power of premodern

icons emerges from this "primitive" emotion-arousing value of human features: in leaning on Levinas for his definition of postmodernity, Bauman may be setting "Marx on his head" as postmodernity returns—like Karl Marx's communism—to its "primitive" cultural origin!

99. Alfred W. Crosby, *The Measure of Reality: Quantification and Western Society, 1250-1600* (Cambridge: Cambridge University Press, 1997). An obsession with measurement also seen by that observer of early modernization trends, William Shakespeare in *King Lear*, with Lear's enraged reaction to his youngest daughter, Cordelia's, refusal to quantify her love for him, a refusal to impose the reign of modernity's sign of the *index* on that premodern code of *filiation* that still governs family love.

100. William J. Bouwsma, *A Usable Past: Essays in European Cultural History* (Berkeley: University of California Press, 1990); William J. Bouwsma, "Calvin and the Renaissance Crisis of Knowing," in *The Organizational Structure of Calvin's Theology*, ed. Richard C. Gamble (New York: Garland, 1992), 226-48. It should be noted that Latin American scholar Enrique Dussel, in his "Beyond Eurocentrism: The World-System and the Limits of Modernity," in *The Cultures of Modernization*, ed. Fredric Jameson and Masao Miyoshi (Durham, N.C.: Duke University Press, 1998), 3-31, has recently launched a Marxizant attack on Joseph Needham's thesis, arguing that it was an economic factor—the gold and silver from Spain's New World empire—rather than Galileo's science, which came later, that launched European modernity. What Dussel ignores is that this economic factor—the European acquisition of American bullion—would not at all have been possible without that prior *cognitive revolution*—the quantitative science of ocean navigation that underlay the "discovery" of America by Christopher Columbus! In my emphasis upon the immense contribution that the science of navigation made to European formulation of a mechanistic "object-permanent" worldview, I should also note the prominence of the symbol of "water" in Carl Jung's psychology in unconscious terror of death and the unknown: the conquest of water—from Archimedes to the steamboat gave Western culture that sense of invincibility in the late nineteenth century, that sense of mastery of the objective world, which was coincidentally first shattered with the sinking in 1912 of the "unsinkable" Titanic! Furthermore, the religion of Christianity so emphasized by Weberian sociology as the primary factor in Europe's breakthrough to modernity is, interestingly, the only major world religion to contain in its founding narratives so many episodes detailing the navigational conquest of water, as in the Gospel accounts of Jesus stilling the storm around the boat, or his walking on water—a point that, while not contradicting Weber, reinforces my hypothesis of Europe's longstanding love affair with waterborne navigation being the container into which prior African and Asian cognitive-technological advances diffused to form the "object-permanent" culture of modernity.

101. I find it particularly interesting that the "postmodern" outlook of Jacques Derrida's deconstructionism—which, as I have pointed out in an earlier note, has been found to be similar to Peirce's philosophy in its insistence on "intertextuality" (i.e., the insistence that any interpretant of a text must itself be another text, with no interpretation possible outside textuality)—should call into question both premodern subjective "presence," by claiming linguistic priority for the written text over oral communication, and modern "objectivity," by insisting on the polysemic multiplicity of relativistic interpretations within all texts. While I find no merit in Derrida's overall theoretical argument—as I point out in chapter 1—the relativism of perspectives is built into semantic texts by the referential nature of language itself, but such a perspectival "noise" is cleared by the pragmatic cooper-

ative structures of communicative intentions. I strongly disagree with Derrida's sleight-of-hand in assimilating oral speech to the ontological priority of the text because, as the Pragmatist tradition from Peirce to G. H. Mead insists, the "signs" of gesture, facial expression, and voice inflection preceded and constructed the semantics of textual language, an insight shared by Peirce's Pragmaticism with Derrida's supposed philosophical master, Martin Heidegger. But while invalid as a theory, Derrida's deconstructionism, like Jean-Paul Sartre's novel *La Nausee* before it, serves as a great phenomenological description of that emotion of near-panic, of nausea, that must have struck the imaginations of those who first grasped the transitoriness—the feeling, as Marx put it, that "all that's solid melts into air"—of modernity's pretensions to cumulative objectivity.

102. Margaret S. Archer, *Culture and Agency* (New York: Cambridge University Press, 1988).

103. Juliet Flower MacCannell, in her *The Regime of the Brother: After the Patriarchy* (London: Routledge, 1991), utilizes Jacques Lacan's psychoanalytical concept of *meconnaissance*—misreading—to illustrate how the narratives of the French Enlightenment's rhetoric of "fraternity" tended to substitute what I call *filiation*, the pre-modern "tyranny of the father" with an equally familisitic "regime of the brother." Luhmann ("The Evolutionary Differentiation between Society and Interaction," 123-25) points out how the *philosophes* of the Enlightenment mistook the systematic coldness of modern rationality for the "semantics of warmth and well-being" of community. Such *meconnaissance* in social theory, according to Luhmann, can only be avoided by theorizing at a "sufficiently abstract level."

104. Anthony Kenny, *Will, Freedom, and Power* (New York: Basil Blackwell, 1975), 123-26; Luhmann, "The Evolutionary Differentiation between Society and Interaction," 113.

105. Mestrovic, *Anthony Giddens*; N. J. Allen, "Effervescence and the Origins of Human Society," in *On Durkheim's Elementary Forms of Religious Life*, ed. Allen; Vernon Reynolds, *The Apes: The Gorilla, Chimpanzee, Orangutan, and Gibbon—Their History and Their World* (New York: E. P. Dutton, 1967), 106-7, 123, 131-32, 181, 271; Harry F. Harlow and R. R. Zimmerman, "Affectional Responses in the Infant Monkey," in *Science* 130, (1959): 421-432.

106. Giddens, *Politics, Sociology, and Social Theory*, 258; Claude Levi-Strauss, *The Savage Mind* (Chicago: University of Chicago Press, 1966), 131; Levi-Strauss, *Introduction to the Work of Marcel Mauss*, 35. Such a concept of unconscious mediation between self and other formulated by Levi-Strauss—called "an objective intersubjectivity" by Levi-Strauss's intellectual heir and exponent, Marcel Henaff (*Claude Levi-Strauss*, 104)—would, of course, be anathema to Giddens, who would excoriate such "society-personality homology" for not recognizing "the skillful and knowledgeable character of the everyday participation of actors in social practices."

107. John G. Watkins and Helen H. Watkins, *Ego States: Theory and Therapy* (New York: Norton, 1997); Paul Federn, in *Ego Psychology and the Psychoses*, ed. E. Weiss (New York: Basic, 1952); Talcott Parsons, *Social Systems and the Evolution of Action Theory* (New York: Basic, 1977).

Until Talcott Parsons, carrying forward Weber's double rejection (and double acceptance) of German idealism and Marxist materialism, provided an alternative, the dominant concept of culture in American social science identified culture with learned behavior. This concept cannot be called "wrong" . . . but . . . it is very difficult to generate analyses of much theoretical power from such a diffuse, empiricist notion.

In place of this near-idea, Parsons, following not only Weber but a line of thought stretching back at least to Vico, has elaborated a concept of culture as a system of symbols by which man confers significance on his own experience.
    —Clifford Geertz, *The Interpretation of Cultures*:
    Selected Essays (New York: Basic Books, 1973), 249-50.

The philosophical problems involved in translating the meanings and the reason of one culture into the language of another, and of explaining super-empirically-oriented beliefs in scientific terms, were not solved by functionalism. They were evaded. Other forms of sociological analysis neglected these issues no less: the use of statistical techniques was often accompanied by mindless lack of interest in the philosophical assumptions involved in social enquiry.
    —Bryan R. Wilson, *Rationality: A Sociologist's Introduction*
    (New York: Harper & Row, 1970), viii.

Rationality comes to explain the unity of mankind despite diverse appearances; relativism comes to explain the moral unity of mankind despite diverse appearances. Then the central issue becomes how to reconcile rational and moral unity.
    —Ian Charles Jarvie, *Rationality and Relativism:*
    In Search of a Philosophy and History of Anthropology
    (London: Routledge & Kegan Paul, 1984), 7.

CHAPTER 1

Agency: Meaning, Perspectivism, and Pragmatics

In 1937, Talcott Parsons had sought—in *The Structure of Social Action*—to arrive at a synthesis of the diverse insights into the nature and dynamics of social action that had hitherto been achieved by Max Weber, Emile Durkheim, Vilfredo Pareto, and T. H. Marshall. That early work by Parsons was still being hailed in 1989 by Charles Camic as the "charter of incorporation" for the going concern of American social science, because it had sought a clear demarcation of agency—referred to by Parsons as "voluntaristic action"—from mere behavior. And such a *demarcation*, marking out the proper subject matter of social science, had begun with Parsons's analysis of the "unit-act" into its four constituent elements:

1. The agent: an act implies an agent or "actor."
2. The goal, or end-of-action: an act must have an "end"—a future state of affairs to which the process of action is oriented.
3. The situation: an act must be initiated in a "situation," which in turn is "analyzable" into two elements—the "conditions" of action over which the actor has no control and the "means" over which he has control.
4. The normative orientation: the act involves a certain mode of relationship between all these elements and this relationship coheres within the "normative orientation" of the action.[1]

But, just as the writing of the U.S. Constitution had drawn the immediate ire of Thomas Jefferson (for its lack of a Bill of Rights) in the eighteenth century, so did Parsons's 1937 "charter of incorporation" immediately call forth *its* "Jeffersonian" critique. For, says Richard Grathoff,

It was either late in 1938 or in the spring of the following year that Professor F. A. Hayek, then editor of *Economica* at the London School of Economics, invited Alfred Schutz to write a review of Talcott Parsons' *The Structure of Social Action. . . .* Though Schutz accepted, he was never himself to publish his essay and critique of Parsons.[2]

That critique, reiterating Schutz's stance on "The Subjective Point of View in the Social Sciences," had focused upon that third element of Parsons's 1937 analysis of the "unit-act," namely, the situation. The "situation" *from whose point of view*, Schutz had asked—the actor's or the observer's?

That Schutz's question of *perspectives* had penetrated to some exposed nerve in the Parsonsian corpus was apparent, for after an extended correspondence between the two most influential social theorists of the twentieth century, edited and published in 1978 by Grathoff, Parsons still found himself years later, in "A 1974 Retrospective Perspective," addressing that "central issue between Dr. Schutz and myself, namely, that of the status of what we have both called 'the subjective point of view.'"[3]

Parsons's definitive reply to Schutz's question of perspectives was this:

It seems to me that Dr. Schutz poses an altogether unrealistically sharp contrast between the point of view of the actor and the point of view of the scientific observer and analyst, virtually dissociating them from each other. . . . Quite the contrary it seems to me that they are closely connected and that "doing" science is an extreme type of action[4]

Ironically, Schutz's question of perspectives, dismissed by Parsons in 1974 as "unrealistic" from what Parsons considered to be a scientific point of view, had earlier been posed by Max Weber within the *Methodenstreit* debate of late-nineteenth-century German social science. In his critical review of the book *Wirtschaft und Recht nach der materialistischen Geschichtsauffassung*, written by Rudolf Stammler in 1896, Weber had said:

And so the obscurity of Stammler's text is perpetuated. Questions of every conceivable sort are posed, only to be confused with one another. Stammler considers the possibility of "conceiving" (note!) an action as one which is "brought about by the actor." But we do not know whether this is the conception of the actor himself or the conception of the "observer" for whom the action is an *object* of knowledge.[5]

Weber's question of perspectives would still resonate a century later, within what Paul Roth would call the "Rationalitatstreit" of late-twentieth-century Western social science, occasioned by changing views of what "doing science" entailed:

The philosophical lessons learned from Willard Orman Quine and Ludwig Wittgenstein (among others) and the historical lessons learned from Thomas

Kuhn and N. R. Hanson (among others) leaves us without the panoply of distinctions (analytic-synthetic, observational-theoretical) required for rendering
scientific method paradigmatic of rational inquiry. One task confronting a
"post-empiricist" epistemology is that of reforming the shattered consensus regarding the canons of rationality. . . . The substance of the dispute concerns
which set or sets of canons of justification qualify as rational.[6]

In other words, according to Roth, it was the hubris of pre-Quine "empiricist" science to imagine that it enjoyed a rigid boundary between "observation"
and "theory" and could therefore speak of the action-situation without falling
into the question of perspectives; but a "post-empiricist" science recognizes that
all observation is "theory-laden" and therefore all "situations" are predefined by
the perspectives of each individual actor or observer. Returning then to Parsons's
1937 analysis of the "unit-act," we see that since Parsons's analytical element of
"the situation" must *itself* be "theory-laden" with the other elements of actor's
"end-of-action" and "normative orientation"—i.e., the very definition of "the situation" is framed by the *selectivity* of each actor's goals and norms—Parsons's
four elements reduce to (a possibly more complex) two: (1) Each Agent and (2)
Each Definition of the Situation.

Weber's "rationality" has also now accepted the bounds of Herbert Simon's
"bounded rationality," according to Jon Elster, and such "bounding," as recognized by the successive debates about "rationality and the social sciences," tends
to replace the scientific *consensus* about the norms of research validity and justification, with the *anarchy* of the relativism of perspectives.[7]

Just how critical this contemporary "Rationalitatstreit" can become to the
definition of social science itself can be gauged from the reversal of the project of
Durkheim brought on by social scientists influenced by Quine and Wittgenstein:
Whereas Durkheim, according to his biographer Steven Lukes, had accepted the
apparent *relativity* of different cultures' norms and customs but had still hoped
for the explanatory *unity* of "objective" science, the "strong programme" in the
sociology of knowledge advocated by Barry Barnes and David Bloor would view
scientific "facts" themselves as contingent constructions of relativistic cultural
styles. We stand again at the divide between Parsons and Schutz. The question of
perspectives, earlier seen by Parsons as "unrealistic" from a certain view of what
"doing" science involved, returns—now that the view of "big science" in the
Western world seems to have itself metamorphosed—with a renewed and very realistic urgency.[8]

Rationality and the Problem of Meaning

To comprehend the full significance of this century-long debate between the up-
holders of that "realism" about what "doing" science involves—such as Talcott
Parsons and, according to our contemporary philosopher of science Warren

Schmaus, Durkheim himself—and their critics who urge a greater sensitivity toward the different *perspectives* (at the least between the viewpoints of the actor
and the observer in any social situation), such as Alfred Schutz (in his critical review of Talcott Parsons's 1937 *Structure of Social Action*) and Max Weber (in his
Critique of Stammler)—we must now attend to that great shibboleth of Western
modernity (i.e., the historical period dating from the time of Descartes, or at least
the eighteenth-century Enlightenment *philosophes*) that philosophers and social
scientists (such as Ian Jarvie or Hollis and Lukes) identify as the prevailing
antonym of the concept of *relativism*: "rationality."[9]

Speaking about the extensive usage of this concept by one of contemporary
social science's nineteenth-century founders in his still very influential writings,
Bryan Wilson says:

> Weber, studying the development of rationality in western science, economy
> and social organization, sought to make explicit the point at which the value
> freedom demanded by scientific rationality could be fully operative in social
> inquiry. Of the classical sociologists he came closest to recognizing the limita-
> tions of rational procedures of inquiry and understanding. But he did not raise
> doubts about the criteria of rationality itself.[10]

What Weber had avoided facing—when he, as Wilson says, "did not raise
doubts about the criteria of rationality itself"—was the troublesome problem
that appears to have haunted Durkheim's 1913-14 course of lectures "Pragmatism and Sociology": that the concept of "rationality" may already have been
emptied of its significance—with Immanuel Kant's "awakening from his dogmatic slumbers" upon reading the works of David Hume—during that eighteenth
century of the Great European Enlightenment. For what "rationality" had then
signified is readily apparent upon even a cursory reading of the great Cartesian
Rationalist Benedictus (Baruch) de Spinoza's great seventeenth-century work,
Ethic: Demonstrated in Geometrical Order. What Spinoza had meant by *more
geometrico* ("geometrical order") had been the "rationality" of Euclid's geometry (and of Aristotle's *Organon* syllogisms), where the *meaning* contained within
deductive premises—those Euclidean *axioms* or "self-evident truths"—was fully
and stably preserved through the process of deduction in the deductive conclusions. The mathematization of the physical world, carried through by Galileo and
Descartes during the seventeenth century, had hoped to transfer this *stability of
meaning* from the necessary "truths of reason" of mathematical geometry to the
natural, physical world which Plato and Aristotle had hitherto suspected of being—as the "sub-lunar realm"—irreducibly irrational. Such a Galilean/Cartesian
rationalization of the world picture then seems to be—according to that current
interpreter of Weber's thought, Wolfgang Schlucter—the "rationality" that Weber
had seen in the era of Western science's breakthrough to the "rationalism of
world mastery."[11]

But that simple equation of Cartesian Rationalism—between the meaning-stability of deductive "truths of reason" and the structure of the natural world—had by the eighteenth century already been challenged and decisively rebutted by David Hume's empiricism, and it was this rebuttal by Hume of the assumption of meaning-stability in Cartesian "rationality" that resonated in Durkheim's formulation of sociological theory, according to Mary Douglas:

> In his skeptical attack on causal theories, David Hume had already posed the question for Durkheim; Hume had asserted that in our experience we only find succession and frequency, no laws or necessity. It is we ourselves who attribute causality. . . . Durkheim also posed the same question to an imaginary audience of apriorist philosophers . . . and his own answer was that the categories of time, space, and causality have a social origin.[12]

What Paul Roth—in a conscious echo of that nineteenth-century German word *Methodensreit*—calls the Rationalitatstreit of late-twentieth-century social science simply follows upon W. V. O. Quine's having carried through Hume's attack on Cartesian "rationality" beyond Hume's own boundaries. For whereas Hume, according to Quine, had stopped short in his assault upon the "rationality" of Descartes—by preserving an analytic realm of meaning-stable "truths of reason" separate and apart from the synthetic contingency of empirical "matters of fact"—Quine's sweeping denial of any such "analytic-synthetic" distinction proceeds to what Christopher Hookway calls the "scientific refutation of science" by leaving *all human rationality* dependent on its "social origins":

> Prompted only by stimulations of sensory surfaces, we construct a complex, sophisticated account of the . . . character of reality. Another speaker, subject to exactly the same stimulations, could have come to assent to a very different set of sentences. Even all possible evidence could not determine that one of us was correct and the other mistaken. Theory is underdetermined by data.[13]

So if, according to Roth, the Rationalitatsreit controversy in current social science follows upon Quine's destruction, at the level of logic, of (what I have called) the *stability of meaning* assumed by Cartesian rationalism, and has been inherited—because of what Bryan Wilson identifies as Weber's negligence in examining the "criteria of rationality itself"—by current Western social science, then all the current debates between the camps of rationalism and relativism really boil down to a debate about their hidden assumptions about the concept of *meaning* itself. For, as the philosopher Max Black explains, "Questions about meaning are, roughly speaking, questions about the functioning of language. They are to be answered by showing how parts of the language can *replace* one another." Whereas the deductive method of Cartesian rationalism preserved the stability of meaning by replacing general concepts *downward* by particulars,

Quine's "post-empiricist" inductive methodology handles such linguistic "re-placement" by constructing meaning *upward*, from the perceived particulars of experience toward the expected meaning-stability of general concepts.[14]

But such an upward replacement of linguistic meaning by the method of empiricist induction—and this inductive method is favored by *both* the empiri-cism of Locke and Hume *and* the post-empiricism of Quine—can only threaten the meaning-stability of that deductive "rationality" defined for the Western in-tellectual tradition by Euclid and Aristotle and extended into our scientific knowledge of the external world by Galileo and Descartes. For induction, as the logician Nicholas Rescher reminds us, is only a weakened or "enthymematic" form of deduction, where an *enthymeme* is defined as "an argument in whose for-mulation some crucially necessary premise is lacking, so that a larger conclusion is based on lesser premises." In his founding statements about the method to be followed by the new science of sociology, Emile Durkheim seemed to have been sharply aware of precisely this weakness, now highlighted by Rescher, in the in-ductive procedures of empiricism, when he reproached empiricists, according to Warren Schmaus, with "obscurantism."

Empiricism, he charged, results in irrationalism, clarifies nothing, and makes the world "unintelligible." Unlike rationalism, according to Durkheim, empiricism does not assume that there are any "internal connections" or "logical relations" among things that "allow one to think of some with the help of and as a function of the others." For the empiricists, he affirmed, concepts like causation "are more or less elaborated sensations," "purely artificial constructions," illu-sory appearances "that correspond to nothing in things." On the assumption of empiricism, he argued, each fact would be like a "stranger" to those that precede or follow it. Science would be reduced to supplying mnemonic devices for re-membering the usual order in which one thing follows another; in other words, he said, it would be "blind."[15]

The result of this weakening of the concept of rationality in the empiricist development of Western thought was the progressive emptying of rationalism's stability of "shared meaning," with all the consequences that such a weakened echo of what had originally been meant by "rationality" implied for the method-ology of social science. Whereas for Weber interpersonal meaning could, suppos-edly, be readily comprehended via the method *Verstehen*—a German concept now loosely translated by Howard Schwartz and Jerry Jacobs as "empathetic un-derstanding"—the application of such a method outside that *gemutlich* social set-ting of (still comparatively firm) "shared meanings" in nineteenth-century Ger-many can only further fragment our "post-modern" situation of unstable meaning and its generalized malaise of maximum mutual misunderstanding—a situation that is, ironically, comprehended rather well by Quine's notion of the "indetermi-nacy of translation."[16]

The problems left by Weber's theoretical legacy for current social science are further compounded by the fact that besides lacking an adequate theorization, according to Bryan Wilson, in that key-concept of rationality most associated with it, Weber's sociological theory *also* lacks, according to Roland Robertson, an adequately nontautological definition of that other key concept most associated with it: "meaning." And it was into this gap within the heart of Weberian sociology, according to Robertson, that Alfred Schutz plunged:

> As vast numbers of sociologists have emphasized "meaning" lay at the heart of Weber's sociology and of his life-philosophy generally. We should recall that Weber tied meaning very closely to his delineation of action. In fact "meaning" tended to make sociological sense for Weber in reference to its actional significance. And vice versa, action was constituted, in contrast to mere behavior, by its subjectivity meaningful significance. For a number of schools of sociology, Weber's emphasis upon subjective meaning has not simply been unproblematic, it has been unequivocally stamped with approval as being the paradigmatic form of interpretive sociology. Unfortunately what Weber meant by meaning has not been adequately discussed by Weber aficionados. The major exception is the critique offered by Schutz and subsequent elaborations of Schutz's work. Weber did not, as Schutz rightly argued, excavate the foundations of social knowledge and the phenomenal attribution of meaning.[17]

Surely no more damning expose of the yawning emptiness of the "Weberian" theory of meaning can be found than this paragraph written by Robertson, himself a "Weber aficionado." Weber's vaunted sociological theory of *meaning*—that master concept that for Weber, and for generations of Weberians, served to differentiate and demarcate social science's focus on *action* from mere *behavior*—stands exposed for the tautological circularity of intuitions that it really is: with "meaning" comprehended through "action" and "action" in its turn defined by "meaning"! The tendency to Western ethnocentrism lurking behind such Weberian tautological circularity—an ethnocentric bias carried, apparently, by the Weberian Talcott Parsons—is also exposed by Robertson:

> There is no doubt that, in Parsons' words, "Weber postulates a basic "drive" toward meaning and the resolution of . . . discrepancies (between normative expectations and actual experiences) on the level of meaning, a drive or tendency which is often held in check by various defensive mechanisms, of which the pre-eminent one (relevant to his sociology of religion) is that of magic." . . . Weber also sketched empirically a path leading from primitive stages of magic and ritual, where Parsons puts it, the quest for meaning was "held in check" to a highly modern, intellectualist situation.[18]

The problem—apparently not seen by Robertson—with such a pseudo-Freudian reading (by Parsons) of Weberian "meaning" in terms of "drive or tendency" is that, besides confounding the requisite intellectual work of definition and elaboration in a theory of meaning with mere imagistic verbiage, such We-

berian (or Parsonsian) assumptions that primitive magic and ritual have meaning
"held in check" also justify suspicions that Weber had substituted nineteenth-century European ethnocentrism for social science's ideal of universalistic comprehension. The result, as Martin Hollis and Steven Lukes explain, is a *reactive pen-
dulum-swing* toward relativism:

> Relativism has always appealed to noble and worthy sentiments. Within an-
> thropology a need and duty have long been felt not only to understand the
> worlds of other cultures form within, but also to respect them: here to interpret
> the world is not to change it. It was easy to suppose that this implied judging
> other cultures by their, not our, standards, especially in the face of the prevail-
> ing ethnocentric assumptions of nineteenth-century anthropology. So Franz
> Boas and his followers forged a cultural relativism which refused to see any hi-
> erarchy among peoples or an evolutionary scale linking the primitive to the
> modern, or early magic and religion to modern science in the manner of Frazer
> and Tylor. Instead, they parceled out humanity into separate cultures, biologi-
> cally and mutually irreducible.[19]

The extension of such Boasian relativism into that generalized revulsion
against the normative ideal of scientific objectivity displayed by Western social
scientists in the second half of the twentieth century may indeed have more to do
with Western feelings of guilt about the earlier ethnocentric excesses of Western
colonialism than with any unbiased consideration of the universalistic applicability of scientific logic itself. For, as Ernest Gellner put it, "Lucidly presented and
(putatively) independent facts were the tools and expression of colonial domination; by contrast, subjectivism signifies intercultural equality and respect."[20]

It must be emphasized that Parsons himself, over the extended span of his
theoretical development, was *not* insensitive to such relativism of perspectives.
As Hans Adriaansens has explained, in *Talcott Parsons and the Conceptual
Dilemma*, Parsons's theoretical move in 1951 from what Adriaansens calls the
"social nominalism" of Weber to the "social realism" of Durkheim was occasioned by Parsons's desire to escape the subjectivistic anomalies of Weber's theoretical formulations. Or, as Niklas Luhmann explains this most criticized, most
misunderstood theoretical move by Parsons in 1951 in *The Social System*, it was a
response by Parsons to the problem he had perceived, of "contingency" of perspectives:

> The index of *Toward a General Theory of Action* contains no entry on "contin-
> gency." The concept has, nevertheless, central significance in Parsons' work,
> without finding adequate attention and elaboration. The main chain of argu-
> ments is reduced to this conception: Social systems need normatively institu-
> tionalized structures to secure complementarity of expectations. This comple-
> mentarity is problematical because of the "double contingency" inherent in
> interaction. The gratification of ego is contingent on the action alter chooses.

Alter's selection among his available alternatives is, in turn contingent on ego's selection. There is then, an infinity problem, as in all relations which can change on both sides. This infinity problem was taken by Parsons to be solved by shared meanings in relatively stable symbolic systems.[21]

Parsons's solution to the problem of contingency of perspectives is, however, also seen by Luhmann as "a halfway position," inasmuch as Parsons, although correctly pointing to the historical evidence of continuing social order in communication and also correctly deducing from that prevalence of order over contingency the existence of a level of "shared meanings," nevertheless failed, according to Luhmann, to elaborate on the crucial point behind such a historical overcoming by human communication of the problems of contingency—the *mechanism* by which meanings are shared, i.e., *a theory of meaning*:

His position may be characterized in a few yes-but statements:

1. *It is true* that Parsons manages to overcome the purely behaviorist standpoint and follow Weber in defining action through intended meaning. *But* the concept of meaning is not analyzed further. Meaning is treated as a property of human action and not as selection out of a universe of possibilities.

2. *It is true* that Parsons no longer presents the problems of order in the way Hobbes did, i.e. with reference to the question of political means, and instead refers to the contingency of intended meaning. Order is not equated with political domination but defined as a normative structure that overcomes this contingency and makes possible the complementarity of expectations. *However*, because the concept of meaning is not functionalized we end up with only such statements as: if order is to exist at all, there must be structures, norms, commonly accepted values, institutions, etc. These statements remain empty and the accompanying analytic-classificatory scheme serves merely to further decompose and elaborate them, not however to give them substance.

3. *It is true* that Parsons can use this approach to apply the techniques of functional analysis within pregiven system structures. *But* he cannot deal with the broader and more fundamental question of the function of systems themselves or of structure as such. He is quite aware of the limitations inherent in such a structural-functional analysis but the attempts to overcome them are restricted to the creation of a gigantic and incredibly complex model of interdependent variables instead of involving a radical reformulation of the entire problem of functionalism.[22]

I personally am convinced that Luhmann's call for a theory of "functionalized meaning" had already been answered—a full century before Luhmann made it!—by that cornerstone of Charles Sanders Peirce's Pragmaticism, the *Pragmatic Maxim,* which Carl Hausman calls Peirce's "criterion of clarity."[23] But, before following Luhmann into such "a radical reformulation of the entire problem of functionalism," I need first to consider the difficulties of that *other*—apparently more obvious—attempted solution to the problems of meaning and the contingency of perspectives: the plunge taken by some social scientists and philosophers into what Peirce would have called *semantics*, the pursuit of meaning-*in*-language.

The Semantic Alternative:
Contingency, Language, and Perspectivism

The 1951 quest by Talcott Parsons, in *The Social System*, for contingency-transcending social order in a Durkheimian conception of "shared meanings" led later to a focus on that immediately apparent locus of such shared meaning: human language. The temptation to posit language as the carrier, or container, of that unobserved *esse* that Durkheim's "social realism" had called *society sui generis* (an association between *langue* and Durkheim's *society* made earlier by the linguist Ferdinand de Saussure, according to Ino Rossi) leaps out from Parsons's own words: "The concept of a shared basis of normative order is basically the same as that of a common culture or a symbolic system. The prototype of such an order is language."[24]

This *linguistic* cue from Parsons is easily recognized in that expanded role for language proposed by Parsons's student Victor Lidz, in the latter's own quest for the "core" of the social system:

> Language has often been discussed as a prototypical instance of the media. . . .
> Here, a functional location for language will be proposed and it will be given
> high theoretical priority as a model for the treatment of other media. Language
> will be discussed as comprising the core of the generalized mechanism of the
> whole system of action. . . . It provides the basis in common meaning by which
> the processes generated by the respective action subsystem media may be co-
> ordinated with one another.[25]

It is this focus by Lidz on language that Jurgen Habermas then proposed—in the second volume of his 1987 work *The Theory of Communicative Action*—as an alternative to Luhmann's approach to the theory of meaning:

> There are, of course two opposed strategies for dealing with this task. On the
> one hand, we can as Lidz does, carry out the analysis of language at the level
> of a theory of communication. In this case we can link up with general linguis-
> tics and with the philosophy of language, as well as with sociological action
> theories that analyze interpretation and mutual understanding as mechanisms
> for coordinating action. This is no longer possible if, on the other hand, once
> cuts beneath the level of language theory and action theory, pursues a systems-

theoretical strategy, and brings the mechanism of linguistic understanding into social theory only from the functionalist perspective of system formation. . . . This is the strategy Luhmann is following.[26]

Since I believe that it is Luhmann's call for a "functionalized" concept of meaning that is the *closest in spirit* to Peirce's Pragmaticism—a personal belief that I will defend in some detail in the next section of this chapter—I can only view the above statement by Habermas as a step backwards from the clarity of his earlier focus on the "dialogue constitutive" universals of Peircean *pragmatics*, into the muddy backwaters of Lidz's slide into linguistic *semantics*.[27]

But given that this plea by Habermas for the linkage between social theory and its sister science of linguistics in the common subject matter they pursue, that is, *meaning*, is validated by precedent in the history of science—as for example, Dalton's atomic theory strengthened and cross-fertilized both chemistry and physics, in that the two sciences shared a common pursuit of the mechanism of atomic bonding—it is important to ask: in what way is the structure of human language *congruent* with the structure of human society? Just so *very* congruent, answers the linguist Michael Halliday, that linguistics and sociology could merge into one single science of "socio-semantics," so that

if we say that linguistic structure "reflects" social structure, we are really assigning to language a role that is too passive. . . . Rather we should say that linguistic structure is the realization of social structure, actively symbolizing it in a process of mutual creativity. Because it stands as a metaphor for society, language has the property of not only transmitting the social order but also maintaining and potentially modifying it. . . . Variation in language is the Symbolic expression of variation in society: it is created by society, and helps to create society in its turn.[28]

In fact, this *co-variation* between the structure of language and the structure of social action runs so deep, argues Halliday, that Parsons's 1937 analytical breakdown of the "unit-act" into its constituent elements merely mirrored the sentence structure—of subject (agent), object (goal, end-of-action), and verb (action-situation)—of linguistic *syntax*.[29]

Why then do I still insist—against the advice of Habermas—on following Luhmann's strategy of cutting "beneath the level of language theory"?[30] It is because of the warning given by another linguist, Dell Hymes, about *linguistic* meaning being a broader concept than *social* meaning. Linguistic meaning, argues Hymes, encompasses *both* "social meaning" and "referential meaning." It is the *conflation* of these two concepts of meaning that led to the relativism of the Sapir-Whorf hypothesis—a hypothesis about linguistic relativity that proposed, according to Steven Lukes, that "we dissect nature along lines laid down by our native languages."[31]

The concepts that Hymes calls "social meaning" and "referential meaning" are respectively studied within that division of labor of Peirce's semiotic instituted by Charles Morris in 1938 as *pragmatics*—the study of Hymes's "social meaning"—and *semantics*—the study of Hymes's "referential meaning." The problems of "referential meaning" in linguistic semantics are likely to make that extensive co-variance between language and society (expected by Halliday) unlikely, because—according to the Peircian philosopher Nicholas Rescher—"referential meaning" makes linguistic structure so very fluid that it not only *fails* to reflect social reality but may also lack any precise congruence with physical reality itself:

> However closely the descriptive machinery of our language—its stock of adjectives, verbs and adverbs—may be tied to reality, the link to reality is broken when we move from universals to particulars and from their features to the things themselves. Once we have enough descriptive machinery to describe real things (such as this pen, which is pointed, blue, 6 inches long, and so on), we are ipso facto in a position to describe nonexistents (a pen in other respects like this one but 10 inches long). It is in principle impossible to design a language in which the descriptive mechanisms suffice for discourse about real things alone, without affording the means for introducing nonexistents into discussion. The mechanisms of reference to nonexistents are an inherent linguistic feature. Any language adequate to a discussion of the real cannot but burst the bounds of reality.[32]

Such slipperiness of "referential meaning" from reality to nonexistent possibilities, which Rescher considers "an inherent linguistic feature"—an instability of meaning which not surprisingly leads to that relativism so common among academics who confuse the evolutionarily stable pragmatics of social structure with the quicksand of linguistic semantics—is only further exacerbated by a social phenomenon: the exponential growth of the division of labor during the second half of the twentieth century. In a trenchant illustration of linguist Hymes's insistence that "linguistics needs the sociologist," the linguistic philosopher Hilary Putman has put forth a recognizably sociological hypothesis to account for the spreading problems of relativism and the Quinean "indeterminacy of translation." The growing division of labor, multiplying the realm of possibilities, says Putman, forces also a growing division of *linguistic* labor that strains language's referential meaning. The word *gold* may have a different meaning for the chemist from the meaning it carries for the jeweler, says Putnam, in exactly the same way as the philosopher and historian of science Paul Feyerabend had earlier argued that the word *mass* meant something incommensurably different in Einstein's theory from what it did in Newton's—within the single profession of theoretical physics.[33]

Where then, does such a growing evaporation of the *semantic* content of referential meaning—into what the postmodernist philosopher Jean Baudrillard has labeled "hyper-reality"—leave sociology's preoccupation with what Wolf-gang Schlucter saw as Max Weber's "rationalism of world-mastery"? What Richard Rorty called the "linguistic turn" in philosophy had led to the discovery in one lifetime—the lifetime of Ludwig Wittgenstein—that the positivist dream of Wittgenstein's earlier writing in the *Tractatus* of an easy fit between linguistic structure and reality was impossible. Another philosophical observer of this linguistic turn, Ian Hacking, sees the death of all "Arch-Rationalism" or "Positivism"—which had hankered after the one canonically strong "Rationality"—and the birth instead of "Anarcho-Rationalism" with "different styles of reasoning":

1. There are different styles of reasoning. Many of these are discernible in our own history. They emerge at definite points and have distinct trajectories of maturation. Some die out, others are still going strong.
2. Proposition of the sort that necessarily require reasoning to be substantiated have a positivity, a being true-or-false, only in consequence of the styles of reasoning in which they occur.
3. Hence many categories of possibility, of what may be true or false, are contingent upon historical events, namely the development of certain styles of reasoning.
4. It may be inferred that there are other categories of possibility than have emerged in our tradition.
5. We cannot reason as to whether alternative systems of reasoning are better or worse than ours, because the propositions to which we reason get their sense only from the method of reasoning employed. The propositions have no existence independent of the ways of reasoning toward them.[34]

Hacking's layout of the "different styles of reasoning" of what he calls our current "anarcho-rationalism" gives me the handle that I need in order to return to the debate between Parsons and Schultz with which I began this chapter, so as to present Peirce's Pragmaticism—to my audience of social scientists—as transcending both horns of that Parsons-Schutz dilemma. Parsons had by 1951 decidedly opted against the possibility that social science should study the *semantic* level of linguistic meaning—which is the import of that view expressed by Parsons in his conclusion to *The Social System*, that social sciences such as

anthropological theory . . . should be clearly distinguished from what in Germany have been called the Geisteswissenchaften. . . . These deal with analysis of the *content* of cultural pattern systems for its own sake without regard to their involvement in systems of action.[35]

Alfred Schutz, on the other hand, had just as adamantly opted to go the other way, restricting his vision to that phenomenological level of the German *Geisteswissenschaften*—the level of the actor's own *semantics*.[36]

I therefore found it rather interesting that, in his 1976 article "Rational Conduct and Social Life," P. S. Cohen chose to analyze Schutz's 1964 paper "The Problem of Rationality in the Social World" so as to contrast the approach of Schutz with that of Parsons, along the lines of what Hacking called "different styles of reasoning":

> Alfred Schutz has argued that the kind of rationality discussed by Parsons, and which one may call "strong rationality," has little relevance for the ordinary, mundane, routine activities carried out by most individuals and groups in most societies. Nevertheless, these routine activities can be seen as containing an inner rationality. . . . The individual can be said to be acting rationally in the sense that what he does follows from the theories and facts which he has at his disposal. . . . Schutz implies in opposition to Pareto, but using a common criterion of rationality, that men's actions *do* follow from their assumptions. . . . Consequently their everyday conduct is not the rational conduct of Parsons or the logical conduct of Pareto, but neither is it the non-logical conduct of Pareto.[37]

In contrast to what he called the "strong rationality" of Parsons, Cohen calls Schutz's concept—of that non-Pareto-optimal reasoning by which human actions may "follow" in a blind, relentless logic from their irrational assumptions—"weak rationality." The relevant question for social science is how far does such a Schutzian process of *weakening* rationality proceed. The answer, readily supplied by Cohen, is all the way to insanity:

> The penultimate type is that in which the actor's unconscious "rationale" leads to the total defeat of those goals which he might consciously wish to pursue using means rather different from those which he does use while in the grip of unconscious motives and fantasy thinking. The final type is that in which the actor retreats almost totally into the inner world of fantasy so that all of his actions have the appearance to the untutored of having neither meaning nor rationale.[38]

And what is the prescribed method of social science when faced with the semantics of a schizophrenic's "word salad"? Apparently, a demand by Cohen and other subjectivists from the 1970s that the scientific observer phenomenologically "bracket" his own norms of rationality or objectivity—in some Husserlian *epoche*—so as to better penetrate into that schizophrenic actor's semantic lifeworld. Or, as Lukes explains about that other relativist from the 1970s, Clifford Geertz:

> More generally, as Geertz remarks, the proper model of explanation, or at least part of it, is "thick description," essentially involving interpretations of actors' interpretations, where the observer is faced with "a multiplicity of complex

conceptual structures, many of them superimposed upon or knotted into one another, which are at once strange, irregular, and inexplicit, and which he must contrive somehow first to grasp and then to render.[39]

Looking back on Geertz's 1973 unveiling of his method of "thick description" from the vantage point of 1999, the South African-born anthropologist Adam Kuper remarks:

Geertz's writings had formed the new generation of anthropologists, just as much as their flirtations with the New Left. . . . It is therefore not altogether surprising that the next turn in American anthropology was toward an extreme relativism and culturalism, the program of Geertz, but stripped of all reservations.[40]

Steven Lukes provides us with his handy label, "perspectivism," which may help encapsulate in a synoptic view that long tradition—from Weber to Schutz to the post-Geertz domination of Western social science—of what I have been referring to, in my writing so far, as the *relativism of perspectives*:

The thought shared by Nagel and Geertz . . . I shall label "perspectivism": namely, that at least some areas of social enquiry are inherently perspectival. By "perspective" I shall mean a more or less closely related set of beliefs, attitudes and assumptions that specify how social reality is to be understood. . . . In applying them, one may explain from some perspective what could not be explained from no perspective.[41]

But the problem with such perspectivism is its social price. Some may believe the claims made by such as Geertz or Schutz that they could, with long immersion in "participant observation," succeed in Edmund Husserl's *epoche*—that phenomenological "bracketing" of their own perspectives—to engage in the "thick description" of their subjects from "within" their own "assumptions" or "complex conceptual structures." But anthropologist Kuper does not. Pointing to instances in Geertz's ethnographic writing when Geertz compares the Balinese cockfight to a production of *Macbeth* or argues that such a cockfight expresses hidden, subversive aspirations and values of Balinese men, Kuper argues that "such interpretations are not derived from any informants, and may be inaccessible to them," thereby accusing Geertz of having been unfaithful to his own methodological prescription of (thick) *description* by adding "a further level of interpretation." Nor does sociologist Alex Thio—who is generally sympathetic to the "humanist" theories of the 1960s and 1970s—accept the claims made by Schutzian phenomenologists that they "keep a totally open mind." Thio simply points to self-reports by decades-long practitioners of Zen meditation to argue that such a phenomenological *epoche* is impossible.[42] Whatever interpretations relativists and subjectivists may produce of 1912 Morocco, or of autistic inner worlds of fantasy, they still face questions about *validity* from other social scientists like Kuper and Thio.

We have seen that supporter of Parsonsian systems theory Niklas Luhmann call this the "infinity problem" of contingency. And we have seen the Peircean philosopher Nicholas Rescher argue that the *semantic slippage* of referential meaning—often to positing the existence of nonexistents—is "an inherent linguistic feature."[43] In that ultimate Peircean context of the evolutionary struggle for survival-fitness, Rescher's biggest argument against relativist semantics is not that it is wrong, but that over-indulgence in its infinity of perspectives may prove prohibitively expensive in that all human action—including the communicative actions of scientific communities—is subject to economistic constraints. In pursuit of their goals, their ends-of-action, humans can only pay a finite price in their exertion-efforts. The efforts of scientific action, as a communal, shared activity in producing and transmitting knowledge, must bear the price of successful communication. Ultimately, social scientists' finite budgets of time and energy will not be able to afford the costs of an infinity of perspectival interpretations. But when we assess perspectivism, not merely from normative *a prioris* (à la Kant) but from instrumental price constraints (à la Peirce), we have already begun to do *pragmatics*.[44]

Pragmatics in Context:
Meaning and Method in the Social Sciences

Consider the theory of meaning outlined by Charles S. Peirce (circa 1905) in his Maxim of Pragmati(ci)sm:

> In order to ascertain the meaning of an intellectual conception one should consider what practical *consequences* might conceivably result by necessity from the truth of that conception; and the sum of these *consequences* will constitute the entire meaning of the conception.[45]

Carl Hausman begins his 1993 book *Charles S. Peirce's Evolutionary Philosophy* by declaring this "so-called criterion of meaning" to be "the part of Peirce's philosophy that is probably most widely known . . . central to what is called Pragmatism, but which in his later thought he preferred to call Pragmaticism." Peirce himself had begun his *Lectures on Pragmatism* with a presentation on what he called "Two Statements of the Pragmatic Maxim," indicating that he had modified his original January 1878 formulation of this maxim, contained within his essay "How to Make Our Ideas Clear," because its comparatively less clear phrasing—especially in its French translation on page 48 of the *Revue Philosophique* 7 (which is precisely the version that Emile Durkheim had read and cited in his *First Lecture* on "Pragmatism and Sociology"!)—had bred a group of "new pragmatists" who had read what he had written, "but were ashamed to confess it" because they found it "humiliating" to confess that they had "learned anything of a logician."[46]

What had immediately struck me about this later, more carefully phrased version of Peirce's Pragmatic Maxim was its clear echo—which seemed to leap out at me from its printed words—of the themes in recent debates in sociological theory. I have purposely italicized the word "consequences" in my citation of this maxim above because I had realized, during my graduate studies in sociology, that if there had been any one single proposition that both the defenders of sociological functionalism, such as Robert Merton, and its opponents, such as Jon Elster, seemed to agree upon, it was precisely the assertion that the perspective of functionalism consisted in the determination of a phenomenon not by its antecedent cause—which had been the mainstay of the method of mechanistic physics since the seventeenth century—but by its consequences. By such a widely accepted definitional criterion, Peirce's Pragmatic Maxim is clearly a "functionalist" theory of meaning. And since, as we have already seen, Niklas Luhmann's "it is true . . . but" criticism of Talcott Parsons's systems theory centers on his perception that in the Parsonsian corpus "meaning is not functionalized," then it necessarily follows that "Luhmannian" sociology is *ipso facto* a *Pragmaticist* sociology.[47]

Further echoes of the debates within sociological theory leap to mind upon reading—three paragraphs after that statement of the Pragmatic Maxim in the preface to the fifth volume of his *Collected Papers*—Peirce's tracing of the "ancestry of pragmatism" to Alexander Bain's definition of "belief" as "that upon which a man is prepared to act." I had earlier criticized Max Weber's circular (tautological) definition, as presented by Roland Robertson, of "meaning . . . in reference to its actional significance. And vice-versa, action . . . by its subjectively meaningful significance," as conceptually (i.e., in its aspect as "pure theory" of social science) empty, but in his practice as a social historian—most notably in his writing of *The Protestant Ethic and the Spirit of Capitalism*—Weber had interpreted Protestant religious belief in precisely this Bain/Peirce/Pragmati(ci)st way, as "that upon which a man is prepared to act."[48]

In contrast to Weber—to whose total *oeuvre* I find myself reacting in a similar way as Peirce reacted to Hegel: as possessing historical insights of "much significance" while being confused in his theoretical formulation[49]—anthropologist Bronislaw Malinowski's formulation of his own theoretical stance seems to prefigure to an uncanny degree my own attempt in this present book to fashion a *Pragmaticist* sociology of *globalization*. While declaring, in *Argonauts of the Western Pacific*, that he had sought to comprehend meaning in such a way as to "understand the world the way in which the natives do" so as "to grasp the native's point of view, his relation to life, to realize his vision of the world," Malinowski had also—in his little-known supportive supplement to the Peirce-inspired book by C. K. Ogden and I. A. Richards, *The Meaning of Meaning*, declared that his "science of symbolism and meaning" would function as a "combined linguistic and ethnological study" within "the conception of the 'context of situation'" in such a way as to grasp the "meaning of words rooted in their pragmatic efficiency."[50]

While I hold no brief within this current book either for or against any of Malinowski's empirical research interpretations—a point I wish to emphasize lest I mislead my reader with my enthusiasm for Malinowski's theoretical formulations—I find his theoretical statements within the two writings that I just cited to be the perfect illustration of my vision of how a *Pragmaticist* social science would transcend that Parsons-Schutz dilemma—between the actor's and the (scientific) observer's points of view—while avoiding the pitfalls of Geertzian relativism. In a "two-level" or "two sides of knowledge" epistemic procedure (as presented by the scientific realists Mario Bunge and Roy Bhaskar, respectively), Malinowski's theory of knowledge would (ideally) first report the empirical observables of the actor's semantics (thus seemingly siding with Schutz in his debate against Parsons, but without risking the contamination of such empirical data by the observer's own premature interpretations, as Adam Kuper accused Clifford Geertz of having done in his Balinese ethnography) and before proceeding to the second step—of hermeneutical interpretation—by classification of such observed semantics within the theoretical (unobserved) framework of a global (or as the early Habermas—following Peirce—would have called it, a "universal") *pragmatics*.[51]

But before I proceed to elaborate upon my two-level scientific-realist epistemic procedure—of the empirical observation of the actor's semantic text, followed by the theoretical classification within global-pragmatic context (without denying the obvious possibility that all such empirical observation may be theory-laden: one need not be a positivist to attempt to accurately and truthfully report another person's semantic statements in that person's own words!)—in a Peircean synthesis of Schutz's phenomenology with Parsons's systemic science (a synthesis that is possible because Peirce was both, a [triadic] phenomenologist as well as a scientific realist), I need to address those critical caveats raised by two other respected philosophers of science against Peirce's Pragmaticism.

The first such caveat—against Peirce's Pragmatic Maxim, or criterion of meaning—was reportedly raised by the co-author of *Principia Mathematica*, Alfred North Whitehead, who complained that the

> Pragmatic test can never work, unless on some occasion—in the future, or in the present—there is a definite determination of what is true on that occasion. Otherwise the poor pragmatist remains an intellectual Hamlet, perpetually adjourning decision of judgment to some later date.[52]

While it is readily apparent that Whitehead's critique of Pragmatism—for lacking "a definite determination of what is true" on any occasion—is really directed at William James rather than at Peirce (who even Emile Durkheim, a non-specialist in philosophy, had acknowledged as having a definite determination of truth to the point of "inevitability"), it is nevertheless also apparent that if the concept of "meaning" is substituted for the phrase "what is true" in this passage from Whitehead that I just cited, then his accusation against the Pragmatist of being "an intellectual Hamlet" might also apply against Peirce for Peirce's insistence—in his later, 1905, version of the Pragmatic Maxim—on meaning's dependence on "the sum" of the "practical consequences" potentially postpones the total determination of the meaning of any concept, into the indefinite future.

It is precisely this very *un*-Hegelian eschewal of "totality" by Peirce—his radical openness to future time's "unlimited community of interpretation"—that leads Karl-Otto Apel to compare Peirce to both Karl Popper and Martin Heidegger. As I have been trying to emphasize so far (to a possibly incredulous reading audience of social scientists accustomed to dichotomizing "scientism" against "hermeneutics"), Peircean Pragmaticism contains within itself both the scientific realism of Popper and the hermeneutic sensitivity of Heidegger.[53]

In a way which calls to mind the phenomenological sociologist Peter Berger's concept of "plausibility structures," Hausman talks about Peirce's theory of meaning as being really about "would-be's":

> Meaning, as general, depends on what Peirce called *would-be's*, which are patterns according to which occur the outcomes of actions and consequences relevant to the idea in question. Would-be's are conditions that function much like rules, by leading to certain kinds of consequences that would be encountered if the general, or rule, were applied to the world. Thus, according to the maxim, the meaning of "hard" is determined by tests such as attempting to scratch it and finding that it will not be scratched by many other substances. Meaning is to be understood as disclosed in dispositional conditions, in habits, according to which the meaning or would-be could be expected to be exemplified if the concept that articulates the meaning were put to the test.[54]

Had Whitehead really been criticizing Peirce's theory of *meaning* in the passage above from his best-known work, *Process and Reality*—as Darrel Christensen's article, "A Hegelian Critique of Peirce" (which Christensen claims to have presented to the Charles Sanders Peirce Society on October 5-7, 1978, at Bloomington, Indiana) asserts—instead of (as I suspect, from his wording) merely limiting the object of his critique to William James's admittedly faulty theory of truth (which Whitehead, like many others, including Durkheim, mistakenly considered the sum total of Pragmatist philosophy), he would in effect only have been denying the "futuricity"—that very openness to time's creative novelty—that he had been claiming for his own "process" metaphysics. It should be noted, however, that Whitehead's "process philosophy" was *not* in any fundamental way opposed to Peirce's Pragmaticism (of which the Pragmatic Maxim had been the key component), as Peirce's Hegelian critic Christensen has claimed, but was really—as that reputed philosophical interpreter of both Peirce and Whitehead, Nicholas Rescher, has noted—very similar to it in its fundamental insistence on the openness of the future, of reality being, not a finished product but a *process*. Whereas "Whitehead has been the dominant figure in recent process philosophy," says Rescher, for Peirce, too, "a through-and-through process of cosmic evolution characterizes the reality we confront in our efforts to understand the world."[55]

A possibly more trenchant criticism—from the perspective of my project in this book of outlining a scientific realist epistemic procedure for a globally applicable social science involving the two levels of observational *semantics* and theoretical *pragmatics*—is logician Willard Van Orman Quine's denial of the feasibility of such a *pragmatics/semantics* conceptual separation. "Charles Morris," says Quine,

> an admirer of Peirce and a fellow admirer of the number three . . . divided the domain of semiotic into *syntax, semantics*, and *pragmatics*. This trichotomy, taken up by Carnap, has been faithfully cited and adhered to for forty years, despite the fact that the separation between semantics and pragmatics is a pernicious error. I suspect that the durability of this trichotomy is due to its trinity.[56]

The "trichotomy" that Quine here refers to is the famous division by Morris in 1938 of Peirce's semiotic into the three separate sciences of *syntactics* (or *syntax*, as Quine prefers to call it), the science of the relationships between signs (as in the rules of grammar); *semantics*, the science of the "referential meaning" between signs and the objects to which they mean to refer (the meanings furnished by standard dictionaries of any language); and *pragmatics*, the science of the relationships between signs and their users.[57]

In the section titled "Meaning," which immediately follows his threefold division of Peirce's semiotic in his *Foundations of the Theory of Signs*, Morris was quick to reassert what he called "the unity of semiotic." Syntactics, semantics, and pragmatics, argued Morris, were useful "abstractions . . . just as biologists study anatomy, ecology and physiology."[58] It is important to understand this point by Morris—that his threefold division of Peirce's science of meaning had been designed for the convenience of practicing scientists, in the same way that biologists also practice a convenient division of labor without thereby denying in any way the underlying conceptual unity of biological science—because, in the passage just cited, Quine does not even notice the contradiction in his statement between his condemnation of the dichotomy between the two sciences of semantics and pragmatics only and his satirical attitude overall to Peirce's and Morris's admiration "of the number three." In other words, Quine would prefer—for his own convenience as a linguist/logician—to maintain that separation between syntax and semantics, while denying the necessity for pragmatics. But, on the other hand, as a sociologist, I see my own convenience as standing "on the other side," so to speak, of Quine. While Quine's linguistic logic needs that interface between syntax and semantics, I believe that social science cannot survive without lodging its theoretical formulation within that other interface that Quine neglects but his fellow philosopher Hilary Putnam has in fact used, as we have already seen, in his appeal to the division of labor to explain the growing relativity of referential meaning, an explanation (by Putnam), which in relating signs to their users, was in fact—regardless of whether Putnam admitted it or not—practicing what Morris had called *pragmatics*.[59]

Indeed, all that Quine's criticism seems to be really implying when he says that the Peirce/Morris "trichotomy . . . has been faithfully cited and adhered to for forty years" because it was "taken up by Carnap" is that Rudolf Carnap, the influential logician and philosopher of science, had (in the middle 1930s, persuaded by Alfred Tarski, the proponent of that "semantic theory of truth" that we have seen in the introduction to this book) accepted the legitimacy of the Peirce/Morris distinction between syntax and semantics. No sociologist has—as yet—persuaded either himself or any other logician of the legitimacy of Morris's definition of a special science of (what Dell Hymes calls) "social meaning" in the pragmatic relationships between signs and their users.[60]

That social science cannot even explain that commonplace social phenomenon of political prejudice without stepping beyond the semantics of objective referential meaning into the pragmatics of the relationships between signs and their users was explained in 1962 by the philosopher of science Arthur Pap:

> Banker X who hates all communists without exception may feel a surge of hatred whenever he hears someone referred to as a communist; nevertheless this hatred has nothing to do with the *semantic meaning* of "communist." . . . Such images constitute part of the *pragmatic meaning* of the expression for that man.[61]

Furthermore, that the *sociology of knowledge*, as practiced from Durkheim and Mauss to Barnes and Bloor, should have been addressing this Peirce/Morris definition of *pragmatics*—the relationship between signs and their users—as separate from truth-conditional *semantics*, was also made clear by Pap:

> Thoughts and other kinds of mental states that are causally connected with a linguistic expression without being directly relevant to the question of truth constitute the *pragmatic meaning* of the expression. Normally, a man who utters the sentence "it will rain" with a tone of conviction believes that it will rain. But whether or not he believes what he said *is irrelevant to the question of whether what he said is true*. Therefore *the belief is no part of the truth-condition of the sentence*.[62]

As I said earlier, in the introduction to this book, *pragmatics*, as defined by Peirce/Morris, is governed by that simple—and well-known—"theorem," supposedly stated by the University of Chicago sociologist W. I. Thomas: if something is *believed* to be true, it will have real *consequences*. That Thomas—like his fellow University of Chicago sociologist, George Herbert Mead—was echoing the Pragmatic Maxim of Charles Peirce is not to be marveled at, given the well-known links between the sociology practiced by the University of Chicago in the 1920s and 1930s and Pragmatist philosophy. What is to be marveled at, instead, is that it has taken sociologists so long to trace that "consequences of belief" theme to its real source—in the Pragmatic Maxim of Charles Sanders Peirce.[63]

But, along with this persistent ignorance on the part of social scientists about what their "neighbors" within the intellectual division of labor, the philosophers of science, have been doing for the last century, we have—as the "other side of the coin" that Emile Durkheim might have held up as the quintessential example of the "anomic" division of labor—the philosophers of science inching toward the appreciation of the linguistic-communicative aspects of science itself, terrified as they discover the pragmatics of science that they might have blundered into social science. For a full appreciation of this *opera buffa* state of affairs between our two protagonists, the social scientists and the philosophers of science, I must for a moment step aside from my "philosophical ignorance of the social scientists" narrative, so as to enable Bryan Skyrms—through his 1984 book, *Pragmatics and Empiricism*—to trace that reluctant journey of twentieth-century philosophy of science chronologically through the semiotic triad of *syntax, semantics* (which is where Quine had last left us, mourning Rudolf Carnap's acceptance of the "trichotomy" of Peirce and Morris), and *pragmatics*.[64]

Beginning with Otto Neurath's 1931 work "Sociology and Physicalism," says Skyrms, the Vienna Circle's rejection of metaphysics had flowered into Carnap's 1936 publication (in German) of *The Logical Syntax of Language*, which had viewed the procedure of science as a relation of signs to other signs, a strict grammar regulating the "deducibility" of all scientific statements from "foundations":

> How can one have a *syntactical* theory of science? Everything must be done in terms of derivability and *syntactic* definability. Confirmation must be explained in terms of the deducibility of certain epistemically privileged sentences . . . from other sentences of the theory, scientific explanation as the deduction of sentences to be explained from suitable explaining sentences and so forth.[65]

Such *syntactic* foundationalism—with strong deductive "rationality"—had collapsed upon the problem of meaning:

> There are perfectly meaningful statements of high-level theoretical physics such that neither they nor their denial are deducible from observation sen-

tences. . . . Restriction to *syntax*, which was thought to be required by the principle of empiricism, made that principle impossible to formulate. . . . By the middle thirties Tarski had convinced Carnap of the legitimacy of *semantics*.[66]

This post-Tarski view of science as *semantics* had, however, faced the *same* problems that we have seen (in this chapter's last section) occurring in our human communication of "referential meaning"—what Niklas Luhmann had referred to as the "infinity problem" of multiple perspectives—with those consequent results of the "indeterminacy of translation."

> For instance there is the proposition that there are *infinitely* many observable objects (or indeed that there are uncountably many observable objects). The propositions would be empirically meaningful in the sense of supervenience but not in the sense of translatability into first-order empiricist language.[67]

But why—we may ask, as relativists do—must science require "translatability"? Because, answers the Peircean Pragmaticist philosopher Nicholas Rescher, scientists do not work alone but in community. Science is perforce subject to constraints of clarity and economy involved in intersubjective communication. This social nature of science forces the scientific pursuit of meaning from its attempted self-restriction to *semantics*—the study of objective "referential meaning"—into *pragmatics*, the recognition of "social meaning." Says Skyrms:

> Perhaps the tendency toward neglect of *pragmatics* stems from the idea that *pragmatics*, being the study of the *relations between signs and their significations to sign users*, must end up being psychology or sociology.[68]

There we have it, the full vision of the "anomic" division of labor between social scientists and philosophers of science. While the former, as we have seen, might quote W. I. Thomas or G. H. Mead because they have been labeled sociologists but shy away from the "logician" Peirce, the latter—according to Skyrms— "neglect pragmatics" because they fear it "must end up being psychology or sociology"! How far we seem to have traveled indeed from the "encyclopedic" interests of Diderot and the other *philosophes* of the French Enlightenment, for whom the integration of all knowledge had been a normative end-in-itself!

Skyrms's shift of our view of science away from the usual vision of its pure search for truth toward a "social" view of communicative efficiency is echoed in Joseph Rouse's book *Knowledge and Power: Toward a Political Philosophy of Science*. Rouse's argument is that the logic of scientific evolution is better comprehended as a social-pragmatic quest for power-knowledge as the capacity to control nature for social needs than as disinterested search for truth. It is this evolutionary pressure that, according to Rescher, moves the history of thought along that Peircean triadic journey, beginning from the *firstness* of "perspectival relativism" at the semantic level of multiple individual truth claims, as

> we stand committed to a quest for the truth as a regulative idea, but this is not something we can ever claim finally and definitively to have in hand . . . Distributively for any individual there is, no doubt a right perspective. But collectively there is none. Reality must embrace individual divergences, but it cannot fuse them. A *plurality of perspectives cannot be made over into one single plurality-embracing perspective.*[69]

But how do we get—as a community—from such relativism of individual perspectives to the "shared meanings" of Peircean *thirdness*? From his own perspective as a professional philosopher, Rescher can only describe this step in broad and very general outline, as occurring with a certain inevitability:

> I have not, would not, and (for my purpose) need not argue that survival is the master value. All that I am committed to argue is that *pragmatic* efficacy and survival-conduciveness are the ultimate controlling-values for monitoring the adequacy of our cognitive instrumentalities. For as long as we are actively and variably involved in interactions with nature for the realization of our purposes, its pressures on our cognitive procedures are bound to tend in the direction of enhanced adequacy.[70]

Unlike his fellow-philosopher Quine, Rescher is perfectly willing to accept, as I do, the distinction established by Morris in 1938 between the semantics and pragmatics of meaning, admitting (as indeed Quine admits, even while denying its validity) that "it is distinctly Peircean in its spirit":

> The truth conditions of a statement are a matter of the *semantics* of a language; the use conditions are a matter of what has come to be called its *pragmatics*. These use conditions are intrinsic components of the language—a part of what children learn about the use of their native tongue at mother's knee. Truth conditions do not have a monopoly on "meaning"—this concept is broad enough to encompass both sorts of conditions.[71]

Rescher's "pragmatic efficacy," whose "economic rationale" constrains human beings to "trust" each other in "communication as cooperation," applies especially to that cooperative enterprise we know as "science," as is readily apparent in the history of physics. Had Isaac Newton not "economized" in unifying the hitherto disparate "perspectives" of falling apples and revolving heavenly bodies, through the explanatory concept of gravity, the evolution of physics would have stalled or stopped. The logician Raymond Nelson has called pragmatics a "metalanguage" incorporating and "explaining" the multiple perspectives of semantic truth claims, and anthropologist Robin Horton echoes this theme in his vision of the function of science's "explanatory theory":

> The quest for explanatory theory is basically the quest for unity underlying apparent diversity: for simplicity underlying apparent complexity; for order underlying apparent disorder; for regularity underlying apparent anomaly.[72]

In an echo of Rescher's statement that pragmatics are "what children learn about the use of their native tongue at mother's knee," Hilary Putnam has also noted that, despite Quine's science-based arguments for the "indeterminacy of translation," in the quotidian world of mundane action translation seems to occur quite efficaciously. Translators are regularly trained and hired by multinational institutions, and, despite the "infinity problem" of perspectivism, children learn to speak the language of their parents, teachers, and friends. Even the relativism of Barnes and Bloor is apparently refuted by their mentor Wittgenstein's insistence about the impossibility of a private language. How does the translation that occurs in our quotidian lives—these *pragmatics* of our "life-worlds"—succeed in bridging over multiple semantic perspectives?

We may begin to answer this question if we move our theoretical vision up a notch, from our consideration of the quotidian world of children and business-companies routinely managing efficacious translation of perspectives toward that example of a *different* society (from our "Westernized" urban milieu) which the Wittgensteinian philosopher Peter Winch had used to illustrate his assertion of the supposed inevitability of perspectival relativism—the Azande, studied by E. E. Evans-Pritchard. We may notice Evans-Pritchard's surprisingly (from Winch's point of view) *non*-relativistic statement in his celebrated 1937 work, *Witchcraft, Oracles, and Magic among the Azande*:

> Zande belief in witchcraft in no way contradicts empirical knowledge of cause and effect. The world known to the senses is just as real to them as it is to us. We must not be deceived by their way of expressing causation and imagine that because they say a man was killed by witchcraft they entirely neglect the secondary causes that, as we judge them, were the true causes of his death. They are foreshortening the chain of events, and in a particular social situation are *selecting* the cause that is *socially relevant* and neglecting the rest.[73]

The crucial theoretical concepts used by Evans-Pritchard—and italicized by me for the reader's convenience—are, it seems to me, "selectivity" and "social relevance." Despite the differences in perspectives that Winch has pointed out between Azande witchcraft and Western science, in his need to "make sense" of this different culture, Evans-Pritchard, the social scientist, appears to me to be using the very same procedure used by children to comprehend their parents. The children (and most effective language translators) "step back" from the observed *semantics* of the situation—the relations of linguistic signs to what they represent—to the *pragmatics*, the contextual relations between signs and their users, which, in this Azande case, are governed (according to Evans-Pritchard) by what, via a process analogous to Immanuel Kant's *transcendental deduction*, Evans-Pritchard has *deduced* to be the particular "selectivity" and "social relevance" of Azande cultural norms.

When Evans-Pritchard speaks of the Zande "selecting" for their belief-system "what is socially relevant," I am reminded of Niklas Luhmann's "functionalized" definition of meaning as "selection out of a universe of possibilities," a "directed-ness" of mind to objects, which Luhmann comprehends within Edmund Husserl's phenomenological problematic of "intentionality," as also does that "speech acts" philosopher of language who had caught Erving Goffman's attention in his posthumously published paper, *Felicity's Condition*: John Searle. Says Searle:

> Many of our mental states are in some sense directed at objects and states of affairs in the world. If, for example, I have a belief, it must be a belief that such-and-such is the case. . . . It is this feature of directedness of our mental states that many philosophers have labeled "Intentionality."[74]

Searle's term *intentionality* is borrowed from the phenomenology of Edmund Husserl. Husserl's "noetic *act*/noematic *content*" conceptual distinction parallels our Peircean pragmatic/semantic separation, and Searle continues Husserl's distinction by substituting the letter *s* for *t* when referring to the semantic content of meaning:

> This account of Intentionality suggests a very simple account of the relationship between Intentionality-with-a-t and Intensionality-with-an-s. Intensionality-with-an-s is a property of a certain class of sentences, statements, and other linguistic features.[75]

But, unlike the triadic phenomenology of Peirce—which had begun in 1868, as I described in the introduction, with his "four denials" against the isolated, individual *ego cogito* of René Descartes—Husserl's phenomenology had remained trapped within a "transcendental" version of Cartesian ego, with drastic consequences for the "intersubjectivity" that Husserl's sociological followers—most notably Parsons's 1938-74 methodological antagonist, Alfred Schutz—sought to comprehend.

As Herbert Reid explains in his "postmodern perspective" entitled "Time, Historicity, and Political Theory":

> Concluding his 1932 study, Schutz expressed his hopes for Husserl's investigations into the problems of intersubjectivity. Yet appropriately, Max Weber re-

ceived the last word. For Schutz erected his interpretive sociology on Weber's methodological individualism. . . . Schutz continued to hold that the social scientist can understand man "only as a personal ideal type without duration and spontaneity." As critics and followers alike have noted, personal ideal types are puppets activated by "thought experiments" with the social scientist as puppet master . . . Schutz's difficulties with Husserl's treatments of the phenomenological problem of the constitution of "intersubjectivity" are well-known. Turning away from Husserl's problematic, Schutz fixed on the world of daily life, with its natural attitude of "common sense" as the archetype of our experience of reality. . . . The point is *not* to argue with Schutz's later assessment of how successfully Husserl traveled from Cartesian egology. Rather the question is whether responding negatively to Husserl's final efforts did not lead Schutz in greater difficulties. When, following Schutz, social science accepts the unproblematic "intersubjectivity" of the everyday life-world as a categorical given, does it not risk greater troubles? For does it not reproduce an ontological dualism between nature and history?[76]

It is precisely such a "dualism between nature and history"—which Reid charges against Schutz's phenomenological sociology—that Peirce's triadic phenomenology had successfully transcended, by adhering to what Carl Hausman calls *evolutionary realism*.[77] Anthony Giddens sees a similar dualism—between internal meaning and external power—as common to all the "interpretative sociologies" that had followed the lead of Schutz's phenomenology, such as Harold Garfinkel's ethnomethodology and Peter Winch's post-Wittgensteinian, meaning-as-rule-following approach:

First each deals with action as meaning rather than with action as praxis—the involvement of actors with the practical realization of interests, including the material transformation of nature through human activity. Second, partly as a consequence of the first, none recognizes the centrality of power in social life. Even a transient conversation between two persons is a relation of power, to which the participants may bring unequal resources. . . . Meanings that are made to count express asymmetries of power.[78]

To return to the two concepts of "selectivity" and "social relevance" that I had previously highlighted in Evans-Pritchard's interpretation of Azande epistemology, we may say that the Cartesian egology of Husserl's phenomenology has persisted in the methodologies of Husserl's sociological followers' focus upon the "selectivity" of individual intentionality, at the cost of losing sight of its "social relevance." But the solution that Giddens offers to these problems of perspectivism of the "hermeneutic circle"—an undefined and unelaborated "double hermeneutic" which "is of considerable complexity" and opposes Schutz's "one-way one"—pales in comparison with the complete socialization of intentionality that is possible within the tradition of Peircean Pragmaticism. For if it is social power that Giddens wants to connect to the comprehension of meaning, then he ought first to notice the definition of such power *as cooperation*—which Richard Bellamy attributes originally to Durkheim's concept of "solidarity"[79]—by Hannah Arendt:

> Power corresponds to the human ability not just to act but to act in concert. Power is never the property of an individual; it belongs to a group and remains in existence only so long as the group keeps together. When we say of somebody that he is "in power" we actually refer to his being empowered by a certain number of people to act in their name.[80]

Having thus guided Giddens and my readers to Arendt's insight about the source of social power in the solidarity of human cooperation, I am now ready to arrive at the principal focus of this chapter: the insight of pragmatics that it is this very solidaristic cooperation that also constructs communicational meaning. For, as presented in H. Paul Grice's formulation of his "Cooperative Principle":

> Our talk exchanges do not normally consist of a succession of disconnected remarks, and would not be rational if they did. They are characteristically, to some degree at least, cooperative efforts. . . . One might label this the Cooperative Principle.[81]

Grice's Cooperative Principle has already featured within sociology as the "turn-taking" phenomenon witnessed by sociologists in "conversation analysis." As Emanuel Schegloff explains:

> When persons talk to each other in interaction, they ordinarily talk one at a time and one after the other. When their talk is not produced serially in this manner, they generally act to restore "order."[82]

In other words, just as Kant's "transcendental deduction" had once sought the nonempirically observable principles that "constituted" *orderly* knowledge, the pragmatics of Grice's "cooperative principle" are what Habermas had called "dialogue constitutive."[83] And the same "cooperative principle" then, as Schegloff asserts, connects the order of micro-interactions between small groups to the macropolitics of nations. For, as the Parsonsian sociologist Guy Rocher points out:

> Parsons in fact recognizes that he has taken the existence of social order as the point of departure for his thinking. But he also insists that in his view order is not an ideal but a problem. As it is posed in the Hobbesian tradition, the question of order amounts to asking how society is possible at all—why do men live together in society instead of destroying each other? . . . He considers the

solution reached about the same time by Freud, Durkheim, Mead and Cooley to be the most important discovery of the century in the social sciences.[84]

The solution to Parsons's question of "the existence of social order" as given by Mead in *Mind, Self, and Society* looks like an extended version of Grice's Cooperative Principle. "Language," says Mead, "is just a part of the *cooperative process*, that part which does lead to an adjustment to the response of the other so that the whole activity can go on."[85]

Such pragmatic cooperation, so that (as Mead phrased it) "the whole activity (of human conversation) can go on" is what constitutes *meaning*, according to Grice. As Grice put it—as his first "generalization" in his celebrated article, "Meaning":

> "A meant something by *x*" is (roughly) equivalent to "A intended the utterance of *x* to produce some effect in an audience by means of the recognition of this intention"; and we may add that to ask what A meant is to ask for a specification of the intended effect (though, of course, it may not always be possible to get a straight answer involving a "that" clause, for example, "a belief that ... ").[86]

Now it does not require the insight of genius (to use a pithy colloquialism) to see the obvious here: that Grice's definition of *pragmatic* meaning—as the "intended effect" of the "recognition" by the listener—of the speaker's "intention" is a paraphrased restatement of Charles Sanders Peirce's Pragmatic Maxim: that meaning consists of the "practical consequences" of an "intellectual conception."[87]

But, as far as I am aware, Grice, the twentieth-century British philosopher of language, did *not* credit Peirce, the late nineteenth-century American philosopher, for having prefigured his Cooperative Principle. In fact, the 1989 collection of Grice's writings, *Studies in the Way of Words*, does not carry even a single reference to Peirce. Furthermore, that otherwise commendable overview of the current situation in linguistic pragmatics, British linguist Jenny Thomas's 1995 book *Meaning in Interaction: An Introduction to Pragmatics*, while helpfully dissecting (for a sociologist like myself not specialized in the debates between linguists) all the theoreticians of language who had attracted the attention of Erving Goffman in his posthumous July 1983 *American Journal of Sociology* article, "Felicity's Condition," also makes only a single reference to either Peirce or to his Pragmatic Maxim.[88]

Having already bemoaned on more than one occasion in this book this strange "anomic" division of intellectual labor—among linguists, philosophers, and social scientists forced to "re-invent the wheel" because of poor institutional memory about the progress in a neighboring discipline!—I will briefly recapitulate, as I had promised in the introduction, Goffman's last journey to the linguists, with the help of Thomas's 1995 introduction to (linguistic) *pragmatics*.

Grice's Cooperative Principle, notes Thomas, emerges from his work "with J. L. Austin at Oxford in the 1940s and 1950s . . . and its related conversational maxims arise from the same tradition of ordinary language philosophy."[89] Austin's "felicity conditions"—the concept which had animated that July 1983 article by Goffman titled "Felicity's Condition"—were the social conventions, norms, and procedures that Austin had listed in his 1962 book, *How to Do Things with Words*, which were required conditions for the successful conversational comprehension of what Austin had called "performative verbs"—verbs that occur in sentences such as "I apologize" that in having no (semantic) truth conditions cannot be comprehended in conversations (the way we comprehend semantically, say, the declarative sentence "My car is white" by checking its truth or falsehood) except by reference to the social conventions governing the use of that verb (as, for example, saying "I apologize" instead of "Happy Anniversary" at a friend's wedding anniversary would change the meaning of the situation).[90]

The three reasons that Thomas adduces for the "collapse of Austin's performative hypothesis"—that there is no grammatical way to distinguish perfomative verbs from other verbs, that the presence of a performative verb does not guarantee that the specified action is performed, and that there are ways of "doing things with words" which do not involve the use of performative verbs—simply illustrate my point that pragmatics is sociology rather than linguistics; or, as the sociolinguist Dell Hymes had put it, "Linguistics needs the sociologist."[91]

In fact, the social scientist may very profitably assimilate Austin's key concepts as elaborations of Durkheim's insights. The "illocutionary force" of Austin's performative verbs, for example, strikes me as a variation on that theme of the social "force" that Durkheim had perceived in religious ritual, and the "infelicitous" situation which results when Austin's "felicity conditions" are not observed is a variant of Durkheim's "anomie."[92]

In her analysis of the "problems" that linguists encounter with the "four conversational maxims"—of quantity, quality, relation, and manner—constituting (as four component parts or aspects of) Grice's Cooperative Principle, Thomas makes a similar point to one which she had earlier made about Austin's work: that any attempt at the successful application of this Cooperative Principle's four maxims almost automatically takes the linguist into sociological explanations of conventional (or other) behavior.[93]

It is in his move from the *semantics of implication*—that valid procedure of deduction as defined in Aristotle's syllogisms, for example, where the conclusions of the syllogism have the same truth value as the premises—to the *pragmatics* of what he called *implicature*, the "implied meaning" that goes beyond the "expressed meaning" of words—a move, as Thomas so aptly puts it, "from what is said to what is meant"—that Grice's formulation of his Cooperative Principle enables the cross-fertilization between linguistics and social science that Goffman had been looking for in "Felicity's Condition." Thus, the 1986 attempt by Don Sperber and Deirdre Wilson to flesh out Grice's third conversational maxim (of relation: "Be relevant") into a full-blown theory of linguistic "relevance" connects conceptually with that concern with "social relevance" that Evans-Pritchard had shown in 1937 in his study of Azande implied meaning.[94]

Similarly, Norbert Elias's extensive delineation of the "history of manners" or "power and civility" in *The Civilizing Process*—which the French cultural historian (and proponent of Levy-Bruhl's methodology of *outillages mentaux*) Roger Chartier adjudges such a milestone in the *histoire des mentalités*—is really only an extended explication of the operation of Grice's fourth conversational maxim—of manner—over that *longue duree* of historical time which French historians from Braudel to Chartier have sought to excavate.[95]

Finally, the intellectual career of the founder of sociology, Emile Durkheim, could itself be considered as an extended quest for Grice's "cooperative principle": Richard Bellamy has shown how Durkheim's 1893 usage of the term "solidarity" developed out of the "solidarism" that Leon Bourgeois had been prescribing for the cooperative movement of French syndicalism. Warren Schmaus has pointed to Durkheim's argument—around page 521 of his 1912 French publication of *The Elementary Forms of the Religious Life*—that the "collective forces" of religious ritual "are the product of cooperation." And, in that final intellectual excursion "only a few years before his death" that Hans Joas considers a logical development of the conceptual trend of that 1912 book on the sociology of religion, the 1913-14 lectures on "Pragmatism and Sociology," Durkheim had begun his *Tenth Lecture* by noting that the Pragmatist philosophy that Ferdinand Schiller's *Studies in Humanism* had imbibed (via William James) required humans to "cooperate" as in "constructing reality."[96]

Lest I mislead my reader—with this display of enthusiasm for Grice's Cooperative Principle—into believing that I am advocating the importation of Gricean linguistics into sociology, I hasten to aver that, conscious as I am that linguists and philosophers of language, such as Wayne A. Davis, have declared the theory of Gricean linguistics to have been a "failure," it is *not* Grice's linguistics *in toto* that I wish to import into social science, but only his insight into—as Nicholas Rescher puts it—*communication as cooperation*.[97]

Believing, as I do, *with* Durkheim—and *against* the Weberian sociologist Dennis Wrong—that the mental habits of Western modernity render an "undersocialized" rather than an "oversocialized" conception of the human actor the real threat to a realist view of society, and also accepting Rescher's argument that a *realist* scientific procedure (i.e., scientific realism) "represents a postulation" of the theoretical entities underlying empirical observation "on *functional* rather than on *evidential* grounds," I merely postulate communicational cooperation à la Grice (and Rescher) without requiring any evidence from linguistics. By pursuing such Durkheimian "solidarity" to that very edge of our cultural texts—that "edge" where even to orally utter meaningful words implies the existence of prior "turn-taking" cooperation—I will utilize such forms of this "cooperative principle" underlying all human communication in a realistic "deconstruction" in my next two chapters of the prevailing semantics of individual *self* and *power*, in order then (in chapter 4) to be able to trace the evolution of Peircean communicational (interpretant) form, from the original tribalism of our ancestors to our current process of *globalization*.[98]

Notes

1. Talcott Parsons, *The Structure of Social Action* (New York: McGraw-Hill, 1937), 44; Charles Camic, "Structure after 50 years," *American Journal of Sociology* 95, no. 1 (July 1989), 38-107.

2. Richard Grathoff, ed., *The Theory of Social Action: The Correspondence of Alfred Schutz and Talcott Parsons* (Bloomington: Indiana University Press, 1978), xvii.

3. Grathoff, *Theory of Social Action*, 44, 115.

4. Grathoff, *Theory of Social Action*, 123.

5. Max Weber, *Critique of Stammler* (New York: Free Press, 1977), 154; Rudolf Stammler, *Wirtschaft und Recht nach der materialischen Geschichtsauffassung: Eine sozialphilosophische Untersuchung* (Leipzig: Veit & Comp., 1896).

6. Paul A. Roth, *Meaning and Method in the Social Sciences* (Ithaca, N.Y.: Cornell University Press, 1987), 2.

7. Jon Elster, *Logic and Society* (Chichester, England: Wiley, 1978); Bryan Wilson, ed., *Rationality* (New York: Harper & Row, 1970); Hollis and Lukes, *Rationality and Relativism*.

8. Barry Barnes, *Scientific Knowledge and Sociological Theory* (London: Routledge & Kegan Paul, 1974). David Bloor, in his *Knowledge and Social Imagery* (London: Routledge and Kegan Paul, 1976), 2-10, had justified the "strong programme" in the sociology of knowledge as a mere extension of Durkheim's own program in the sociology of knowledge to its logical conclusions. Whereas Durkheim, argued Bloor, had proposed the causal explanation of all collective representations by external social events, except for the representations of science itself, the "strong programme" of Barnes and Bloor was merely seeking consistency by also including scientific knowledge under that purview of Durkheim's external causation. To the imputation by Bloor of his relativism to Durkheim, Schmaus (*Durkheim's Philosophy*, 256, 264) responds that Bloor has confused social interests or *purposes*—which are the external factors that the "strong programme" uses to explain the discovery of scientific facts—with the social *causes* that Durkheim sought. "In sum," says Schmaus, "although I agree with David Bloor that there are fruitful insights in Durkheim that contemporary sociologists of scientific knowledge should follow up, I disagree about what those insights are. What I like about Durkheim is that he did not maintain the absurdity of being a realist about the explanatory concepts of sociology while denying any reality to the concepts of natural science. . . . I also approve of the way that he avoided relativism. He defended the idea that all human beings think alike without committing himself to the view that we are all perfect logicians."

9. Hollis and Lukes, *Rationality and Relativism*; Jarvie, *Rationality and Relativism*.

10. Bryan R. Wilson, ed., *Rationality* (New York: Harper & Row, 1970), vii.

11. Aristotle, *The Organon* (Cambridge, Mass.: Harvard University Press, 1938); Benedictus de Spinoza, *Ethic: Demonstrated in Geometrical Order and Divided into Five*

Parts (London: Trubner & Co., 1883); Wolfgang Schlucter, *The Rise of Western Rationalism: Max Weber's Developmental History* (Berkeley: University of California Press, 1981), 9-22.

12. Mary Douglas, *How Institutions Think* (Syracuse, N.Y.: Syracuse University Press, 1986), 11-12.

13. Hookway, *Quine*, 199.

14. Roth, *Meaning and Method*, 2; Wilson, *Rationality*, vii; Max Black, *Perplexities: Rational Choice, the Prisoner's Dilemma, Metaphor, Poetic Ambiguity, and Other Puzzles* (Ithaca, N.Y.: Cornell University Press, 1990), 29 (italics added).

15. Schmaus, *Durkheim's Philosophy*, 63; Nicholas Rescher, *Induction: An Essay on the Justification of Inductive Reasoning* (Pittsburgh: Pittsburgh University Press, 1980), 10.

16. Howard Schwartz and Jerry Jacobs, *Qualitative Sociology: A Method to the Madness* (New York: Free Press, 1979), 17. Hookway (*Quine*, 128-45) offers a comprehensive discussion of the meaning and consequences of Quine's now-famous concept of the "indeterminacy of translation."

17. Roland Robertson, *Meaning and Change: Explorations in the Cultural Sociology of Modern Societies* (New York: New York University Press, 1978), 77.

18. Robertson, *Meaning and Change*, 78.

19. Hollis and Lukes, *Rationality and Relativism*, 2.

20. Gellner, *Postmodernism, Reason, and Religion*, 26-27, cited in Kuper, *Culture: The Anthropologists' Account* (Cambridge, Mass.: Harvard University Press, 1999), 220.

21. Niklas Luhmann, "Generalized Media and the Problems of Contingency," in *Explorations in General Theory in Social Science*, ed. Jan C. Loubser et al. (New York: Free Press, 1976), 508; Hans P. M. Adriaansens, *Talcott Parsons and the Conceptual Dilemma* (Boston: Routledge, 1980).

22. Niklas Luhmann, "Modern Systems Theory and the Theory of Society," in *Modern German Sociology*, ed. V. Meja, D. Misgeld, and N. Stehr (New York: Columbia University Press, 1987), 178 (italics in original).

23. Hausman, *Charles S. Peirce's Evolutionary Philosophy*, 6. Referring to that famous *Pragmatic Maxim* from Peirce's 1878 article, "How to Make Our Ideas Clear"— cited by Durkheim, *Pragmatism and Sociology*, 5—Hausman calls it the "so-called pragmatic maxim of meaning, which Peirce proposes as a criterion of clarity."

24. Rossi, *From the Sociology of Symbols*, 133; Talcott Parsons, *Social Systems and the Evolution of Action Theory* (New York: Free Press, 1977), 168.

25. Victor M. Lidz, "Introduction to Part II: Generalized Action Analysis," in *Explorations in General Theory in Social Science*, ed. J. Loubser et al. (New York: Free Press, 1976), 125.

26. Jurgen Habermas, *The Theory of Communicative Action*, vol. 2: *Lifeworld and System: A Critique of Functionalist Reason* (Boston: Beacon Press, 1987), 260-61.

27. Luhmann, "Modern Systems Theory," 178. Thomas McCarthy, in *The Critical Theory of Jurgen Habermas* (Cambridge, Mass.: MIT Press, 1978), 275, 425 nn. 3 and 5, 427 n. 21, cites Habermas's statements in "Universal Pragmatics"—in Habermas, "Was heisst Universalpragmatik?" in *Sprachpragmatik und Philosophie*, ed. Karl-Otto Apel (Frankfurt, 1976), 205-13—to the effect that "semantic theory cannot be completely carried out in the attitude of the linguist, under an abstraction from pragmatic aspects." In my attempt to understand why Habermas was backsliding by 1987 from this earlier focus on

96 Chapter 1

"universal pragmatics" to that semantic focus of Lidz and of linguistics, I could not help but notice that Hans Joas, in "The Unhappy Marriage of Hermeneutics and Functionalism," in *Communicative Action: Essays on Jurgen Habermas's The Theory of Communicative Action*, ed. Axel Honneth and Hans Joas (Cambridge: Polity Press, 1991), 98-103, while linking Durkheim to an "intersubjectivistically oriented pragmatism," critiques Habermas for "his unfortunate joining together of hermeneutics and functionalism" by citing three of the original founders of Pragmatism—William James, George Herbert Mead, and John Dewey—but does not mention that greatest contributor to that "intersubjectivistically oriented pragmatism," Charles Sanders Peirce, even once! I can only conclude that both Habermas and Joas have failed to comprehend the full sociological significance of the thought of Peirce, simply because they both depend so heavily for their knowledge of Peirce's writings on the German writings of Apel. While I tend to be in complete agreement with Apel's reading of Peirce in almost every aspect, I am convinced that the nebulous understanding of Peirce's sociology, shown by German readers of Apel such as Joas and Habermas, stems from the fact that Apel's seminal book *Charles S. Peirce: From Pragmatism to Pragmaticism*, first published in Frankfurt in 1967 and available since 1981 in that English translation (published by the University of Massachusetts Press) which I read, lacks all awareness of those early, specifically sociological writings by Peirce—such as his 1861 "I, It and Thou," or that November 12, 1863, oration "The Place of Our Age in the History of Civilization" (which prefigures my own three "pragmatic codes" defined in chapter 4), which became available in print to a wider audience only with Max Fisch's edited volume, *Writings of Charles S. Peirce*, 45-46, 101-13.

28. Michael A. K. Halliday, *Language as Social Semiotic: The Social Interpretation of Language and Meaning* (Baltimore, Md.: University Park Press, 1978), 25-122, 186.

29. Halliday, *Language as Social Semiotic*, 142.

30. Habermas, *The Theory of Communicative Action*, 2:260-61.

31. Dell Hymes, *Foundations in Sociolinguistics: An Ethnographic Approach* (Philadelphia: University of Pennsylvania Press, 1974), 63. Of note is the fact that this book by Hymes is dedicated to the anthropologist Edward Sapir, co-framer, with linguist Benjamin Whorf, of the Sapir-Whorf hypothesis of linguistic relativity. See also Lukes, "Relativism in Its Place," 267. For a Peirce-inspired critique of the relativistic interpretations of the Sapir-Whorf hypothesis, see Ferrucio Rossi-Landi, *Ideologies of Linguistic Relativity* (The Hague: Mouton, 1979).

32. Nicholas Rescher, "The Ontology of the Possible," in *The Possible and the Actual: Readings in the Metaphysics of Modality* (Ithaca, N.Y.: Cornell University Press, 1979), 179.

33. Hilary Putnam, *Meaning and the Moral Sciences* (London: Routledge & Kegan Paul, 1978); Paul Feyerabend, "Realism and Instrumentalism: Comments on the Logic of Factual Support," in *The Critical Approach to Science and Philosophy*, ed. Mario Bunge (London: Collier-MacMillan, 1964). See also social psychologist Fathali M. Moghaddam's *The Specialized Society: The Plight of the Individual in an Age of Individualism* (Westport, Conn.: Praeger, 1997), 7; Moghaddam argues that the current global division of labor would have been seen by Emile Durkheim as "anomic."

34. Ian Hacking, "Language, Truth, and Reason," in *Rationality and Relativism*, ed. Martin Hollis and Steven Lukes (Cambridge, Mass.: MIT Press, 1982), 64-65; Jean Baudrillard, *Simulations* (New York: Semiotext(e), 1983); Schlucter, *The Rise of Western Rationalism*, 9-22; Richard Rorty, ed., *The Linguistic Turn: Recent Essays in Philosophical*

Method (Chicago: University of Chicago Press, 1967); Ludwig Wittgenstein, *Tractatus Logico Philosophicus* (London: Routledge & Kegan Paul, 1933).

35. Talcott Parsons, *The Social System* (New York: Free Press, 1951), 554 (italics added).

36. Alfred Schutz, *Life Forms and Meaning Structure* (London: Routledge & Kegan Paul, 1982).

37. P. S. Cohen, "Rational Conduct and Social Life," in *Rationality and the Social Sciences*, ed. S. I. Benn and G. W. Mortimore (London: Routledge & Kegan Paul, 1976), 141 (italics in original).

38. Cohen, "Rational Conduct," 153.

39. Lukes, "Relativism in Its Place," 301; Clifford Geertz, "Thick Description: Toward an Interpretive Theory of Culture," in Geertz, *The Interpretation of Cultures: Selected Essays* (New York: Basic Books, 1973).

40. Kuper, *Culture*, 206.

41. Lukes, "Relativism in Its Place," 301-5.

42. Kuper, *Culture*, 112, citing Geertz, *The Interpretation of Cultures*, 452; Alex Thio, *Deviant Behavior* (New York: Longman, 1998), 40, 42. I find it particularly interesting that these two skeptics about Western subjectivist claims should *both* emphasize their "outsider" status in mainstream Western culture: Kuper as a South African and Thio as being of Chinese descent.

43. Luhmann, "Generalized Media and the Problem of Contingency," 508; Rescher, "The Ontology of the Possible," 179.

44. Nicholas Rescher, *Peirce's Philosophy of Science: Critical Studies in His Theory of Induction and Scientific Method* (Notre Dame, Ind.: University of Notre Dame Press, 1978); *Cognitive Economy: The Economic Dimension of the Theory of Knowledge* (Pittsburgh, Pa.: University of Pittsburgh Press, 1989). In my previous chapter, I had presented a similar argument made by Rescher against relativism—the *constraining* effects of our *goals* upon the potentially infinite multiplicity of our subjective interpretations—in Rescher, *Objectivity*, 73.

45. Peirce, *Collected Papers*, 5.9 (italics added).

46. Hausman, *Charles S. Peirce's Evolutionary Philosophy*, 2; Peirce, *Collected Papers*, 5.14-18; Durkheim, *Pragmatism and Sociology*, 5.

47. Luhmann, "Modern Systems Theory," 178; Robert Merton, "Latent and Manifest Functions" in *Social Theory and Social Structure* (New York: Free Press, 1957); Elster, *Logic and Society*. Peirce (*Collected Papers*, 5.467) emphasizes that "I understand pragmatism to be a method of ascertaining the meanings, not of all ideas, but only of what I call 'intellectual concepts.'" As examples, he excludes color words, such as *red* or *blue*, from the purview of his maxim, since they are "mere subjective feelings," while including *hard* and *soft* because they "express the factual behavior of the thing under the pressure of a knife-edge." Such an *operationalizing* restriction on the applicability of his Pragmatic criterion of meaning should be found acceptable by a social sciences—such as sociology—that routinely insist upon *operational* definitions of concepts in their research methodology.

48. Peirce, *Collected Papers*, 5.12; Max Weber, *The Protestant Ethic and the Spirit of Capitalism* (New York: Scribner, 1958); Robertson, *Meaning and Change*, 77.

49. Peirce, *Collected Papers*, 5.436, titled "Pragmaticism and Hegelian Absolute Idealism," is just one of several references to Hegel's work by Peirce. While constantly ac-

Chapter 1

knowledging Hegel's philosophy of history as a major spur and inspiration in the development of his own thought, Peirce declares that "pragmaticism is closely allied to the Hegelian absolute idealism, from which, however, it is sundered by its vigorous denial that the third category (which Hegel degrades to a mere stage of thinking) suffices to make the world, or is even so much as self-sufficient. Had Hegel, instead of regarding the first two stages with his smile of contempt, held on to them as independent or distinct elements of the triune Reality, pragmaticists might have looked up to him as the great vindicator of their truth."

50. Bronislaw Malinowski, "The Problem of Meaning in Primitive Languages," in *The Meaning of Meaning*, eds. C. K. Ogden and I. A. Richards (New York: Harcourt, Brace, Jovanovich, 1946), 296-97; Bronislaw Malinowski, *Argonauts of the Western Pacific* (New York: Dutton, 1961), 24-25.

51. Bhaskar, *Philosophy and Scientific Realism*, 16; Bunge, *Metascientific Queries*; Kuper, *Culture*, 112; Thomas McCarthy, "The Idea of a Universal Pragmatics," in McCarthy, *The Critical Theory of Jurgen Habermas*, (Cambridge, Mass.: MIT Press, 1978), 272-91.

52. Alfred North Whitehead, *Process and Reality* (New York: Free Press, 1978), 181; cited in Darrel E. Christensen, "A Hegelian Critique of Peirce," in *Hegelian/Whiteheadian Perspectives* (Lanham, Md.: University Press of America, 1989), 104.

53. Apel, *Charles S. Peirce*, 3, 188, 197 n. 3, 247 n. 108, 248 n. 8.

54. Hausman, *Charles S. Peirce's Evolutionary Philosophy*, 7 (italics in original). See also Peter Berger, "Plausibility Structures," in *Religion: North American Style*, ed. Thomas E. Dowdy and Patrick H. McNamara (New Brunswick, N.J.: Rutgers University Press, 1997), 20-22; *The Heretical Imperative: Contemporary Possibilities of Religious Affirmation* (Garden City, N.Y.: Anchor Press, 1979).

55. Nicholas Rescher, *Process Metaphysics: An Introduction to Process Philosophy* (Albany: State University of New York Press, 1996), 14, 20; Christensen, *Hegelian/Whiteheadian Perspectives*, 104.

56. W. V. O. Quine, *Quiddities: An Intermittently Philosophical Dictionary* (Cambridge, Mass.: Belknap Press, 1987), 211. It should be noted that though the work by Morris cited here by Quine is the 1946 edition of *Signs, Language, and Behavior*, this threefold division—into *syntax, semantics* and *pragmatics*—of Peirce's semiotic had been carried through earlier by Charles Morris, *Foundations of the Theory of Signs* (Chicago: University of Chicago Press, 1938).

57. Morris, *Foundations of the Theory of Signs*, 13-42.

58. Morris, *Foundations of the Theory of Signs*, 43.

59. Putnam, *Meaning and the Moral Sciences*.

60. Quine, *Quiddities*, 211; Morris, *Foundations of the Theory of Signs*, 29-42; Dell Hymes, *Foundations in Sociolinguistics*, 63.

61. Arthur Pap, *An Introduction to the Philosophy of Science* (New York: Free Press of Glencoe, 1962), 10 (italics added).

62. Pap, *Introduction*, 10 (italics added). See also Emile Durkheim and Marcel Mauss, *"De Quelques Formes primitives de classification"* (1903), English translation: *Primitive Classifications*, ed. Rodney Needham (London: Cohen and West, 1963); Barry Barnes and David Bloor, "Relativism, Rationalism, and the Sociology of Knowledge," in *Rationality and Relativism*, ed. Hollis and Lukes.

63. Peirce, *Collected Papers*, 5.9.

64. Brian Skyrms, *Pragmatics and Empiricism* (New Haven, Conn.: Yale University Press, 1984). It should be noted that in his later work—see, for example, his final chapter, "The Evolution of Meaning" in Brian Skyrms, *Evolution of the Social Contract* (Cambridge: Cambridge University Press, 1996), 105-11—Skyrms moves very close to the theory of the evolution of meaning I develop in chapter 4. In another display of what I see as the "anomic" division of labor between philosophy of science and sociology, Skyrms seems rather unaware of the efforts of Durkheim's tradition in sociology to develop a historical view of the evolution of collective representations and is therefore unable to develop that "marriage" of Durkheim's sociology with Peirce's pragmaticism that I am proposing here. See also Quine, *Quiddities*, 211.

65. Skyrms, *Pragmatics*, 4 (italics added).

66. Skyrms, *Pragmatics*, 5 (italics added).

67. Skyrms, *Pragmatics*, 8 (italics added). Compare Rescher, "Ontology," 179; Luhmann, "Generalized Media," 508; Hookway, *Quine,* 127-45.

68. Skyrms, *Pragmatics*, 11 (italics added).

69. Nicholas Rescher, "Responses," in *Praxis and Reason: Studies in the Philosophy of Nicholas Rescher* (Washington, D.C.: University Press of America, 1982), 106-7 (italics added).

70. Rescher, "Responses," 132-33 (italics added).

71. Nicholas Rescher, *Communicative Pragmatism and Other Philosophical Essays on Language* (Lanham, Md.: Rowman & Littlefield, 1998), 1, 66 (italics in original).

72. Robin Horton, "African Traditional Thought and Western Science," in *Rationality*, ed. Bryan Wilson, 132; Raymond J. Nelson, *The Logic of Mind* (Dordrecht, Holland: D. Reidel, 1982), 212, 263; Rescher, *Communicative Pragmatism*, 13-24.

73. E. E. Evans-Pritchard, *Witchcraft, Oracles, and Magic among the Azande* (Cambridge: Cambridge University Press, 1976), 25 (italics added). See also Peter Winch, "Understanding a Primitive Society," in *Rationality*, ed. Bryan Wilson, 78.

74. John Searle, "What Is an Intentional State," in *Husserl, Intentionality, and Cognitive Science*, ed. Hubert Dreyfus (Cambridge, Mass.: MIT Press, 1982), 259.

75. Searle, "Intentional State," 268. Jenny Thomas (*Meaning in Interaction*, 93) traces this distinction between semantic truth content and semantic use through dual formulations in several analysts of language: "Searle distinguishes between 'propositional content and 'illocutionary force' (cf. Austin's 'locution' and 'illocution' and Grice's 'what is said' and 'what is meant')."

76. Herbert G. Reid, "Time, Historicity, and Political Theory," in *Tradition, Interpretation, and Political Science*, ed. John S. Nelson (Albany: State University of New York Press, 1986), 223-24; Peirce, "Some Consequences of the Four Incapacities," 1868, in *Writings of Charles S. Peirce* 2:211-42; Hookway, *Peirce*, 19-30.

77. Hausman, *Charles S. Peirce's Evolutionary Philosophy*, 2, 140-224. See also Apel, *Charles S. Peirce*, 134-90.

78. Anthony Giddens, *New Rules of Sociological Method: A Positive Critique* (New York: Basic Books, 1976), 53-57, 162.

79. Richard Paul Bellamy, "France: Liberalism Socialized," in *Liberalism and Modern Society: A Historical Argument* (University Park: Pennsylvania State University Press, 1992), 72-104.

80. Hannah Arendt, *On Violence* (New York: Harcourt Brace & World, 1970), 44.

81. H. Paul Grice, "Logic and Conversation," in H. Paul Grice, *Studies in the Way of Words* (Cambridge, Mass.: Harvard University Press, 1989), 26.

82. Emanuel A. Schegloff, "Between Macro and Micro: Contexts and Other Connections," in J. Alexander et al., *The Micro-Macro Link* (Berkeley: University of California Press, 1987), 207.

83. See Thomas McCarthy, *The Critical Theory of Jurgen Habermas*, 425, 425 n. 5, on the "Universal Pragmatics" of Habermas.

84. Guy Rocher, *Talcott Parsons and American Sociology* (New York: Barnes and Noble, 1975), 161.

85. George Herbert Mead, *Mind, Self, and Society from the Standpoint of a Social Behaviorist* (Chicago: University of Chicago Press, 1934), 74 (italics added).

86. Grice, "Meaning," 220. It should be noted that Grice's caveat—put in parentheses at the end of the paragraph that I just cited—that "it may not always be possible to get a straight answer . . . " confirms Karl-Otto Apel's argument (*Charles S. Peirce*, 129-30) that the *pragmatics* of meaning cannot be reduced, as Apel accuses Charles Morris of having done, to positivistic or behavioristic observation. Morris was the editor of Mead's *Mind, Self, and Society* 1934 edition, whose title defined itself "from the standpoint of a social behaviorist." Talcott Parsons' "Some Problems of General Theory in Sociology," in *Theoretical Sociology: Perspectives and Developments*, ed. J. C. McKinney and E. A. Tiryakin (New York: Appleton-Century-Crofts, 1970), 46-62, echoes Grice's pragmatics of "recognition" when he attempts to begin a general theory of media with "two of W. I. Thomas's four wishes, for response and recognition. . . . If response were to be included, it seemed logical that recognition also ought to be—here I differ from Victor Lidz. . . . The best terminological solution I have come upon so far is performance capacity."

87. Peirce, *Collected Papers*, 5.9.

88. Grice, *Studies in the Way of Words*, 387-94 (index); Thomas, *Meaning in Interaction*, 219-24 (index); Erving Goffman, "Felicity's Condition," *American Journal of Sociology* 89, no. 1 (July 1983).

89. Thomas, *Meaning in Interaction*, 56.

90. J. L. Austin, *How to Do Things with Words* (Oxford: Oxford University Press, 1962), 14-15, cited in Thomas, *Meaning in Interactions*, 32-41.

91. Thomas, *Meaning in Interaction*, 44; Hymes, *Foundations in Sociolinguistics*, 69.

92. Thomas (*Meaning in Interaction*, 36-51) echoes Durkheim's *Elementary Forms* in speaking of "ritual" performatives. See Schmaus, *Durkheim's Philosophy*, 217-19, for analysis of Durkheim's concept of the "force" of religious ritual. By asserting that for Durkheim such "forces . . . are the product of cooperation," Schmaus is in fact mutually assimilating the linguistic pragmatics of Austin/Grice's "cooperative principle" and Durkheim's sociology. Jurgen Habermas, *The Theory of Communicative Action*, also links Durkheim with what Habermas calls the "linguistification of the sacred."

93. Thomas, *Meaning in Interaction*, 61-93. Rescher (*Communicative Pragmatism*, 12-13, 46 n. 2, 74 n. 1) has adapted Grice's maxims into his own four "injunctions" or "governing principles" of the "economy . . . of communication."

94. Thomas, *Meaning in Interaction*, 56-57; Aristotle, *The Organon*; Dan Sperber and Deirdre Wilson, *Relevance: Communication and Cognition* (Oxford: Basil Blackwell, 1986); Evans-Pritchard, *Witchcraft*, 25.

95. Norbert Elias, *The Civilizing Process*, vols. 1 and 2 (New York: Pantheon Books, 1982); Roger Chartier, *Cultural History*; Roger Chartier, *On the Edge of the Cliff: History, Language, and Practices* (Baltimore: Johns Hopkins University Press, 1997), 124-44.

96. Bellamy, *Liberalism*, 66-75, citing Leon Bourgeois's 1895 book, *Solidarite*; Schmaus, *Durkheim's Philosophy*, 218-19; Joas, *Pragmatism and Social Theory*, 55; Durkheim, *Pragmatism and Sociology*, 54.

97. Wayne A. Davis, *Implicature: Intention, Convention, and Principle in the Failure of Gricean Theory* (Cambridge: Cambridge University Press, 1998); Rescher, *Communicative Pragmatism*, 13.

98. Dennis Hume Wrong, *The Oversocialized Conception of Man* (New Brunswick, N.J.: Transaction, 1999). Rescher (*Communicative Pragmatism*, 29-30) says: "We do not learn or discover that there is a mind-independent reality, we *presume* or *postulate* it. As Kant clearly saw, objective experience is possible only if the existence of such a real, observer-independent world is presupposed from the outset rather than seen as something that must be a matter of post facto discovery about the nature of things" (Rescher's italics).

Provided some rather restrictive assumptions are met, the concept of power and a simple force model represent a reasonable approach to the study of social choice. Provided some rather substantial estimation and analysis problems can be solved, the concept of power and more elaborate force models represent a reasonable approach. On the whole, however, power is a disappointing concept. It gives us surprisingly little purchase in reasonable models of complex systems of social choice.

—James G. March, "The Power of Power,"
in *Varieties of Political Theory*, ed. David Easton
(Englewood Cliffs, N. J.: Prentice-Hall, 1966), 70.

The systems approach searches for control relationships, that is, it focuses on behaviors that are controlled by the structure of the system and its environment. The systems approach is concerned with developing vocabularies and theoretical constructs that focus on the relations between structure and process.

—Patrick Doreian and Norman Hummon,
Modeling Social Processes (New York: Elsevier, 1976), 4

Theoretical progress in this problem area would seem to hinge upon a more complete and elaborate comprehension of the direction of flows and interchanges. . . . The basic idea is that deflation and inflation of power are conditioned by the form in which power is gained by a government and the aspect (functionally speaking) of the society upon which the government acts. In other words, we are attempting to isolate of what, in terms of specific subsystems, the government is the pivot.

—Roland Robertson, "Societal Attributes and
International Relations," in *Explorations in General
Theory in Social Science: Essays in Honor of
Talcott Parsons*, Volume Two, ed. Jan J. Loubser,
Rainer C. Baum, Andrew Efrat, Victor Meyer Lidz
(New York: The Free Press, 1976), 731.

CHAPTER 2

Social Power: The Signifying Context of Communicative Meaning

Social science studies human agency not in a vacuum, but within a social "context." From Karl Marx's dictum that "men make history, but not exactly as they please," to the contemporary mathematical-modeling methodology of Patrick Doreian and Norman Hummon, whose "systems approach searches for control relationships . . . [and] focuses on behaviors that are controlled by the structure of the system and its environments," the social science has sought to delineate that "context" within which human agents act. Our empirical knowledge of the social context of "control relationships" proceeds from our experience of power—an experience, according to the philosopher of action Myles Brand, that John Locke's 1690 *Essay Concerning Human Understanding* had traced to our awareness of human "volition" or "willing."[1]

It is to that idea of the will as the source of our experience of power that Emile Durkheim had referred when, in *The Elementary Forms of the Religious Life*, he had granted that, "in willing, it is said, we perceive ourselves directly as a power in action." But, he had pointed out, it is in that very exercise of our volition that we also become aware of constraints on our individual powers: "When I throw myself against an obstacle, I have a sensation of hindrance and trouble."[2] It had been by appeal to such experiences of constraint on volitional power that Durkheim had earlier defined the "facts" of our social context. Constraint, he had argued, was

> intrinsically a characteristic of facts. . . . The proof of this is that it asserts itself as soon as I try to resist. If I attempt to violate the rules of law, they react against me so as to forestall my action. . . . In other cases the constraint is less violent; nevertheless it does not cease to exist. . . . If I do not conform to ordinary con-

ventions . . . the laughter I provoke, the social distance at which I am kept, produce, although in a more mitigated form, the same results as any real penalty.[3]

Durkheim's delineation of the constraint that "social facts" exert on the agent's volitional power had informed the development of twentieth-century social science's concept of social structure. But, it is at the end of the twentieth century that another French writer, Michel Maffesoli, has appealed to Durkheim's concept of "effervescence" to define a type of social power—*puissance*—as the "opposite" of the power of politico-economic structure. As Maffesoli's translator, Don Smith, explains:

> The term 'puissance' in French conveys the idea of the inherent energy and vital force of the people, as opposed to the institutions of 'power' ('pouvoir'). Maffesoli makes a clear distinction between these two terms, both of which are usually rendered as 'power' in English. I have chosen to leave the term 'puissance' in the original French, in order to maintain this distinction.[4]

Echoing Hannah Arendt's definition of power as the ability "to act in concert," Maffesoli, a professor of sociology in Paris, defines *puissance* by reference to Durkheim's sociology of religion as insisting "above all . . . on the being-together, on what I called 'immanent transcendence'—another way of describing the *puissance* which binds small groups and communities."[5]

Social power as *puissance*—that collectively generated power that Durkheim had seen in religious ritual as "the product of cooperation"—corresponds to that "cooperative principle" of H. Paul Grice's pragmatics, which also generates meaning. Such a concept of power does not fall into that dichotomizing of meaning against power that Anthony Giddens had accused Alfred Schutz's phenomenology of propagating.[6]

But, as Smith, Maffesoli's translator, is aware, the two French terms, *puissance* and *pouvoir*, that Maffesoli uses are both "usually rendered as 'power' in English." In what may well be the ultimate irony of what Willard Van Orman Quine has called the "indeterminacy of translation," it is only *pouvoir*—what Max Weber had defined as "the probability that one actor in a relationship will be in a position to carry out his own will despite resistance"—that seems to have survived in the English-language semantics of "social structure." It is to that historical analysis of the social structure of *pouvoir*—an analysis that I hope will lead us back to the Peirce-Durkheim pragmatics of *puissance*—to which I must now turn.[7]

Structure and Power:
Family Resemblances and Conceptual Relations

George Stocking's 1984 essay, "Radcliffe-Brown and British Social Anthropology," traced the development of structural functionalism "at midcentury" through the conflict for Durkheim's heritage of sociological method between Bronislaw Malinowski, whose "functionalism" had emphasized the study of culture shaped by the constraints of social "needs," and Alfred Reginald Radcliffe-Brown, whose "hyphenated functionalism" had stressed instead a "natural Science of society." Malinowski's earlier death in 1942, said Stocking, had left Radcliffe-Brown's "natural science" approach to the definition of social structure in undisputed influence over the subsequent work of functionalist social scientists such as Meyer Fortes and Raymond Firth.[8]

Radcliffe-Brown's project of studying "the social system" within "natural laws" had demanded "a taboo on the word *culture*, as well as on process." Radcliffe-Brown's focus, supported by numerous examples from physiology, had been on persistence and continuity: "The characteristic of any persistent system is that it maintains through a certain lapse of time its structural continuity." Hence, he had argued, "a social structure is a natural persistent system," and "the word 'change' (and more particularly 'process') is ambiguous in relation to society. . . . There is change *within* the structure of society. But it does not affect the structural form of the society." And even culture was defined—when the taboo was "revoked" after his physiological-skeletal analogy of "structure" has been established—by its relation to persistence, as the "standardization" of behavior:

> The word "culture," then, as I am going to use it, is a term which obviously refers to a certain standardization of behavior, inner and outer, in a certain group of human beings, in a society. That is the primary significance of the word.[9]

This conservative bias towards persistence, and against change and process, which critics such as Walter Buckley imputed to the methodological vision of structural functionalism could be seen, despite the lack of specific references to Radcliffe-Brown, in Talcott Parsons's structural-functional book (whose title, *The Social System*, seemed to echo Radcliffe-Brown):

> A particularly important aspect of our system of categories is the "structural" aspect. We simply are not in a position to "catch" the uniformities of dynamic process in the social system except here and there.[10]

Parsons would later argue that "the hyphenated label 'structural-functionalism' has seemed to me decreasingly appropriate," and that

> we do not wish to hypostatize structure. . . . Process, then, is the correlative concept designating the respects in which the state of a system or the relevant part or parts of it changes within the time span relevant and significant for the particular cognitive purpose in mind. A physiologist studying the process of digestion does not assume that the input of food substances from the environment will remain constant over a period of, let us say, several hours.[11]

But even then Parsons still shared Radcliffe-Brown's critical view of Malinowski's concept of function, and admitted:

> As between the two leading British social anthropologists of that generation, I found myself strongly leaning to the side of Radcliffe-Brown, as a theorist of social systems in something like my own sense. Of course the influence of Durkheim, which was so prominent in Radcliffe-Brown may be seen to have influenced me greatly, an appraisal shared by my other London teacher, Ginsberg.[12]

But just how exaggerated that appraisal by Parsons's London teacher—about Durkheim having been the prominent influence over Radcliffe-Brown—was, is apparent in Stocking's other 1984 essay, "Dr. Durkheim and Mr. Brown: Comparative Sociology at Cambridge in 1910":

> Until recently, the Durkheimian influence, however "true" to the original, has been generally assumed to have been critical to the formation of Radcliffe-Brown's anthropology. That assumption has recently been challenged.[13]

Stocking's assessment of the degree of Durkheim's influence visible in the work of Radcliffe-Brown seems to echo that division, made by Parsons himself, and by Jeffrey Alexander, between an "earlier" and a "later" Durkheim:

> It is not clear that he had yet fully assimilated all the implications he was to derive from the *Rules of Sociological Method* (1895); but he had read *Suicide* (1897), and the role of *The Division of Labor* (1893) in his interpretation of "primitive" social forms is absolutely critical. . . . In this context, it would seem, then, that the earliest extant formulation of Radcliffe-Brown's lifelong project for a "Comparative Sociology" was, as both his memory and conventional interpretation have insisted, already very much in a Durkheimian mode—although as some would have surmised, it is strongly that of "early" Durkheim.[14]

So, apparently believing that he was following the "early" Durkheim, Radcliffe-Brown had placed "a taboo on culture" and had argued for "a natural science" approach to the study of social structure:

> In the first place, I regard as a part of the social structure all social relations of person to person. For example the kinship structure of any society consists of a number of such dyadic relations, as between a father and a son, or a mother's brother and his sister's son . . . Secondly, I include under social structure the differentiation of individuals and of classes by their social role.[15]

But Radcliffe-Brown's "natural science" approach to social structure had been challenged by the French anthropologist Claude Levi-Strauss. Levi-Strauss had argued that, in distinguishing between *parenté* and *consanguineté*, Durkheim had already placed kinship (*parenté*) beyond mere biological relationship (*consanguinité*). Kinship, in Levi-Strauss's reading of Durkheim, was not a biological fact to be readily observed by natural science but a cultural construct. And since even such elementary, premodern social structures could only be studied as cultural constructs, it logically followed that all social structures must be studied not as empirically given but as mental constructs.[16]

That such radically divergent interpretations of Durkheim could bring communication in social science to a stop had been recognized in Radcliffe-Brown's 1953 letter to Levi-Strauss:

> As you have recognized, I use the term "social structure" in a sense so different from yours as to make discussion so difficult as to be unlikely to be profitable.[17]

By 1975 the disagreements between social scientists about the definition of *social structure* had apparently become so vast that the sociologist Peter Blau had issued an almost Wittgensteinian plea for social scientists to respect the family resemblances between each other's "use" of the concept:

> Since the concept of social structure is often defined implicitly by the way it is used in the analysis, not explicitly, one way to infer its meaning for various authors is to examine its antithesis, the counterpoint that serves as background for bringing out the features of social structure. An elementary contradistinction to structure in social life is chaos, formlessness, idiosyncratic human behavior that exhibits no regularities and hence is unstructured. Only if social behavior reveals some consistent, more or less persisting regularities can we begin to speak of it as being structured.[18]

But even such minimally "consistent, more or less persisting regularities" in social behavior could present, according to Hubert Blalock's 1984 book, *Basic Dilemmas in the Social Sciences*, "the challenge" of "a combination of complexities:"

> First, virtually all social processes are far more complex than we often realize. . . . Second, measurement problems in the social sciences are formidable. . . . Third, as is also common within the physical sciences, rates of change in social phenomena are sometimes far too rapid to be studied with present resources, sometimes they are far too slow. . . . Fourth, there is a tremendous variety of behaviors and other phenomena we wish to explain.[19]

Such complexities would militate, according to Blalock, against Radcliffe-Brown's project of assimilating the study of social structure within "natural science":

The social sciences, lodged as they are between the natural sciences and humanities, have almost inevitably become a battleground over the suitability of natural science models and approaches to the study of human behaviors and social processes.[20]

Against the *naïve realism* of Radcliffe-Brown—who, while excoriating Levi-Strauss for having "built up" models of social structure that had "nothing to do with reality," had peremptorily declared, "I regard the social structure as a reality"—Blalock recognized the "complications produced by multiple causation," exacerbated by "further ambiguities in the real world," and the "limitations imposed by a fuzzy reality" that lead to "complications in dynamic analyses." Instead of that problem-free directness of perception that Radcliffe-Brown's *naïve realism* had earlier expected, Blalock's 1984 solution to the complexities of reality was to rely instead on "indirect measurement":

> Since the testing of scientific theories relies on some kind of assessment of the goodness of fit between theoretical predictions and empirical evidence that must inevitably be filtered through our human sensory organs, all measurement must be indirect, though to varying degrees.[21]

But such an "indirect" approach to the study of "social structure" had already been pioneered—before Blalock had suggested it in 1984—by another anthropologist, who, unlike Radcliffe-Brown, had made no pretense of following Durkheim. As the mathematical sociologist Harrison White explained in his 1970 attempt to model mobility within modern organizations:

> There is much to do and little guidance in the literature, with the notable exception of *The Theory of Social Structure* by S. F. Nadel. He understood enough to be baffled by the problem of even defining social structure. It is with one of his suggestions, that of defining structure *indirectly* through the analysis of recruitment patterns, that the current book is consonant.[22]

Recruitment defines a *relation* between human actors, also specifying the actors' complementary roles of recruiter and recruitee. Recruitment patterns therefore satisfy Radcliffe-Brown's stipulation to "include under social structure the differentiation of individuals and of classes by their social role." But recruitment is also an *action* and can therefore be studied within Max Weber's Action Paradigm. According to Jana Salat's study of anthropologist S. F. Nadel's life and work, Nadel had, in operationalizing the concept of structure, preferred to abandon Radcliffe-Brown's supposedly Durkheimian focus to depend instead on Weber's Action Theory to define criteria of structural placement in roles. "According to Nadel," says Salat, such criteria would be in "command over one another's actions" and in "command over existing benefits or resources." This meant that factors had to be identified which clearly underlined the power positions that certain individuals had over others.[23]

Salat accepts the assertion made by Nadel's critic Morris Freilich in 1966 that "Nadel's social structure is basically power structure." Beginning with Radcliffe-Brown's attempt to comprehend Durkheim's concept of social-structural "constraint" over human agency within the frame of "natural science," social science had come around—with the "indirect" approach to social structure in the anthropology of Nadel—to Weber's definition of power as "the probability that one actor in a social relationship will be in a position to carry out his own will despite resistance." It is therefore to the scrutiny of Weber's concept of power that we must now turn, if we are to come to grips with that stricture by Anthony Giddens against hermeneutic phenomenology's "interpretative sociology": that it neglects "the centrality of power in social life."[24]

Domination: The "First Face" of Power

In his 1986 book *Power and the Division of Labour*, Dietrich Rueschemeyer focused on what he called "Durkheim's problem." Durkheim's celebrated 1893 study of *The Division of Labor in Society*, argued Rueschemeyer, while overtly aiming to transcend Adam Smith's and J. S. Mill's utilitarian explanation of "social needs" causing social role differentiation, had really ended up covertly smuggling a tacit form of utilitarianism back into sociology, through the concept of the "function." A "function" of society, as Malinowski was aware, can be understood as a "social need." To overcome Durkheim's "problem," Rueschemeyer appealed to Max Weber.[25]

In turning from Durkheim to Weber, Rueschemeyer was not the first social scientist to "jump ship" from Durkheim's social realism when the (conceptual) going got tough. As we have seen, this theoretical gambit had been played before by the anthropologist S. F. Nadel, and even earlier, as W. Paul Vogt pointed out, from within Durkheim's own circle of early French sociology, by Durkheim's student Celestin Bougle. More recently, French social scientist Raymond Boudon has been a vociferous proponent of the "methodological individualism" of Weber. What Rueschemeyer, in his 1986 book, had hoped to grasp—through that switch in theoretical perspective from Durkheim's social realism to Weber's methodological individualism—was the "proximate" cause of the division of labor, i.e., power.[26]

But, as Barry Barnes's 1988 study *The Nature of Power* reminded us, the concept of "power" in the social sciences, like the concepts of "gravity" and "electricity" in the natural sciences, has been easier to explicate only by describing its consequences:

> Power is one of those things, like gravity and electricity, which makes its existence apparent to us through its effects, and hence it has always been easier to describe its consequences than to identify its nature and its basis.[27]

Now, I need hardly remind my reader that Charles S. Peirce's 1905 version of the Pragmatic Maxim had also used the word that Barnes used—*consequences*—in order to "ascertain the meaning of an intellectual conception," but Peirce had also specified that it is "the sum of these consequences" that "will constitute the entire meaning of the conception." So it behooves us to check whether Rueschemeyer's quest for structural role differentiation's "proximate" cause in "power"—as Weber had defined it—meets this Peircean criterion of meaning. After paying due respect to Weber's recognition of the definitional difficulty of power as an "amorphous" concept, Rueschemeyer proceeds to lay out for us Weber's indirect perception of power through its consequences:

> Power is the probability that one actor in a social relationship will be in a position to carry out his own will despite resistance, regardless of the basis on which this probability rests.[28]

Now, in our postmodern era when the airwaves of academia have been saturated by Michel Foucault's insistence on the "productive" aspect of power, it is readily apparent that that crucial last phrase in Weber's definition of power, "regardless of the basis on which this probability rests," forecloses on precisely that "knowledge" aspect of Foucault's "power/knowledge" complex—what Weber's own acute historical insight would elsewhere highlight as the "legitimation" problem of dominating power—and it is precisely to this neglected "productive" aspect of power that Barnes appeals by pointing to that "power to" act—in contrast to Weber's "power over" regardless of the basis upon which such domination rests—that had been emphasized by Talcott Parsons:

> Finally, the power of the individual is manifest in its *effects* upon other individuals—in their compliance, whether willing or reluctant, with the will of the power-holder: power is defined as "power over" rather than "power to." Once more Parsons is the outstanding deviant from the mainstream view.[29]

The occasion for what Barnes saw as Parsons's "deviance" from the Weberian "mainstream"—by defining "power as a generalized capability not tied to a few specific relationships"—had been Parsons's critique in 1960 of C. Wright Mills's celebrated 1956 concept of the "Power Elite." Rebuking Mills, Parsons had pointed out that power is mobilization above all, of the action of persons and groups, which is *binding* on them by virtue of their position in society. Thus within a much larger complex, Mills concentrates almost exclusively on the distributive aspect of power. He is interested only in *who* has power and on what *sectoral* interests he is serving with his power, not in how power is generated or in what communal, rather than sectoral, interests are served.[30]

Since Mills had only been using Weber's concept of individual (or sectoral) "power (over)"—as "the probability that one actor in a social relationship will be in a position to carry out his will despite resistance, regardless of the basis on which this probability rests"—Parsons's attack on Mills had in effect demonstrated why Weber's definition of power (despite Roland Robertson's 1978 attempt to assimilate Weber to the philosophical tradition of Pragmatism, in that "'meaning' tended to make sociological sense for Weber in reference to its actional significance") *fails* to pass the test of Peirce's criterion of meaning. As Parsons had pointed out, by focusing solely on the domination-consequences of power, Weber's definition neglects power's most important consequences of "mobilization," and thereby misses Peirce's stricture on meaning having to contain the "sum" of the practical consequences of an intellectual conception.[31]

Ironically, in the resulting controversy within mainstream American social science, the pluralist reply to Mills's elitist view—delivered by Robert Dahl's 1961 study of New Haven's community power structure, *Who Governs*—had also reflected Weber's "power over" view, for Dahl had earlier written in "On the Concept of Power": "A has power over B to the extent that he can get B to do something that B would not otherwise do."[32]

This irony, of Mills's and Dahl's opposing political standpoints sharing the same Weberian conception of power, is best appreciated when viewed in the light of methodologist Hubert Blalock, whose 1984 book, *Basic Dilemmas in the Social Sciences*, we have previously considered. The problems of measurement, said Blalock, which social science might otherwise be seen as sharing with some physical sciences such as particle physics, are really exacerbated beyond any level physical science might experience by the problem of ideology. Ideological debates which filter from the social scientists' personal views into their scientific theorizing feed on and in turn reinforce the scientific problems of measurement. The "community power" debate of the late 1950s and early 1960s had been fueled by the conflicting ideological passions then burning around Mills's "left-wing populist" attack on American "pluralist" pretensions and by Dahl's rallying to the defense of established views on American pluralism, but it was the unfolding of this debate into a running ideological-cum-methodological battle beyond the 1960s which in its turn exposed problems of definition and measurement entailed in the protagonists' common "Weberian mainstream" of "power-over" views.[33]

C. Wright Mills's hypothesis about "elitism" within modern America's socio-economic structure had been posed within the deductive framework of Max

Weber's theory of "domination" emerging from within the modern rationality-imperative of bureaucracy. According to Weber, argues John Hughes, modern bureaucratic rationality had implied extensive gradations of dominating "power over" because bureaucracy had been characterized as:

1. a hierarchically arranged organization of specialized administrative appointments,
2. occupied by those whose full-time occupation it is and whose income is derived solely from it,
3. those who are themselves trained and specialized in administrative skills,
4. those whose conduct is regulated by impersonal and written rules, and
5. those whose relationships within the organization are regulated in terms of super and subordination.[34]

But if it is indeed the case that these five points accurately describe the functioning of modern bureaucracy, argues Bob Anderson, then the following sets of interlinked propositions logically follow:

1. Under the ethos of rational efficiency guiding the rapid social and economic changes taking place in the industrialized and industrializing world, all activities in every sphere of life were being subjected to organization in terms of the effective achievement of goals, allocation of delimited responsibilities, hierarchical structures of power and decision-making, and the centralization of control.
2. Since modern societies have sought to make the mechanisms of distribution more efficient, and the asymmetric distribution of power and rewards which all societies display is a reflection of the need to distribute effectively the reservoir of natural talent within any society, the efficient allocation of individual talents and capacities necessitates an unequal distribution of power and rewards.
3. Furthermore, since modernization implies a social transformation from a collectivist to an individualist basis for society—and such a movement threatens the "atomizing" of society, the breakdown of all the major intermediary groupings, and the consequent irrational sway of masses by charismatic leaders or authoritarian propaganda—the domination of Pareto's logical elites is justified and legitimated.[35]

"Taking these three together," argues Anderson in "The Empirical Study of Power," helps place what Mills had been doing in his 1956 study, *The Power Elite*, in its proper context:

> What we have is a fear that the rationalization of activities and ideas, rather than leading to tolerance, pluralism and the end of ideology, would result in the

concentration of power and ultimately totalitarianism. That these processes were in train was attested by a whole range of studies of local community life and of political parties, movements and systems. . . . Against this background, Mills' choice to study the occupants of what he terms the "command posts" of society becomes understandable.[36]

What Mills had seen was that in the three major administrative blocs which, he claimed, dominated contemporary American life—the military, industrial-economic, and political-administrative structures—there were indeed "command posts" within each structure, occurring through centrality within networks of shared group memberships, interlocking directorships, committee memberships, and so forth, and these command posts were occupied by an elite whose similarity in social background, education, and intermarriages made an assumption of homogeneity (in terms of sharing a common set of attitudes and orientations) plausible.

However, argues Anderson, in a direct echo of Parsons's 1960 critique of Mills:

It has to be said that although the evidence which Mills offers is voluminous and much of it is quantified, none of it is really conclusive. The statistics which are cited are nearly all descriptive in nature and have not been subjected to any kind of testing. Mills' argument, if it convinces, does so because of the weight of the material brought to bear, the welter of examples offered, and not because of the systematicity of its collection nor the rigor of his analytic methods. . . . What remains at issue is the central question of whether the power elite can and does exercise its power in its own sectional interest. Neither Mills nor any of his followers offers any evidence that this is indeed the case.[37]

Mills's methodological approach had been "reputationalist," in the sense that it was based upon reputations and beliefs about who occupied positions of power and not on observations about what they actually did, and this was the thrust of Robert Dahl's counterargument in his 1958 paper, "A Critique of the Ruling Elite Model." If, as was the case, argued Dahl, the central propositions of the power elite case were (1) power is accumulated across the range of policy formation, (2) the elite acts as a cohesive group against the interests of the majority, and (3) crucial control of decision-making was in the hands of the elite, then the power elite proponents, such as Mills, would have had to demonstrate their case not just through reputations but by showing that all three propositions held true in actual cases of decision-making. And such a rigorous test of the power elite case through empirical observation of actual decision-making was provided by Dahl in his own 1961 New Haven study, whose examination of decisions had revealed not a unified, cohesive elite deciding its own interests but conflicting interests between several economic, social, and political elites. New Haven politics, Dahl had concluded, revealed no power elite, but only a system of "dispersed inequalities" and "polyarchic" government.[38]

Yet inadvertently, while basing his pluralist case against Mills on the strengths of empirical observation, Dahl had exposed the weakness of empiricism in social science's comprehension of "power over" domination. For, unlike the Kaiser-Reich of Weber's Germany, where the domination of an elite was not denied even by that elite, a power elite within a self-defined democracy would, by necessity, have to mask its domination. The problem this creates for measurement reliability is explained by Anderson: the essence of Dahl's empiricist argument was his demand that the researcher cite observed cases of elite control. But, for such empirical observation, the researcher would have needed access to all those inner sanctums—including private clubs and residential quarters—wherein the policy-making groups of a self-defined democracy actually reach their decisions. And such empiricism, argues Anderson, then faces the dilemma that

> if an elite was exercising control of the kind the power elite argument requires, it would, given the rhetoric of democratic systems, have to be pretty politically inept to allow such an investigator to see it exercising centralized control. And if it were so inept it could hardly pose the political threat to the interests of the majority that Mills and his followers suppose. . . . As a consequence, no matter what Dahl had done, and no matter how he had formulated his investigative strategy, his conclusions were always likely to be open to the allegation either that he had failed to find the real center of power or that he could not hope to offer an unequivocal demonstration of its existence. Dahl's study would be condemned either for reactionary apologetics or for muddleheadedness.[39]

Dahl's empiricist project of observing Weberian "power over," i.e., power as domination, had run into the "theory-laden" problems of empirical observation: in that peculiarly reflexive manner in which such problems tend to manifest themselves in social science, the empirical observer had been snared within the social definition of the situation that had "generated" that very power which he had sought to observe.[40]

Power's Other "Faces": From the Empirical Mismeasure of "Power Over" to the Theoretical Definition of "Power To"

Robert Dahl's "Critique of the Ruling Elite Model," in 1958, had criticized the assertion that C. Wright Mills had made in 1956 about the existence of a "power elite" dominating American society, on the *empiricist* grounds that Mills's reliance upon a person's *reputation* for having power had not involved the direct empirical observation of such power being exercised in concrete decisions. "I do not see," Dahl had said, "how anyone can suppose that he has established the dominance of any specific group in a community or nation without basing his analysis on the careful examination of a series of concrete decisions."[41]

But Dahl's empiricist assumption about what the scientific analysis of power involved was soon challenged by the notion of a "second face of power"—less "obvious" to empirical observation—introduced in 1962 by Peter Bachrach and Morton Baratz in "The Two Faces of Power." The views of Bachrach and Baratz, presented comprehensively in their 1970 book *Power and Poverty*, drew overtly upon post-empiricist (post-positivist) philosophy of science to argue that, since all science involves the making of judgments of significance deriving from the scientist's theoretical perspective, social science should consider those aspects of political life that are covert and "nonobvious." In criticizing Dahl's empiricist focus on actual decisions and overt conflict, Bachrach and Baratz put forward the concept of the "nondecision," which they defined as "a decision that results in suppression or thwarting of a latent or manifest challenge to the values or interests of the decision-maker."[42]

That "second face" of domination, according to Bachrach and Baratz, was therefore to be sought not in the observed decisions that Robert Dahl had conflated with the entirety of power but in those subterranean patterns of social organization's "mobilization of bias" in favor of dominant interests:

> Political systems and sub-systems develop a "mobilization of bias," a set of predominant values, beliefs, rituals, and institutional procedures ("rules of the game") that operate systematically and consistently to the benefit of certain groups and persons at the expense of others. Those who benefit are placed in a preferred position to defend and promote their vested interests.[43]

But, in another version of that "central question" Bob Anderson had posed in "The Empirical Study of Power"—the question "of whether the power elite can and does exercise its power in its own sectional interests"—Dahl's fellow-pluralist Nelson Polsby inquired whether Bachrach and Baratz's "second face of power" was, in principle, amenable to empirical study.

> The central problem is this: Even if we can show that a given status quo benefits some people disproportionately (as I think we can for any real world status quo), such a demonstration falls short of showing that the beneficiaries created the status quo, act in any meaningful way to maintain it, or could in the future, act effectively to deter changes in it.[44]

So, asked Polsby, "How to study this second face of power? To what manifestations of social reality might the mobilization of bias refer? Are phenomena of this sort in principle amenable to empirical investigation?"[45]

"No," answered Anderson in "The Empirical Study of Power." Referring to the "empirical" studies of poverty and the noninvolvement of minorities in decision-making in Baltimore in Bachrach and Baratz's *Power and Poverty*, Anderson argued that the authors had

returned to the actual events which they could observe. They focused on decisions and ignored to a large extent, non-decisions. They did this because it
proved to be impossible to specify what exact courses of action were open to
decision-makers at any time, and what were the precise reasons whereby one
line was chosen rather than another.[46]

The result of this dilemma—that the full extent of the domination by modern elite groups could be theoretically inferred but not empirically observed—
was the 1974 suggestion by Steven Lukes, in *Power: A Radical View*, that social
science abandon its commitment to the empirical observation of overt conflict
situations and consider instead the presence of social institutions whose structural and cultural patterns cannot be directly observed in individual behavior. Of
the "non-decision" approach of Bachrach and Baratz, Lukes argued that it had
been "still committed to behaviorism" in its study of overt, "actual behavior" (in
both decisions and "non-decisions") within paradigmatic conflict situations. But,
said Lukes,

> Decisions are choices consciously and intentionally made by individuals be-
> tween alternatives, whereas the bias of the system can be mobilized, recreated
> and reinforced in ways that are neither consciously chosen nor the intended re-
> sult of particular individuals' choices. . . . Moreover, the bias of the system is
> not simply sustained by a series of individually chosen acts, but also, more im-
> portantly, by the socially structured and culturally patterned behavior of
> groups, and practices of institutions which may indeed be manifested by indi-
> viduals' inaction.[47]

What Lukes had really been arguing, suggested Anderson, was "that conflict and conflict management may not always be strictly observable. Culturally
accepted norms and values may express and channel latent conflicts." But if for
Lukes "power involves more than power behavior," asked Anderson, "how then
might we go about studying these non-observable, non-measurable aspects of
power?"[48]

For an answer, Lukes had pointed to Matthew Crenson's 1971 empirical
study *The Unpolitics of Air Pollution*, whose contention had been that in Gary,
Indiana, U.S. Steel's "power reputation" as Gary's dominant power had prevented
air pollution from becoming a major issue and had ensured that when pollution
regulations had been framed, they had been neither costly nor effective. But
Crenson had also admitted that U.S. Steel had never actively involved itself in
opposing pollution regulations and that it had, in fact, repeatedly said that the
company would neither support nor oppose the effort to legislate on the issue but
would conform to whatever local regulations were enforced. For Crenson, such
inaction by U.S. Steel had itself been significant. "What U.S. Steel did not do
was probably more important than what it did do," Crenson had argued, in return-

ing to the "reputationalist" method of C. Wright Mills—i.e., the procedure of accusing a social group whose reputation is of having domination of in fact exercising such domination without producing any other evidence than its "reputation for power."[49]

Pointing then to the absurdity inherent in the apparent demand that Lukes had made (in his 1974 critique of the positions taken by Bachrach and Baratz in 1970), that *latent* power-conflicts—which are, by definition, unobservable—be empirically observed, Anderson had ended his 1984 article by demanding that social science cease this fruitless quest for the empirical observation of Weberian domination and focus instead on

> another concept which is surprisingly underused in political sociology, namely the idea of a negotiated order. . . . We can ask how it is that the orderliness, the respecting of the rules, is brought about and reproduced by the things that the actors themselves do. How are the images and definitions of the nature of the game and the parties involved projected and sustained, amended or changed.[50]

It is precisely this concept of social power as "negotiated order" that animated the argument of the 1987 book *Power and Marxist Theory: A Realist View* by Robert Dahl's student Jeffrey Isaac. In a helpful summary of the issues involved in that extended debate about "community power" that had begun with Dahl's 1957-61 critiques of Mills's concept of the "power elite," Isaac argued:

> Both Bachrach and Baratz, and Lukes, have failed to develop the structural dimension of power they rightly point to. This is not a problem for Dahl, who never raises the question of a structural dimension of power. In this sense, it may well be true that Dahl's view, which March has called a "simple force" model, is the most consistent. Its consistency is purchased at a price, however—its inability to conceptualize the way power is implicated in the constitution of the conditions of interaction.[51]

I need hardly remind my readers at this point that by conceptualizing power as "implicated in the constitution of the conditions of interaction," Isaac was traversing that well-trodden ground of Hans-Otto Apel and the early Jurgen Habermas, looking to Charles S. Peirce's philosophy for the "dialogue-constitutive" pragmatics. I have already linked the meaning-constituting "cooperative principle" of H. Paul Grice's linguistic pragmatics with the (cooperative) power that Hannah Arendt had conceptualized as "the human ability not just to act but to act in concert." It is in a stunning echo of Arendt's 1970 assertion that "when we say of somebody that he is 'in power' we actually refer to his being empowered by a certain number of people to act in their name," that Isaac questioned that "traditional idiom" of power-as-domination that had perdured from Max Weber to Steven Lukes:

Lukes is explicit in his rejection of the locution "power to," and instead accepts an exclusive emphasis on "power over." For him power is exhausted in interaction, in the regularity with which A can get B to do something, thus having power over B. . . . He justifies inattention to the locution "power to" by arguing that it is "out of line with the central meaning of power as traditionally understood and with the concerns that have always preoccupied students of power." But it is precisely this traditional idiom that I question. An adequate formulation of the concept of power one agent exercises "over" another agent in interaction is parasitic upon the relatively enduring powers to act that the agents possess.[52]

Isaac specifically linked his positing of such "enduring" interaction-constitutive cooperative "power to" (act) to the methodology of *scientific realism*:

In the realist view power, as those capacities implicated in on-going social practices, is a necessary feature of social interaction; where there is society there is social power. However, "power over" or domination, is *not* therefore a necessary feature of society.[53]

This *realist* view of social power—those social "capacities" for action that are "a necessary feature of social interaction"—had been occluded, argued Isaacs, by the *empiricist* tradition in American social (political) science having "co-opted" the historical insights of Weber's methodological individualism (which, as I will argue in greater detail in chapter 3, is also inherently empiricist, rather than realist):

Weber's conceptualization of domination was an early casualty of behavioralism in political science, having been co-opted into the attempt to "operationalize" the concept of power. This is understandable insofar as Weber, operating within the tradition of methodological individualism, emphasizes the dimension of will and intentionality or, in Lukes' terms, action. . . . On the empiricist view to say that master has power over slave, or dominates slave, means that the behavior of the master causes the behavior of the slave, that is, it regularly antecedes it. According to the realist position it is not the behavior of the slave that is caused by the behavior of the master; rather, the master-slave relationship is the material cause of the behavior of both the master and the slave, and the specific way the master *and* the slave (an equally purposive agent) choose to act out the relationship is the efficient cause. For empiricism there are only efficient causes; but the consequence of this is an inability to explain both the mutual identities available to parties to social relationships. On my view the master, while dominant, operates under constraints just as the slave does. And the slave, though subordinate, is also causally effective in determining the outcomes of his encounters with his master.[54]

Ironically, while employing that very language about "constraints," external to agency, which Anthony Giddens had excoriated in the sociological theory of

Emile Durkheim—"On my view the master, while dominant, operates under *constraints* just as the slave does," Isaac had said in the passage that I just cited— Isaac traced his concept of social power-as-negotiated order to Giddens and to Hegel:

> This recognition also enables us to incorporate directly into the conceptualization of power the chronic *negotiation* attending its exercise. Giddens calls this the "dialectic of control." . . . The emphasis on the mutuality of power relations, and on the genuine agency of the subordinate, is an important theme within the (Hegelian) tradition. Thus in Hegel's famous chapter "Lordship and Bondage" in *The Phenomenology of Mind*, while the slave appears to the master as "inessential," a wholly dependent instrument of the master's will, it becomes "evident that this object does not correspond to its notion"— that it is the master who is dependent on the slave's activity."[55]

While I have already had occasion in this book to criticize the emptiness of the sonorous phrases Giddens likes to use—such as, for example, that "double hermeneutic" in whose name he had criticized Alfred Schutz's phenomenology in his 1976 book, *New Rules of Sociological Method*—I will again return to that critique of Hegelian idealism offered by Charles S. Peirce, that although his "Pragmaticism is closely allied to the Hegelian absolute idealism . . . it is sundered by its vigorous denial that the third category (which Hegel degrades to a mere stage of thinking) suffices to make the world." In the meantime, it is imperative to analyze Isaac's scientific-realist conception of social power as negotiated order further, so as to place it within its proper locus within that marriage of Durkheim's sociology with Peirce's Pragmaticism which I am proposing.[56]

The Social Order of *Puissance*:
Negotiation, Communication, and Closure

"The word *power*," argued Isaac, "derives from the Latin word *potere*, meaning 'to be able.' It is generally used to designate a property, capacity, or the wherewithal to affect things." This etymological connection of the concept of "power" to its Latin cognates of "capacity," or "being able to"—i.e., all the relations of the conscious awareness of "I/we can," behind and before the actor's perception of "I/we act"—permitted Isaac to "thus define social power as those capacities to act possessed by social agents in virtue of the enduring relations in which they participate."[57]

We may compare Isaac's *scientific realist* view of power as *potentia*—also from the Latin *potere*—meaning "those capacities to act possessed by social agents in virtue of the enduring relations in which they participate," to that *puissance* (a word from the Latinate French language that corresponds to the Latin *potentia*) that the Parisian sociologist Michel Maffesoli so helpfully defines through an "image" that he borrows from the postmodernist Jean Baudrillard's book *L'Amerique*:

> Let us evoke an image: in describing the beauty of the American highway and its traffic, Baudrillard reports on this strange ritual and the "regularity of these flux(es) which put an end to individual destinies." For him, "the only true society, the only warmth present, is that of a propulsion, a collective compulsion." This image can provide food for thought. In an almost animal way, we can feel a *puissance* which transcends individual trajectories or rather which situates them as part of a vast ballet. . . . This is the arabesque of sociality.[58]

That very image—of the choreography of "a vast ballet"—suggested by Maffesoli in his explication of power as *puissance* suggests its kinship to that meaning-constitutive "cooperative principle" of H. Paul Grice's linguistic pragmatics. In talking further about the "sequential aspect" of *puissance*, "that allows me to talk of the surpassing of the principle of individuation," Maffesoli directly evokes the *sequential* "turn-taking" visible in that sociological observation of Grice's Cooperative Principle in action by Emanuel Schegloff:

> When persons talk to each other in interaction, they ordinarily talk one at a time and one after the other. When their talk is not produced serially in this manner, they generally act quickly to restore "order."[59]

This social order of cooperative "sociality's *puissance*," asserts Maffesoli—in an echo of Jeffrey Isaac's conceptual opposition of the realist "power to" to the empiricist/methodological individualist, dominating "power over"—"is the opposite of the politico-economic power." Such *puissance*, conceptually different from the *pouvoir* of politico-economic domination, is traced by Maffesoli to Emile Durkheim's concept of religious "effervescence . . . which above all insists on the being-together, on what I called 'immanent transcendence'—another way of describing the *puissance* which binds together small groups and communities."[60]

Indeed, such cooperative *puissance*, which Maffesoli's linkage to Durkheim's concept of religious "effervescence" would suggest was conceived of only in Durkheim's 1912 writing of *The Elementary Forms of the Religious Life*, is traced by Richard Bellamy all the way back to that concept of communicational "solidarity" within occupational groups—the solidarity that Phillipe Schmitter had termed "societal corporatism," to differentiate Durkheim's meaning from the "state corporatism" of later fascist political regimes that Durkheim had outlined in his 1893 writing of *The Division of Labor in Society*.[61]

If we then consider that periodization offered by Hans Adriaansens of that forty-year authorial trajectory of Talcott Parsons between 1937 and 1977 as being marked most of all, by Parsons's conceptual move in 1951—in *The Social Sys-*

tem—from his earlier discipleship of Weber's "social nominalism" towards the "social realism" of Durkheim, then it is to Durkheim's influence that we must credit Parsons's insightful critique in 1960 of that Weberian power-as-domination theme in C. Wright Mills's 1956 book, *The Power Elite*. For the concept of power-as-(collective/social) capacity, which Isaac attributes to Giddens, was, as Michael Mann recognized in his 1986 book *The Sources of Social Power*, defined (within the context of sociological works written in the English language) by Parsons. Giddens himself has acknowledged Parsons's linkage of such power to the concept of "collectivity":

> Among the many interpretations of power in social and political theory, two main perspectives appear. One is that power is best conceptualized as the capability of an actor to achieve his or her will, even at the expense of that of others who might resist him—the sort of definition employed by Weber among many other authors. The second is that power should be seen as a property of the collectivity: Parsons's concept of power, for instance, belongs to this latter category.[62]

If we remember the phrasing of Hannah Arendt's statement in her 1970 book, *On Violence*, that "Power corresponds to the human ability not just to act but to *act in concert*" (my italics), it is significant that Parsons—whose critics argue "that his sociology could not address the general problem of power in a way which was analytically satisfying and sensitive to empirical circumstances"[63]— had already used a phrase very similar to Arendt's in 1951, that same year that Adriaansens has marked as the year of Parsons's turning point from Weber's "social nominalism" to Durkheim's "social realism":

> A social system having the three properties of collective goals, shared goals, and of being a single system of interaction with boundaries defined by incumbency in the roles constituting the system, will be called a *collectivity*. The action of the collectivity may be viewed as the *action in concert* of a plurality of individual actors."[64]

I indicate this similarity in the phrasing around that concept of "action in concert" between the 1970 writing of Arendt and that 1951 writing by the recently converted "Durkheimian" Parsons not to accuse Arendt of plagiarism (for I do not know if Arendt had, when she wrote *On Violence*, ever read the 1951 publications of Parsons), but to place in context what Jurgen Habermas views as a dialectical movement of opposites or contradictories between power-as-domination, -coercion, or -force between individuals (Weber's conception), and power-as-consent or as socially communicated and negotiated agreement (Arendt's conception) with Parsons's view of power emerging as the synthesis between the Weber-Arendt, coercion-consent antitheses:

Max Weber takes the teleological models of action as his point of departure: an individual subject (or group that can be regarded as an individual) chooses the appropriate means to realize a goal that it has set for itself . . . To the extent that his success depends on the behavior of another subject, the actor must have at his disposal the means to instigate the other to the desired behavior. Weber calls this disposition over means to influence the will of another "power." Hannah Arendt reserves for it the term "force (*Gewalt*)."[65]

The whole thrust of Arendt's argument in *On Violence* had indeed been that the concept of "force"—"which we often use in daily speech as a synonym for violence"—should be sharply differentiated from the concept of "power":

Power needs no justification, being inherent in the very existence of political communities; what it does need is legitimacy. The common treatment of these two words as synonyms is no less misleading and confusing than the current equation of obedience and support. Power springs up whenever people get together and act in concert, but it derives its legitimacy from the initial getting together rather than from any action that may then follow. Legitimacy, when challenged, bases itself on an appeal to the past, while justification relates to and ends that lies in the future. Violence can be justifiable, but it can never be legitimate.[66]

Force or violence, Arendt had argued—using the then-recent 1968 Soviet invasion of Czechoslovakia as her primary example—was a manifestation not of a growth or gain of power but rather of its loss or *shrinkage*:

Power and violence, though they are distinct phenomena, usually appear together. Whenever they are combined, power, we have found is the primary and predominant factor. The situation is however, entirely different when we deal with them in their pure states—as for instance, with foreign invasion and occupation . . . Violence can always destroy power: out of the barrel of a gun grows the most effective command, resulting in the most instant and perfect obedience. What can never grow out of it is power. . . . Rule by sheer violence comes into play where power is being lost; it is precisely the shrinkage of power of the Russian government, internally and externally, that became manifest in its "solution" of the Czechoslovak problem—just as it was the shrinkage of power of European imperialism that became manifest in the alternative between decolonization and massacre. To substitute violence for power can bring victory, but the price is very high; for it is not only paid by the vanquished it is also paid by the victor in terms of his own power.[67]

It should be noticed that Arendt, like Weber before her, focused upon individual actors—either as individual persons or groups—*within* power-relationships, rather than as systemic totalities or collectivities. Even while disagreeing with Weber on terminology—what Weber would call *power*, the predominance or domination of one individual's will over another's, Arendt would see as power's antithesis, *force*—Arendt had still been hewing, at least in her example of one individual nation's (the Soviet Union's) use of force against another (Czechoslovakia) to an extension of Weber's methodological individualism. A switch in methodological perspective—from the micro-distributions of collective power-capacity between several individuals or groups to the macro-panorama of the collectivity itself as actor—could obliterate or minimize Arendt's distinction between power and force, and this is what Habermas accuses Parsons of having done in switching from the Weber-Arendt perspective of individual/group micro-actor's perspective to the macro-panoramic view of the collective system's action-perspective:

> Parsons can bring the two phenomena which Arendt contrasts as power and force under one unified concept of power because he understands power as the property of a system which behaves toward its own components according to the same schema that characterizes the behavior of the purposive-rational actor toward the external world. . . . He repeats at the level of systems theory the same teleological concept of power (as the potential to realize goals) that Weber pursued at the level of action theory.[68]

Habermas declares Parsons's attempted systems-theoretic synthesis (of the Weber-Arendt actor-centered power/force antitheses) to have been unsuccessful and theoretically illegitimate, defending thereby what he perceives as Arendt's strict separation of power from force against both Parsons and Weber:

> In both cases, what is specific to the power of unifying speech, what separates it from force, is lost. The power of agreement-oriented communication to produce consensus is opposed to this force, because seriously intended agreement is an end in itself and cannot be instrumentalized for other ends.[69]

Just how mistaken is Habermas's attempt—based on his over-idealized distinction between consent and coercion, between freely agreed-upon consensus and domination by force—to contrast Arendt's view of power with Parsons's can be grasped by focusing upon the analogy which Parsons had used to develop his systems-theoretic conception of power as the "generalized capacity to secure the performance of binding obligations by units in a system of collective organization when the obligations are legitimized with reference to their bearing on collective goals": the analogy of power with money.[70] Just as money can, in a situation of economic confidence, facilitate economic transactions through the expansion or inflation of fiduciary credit over and above existing gold or specie reserves, so power too could, Parsons had argued, in a situation of political confidence, facilitate sociopolitical action (in concert) beyond existing reserves of authoritative coercion or force. But what might happen, asked Barry Barnes—who welcomed Parsons's analogy on the basis of Mary Hesse's studies of analogical reasoning in scientific inference—"if confidence is forfeited"?

> And a possible answer is immediately suggested: just as loss of confidence forces economies back upon gold and monetary metal, so it forces a polity back upon the expedient of direct coercion and the use of violence.[71]

But that had been *exactly* what Hannah Arendt had said with her example of the Soviet invasion of Czechoslovakia: not, as Habermas misreads her, that force is the opposite of power as consent, but only that power "can never grow out of" violence. Like Parsons in his post-1951 Durkheimian phase, Arendt had argued only that "rule by sheer violence comes into play where power is being lost," as in the "shrinkage of power of the Russian government . . . that became manifest in its 'solution' to the Czechoslovak problem."[72]

That Parsons—like Arendt—was in a minority arguing for power's cooperative basis against the majority of social scientists' insistence upon its identity with coercive domination, can be seen in his conception of "non-zero-sum" power in his 1960 essay "The Distribution of Power in American Society," which he had written in critique of Mills's *The Power Elite*. That 1960 conception by Parsons of the non-zero-sum nature of power, says Barnes,

> represents a particularly insightful and significant suggestion on Parsons' part, since it is usual to think that an increase in the power of one person must necessarily be obtained at the expense of another. . . . But Parsons shows that this "zero-sum" conception of power is . . . unlikely to prove an adequate means in modern societies with differentiated political systems.[73]

This "insightful and significant" conception of power by Parsons—power-as-capacity—has now been used by Michael Mann in volume 1 of his ambitious book *The Sources of Social Power* to study the *longue duree* of power from the beginning to 1760. Mann notes that beyond the accepted Weber-inspired definitions that "restrict power to its *distributive* aspects, power by A *over* B," "Parsons noted correctly a second *collective* aspect of power, whereby persons in cooperation can enhance their joint power over third parties or over nature."[74] Basing his view of history on this collective non-zero-sum power-as-capacity generated by "cooperation," Mann—in an impressive though unintended echo of Grice's Pragmatics' quest for the Cooperative Principle behind human meaning—proceeds to grasp *all* human history across *all* civilizations through 1760 in a simple "IEMP" model of four principles of cooperation based on *Ideological, Economic, Military,* and *Political* power forms.

Habermas faults Parsons on the grounds that "unlike money . . . power is not 'by nature' a circulating medium." And Barnes admits that "money is not the ideal basis for an explanatory analogy because money itself is something the operation of which has not been satisfactorily explained."[75]

Indeed, given that Parsons's analogy rests on the basis of collective confidence underlying the operation of both power and money, it is significant that financial experts' fumbling impotence in the face of the volatility of financial markets only reveals how little understood the basis of "confidence" in monetary systems is. That monetary analogy aside, however, there is no denying the substance behind Parsons's insight into the "non-zero-sum" generation of power by collective cooperation, and the synergy it would allow between my Peircean evolutionism and other variants of cultural evolutionism, such as that of Leslie White. White had built his neo-evolutionist anthropology precisely on such measures of increased power-as-capacity (i.e., measures of, literally, the usage of "power" as inanimate energy) through the increased cooperation occasioned by human culture. Compared to other animals, human beings seem capable of ever greater forms of cooperation that increase the collective "non-zero-sum" power to act, i.e., the capacity to achieve collective goals.[76]

Barnes pursued his 1988 quest into *The Nature of Power* beyond his critique of Parsons's power-money analogy, towards the critique—which Barnes shared with Niklas Luhmann—of Parsons's "normative" basis of "shared meaning" (on the grounds that Parsons's refusal to inquire into the origins and basis of the norms themselves had cast doubts upon the very validity of such a normative basis of meaning) into the cooperative basis of human knowledge, the "social order as cognitive order."[77]

But in a conference sponsored by the theory sections of the German and American sociological associations held on June 21-24, 1987—the year just before the publication of *The Nature of Power* by Barnes—Luhmann had already declared the deeper implications of such a *cognitive* view of social order:

> Social systems, according to this theory, consist of communications and nothing but communications—not of human beings, not of conscious mental states, not of roles, not even of actions. They produce and reproduce communications by meaningful reference to communications.[78]

Such a view of social science as the study of "communications and nothing but communications," as laid out by Luhmann in 1987, conforms to the philosophical tradition stemming from Peirce's Pragmaticism that Nicholas Rescher has characterized as "Communicative Pragmatism," whose fundamental questions are "What conditions must be satisfied for the achievement of effective communication to become possible at all?" and "What are the conditions under which effective communication *can optimally be realized?*"[79]

While Rescher's 1998 philosophical "deliberations" into Communicative Pragmatism refrain from undertaking "an *empirical* inquiry into how people actually go about communicating," the conceptual framework for such empirical inquiry is evident in Emanuel Schegloff's sociological observation about the "turn-taking" conditions of effective communication: that when people talk to each other "they ordinarily talk one at a time and one after the other. When their talk is not produced serially in this manner, they generally act quickly to restore 'order.'"[80]

How would Schegloff's empirically observable negotiated order of communication proceed if the "turn-taking" group of talkers increased, say, from a small group of three or four communicators to millions of people all attempting to talk to one another within the same conversation? It is evident that such a crowd of several million simultaneous talkers could only "act . . . to restore 'order'" by engaging in those processes of dual "closure" outlined by Frank Parkin: "exclusion" of others and "usurpation" into the core group of successful communicators.[81]

In his "bourgeois critique" of Marxian class theory, Parkin had deployed this concept of "closure" by borrowing it from the writings of Max Weber. But, as is clear from Richard Bellamy's historical analysis of "Emile Durkheim, the division of labor, and the sources of organic solidarity," Durkheim's focus on the *corporatist* nature of modern occupational groups displayed Durkheim's awareness of precisely such closure—as I have used the concept to apply it to communicative practice—despite his not having overtly used this Weberian term.[82]

It is ironic, therefore, that while I point to the concept of what Bellamy calls "Durkheim's naturally consensual society" to emphasize my application—in Durkheim's name—of Weber's concept of closure to the processes of human communication, I should also fault that self-proclaimed consensualist follower of Weber, Jurgen Habermas, for having fallen behind in his comprehension of "social systems" as consisting "of communications and nothing but communications," for the "ideal speech situation" of Habermas—echoing in its very phrasing, the "ideal types" of Weber—is not subject, by its very ideality, to what I see as the "Durkheimian closure" of *real* human communication.

The escape by Habermas from Durkheim's "social realism" into the ideality of unreal, perfectly idealized "speech situations" emerges from his idealized strict separation, conceptually, of "consensus" from coercive "force"—that separation which we have seen Habermas projecting into the writing of Hannah Arendt.[83]The problem is that such a strict ideal of separation of "agreement-oriented communication" from coercive "force" finds no counterpart in real life where the two often meet, as in, for example, the notorious tendency of victims of abuse—even such apparently non-"forceful" forms of abuse as nonphysical or verbal insult—to "agree" with their abusers. First disseminated into the limelight of public attention in the decades of the 1960s and 1970s when the rash of terrorist hostage-taking episodes had focused upon what had then been called the "Stockholm syndrome"—in which the hostage/victim "agreed" with her captor/abuser—such an "agreement" or "consensus" between the victim and perpetrator of even mildly forceful abuse is now a commonplace of feminist and other advocates of the rights of victims. Not only does Habermas's *ideal* of "undistorted communication" pale before such a *real* continuum between his polar opposites of "consensus" versus coercive "force," but his own insistent splitting of ideal consensus from real coercion itself smacks of those very mechanisms of "splitting" and "idealization" that object-relations psychologists who treat such victims of traumatic force see (with "projection" and "denial") as the typical "defense mechanisms" of the "borderline personality" lacking in "reality testing."[84]

But in appealing to an object-relations psychologist such as Otto Kernberg to dispute that pragmatic reality-testing function of Habermas's split between ideal and real, I have already proceeded into the subject matter of my next chapter: I continue my journey deeper into that realism of Durkheim and Peirce where the reality of cooperative forms older than human history (as has been communicated to us in either written or oral form) that underlies the mere appearance of subjective agency—where communicative cooperation constructs that very entity I perceive as my "self"—is analyzed. For if, as Hannah Arendt had argued, when we refer to a powerful individual, "we actually refer to his being *empowered* by a certain number of people to act in their name," the ultimate *empowerment*—not analyzed even by Arendt—is the subject of chapter 3: *the social construction of the self.*[85]

Notes

1. Myles Brand, *Intending and Acting: Toward a Naturalized Action Theory* (Cambridge, Mass.: MIT Press, 1984), 9; Patrick Doreian and Norman Hummon, *Modeling Social Processes* (New York: Elsevier, 1976), 4.

2. Durkheim, *Elementary Forms of the Religious Life*, 364-65.

3. Durkheim, *The Rules of Sociological Method*, 51.

4. Michel Maffesoli, *The Time of the Tribes: The Decline of Individualism in Mass Society* (London: Sage, 1996), 1 *transl. note,* 4, 58.

5. Maffesoli, *Time,* 58-59; Arendt, *On Violence,* 44.

6. Giddens, *New Rules,* 53; Schmaus, *Durkheim's Philosophy,* 218-19; Grice, *Studies,* 26.

7. Maffesoli, *Time,* 1 *transl. note*; Max Weber, *The Theory of Social and Economic Organization* (Chicago: Free Press, 1947), 152; Hookway, *Quine,* 127, citing Quine, *Word and Object,* 27.

8. George Stocking, "Radcliffe-Brown and British Social Anthropology," in George Stocking, Jr., *Functionalism Historicized: Essays on British Social Anthropology* (Madison: University of Wisconsin Press, 1984), 131, 170-73, 175-80.

9. Alfred Reginald Radcliffe-Brown, *A Natural Science of Society* (Glencoe, Ill.: Free Press, 1957), 12-55, 91-92.

10. Talcott Parsons, *The Social System* (New York: Free Press, 1951), 20-21; Walter Buckley, *Sociology and Modern Systems Theory* (Englewood Cliffs, N.J.: Prentice-Hall, 1967).

11. Talcott Parsons, *Social Systems and the Evolution of Societies* (New York: Free Press, 1977), 100-103.

12. Parsons, *Social Systems and the Evolution*, 19, 89.

13. Stocking, *Functionalism Historicized*, 106.

14. Stocking, *Functionalism Historicized*, 109-10; Parsons, *The Structure of Social Action*, 410, 420-27; Alexander, *Theoretical Logic in Sociology*, 2:232-33.

15. A. R. Radcliffe-Brown, "On Social Structure," in *The Social Anthropology of Radcliffe-Brown*, ed. Adam Kuper (London: Routledge and Kegan Paul, 1977), 28.

16. Claude Levi-Strauss, *Les Structures elementaires de la parente* (Paris: Presses Universitaires de France, 1949).

17. A. R. Radcliffe-Brown, "Letter to Levi-Strauss," in Kuper, *The Social Anthropology of Radcliffe-Brown*, 42.

18. Peter Blau, *Approaches to the Study of Social Structure* (New York: Free Press, 1975), 7.

19. Hubert M. Blalock, Jr., *Basic Dilemmas in the Social Sciences* (Beverly Hills, Calif.: Sage, 1984), 17-19.

20. Blalock, *Basic Dilemmas*, 23.

21. Blalock, *Basic Dilemmas*, 47, 60-81; Radcliffe-Brown, "Letter to Levi-Strauss," 42.

22. Harrison White, *Chains of Opportunity: System Models of Mobility in Organizations* (Cambridge, Mass.: Harvard University Press, 1970), 330 (italics added).

23. Jana Salat, *Reasoning as Enterprise: The Anthropology of S. F. Nadel* (Gottingen: Edition Herodot, 1983), 107; Radcliffe-Brown, "On Social Structure," 28.

24. Salat, *Reasoning*, 107; Weber, *The Theory*, 152. Giddens, *New Rules*, 53.

25. Dietrich Rueschemeyer, *Power and the Division of Labour* (Cambridge: Polity, 1986), 41.

26. Rueschemeyer, *Power*, 11; W. Paul Vogt, "Durkheimian Sociology versus Philosophical Rationalism," in *The Sociological Domain: The Durkheimians and the Founding of French Sociology*, ed. Phillipe Besnard (Cambridge, Mass.: Cambridge University Press, 1983), 231; Raymond Boudon, *The Logic of Social Action: An Introduction to Sociological Analysis* (Boston: Routledge, 1981).

27. Barry Barnes, *The Nature of Power* (Urbana: University of Illinois Press, 1988), ix.

28. Rueschemeyer, *Power*, 11, citing Weber, *The Theory*, 152; Peirce, *Collected Papers*, 5.9.

29. Barnes, *The Nature*, 6 (italics in original); Michel Foucault, *Power/Knowledge: Selected Interviews and Other Writings, 1972-1977* (New York: Pantheon Books, 1980).

30. Talcott Parsons, *Structure and Process in Modern Societies* (Glencoe, Ill.: Free Press, 1960), 221 (italics in original); Barnes, *The Nature*, 6; C. Wright Mills, *The Power Elite* (New York: Oxford University Press, 1956).

31. Parsons, *Structure*, 221; Robertson, *Meaning*, 1978; Peirce, *Collected Papers*, 5.9.

32. Robert Dahl, "On the Concept of Power," *Behavioral Science* 2, (1957), 202-3.

33. Blalock, *Basic Dilemmas*, 130.

34. John Hughes, "Bureaucracy," in *Applied Sociological Perspectives*, ed. R. J. Anderson and W. W. Sharrock (London: Allen & Unwin, 1984), 108.

35. Bob Anderson, "The Empirical Study of Power," in Anderson and Sharrock, *Applied Sociological Perspectives*, 170.

36. Anderson, "The Empirical Study," 170.

37. Anderson, "The Empirical Study," 171-73.

38. Robert Dahl, *Who Governs? Democracy and Power in an American City* (New Haven, Conn.: Yale University Press, 1961); "The Critique of the Ruling Elite Model," *American Political Science Review* 52, (1958), 263-64.

39. Anderson, "The Empirical Study," 175-76.

40. Parsons, *Structure and Process*, 221: in defining his "non-zero-sum" concept of power against the "distributive" or "zero-sum" concept of power that C. Wright Mills had borrowed from Max Weber, Parsons had used the word *generated*, as in accusing Mills of being "interested only in *who* has power . . . not in how power is generated or in what communal, rather than sectoral, interests are served" (Parsons's italics).

41. Dahl, *The Critique*, 463-64.

42. Peter Bachrach and Morton S. Baratz, *Power and Poverty: Theory and Practice* (New York: Oxford University Press, 1970), 43-44; Peter Bachrach and Morton S. Baratz, "The Two Faces of Power," *American Political Science Review* 56 (1962), 947-52.

43. Bachrach and Baratz, *Power*, 43-44.

44. Nelson W. Polsby, *Community Power and Political Theory* (New Haven, Conn.: Yale University Press, 1980), 208.

45. Polsby, *Community Power*, 190.

46. Anderson, "The Empirical Study," 179-80.

47. Steven Lukes, *Power: A Radical View* (London: MacMillan, 1974), 22-23.

48. Anderson, "The Empirical Study," 181-82.

49. Matthew A. Crenson, *The Unpolitics of Air Pollution: A Study of Non-Decisionmaking in the Cities* (Baltimore, Md.: Johns Hopkins University Press, 1971), 77.

50. Anderson, "The Empirical Study," 183-88.

51. Jeffrey C. Isaac, *Power and Marxist Theory: A Realist View* (Ithaca, N.Y.: Cornell University Press, 1987), 39.

52. Isaac, *Power*, 38; Arendt, *On Violence*, 44; Grice, *Studies*, 26; Thomas McCarthy, *The Critical Theory*, 425 nn. 3 and 5, synoptically explains the efforts by Apel and Habermas in 1976 to develop a "universal pragmatics" of "dialogue-constitutive" functions based on Charles Peirce's Pragmaticist philosophy.

53. Isaac, *Power*, 83-84.

54. Isaac, *Power*, 84-86.

55. Isaac, *Power*, 89. See Anthony Giddens, *Central Problems in Social Theory: Structure and Contradiction in Social Analysis* (Berkeley: University of California Press, 1979), for his critique of Durkheim's concept of the "constraint" that "social facts" exert on human agency.

56. Peirce, *Collected Papers*, 5.436; Giddens, *New Rules*, 162.

57. Isaac, *Power*, 74-80.

58. Maffesoli, *Time*, 76, citing Jean Baudrillard, *L'Amerique* (Paris: Grasset, 1986), 107.

59. Schegloff, "Between Macro and Micro," 207; Maffesoli, *Time*, 76; Grice, *Studies*, 220.

60. Maffesoli, *Time*, 4, 58-59; see also p. 1 for translator's note explaining how—since Maffesoli's two French words *puissance* and *pouvoir*, respectively, had only one English cognate, "power"—he had consistently translated only *pouvoir* as "power" while maintaining the French *puissance* throughout the English translation.

61. Bellamy, *Liberalism*, 95-101; 277 nn. 142, 144-45; 278 n. 148. Philippe C. Schmitter, *Corporatism and Public Policy in Authoritarian Portugal* (Beverly Hills, Calif.: Sage, 1975).

62. Giddens, *Central Problems*, 69. Mestrovic (*Anthony Giddens*, 41-46) accuses Giddens of having read Durkheim "superficially . . . as a precursor to Parsons." See Parsons, *Structure and Process*, 221; Adriaansens, *Talcott Parsons*; Michael Mann, *The Sources of Social Power*, vol.1: *A History of Power from the Beginning to A.D. 1760* (Cambridge, England: Cambridge University Press, 1986), 6.

63. Roland Robertson and Bryan Turner, "Talcott Parsons and Modern Social Theory: An Appreciation," *Theory, Culture, and Society* 6 (1989): 546; Arendt, *On Violence*, 44.

64. Talcott Parsons and E. A. Shils, eds., *Towards a General Theory of Action* (Cambridge, Mass.: Harvard University Press, 1951), 192 (italics added).

65. Jurgen Habermas, "Hannah Arendt's Communications Concept of Power," in *Power*, ed. Steven Lukes (Oxford: Basil Blackwell, 1986), 75.

66. Arendt, *On Violence*, 52.

67. Arendt, *On Violence*, 52-53.

68. Habermas, "Hannah Arendt's," 76.

69. Habermas, "Hannah Arendt's," 76-77.

70. Talcott Parsons, *Sociological Theory and Modern Society* (New York: Free Press, 1967), 308.

71. Barnes, *The Nature*, 15-16.

72. Arendt, *On Violence*, 52-53.

73. Barnes, *The Nature*, 18.

74. Michael Mann, *The Sources of Power*, 6.

75. Barnes, *The Nature*, 19; Habermas, *The Theory of Communicative Action*, 270.

76. Leslie A. White, *The Science of Culture* (New York: Farrar, Straus and Giroux, 1949).

77. Barnes, *The Nature*, 22-39.

78. Luhmann, "The Evolutionary Differentiation," 113.

79. Rescher, *Communicative Pragmatism*, 3-4 (italics in original).

80. Schegloff, "Between Macro and Micro," 207; Rescher, *Communicative Pragmatism*, 3 (italics in original).

81. Frank Parkin, *Marxism and Class Theory: A Bourgeois Critique* (New York: Columbia University Press, 1979); Schegloff, "Between Macro and Micro," 207. As anyone who has observed the communicative interactions between teenagers in high school will realize, my application of Parkin's processes of *dual closure* to peer group pressures is more than just a "thought experiment." Teenagers in American culture routinely apply Parkin's dual closure processes of "exclusion" and "usurpation" in order to fit in with their "in groups."

82. Bellamy, *Liberalism*, 95-101.

83. Habermas, "Hannah Arendt's," 76-77.

84. John F. Clarkin and Otto F. Kernberg, "Developmental Factors in Borderline Personality Disorder and Borderline Personality Organization," in *Borderline Personality Disorder: Etiology and Treatment*, ed. Joel Paris, M.D., 170-72; Jurgen Habermas, *Theory and Practice* (Boston: Beacon Press, 1973), 17, cited by Thomas McCarthy, *The Critical Theory*, 94,98.

85. Arendt, *On Violence*, 44 (italics added).

American individualist sociology appears to be comprised of one banality af-
ter another. Initially we are told that people do things because they want to.
Then we are told that because social reality is complicated, it cannot be ex-
plained, at least not now. Ultimately we are told that, since people have free
will, why bother to explain anything anyway? Individualist sociology takes its
banalities largely from Western middle-class ideology. There is nothing wrong
with that. The origin of ideas is irrelevant to their sociological value. But in-
stead of subjecting these banalities to critical inquiry, American sociologists
have been satisfied with merely repeating them. That is the problem.
>—Bruce Mayhew, "Structuralism vs. Individualism:
>Ideological and Other Obfuscations," Part II,
>*Social Forces*, 59/3 (March 1981), 644.

A minimal notion of the agent is required for the present view of agency. A
Cartesian ego, transcendental self, and the like are replaced with a naturalis-
tic conception of the agent as a physical locus of first-personal purposeful-
ness in the flux of agency and activity; this locus is signaled, in English, in the
use of the first person singular pronoun. As Wittgenstein urged, the pronoun
is eliminable; some demonstrative, ostensive term or signal with the use of an
indexical is however, ineliminable.
>—Donald Gustafson, *Intention and Agency*
>(Dordrecht, Holland: D. Reidel Pub. Co., 1986), 162.

In a sense, James and Peirce cut through the structured rigidity of the Euro-
pean thought of their time to bring the whole self-object system into a new
flux. Particularly in view of the "scientistic" trends in American thought,
pragmatism raised questions about the self which were particularly important.
James introduced a distinctively un-Cartesian pluralism into the concept: be-
sides the I, which thought, there were an I, a me *and various other possible*
selves.
>—Talcott Parsons, "Pragmatism and the Nature of the Self"
>(Essay 7: "Social Interaction"), in *Social Systems and*
>*the Evolution of Action Theory* (1977), 164.

CHAPTER 3

Empowerment: The Social Construction of the Self

The difficulty in overcoming what Steven Lukes calls the "traditionally under-stood" view of power—i.e., that view of social power as a relation of "power over" domination between individuals, which, as we have seen in the last chapter, seems to predominate in Western sociology despite its notorious problems of em-pirical measurement—lies in its being couched within an overall individualist perspective, whose change would involve nothing less than one of those dizzying conceptual revolutions that T. S. Kuhn called "paradigm-shifts." This revolution-ary change in perceptual (and conceptual) focus, from individual subjects to the collective structure, is particularly painful because it upsets deep-rooted human-istic dispositions of "common decency": zoologists and animal-ecologists have to overcome their natural feelings for particular, individual animals to focus on the collective species, and sociologists may need more than citations from the clas-sics to convince them that the important explanatory variable in the study of so-cial process is not in individual attitudes toward other individuals, however differ-ent the individual's attitude of "love" may be from that of "force" or "violence," but in the collective capacity to cope with the exigencies of the human condition.

Indeed, writing about those two early social thinkers who did focus upon the collective, Emile Durkheim and George Herbert Mead, Jurgen Habermas used Kuhn's language of scientific revolutions, viewing this revolution as having oc-curred against a particularly "German" tradition:

> Whereas the problematic of rationalization/reification lies along a "German" line of social-theoretical thought running from Marx through Weber to Lukacs and Critical Theory, the paradigm shift from purposive activity to communica-tive action was prepared by George Herbert Mead and Emile Durkheim.[1]

That Mead's Pragmatist theory of meaning—which, as I have pointed out before, is identical, as far as I see it, with what Niklas Luhmann would call "functionalized meaning"—involved a de-centering of the human subject equivalent to the research procedures of animal ethology has been recognized by Habermas:

> Interaction between animals that is mediated through gestures is of central importance in genetic considerations if one starts, as Mead does, with the concept of objective or natural meaning. He borrows this concept of meaning from the practice of research into animal behavior. . . . The familiar functional circuits of animal behavior serve as a foundation for these ascriptions of meaning: search for food, mating, attack and defense, care of the young, play, and so on. Meaning is a systemic property. In the language of older ethology: meanings are constituted in species-specific environments (von Vexkull), they are not at the disposition of the individual exemplar as such.[2]

Habermas has also recognized that Mead inherited from the Pragmati(ci)sm of Charles Sanders Peirce an integrated intellectual tradition which later split into two separate academic disciplines, social psychology and the philosophy of language and of science, which have since "gone their separate ways":

> Mead's theory of communication also recommends itself as a point of intersection of the two critical traditions stemming from Peirce. Although Mead took no notice of the linguistic turn in philosophy, looking back today one finds astonishing convergences between his social psychology and the analysis of language and theory of science developed in formal-pragmatic terms.[3]

But the formal-pragmatic theory of global cultural evolution—based upon a combination of the Peirce-to-Mead and Durkheim-to-Lacan traditions—which I delineate in the next chapter is not a point toward which the interest that Habermas had earlier displayed in "universal pragmatics" proceeded to develop, because he had along the way recoiled against the deconstruction of individual subjectivity crafted by the poststructuralist (or postmodernist) followers of Jacques Lacan.

As the 1998 book—influenced by Lacan's erstwhile disciple Julia Kristeva—by Kelly Oliver, *Subjectivity without Subjects*, declares:

> By now the strange predicament of the subject in contemporary continental philosophy is quite familiar. Traditionally "the subject" is the epistemological corollary of phenomenology's intentional object. . . . In its variety of formulations, from Descartes's *cogito* through Husserl's transcendental ego, the subject has been the home of consciousness. . . . Through its permutations and complex operations, the subject remains unified. . . . As we know, since Nietzsche, Marx, and Freud, the unified "subject" hangs perilously between quotation marks that

both protect and threaten it. Nietzsche suggests that "the subject" is a fiction of grammar. Marx suggests that it is a historical product. And Freud suggests that it is a construct set up against the unconscious. The subject then, loses both its connection to consciousness and its unity. . . . Some post structuralist theorists have taken advantage of the precariousness of the subject.[4]

Or, as Habermas had previously expressed it: "In the discourse of modernity, the accusers raise an objection that has not substantially changed from Hegel and Marx down to Nietzsche and Heidegger, from Bataille and Lacan to Foucault and Derrida. The accusation is aimed against a reason grounded in the principle of subjectivity" For Habermas the contemporary accusers against "reason grounded in the principle of subjectivity" are "easily recognizable by a prefix, by the neologisms formed by the prefix 'post.'" He would, he declared, have no truck with these postmodernist deconstructionists of subjectivity who take their "critique out of the hands of reason."[5]

This defense of individual subjectivity and agency proffered by Habermas against Lacanian postmodernism's attempts to deconstruct the subject appears to repeat in the late twentieth century those outraged accusations of "sociologism" and "the oversocialized conception of man" that had earlier been leveled against Durkheim and that 1951 move by Talcott Parsons from what Hans Adriaansens called his earlier "social nominalism," à la Max Weber, to Durkheim's "social realism." While we have earlier seen, with Niklas Luhmann, why Parsons had to move from Weberian individualism to Durkheim's social realism to escape the "infinity problem" of the "double contingency" of perspectives, it is now time—along our journey toward that confluence between the intellectual traditions of Peirce-Mead and Durkheim-Saussure-Levi-Strauss-Lacan in the concept of the "social self"—for us to focus sharply upon why the logic of science itself would *require* this move from observed individuals to those theorized principles of cooperation underlying their subjectivity.[6]

The Scientific Logic of Abstraction

Writing while Parsons still lived, Adriaansens expressed surprise that Parsons had not responded to Don Albert Martindale's critique of his 1951 move from individualism to collectivism:

> Meanwhile, Parsons still has not responded to Martindale's expectations and explained why he deserted social behaviorism for macro-functionalism, social nominalism for social realism or, according to Martindale, Weber for Durkheim. This seems strange since Parsons is not the kind of man to be unaware of such important shifts of position in his own work.[7]

That Parsons had not replied to Martindale's critical query about the rationale of his move from his earlier Weberian individualism to Durkheim's social realism may have had more to do with the paucity of his capacities as a philosopher of science than with anything else. His philosophical interlocutors, from Max Black in 1961 to Stephen Savage in 1981, have found his exposition of the methodology of "analytical realism," which Parsons had claimed to have borrowed from the philosophy of Alfred North Whitchead, either puzzling or "unacceptable." Bruce Mayhew's spirited polemics against individualism in sociology in the 1980 and 1981 issues of the journal *Social Forces* had analyzed all versions of structuralism, Anglo-Saxon as well as French, but had refused to even consider the structural-functionalism of Parsons because, like other critics of Parsons such as C. Wright Mills and Stanislav Andreski, he had found the written language of Parsons incomprehensible. Even admirers of Parsons's work such as Roland Robertson and Bryan S. Turner have admitted that "the status of his legacy and the scientific value of his work are still topics of considerable debate and controversy."[8]

That Parsons, in his turn to Durkheim's "social realism," had been aiming at what today we would call "scientific realism" is apparent in the way he interpreted Durkheim's *Rules of Sociological Method*: "The principal defining attributes of Durkheim's 'social facts'—exteriority and constraint—were only variations of the ones used by Descartes to define the 'external world'."[9]

In *The Conceptual Foundations of Contemporary Relativity Theory*, John Graves defines in five points how the approach of scientific realism in physics proceeds in its knowledge of such an "external world" toward the postulation of "theoretical entities:"

1. There is an external world independent of anyone's perception of it.
2. This world may contain entities and processes radically different from those which seem directly disclosed in sense perception.
3. We can, however, attain some degree of knowledge of this external world even though we may never be entitled to claim perfect knowledge.
4. Science is the attempt . . . to understand the structure of this external world, both in its general outline and in the complexities and details of its operation. It thus seeks to transcend the contents of immediate experience, while at the same time explaining them.
5. Scientists do this by developing theories, which postulate "theoretical entities" named by "theoretical terms." In doing so, they hope to achieve as close a correspondence as possible between their postulated entities and the actual elements of the real (or external, or objective) world.[10]

And it is precisely in the terms of such a philosophy of physics—which Descartes, as Parsons was aware, had begun to fashion in order to shore up the conceptual foundations of Galileo's physics—that the attempts by Anthony Giddens to fashion *New Rules of Sociological Method* to overcome Durkheim's emphasis on structure-as-constraint by a "duality of structure" (both constraining and enabling) are criticized by Bryan Turner and Joseph Smith:

> The notion of the duality of structure seems to us to involve a vitiating circularity. According to Giddens, social structures are constituted by human agency as well as simultaneously being the medium of such constitution. We will show that action is taken as a (prior) necessary condition for structure and structure as a (prior) necessary condition for action, so that we are forced to turn in an impossible circle. Now social structures are said to be a medium of their constitution or construction, but Giddens nowhere tells us that he is giving terms such as "medium" and "constitution" a theoretical sense which is substantially different from their natural language sense. . . . So let us ask what is involved in X being a medium for Y to occur. In pre-relativistic physics, the aether pre-existed the propagation of the waves. Air and other material substances are said to be a medium for the propagation of sound. Air certainly can pre-exist the occurrence of a particular sound. Now if social structures are also a medium for the propagation of social action, then they must also pre-exist occurrence of any particular social action.[11]

We may pursue Smith and Turner's focus upon the prerelativistic "aether" of physics further by returning to Graves's *Conceptual Foundations of Contemporary Relativity Theory* to notice how scientific realism has historically pursued its "theoretical entities" into increasing levels of abstraction from the concrete, empirical observation of moving bodies. The comprehension of physical movement had already hit the paradoxes of rest vs. motion with the classical Greek physics of Zeno and Parmenides, and such paradoxes were in turn reflected in the debate between Copernican heliocentrism and Ptolemaic geocentrism on whether the earth or the sun moved. The solution offered by Galileo and Newton had involved an abstraction reversing "common-sense:" not rest, but movement in a straight line with constant velocity (i.e., inertia), was matter's natural state, with outside forces, such as gravity, producing acceleration or change from that inertial state. Finally, says Graves, Einstein's relativity theory reduced gravity to a form of inertia in a rounded space: the four theoretical concepts of matter, motion, time, and space that in Newton's theory still bore some resemblance to the perceptions of ordinary sensory observation were reduced in the "geometrodynamics" of General Relativity Theory to forms of multidimensional space. Thus, the process of increasing levels of abstraction in physics reduced the phenomena of ordinary perceptions, i.e., moving bodies, to the "theoretical entity" of the abstract geometry of space.[12]

We may compare this progression of increasing abstraction in physics—from the observation of bodies-in-interaction to the pure geometry of space in General Relativity Theory—to what happens in social science when we attempt to explain our "commonsensical" or "lifeworld" observation of agency. In an ap-

peal to what sociologists call "socialization," Raziel Abelson traces our phenomenological awareness of our own power of agency: "It is from Mommy and
Daddy or their surrogates that, early in life, we form the concept of agency and
acquire some skill at psychological understanding of ourselves and others."[13]

Pointing out that the British psychologist John Bowlby had discovered that
the strength of one's personal sense of agency correlated directly with the degree
of the security of *attachment* in early infancy to such caregivers, and that such
"attachment, whether secure or insecure, avoidant or ambivalent, can be observed, rated, measured, correlated," Jeremy Holmes informs us that the British
pediatrician and psychoanalyst Donald Woods Winnicott, who "like Bowlby . . .
was primarily concerned with the welfare of children," declared of Bowlby's concept of infant-to-mother attachment: "There is no such thing as an infant. . . .
Wherever one finds an infant one finds maternal care and without maternal care
there would be no infant."[14]

Finally, in this scientific realist progression toward abstraction away from
the observed phenomena of individual agency, object relations psychologist—
and critic of the psychology of Lacan—Peter Rudnytsky says:

> Winnicott, after all, places the individual in a social context with his famous
> apothegm *"There is no such thing as a baby,"* for he forces us to recognize that
> a baby is always *with someone* and hence cannot be understood apart from its
> relationship with its primary caretaker. But . . . Andre Green, still under Lacan-
> ian influence, challenges Winnicott's model by contending that "there is no
> such couple formed by the mother and the baby, without the father," both be-
> cause the child "is a figure of the union between mother and father" and be-
> cause the father "is always somewhere in the mother's unconscious." Green
> moves from the dyad to the triangle, but he remains within the psychoanalyti-
> cal confines of the family. Consequently Deborah Anna Luepnitz issues a fem-
> inist rebuke to both Winnicott and Green by insisting that *"nothing* that a
> mother does is comprehensible" if removed from the contexts of "class, race,
> and the culture of patriarchy."[15]

The moral that Rudnytsky draws from this deepening progress of scientific
abstraction whereby the observation of the individual infant's action leads almost
inevitably to "class, race, and the culture of patriarchy" is that "with regard to
Fredric Jameson's attempt to proscribe 'individualistic categories of interpretation' . . . it is doubtless appropriate to adopt a more collective perspective. Everything depends on the aims of the analysis."[16]

The scientific realist philosopher Mario Bunge would agree. In the article
"Phenomenological Theories," which he had contributed to a Festschrift to Karl
Popper, Bunge argued, by appealing to examples from the history of science, that
whether a science opts to stick to the phenomenological level of observation or
chooses instead to plunge into the "black box" of unobserved "theoretical entities" depends on its level of maturity: Young, immature sciences, argued Bunge,

tended to stick to the level of observation, at the cost of remaining at a shallow level of explanation having low predictive power. More mature sciences, on the other hand, he argued, strive for a depth of predictive and explanatory range, by moving beyond the level of observation to the deduction of unobserved "theoretical entities." While Bunge had pointed to behaviorism, social science's equivalent of the level of purely observational positivism (in that behavior is the observable movement of living bodies), I find Weber's and Schutz's observations of the semantics of subjective meaning to be the real equivalents of Bunge's "phenomenological theories," because social scientific observation—unlike natural science's observation which is stuck to observing moving-but-not-speaking objects—has the verbalized semantics as well as the (behavioral) movements of the agent's body to observe.[17]

Just as the paradoxical anomalies of observation in the natural sciences push them toward the abstract depth of explaining such apparent contradictions by the unobserved influence of "theoretical entities," so does the similar problem of paradox arise in social science when conscious, subjective meaning is contradicted by "unconscious" motivation. Paul Ricoeur calls Sigmund Freud's psychoanalysis of unconscious motives a phenomenology of "suspicion," and even the phenomenological sociologist Peter Berger began his 1963 book *Invitation to Sociology* by emphasizing that sociology "presupposes" such suspicion of subjective meanings, as it

> presupposes that one is interested in looking some distance beyond the commonly accepted or officially defined goals of human actions. It presupposes a certain awareness that human events have different levels of meaning, some of which are hidden from the consciousness of everyday life. It may even presuppose a measure of suspicion about the way in which human events are subjectively interpreted.[18]

That what Berger called "different levels of meaning" could also be "hidden" within the structures of authoritative social conventions is recognized in *Rules and Meanings*, by the Durkheim-inspired social scientist Mary Douglas:

> The moral order and the knowledge that sustains it are created by social conventions. If their man-made origins were not hidden, they would be stripped of much of their authority. The conventions themselves are, therefore, not merely tacit but often extremely inaccessible to investigation.[19]

But if the meanings underlying human action are in good part "incomprehensible," "hidden," or "inaccessible" to the actors themselves, then social science must bypass the individual actors and move to study the more abstract level of the structure of social cooperation beyond direct perception of the individuals involved. So, concluded *The Process of Social Organization* by Marvin E. Olsen:

> The crucial point concerning all . . . human characteristics is that they are
> taken for granted in the study of social organization. They are given constants,
> or parameters for the study of organization, but they are not themselves vari-
> ables to be investigated or explained. Put more directly, from the point of view
> of social organization all individuals are interchangeable.[20]

We have arrived, with Olsen's focus on such social organization regardless
of individual characteristics, at what Durkheim had meant when he spoke of society being *sui generis*. And we have gotten there not through mere denial of the individual's subjectivity but through that scientific realist move beyond the level of
observation, to what Claude Levi-Strauss had called "a different level of reality,"
at which

> Marxism seemed to me to proceed in the same manner as geology and psycho-
> analysis (taking the latter in the sense given it by its founder). All three demon-
> strate that understanding consists in reducing one type of reality to another;
> that true reality is never the most obvious; and that the nature of truth is al-
> ready indicated by the care it takes to remain elusive.[21]

Agreeing as I do with Levi-Strauss, that "true reality is never the most obvious; and that the nature of truth is already indicated by the care it takes to remain
elusive," I will proceed cautiously to "reduce" or "deconstruct" the observed "reality" of individual agents to its deeper "theoretical entities"—the forms of human cooperation—by first demonstrating how the opposite process works: how,
that is, human cooperation constructs the individual sense of self.

Social Theory's First Encounter with the
Mirror Concept: Cooley and Mead

By appealing to the work of Donald Winnicott and other object-relations psychoanalysts to illustrate the inevitable progress—along the lines of scientific realism—from the empirical observation of individual agency to the "theoretical entities" of intersubjective cooperation, I may well have been traversing the route
that Parsons himself had taken in his 1937-51 theoretical odyssey from Weberian
individualism to Durkheim's social realism. Edwin Wallace's *Freud and Anthropology: A History and Reappraisal* in fact cites an article written by Parsons in
1952, "The Superego and the Theory of Social Systems," to show that Parsons
had been aware of the similarity between the Freudian usage of the concept of
"internalization" and "Durkheim's concept of the internalization of moral values," even though Parsons may not have been aware, as Wallace asserts, that this
similarity between the theories of Freud and Durkheim may have been more than

mere coincidence "since Durkheim's theory is clearly stated in *Les Formes elementaires de la vie religieuse*, a book Freud had read by 1913."[22]

C. Fred Alford's 1989 book *Melanie Klein and Critical Social Theory*, in fact, uses Winnicott's concept of maternal "holding"—which Alford claims the *social group* does to the *adult* individual's negative emotions, just as Winnicott's *mother does* to the *infant*'s similar emotions—to criticize the methodology of methodological individualism, which Alford defines as the demand "that the behavior of groups should be explained by reference to the behavior of individuals within them," of Weberian sociology. How is one to explain, asks Alford—referring to that problem that haunted Jurgen Habermas, of post-Hitler Germany's refusal to accept collective guilt for its Nazi past—"that while many individuals practice reparative morality, most groups do not?"[23]

Melanie Klein, say Stephen Mitchell and Margaret Black in their 1995 book *Freud and Beyond: A History of Modern Psychoanalytic Thought*, redefined Freud's concept "of 'drive' to include built-in human objects," thus pioneering "the British Object Relations School" of W. R. D. Fairbairn and Winnicott, for whom Freud's concept of internalization became specifically "internal object relations." In light of the recent criticism by Anthony Giddens of the concept of "internalization" by Durkheim and the post-1951 Durkheimian Parsons (and that "more than an echo" of Parsons is "to be found in Habermas," according to Giddens), I can only refer any sociological readers of this book who may be unfamiliar with the Freudian tradition's development of Durkheim's concept of internalization to the works of two psychoanalysts within the Freudian tradition: the 1968 *Aspects of Internalization* by Roy Schafer and the 1981 *Internalization in Psychoanalysis* by W. W. Meissner, both of which ignore Durkheim but specifically refer to the use by Parsons of the (in their view, "Freudian") concept of internalization.[24]

Referring to the way Parsons had used the concept of "internalization" in 1958 in his article "Social Structure and the Development of the Personality," the Freudian Schafer marvels, "Despite his reliance on a learning theory that gives little or no place to persisting infantile fantasy and to aggression, he adds a major dimension to the theory of internalization." That "learning theory" that Schafer had found, to his obvious amazement, displacing the Freudian tradition in Parsons's explication of Durkheim's concept of "internalization" had been the American Pragmatist philosophy, as explicated by Charles Horton Cooley and George Herbert Mead. In fact, in response to that question posed by Hans Adriaansens—as a call for Parsons to respond to his critic, Martindale, about why Parsons had, in 1951 "deserted . . . Weber for Durkheim"—Parsons himself seemed to have already replied, in 1968, that it had been his reading of Cooley (and Mead) that had led him from Weber's methodological individualism to Durkheim's social realism:

> Thus, I believe Weber was in error when he first defined action as "all human behavior when and in so far as the acting individual attaches a subjective

meaning to it"—and then defined "social action" as a subtype in which the action of others is taken into account. Cooley, however, maintained quite correctly that "general" action is both social and individual, and that Weber's two subtypes should be treated as products of processes of differentiation from "action in general," which is neither individual nor social. However, this is true not only of action in its mental aspect, but also of action as a modality of objects. Here Cooley needs to be supplemented by Durkheim. As *object*, "society," in Durkheim's original sense, is just as immediately primordial, just at given," as is the individual or his own personality.[25]

Unlike Weber, but like Durkheim, Cooley had gone to great lengths to theorize the social construction of individuality. Of the individual, Cooley had written at the beginning of his book *Human Nature and the Social Order*, "The social origin of his life comes by the pathway of intercourse with other persons," an insight that he had further elaborated by denying that heart of individual agency, the "sense of 'I' . . . without its correlative sense of you, or he, or they."[26]

To explain such "internalization" of the social process by the individual, Cooley had appealed to the analogy of the mirror or looking glass:

> As we see our face, figure, and dress in the glass, and are interested in them because they are ours, and pleased or otherwise with them according as they do or do not answer to what we should like them to be, so in imagination we perceive in another's mind some thought of our appearance, manners, aims, deeds, character, friends, and so on, and are variously affected by it.[27]

And imagination, for Cooley, had been only the first of three mental processes leading to such a social construction of the self, the other two being judgement and feeling: "The imagination of our appearance to the other person, the imagination of his judgement of that appearance, and some sort of self-feeling, such as pride or mortification."[28]

Not only had Cooley analyzed this "looking glass" mechanism of the social construction of the individual self, but he had also specified the precise social locus for the joint emergence of large-scale (macro) society and the individual self: "Self and society are twin-born," Cooley had written in *Social Organization*, within the "primary group."[29]

Cooley explained his concept of this birthing locus for all human social-learning:

> By primary groups I mean those characterized by intimate face-to-face association and *cooperation*. They are primary in several senses but chiefly in that they are fundamental in forming the social nature and ideals of individuals. The result of intimate association, psychologically, is a certain fusion of individualities in a common whole, so that one's very self, for many purposes at least, is the common life and purpose of the group.[30]

There, within that "cooperation" of Cooley's social womb, giving birth to both individual and society, we can see the conceptual source of both the "co-operative principle" of linguistic meaning in H. Paul Grice's pragmatics and the macrosociological reach of Parsons's power as "generalized capacity." Ultimately, it is only through this conception by Cooley of the "primary group" that we can clearly see as never before why it is that, as Durkheim had argued against the Utilitarians, and Parsons had seen, even in his supposedly Weber-inspired 1937 book *The Structure of Social Action*, the power behind a social order conceived as merely a society of self-interested individuals makes no sense:

> The ultimate source of the power behind sanctions is the common sense of moral attachment to norms—and the weaker that becomes, the larger the minority who do not share it, the more precarious is the order in question . . . A social order resting on interlocking of interests alone, and thus ultimately on sanctions is hence hardly empirically possible.[31]

In a definition of human communication as a cooperative process long antedating similar statements in the more recent philosophical publications of Grice, Nicholas Rescher, or Jurgen Habermas, Cooley had described the process of "public opinion," which he had seen as cementing social bonds, as a process of constant creation and re-creation of a negotiated consensus, not

> a mere aggregate of separate individual judgements, but an organization, a cooperative product of communication and reciprocal influence. It may be as different from the sum of what the individuals could have thought out in separation as a ship built by a hundred men is from a hundred boats each built by one man.[32]

This "organic process" of the formation of social norms—through the constant debate and negotiation of human communication—had been compared by Cooley, in his later book *The Social Process*, to the biological process of evolutionary selection: "Communicated differences are the life of opinion, as cross-breeding is of natural stock."[33]

"So strong is the individualist tradition in America and England," Cooley had lamented in that publication of his later years, that it seemed unable to overcome the dichotomies between coercion and consent, or conflict and cooperation, that such individualism had begotten:

> The more one thinks of it the more he will see that conflict and cooperation are not separable things, but phases of one process which always involves something of both. . . . You can resolve the social order into a great number of cooperative wholes of various sorts, each of which contains conflicting elements within itself upon which it is imposing some sort of harmony with a view to conflict with others.[34]

That Georg Simmel-like insight that Cooley had had in 1918, about the interpenetration of conflict and cooperation, might well have been applied to the Weberian methodological individualism which still constrains Habermas to isolate his "ideal speech situation" from the reality of human conflict, as it had been used by Cooley in his critique of earlier Anglo-Saxon individualism. I find it ironic, therefore, that when comparing Cooley's thought with the French sociological tradition of Emile Durkheim, Talcott Parsons had seen Cooley's thought as still struggling with the binding coils of that Anglo-Saxon individualism:

> Thus I would suggest that Cooley, as the first to exploit James's initiative in the social direction, is closer to Durkheim than to the other two great theorists of internalization, Freud and Weber. There is indeed a sense in which the primary background of both Durkheim and Cooley is Cartesian and in which, within this frame of reference, each is the obverse of the other. Thus Durkheim was the theorist of society as an object in the external world; Cooley was the theorist of society as part of the individual self.[35]

By making such an accusation of quasi-Berkeleyan subjectivistic idealism against Cooley, Parsons—who had proceeded to hail George Herbert Mead for having refashioned Cooley's insights in a manner "comparable" with Durkheim's social realism—had been merely echoing the criticism of Cooley that Mead himself had proffered in his introduction to Cooley's book *Human Nature and the Social Order*, that

> by placing both phases of this social process in the same consciousness, by regarding the self as the ideas entertained of him by the self, and the other as ideas entertained of him by the self, the action of the others upon the self and of the self upon the other becomes simply the interaction of ideas upon each other within mind.[36]

Parsons's complaint was that, besides Cooley's needed supplementation by Durkheim,

> Cooley also needs to be supplemented by other points of view, as Mead suggested from both psychoanalytic and behavioristic directions, in neither of which Cooley felt inclined to follow. Another of Mead's points was that Cooley's "mentalistic" orientation tended to make him uninterested in the use of more rigorous scientific methods in the study of social phenomena, since he found the introspective approach so well suited to his purposes.[37]

Unlike Cooley, Mead has received a flood of scholarly attention, of which the recent German literature by Hans Joas, Ernst Tugendhat, and Habermas has been only the latest of a long outpouring of critical interest. Indeed, discussing "Cooley's heritage," Lewis Coser had been moved to lament:

The notion of the social and reflected nature of the self has become, though usually in its Meadian version rather than in Cooley's, a constituent part of current sociological theory. There is hardly a textbook in sociology or social psychology that does not discuss it. Matters are somewhat different with the notion of the primary group.[38]

The focus by social science has been upon Mead's book *Mind, Self, and Society*, which had been edited and published in 1934 by Charles Morris on the basis of two sets of lecture notes from the years 1927 and 1930, and had borne thereby what Joas has characterized as "all the defects one would expect from its origin in posthumously published transcripts of Mead's lectures: unreliability, insufficient precision in the recording of Mead's words, and obfuscation of the coherence of Mead's thought."[39]

But this editorial organization of Mead's lectures by Morris in 1934 allows us to enjoy a sufficiently coherent vision of the continuity of Mead's theory with that of Cooley and the pragmati(ci)sm of Charles S. Peirce. Thus, we may split the book's original four sections into two halves so as to summarize Mead's extensively analyzed message in two succinct points: First, the extension of Cooley's "co-operative process" beyond Cooley's restrictions to human mental process and into the wider realm of Darwin's Evolutionary nature; and second, Mead's social process within the self between the "I" and "me."

With regard to the first point, by overtly citing Charles Darwin's book *The Expression of the Emotions in Man and Animals* (originally published in London in 1872), Mead had broadened Cooley's "conscious experience" into the animal world:

> Here Darwin carried over his theory of evolution into the field of what we call "conscious experience." What Darwin did was to show that there was a whole series of acts or beginnings of acts which called out certain responses that do express emotions. If one animal attacks another, or is on the point of attacking, that action calls out violent responses which express the anger of the second dog. There we have a set of attitudes which express the emotional attitude of dogs; and we can carry this analysis into the human expression of emotions.[40]

The purpose of this "social behaviorist" strategy (as labeled by Mead's editor, Morris), risking conflation of dogs and humans, is seen in Mead's second section on "Mind." Mead avoided pursuing meaning *into* human language, i.e., into the relativistic arbitrariness of *semantic* reference with all its movement to and fro between universals and particulars that the contemporary Pragmatist philosopher Nicholas Rescher had warned us about, sticking instead to the *pragmatics* of evolutionary intra-species cooperative communication:

> If you conceive of the mind as just a sort of conscious substance in which there are certain impressions and states, and hold that one of those states is a universal, then a word becomes purely arbitrary—it is just a symbol. You can then

take words and pronounce them backwards, as children do; there seems to be absolute freedom of arrangement and language seems to be an entirely mechanical thing that lies outside of the process of intelligence. If you recognize that language is, however, just a part of the *co-operative* process, that part which does lead to an adjustment to the response of the other so that the whole activity can go on, then language has only a limited range of arbitrariness.[41]

Echoing Peirce's Pragmatic Maxim's definition of meaning by its "practical consequences"—and gifting social science thereby with a full-blooded theory of meaning such as neither Max Weber nor the Edmund Husserl/Alfred Schutz variant of phenomenology had given it (which perhaps accounts for that recent German interest in Mead)—Mead had ensconced those Peircean "practical consequences" firmly within Peirce's evolutionary realism of communicating "organisms":

Meaning arises and lies within the field of the relation between the gesture of a given human organism and the subsequent behavior of this organism as indicated to another human organism by that gesture. If that gesture does so indicate to another organism the subsequent (or resultant) behavior of the given organism, then it has meaning. . . . Meaning is thus a development of something objectively there as a relation between certain phases of the social act; it is not a psychical addition to that act and it is not an "idea" as traditionally conceived. A gesture by one organism, the resultant of the social act in which the gesture is an early phase, and the response of another organism to the gesture, are the relata in a triple or threefold relationship . . . and this threefold relationship constitutes the matrix within which meaning arises, or which develops into the field of meaning. . . . Meaning is implicit—if not always explicit—in the various phases of the social act to which it refers, and out of which it develops. And its development takes place in terms of symbolization at the human evolutionary level.[42]

With Mead's subsequent statement that "the language symbol is simply a significant or conscious gesture," he had, by the time his book was published in 1934—like Charles Sanders Peirce before him—effectively achieved what Niklas Luhmann would later call a sociological theory of "functionalized" meaning, as an evolutionary "selection out of a universe of possibilities."[43]

Turning to Mead's social process within the self between the "I" and "me," the last two sections, on "The Self" and "Society," of Mead's posthumous 1934 book *Mind, Self, and Society,* had outlined and elaborated his celebrated theory of the self as "two distinguishable phases" of the "I" and the "me." In Mead's main concept of "the generalized other" we can recognize Peirce's historically extended community of human communicators, as well as Cooley's "primary group":

The organized community or social group which gives to the individual his unity of self may be called "the generalized other." The attitude of the generalized other is the attitude of the whole community.[44]

An organized community is a totality of individuals, said Mead, who stand in a relation of "cooperation," and

it is in the form of the generalized other that the social process influences the behavior of the individuals involved in it and carrying it on, i.e., that the community exercises control over the conduct of its individual members; for it is in this form that the social process or community enters as a determining factor into the individual's thinking.[45]

And it is this awareness of the community's "generalized other" as a "determining factor," according to Mead, that produces the "self-feeling" of the "me":

What we mean by self-consciousness is an awakening in ourselves of the group of attitudes which we are arousing in others, especially when it is an important set of responses which go to make up the members of the community.[46]

The implications Mead drew from this process of the awakening of self-consciousness involved, first of all, the logical and temporal priority of the existence of society over the individual's existence: "The process out of which the self arises is a social process which implies interaction of individuals in the group, implies the pre-existence of the group."[47] Secondly, argued Mead, the nature of this socially constructed human self involved, in its deepest aspects of cognition and thinking, inescapably social characteristics:

The essence of the self, as we have said, is cognitive: it lies in the internalized conversation of gestures which constitutes thinking, or in terms of which thought or reflection proceeds. And hence the origin and foundations of the self, like those of thinking, are social.[48]

This "internalization" of the social process of conversation then defined the subjective, spontaneous "I" in relation to the objective socially organized "me":

The "I" is the response of the organism to the attitudes of the others; the "me" is the organized set of attitudes of others which one himself assumes. The attitudes of the others constitute the organized "me," and then one reacts toward that as an "I."[49]

Mead's whole concept of the human self was therefore the organism's "internalization" of social process:

The "I" both calls out the "me" and responds to it. Taken together they constitute a personality as it appears in social experience. The self is essentially a social process going on with these two distinguishable phases.[50]

But a weakness or hesitation in Mead's conceptual socialization of the individual self was perceived by Jurgen Habermas:

While the concept of the "me" is fixed, Mead vacillates in the expression "I."
He presents it as something that sets itself off from the representatives of social norms in the self, and that raises the self "beyond the institutionalized individual."[51]

Habermas was not wrong in questioning Mead's presentation of the "I" as the vehicle of time and "novelty," set off—like some lone ranger yelling "don't fence
me in" on the Western frontier—against the social, law-abiding "me." For Mead
had indeed presented his "I" as being in that need of "social control" and the "setting of limits" that would today be seen in unruly juveniles in need of adult super-
vision:

Social control is the expression of the "me" over against the expression of the
"I." It sets the limits, it gives the determination that enables the "I," so to
speak, to use the "me" as the means of carrying out what is the undertaking
that all are interested in.[52]

And, in a drastic overturning of that first of four anti-Cartesian denials that
Peirce had hammered home in 1868—"We have no power of introspection,"
Peirce had argued, "but all knowledge of the internal world is derived by hypothetical reasoning from external facts"—Habermas was able to use this imagery
by Mead, of "social control," to claim that Mead "draws an increasingly clear
boundary between an *external world*, which has consolidated into an institutional
reality, and an *inner world* of spontaneous experience."[53]

But Mead's final section, "Society," in his book *Mind, Self, and Society*,
spoke of "the fusion of the 'I' and the 'Me' in social activities," and, as we have
seen, he had insisted that "what I want particularly to emphasize is the temporal
and logical pre-existence of the social process to the self-conscious individual
that arises in it."[54]

Such a "logical pre-existence" of society, however, is in no way assured if
one phase of Mead's "individual importation of the social process," his "I," remains forever undefined by social process, as the bearer of "novelty" and "spontaneous experiences" outside "social control." We sociologists are therefore fortunate that the intellectual tradition begun by American Pragmatism's 1913-14
interlocutor, Emile Durkheim, had through a dual flow—the borrowings from
Durkheim by the linguistics of Ferdinand de Saussure and the psychology of Sig-

mund Freud—re-emerged, via the structuralist anthropology of Claude Levi-Strauss and the object-relations school of psychoanalysis established by Melanie Klein, respectively, to flower in Jacques Lacan's completion of the Cooley-Mead project of the "social self."[55]

Social Theory's Second Encounter with the Mirror Concept: Lacan

Jean-Marc-Gaspard Itard became physician to the institution for deaf-mutes in Paris in 1800, at the age of twenty-five. That year a boy of eleven or twelve who had been found running wild in the woods around Aveyron was brought to the institution. The boy was an object of great scientific as well as public curiosity. After his capture scientists came from all over the world to see the "natural man." What they saw was a creature more like an animal than a man, expressionless, rocking back and forth, locked in his own world, unable to do anything for himself, helpless, uncommunicative. There seemed to be no way to reach him, no way for him to learn.[56]

This dramatic description of Dr. Jean Itard's introduction to Victor, the "wild boy of Aveyron," in 1800, is contained in Rita Kramer's biography of Maria Montessori, whose celebrated Montessori method of educating young children developed out of Itard's experiences with this wild child. Since I have not yet found even a single reference to Itard in the writings of Emile Durkheim, I cannot prove that Itard's encounter with this "wild boy" was the decisive factor in the development of Durkheim's "social realism," but I can surmise—based on the statement by Lucien Malson (the editor, in 1964, of Itard's 1801 and 1807 published reports on his wild child's progress) that Itard's 1801 report, titled "Of the First Developments of the Young Savage of Aveyron," had "made the child famous throughout Europe"—that Durkheim, writing at the end of that same century which had begun by providing such dramatic evidence against both the French extremes of Cartesian individualism and Rousseau's anticulturalism, could not have been unaware of this drastic empirical lesson taught by Itard's wild boy: that a twelve-year old human child growing up isolated from all human society can in no way develop that cogitating faculty of Cartesian individuals.[57]

It may well have been that that single "well-made experiment," the appearance of the wild boy at the end of the eighteenth century furnished to France's centralized (Parisian) academic tradition, enabled the French sociological tradition to arrive at such a decided consensus about the relations between society and human individuality. Roland Robertson has pointed to the remarkable stability of French social science's granting of logical and ontological priority to society over the individual—an orientation which, according to Robertson, is the polar opposite of American sociology's bias toward individualism. When the popularity

of the French existentialism of Jean-Paul Sartre had threatened to diffuse its re-
furbished Cartesian individualism to the French reading public, it had been opposed by the Durkheimian structuralism of Claude Levi-Strauss, and when the
post-1956 popularity of the individualizing humanism of the "young Marx" had
threatened to overwhelm even the anti-individualist political tradition of French
Marxism, it had been the "structural" Marxism of Louis Althusser—the very
same theoretical source that Joseph Smith and Bryan Turner appealed to in their
1986 polemic against the concept of unlimited agency in the structuration theory
of Anthony Giddens—that had in turn arisen to do battle, in the name of (social)
science, against the Hegelian takeover of French Marxism.[58]

It is therefore not surprising that, in attempting to explain to an English-
speaking audience the psychoanalytical philosophy of Althusser's other source of
intellectual influence (i.e., besides the French philosopher of science, Gaston
Bachelard), Jacques Lacan, Ellie Ragland-Sullivan illustrated the "cultural de-
pendency" that governs the six-to-eighteen-month-old human infant's efforts to
develop a sense of self through parental identification, by appealing to the early
nineteenth century case of "Itard et son sauvage."[59]

Despite claims made by Lacan's opponents from within the American tradition of psychoanalysis known as "ego psychology" that Lacan's theory had a "linguistic bias" against the organism/environment conceptualizations of biological
science, Ragland-Sullivan pointed out that Lacan's seminal 1949 essay—titled
"The Mirror Stage as Formative of the Function of the I as Revealed in the Psychoanalytic Experience" and presented to the sixteenth International Congress of
Psychoanalysis at Zurich—had been based upon the animal ethology of Konrad
Lorenz and Nikko Tinbergen and the "studies of children about eight months of
age, who mirror each other's gestures, as observed by Charlotte Buhler, Elsa
Kohler, and the Chicago School of the 1930s."[60]

The parallels between Lacan's terminology and that used by the Chicago
School of sociologists is impressive: not only does Lacan's celebrated "mirror-
stage theory" of 1949 resemble George Herbert Mead's in this conceptual connection between the human neonate's process of developing a sense of identity by
"mirroring" its care-giving parents, and the evolutionary processes of animal biology (ethology), but also, as Ragland-Sullivan pointed out, that 1949 presentation had, in its turn, been based upon a previous essay by Lacan—now, unfortunately, lost—titled "Le stade du miroir" and "supposedly" presented at the
fourteenth International Congress of Psychoanalysis at Marienbad in 1936 and
"allegedly published" in 1937 in the *International Journal of Psychoanalysis* under the title—reminiscent of the phraseology of Charles Horton Cooley—"The
Looking-Glass Phase."[61]

Indeed, that this resemblance between the theoretical phraseology of Lacan
and that of the Pragmatist sociologists of the Chicago School may have been
more than coincidental was suggested by Ragland-Sullivan's denial that Lacan's
concept of the "mirror" had been borrowed by Lacan—as had been done by other

psychoanalysts such as Donald Winnicott and Heinz Kohut—from Freud's use in 1920 (in his book *Beyond the Pleasure Principle*) of the example of a child dealing with its anxiety about its absent mother by playing peek-a-boo with a mirror, and her suggestion, instead, of its similarity to the "sociological treatise" of George H. Mead's 1934 *Mind, Self, and Society*. Such a similarity between the theoretical statements of Mead and Lacan can be seen in the easy translatability between Lacanian and Meadian theoretical propositions—as, for example, in Ragland-Sullivan's statement, "The difficulty of the *moi/toi* relation (with its implicit narcissistic and aggressive fusions) forces upon the Symbolic order dealings that Lacan has called the 'general notion of the other,' a notion marked by 'normal distance,'" which, to my own Meadian-attuned ears, sounds suspiciously like a Meadian insight about the normal conflicts of the child's interactions with significant others during the earlier "play stage" leading the child to develop linguistically in the later "game stage," its conception of the "generalized other"!—and Ragland-Sullivan therefore blamed the strangeness to the ears of American psychoanalysts of Lacan's *je/moi* terminology, which resembles Mead's "I-me" phrasing far more than it does the traditional "ego-id" terminology of English translations of Freud's writings, for those French-to-English "mistranslations, which also keep A from 'hearing' Lacan (e.g., the *moi* has been rendered as the id)."[62]

But even Francophones who are more familiar with their native idiom than I am may find it almost impossible to plough through that Lacanian style of writing that even a Lacanian admits to being "impossible." For, as Judith Gurewich says, in presenting her introductory essay "The Lacanian Clinical Field: Series Overview" in the Lacanian Maud Mannoni's book, *Separation and Creativity*,

> Lacan felt that Freud's clarity and didactic talent had ultimately led to distortions and oversimplifications, so that his own notoriously "impossible" style was meant to serve as a metaphor for the difficulty of listening to the unconscious. Cracking his difficult writings involves not only the intellectual effort of readers but also their unconscious processes; comprehension will dawn as reader-analysts recognize in their own work what was expressed in sibylline fashion in the text. Some of Lacan's followers continued this tradition, fearing that clear exposition would leave no room for the active participation of the reader.[63]

Since I am neither a psychoanalyst nor am I engaged, in this book, in a case of clinical psychoanalysis, the reader should excuse my heavy dependence—in my pursuit of what I see as the fortunate reincarnation of Mead's sociological theory in the psychoanalytical writings of Lacan—on the clear English interpretation by this professor of English, Ellie Ragland-Sullivan, of those two principal sources of Lacan's ideas, the thirty-three essays published in 1966 as the *Ecrits* and the "Seminars" held by Lacan "from 1953 to the late 1970s."[64]

Lacan conceptualized the "mirror stage," according to Ragland-Sullivan, to comprehend the specifically human phenomenon—occurring at the age of six months—to acquire a body image through identification with a fantasy of what the care-giving parent desires, in order to acquire that integrated motor coordination that other animals appear to have at birth:

> Lacan has called the first six months of human life the pre-mirror stage and describes it as a period in which an infant experiences its body as fragmented parts and images. During this time the infant has no sense of being a totality or an individual unit, because a pre-maturation at birth (by comparison with other animals)—a phenomenon termed *fetalization* by embryologists—marks human babies as uncoordinated and physically helpless. . . . Nonetheless, the infant perceives the world around it from the start of life.[65]

That last sentence "the infant perceives the world around it from the start of life"—forms the principal bone of contention between the psychoanalytic school of Lacan and the British school of "object-relations theory" that developed from the work of Melanie Klein. Lacan's empirically based assertion about the efficacy of the neonate's independent perceptual apparatus being apparent "from the start of life," according to Ragland-Sullivan, "casts doubt on the static aspect of object-relations theory (of Klein, Donald Winnicott, and W. Ronald D. Fairbairn, among others), which depicts the infant as fused with the mother and, consequently, the 'same' as she is." Not only had subsequent research on the perceptual abilities of neonates confirmed Lacan's assertion of neonatal perceptual independence from the mother from the beginning, according to Ragland-Sullivan, but even *a priori* logic should have exposed the conceptual confusion of Lacan's British rivals, for the "logical impasse is obvious: how does one bring a monad enclosed in and upon itself to the progressive recognition of others?"[66]

But therein lies the potential tragedy of the human animal: for while being independent—and individuated—in its perceptual capacities from life's very beginning, *like* other animals, the human infant nevertheless, *unlike* other animals, lacks an integrated system of motor coordination at birth. And it is in the process of acquisition of such lacking motor skills that human infants are uniquely dependent upon the cultural processes of social identification, for

> the human infant cannot walk, talk or obtain food on its own, but spends much time gazing and learning. Lacan has therefore stressed that earliest perception is inseparable from the effects of the outside world, both linguistic and visual. He thinks, furthermore, that since the primordial subject of unconsciousness is formed by identification with its first images and sensory experiences, it will thereafter reflect the essence of these images and objects in identity. The radical idea that the infant actually *becomes* the image or object in primordial fantasy is an experience Lacan calls primary identification, while pointing out that the nature of symbolic incorporation is generally misunderstood.[67]

What Ragland-Sullivan had labeled as the "generally misunderstood" aspect of Lacan's theory could still be seen in Peter Rudnytsky's accusation against Lacan—on behalf of the American school of "ego psychology"—of having neglected "preverbal experience."[68] But rather than neglecting preverbal experience, as psychoanalysts from rival schools mistakenly accuse Lacan of having done, it is that very preverbal experience which features at the heart of Lacan's master concept of the mirror stage. For, not being linguistically accomplished as yet, between the ages of six and eighteen months, when the mirror stage of identification occurs, the infant's sense of identity is cognitively processed in the form not of words but of images, thereby laying the groundwork—as subsequent linguistic development pushes those images of subjective identity out of the range of linguistically governed short-term memory and into the hallucinatory penumbra of the "unconscious"—for what Fredric Jameson has, in his essay "Imaginary and Symbolic in Lacan," called "the problem of the subject." One's primordial sense of self—one's identity—slips beyond the range of linguistic communication, thereby creating, in our postmodern situation of the surfeit of media images, all those "borderline personality" automatisms, wherein one's unconscious identity may respond (image-to-image) to the seductions of the media (as in the wave of high school shooting massacres that we have heard so much about recently) without the controlling mediation of linguistic reflection.[69]

That controlling influence of language arrives, according to Lacan—who, in an unintended echo of Georg Simmel, had sociality residing in triadic relationships rather than in the (mother-infant) dyad—with the child's growing perception of the father's influence (as in that celebrated Lacanian phrase, "the Name-of-the-Father") upon its bond to its mother (and its narcissistic desire to continue inhabiting the image of itself as the fulfilled object of its mother's desire). While we may pause to note that Lacan's concept of the father-mother-child (Simmelian) triad may have much to inform us about the current epidemic of "poor impulse control" in the "borderline personality disorder"—that appears to statistically increase with every increase in the number of single-parent families—it is not such psychiatric epidemiology upon which I must now focus, but upon the reversal that Lacan had wrought upon the Meadian relationship of the "I/*Je*" part of the personality with its "Me/*Moi*" counterpart. For, whereas, according to Mead, "social control is the expression of the 'me' over and against the expression of the 'I,'" and it had been Mead's "me" that "sets the limits," for Lacan on the contrary, according to Ragland-Sullivan,

> As the subject of linguistic distinctions and differences, the *je* stabilizes the *moi* by anchoring its sliding identifications and spontaneous fusions through naming and labeling these responses. In this way, the speaking *je* provides a sense of unity to the opaque yet potent force. Although the narcissistic and aggressive structure of the *moi* pushes it to obliterate differences and perpetuate identificatory sameness, the subject of language tempers these intentions by

rules and cultural conventions. It is increasingly evident, therefore, how crucial is the role of the *je*. Even though intrinsically unified, the *moi* has no guarantees that its question of identity will be answered by others' reinforcement, which renders its existential condition unstable. . . . The *moi* depends on others to validate it in the Real, and on the *je* to "translate" it—to give it shape and form—in the Symbolic, even though the *je* performs this function unawares.[70]

This passage, from Ellie Ragland-Sullivan's 1987 book *Jacques Lacan and the Philosophy of Psychoanalysis*, really encapsulates the heart of *my* book. I can only communicate my feeling of intellectual effervescence (upon my first having read it years ago) to my reader by explicating its profound significance in two separate, but interrelated, points:

First was its completion of Mead's "I/me" theory of personality by reversal of Mead's "control" equation. I have already intimated to my reader how Lacan's *je/moi* theory of personality reverses the Meadian model of control, in that for Lacan, in contrast to Mead, it is the "I" (*je*) which controls the "me" (*moi*). The reader may now notice for himself or herself that in identifying the Meadian "I" as the "speaking *je*," Ragland-Sullivan's Lacan had really "socialized" that under-socialized "I" of the Meadian personality that Jurgen Habermas had described "as something that sets itself off from the representatives of social norms in the self," raising it thereby "beyond the institutionalized individual." As if in response to Habermas, Lacan—as Ragland-Sullivan interpreted him in the passage just cited—said of this "I/je" that "the subject of language tempers these intentions (of the potentially anarchic '*me/moi*') by rules and cultural conventions." As (the later) Wittgenstein had recognized, there cannot exist a private language: by clarifying that the "I/je" speaks, Lacan had also established that it—the "I"— rather than Mead's "me," was the real socializing force within the individual, because, as Ragland-Sullivan emphasized later on, "in Lacan's theory . . . the use of language is an end in itself." In those three interpretant (or pragmatic) codes that I will define in my next chapter as the cybernetic controls of global cultural evolution, the reader may recognize what Ragland-Sullivan called "*je* codes."[71]

The second point is that Lacan's "Theory of Cognition" is *identical* to Peirce's. Ragland-Sullivan had dedicated the third of her five chapters to an extended explication of "Lacan's Three Orders" of cognition. By now drawing my reader's attention back to that single passage about the "speaking *je*" that I just cited from Ragland-Sullivan, I can more simply enable the reader to see for himself or herself how the three-step process of the emergence of Lacan's "speaking *je*"—from the "Imaginary" realm of the *moi* fantasized mirror-image, through the frustration of *moi*'s intentions by social others unwilling to "validate it in the Real," to the *je*'s linguistic "translation" of *moi*'s desires in the realm of the (Lacanian) "Symbolic"—recapitulates *in exact sequence* that Peircean three-step cognitive journey that I had outlined in this present book's introduction: from (Peirce's) iconic *Firstness*, functioning like Lacan's Imaginary order of cognition through metaphoric processes of similarity perceptions, to (Peirce's) indexical *Secondness*, functioning like Lacan's Real by metonymic frustration of subjective desire, into that *Thirdness* of the competent linguistic usage of the process of generalization that both Peirce and Lacan call the "Symbolic." Indeed, critics of Lacan's supposedly linguistic bias and neglect of the preverbal experience of the infant—from American ego psychologists to Lacan's erstwhile Parisian follower Julia Kristeva, whose celebrated feminist theory is premised upon the possibility that in the infant's preverbal experience before the father's irruption into the mother-infant dyad lies the model of liberation from patriarchal law—misundeLacan *because* they have no comprehension of that Peircean three-step logic of cognition by which "the use of language," as Ragland-Sullivan phrased it, "is an end in itself," or, to paraphrase Martin Heidegger, that being human is really *being-toward-communication.*[72]

Rather than grant credit to Lacan, as I do, for having, like Christopher Columbus, stumbled upon his most important discovery—in Lacan's case, his apparently independent rediscovery of Peircean triadic phenomenology—not by design but by the practical exigencies of his exploratory journey into heretofore uncharted or poorly charted waters, Ragland-Sullivan had preferred to brush past Peirce with a brief mention about the similarity between Peirce's *icons* and Lacan's Imaginary (without then mentioning Peirce's name in her book's index) to focus her critique, instead, on the "thoughtlessness" of those who associate Lacan's name with "static Saussurean structuralism." While not denying the overt borrowing by Lacan from Saussure that others have also pointed out—such as, for example, the "Saussurean bar which Lacan borrowed to depict a separation between conscious and unconscious discourse," or that Saussurean conceptual distinction between *langue* and *parole* which Lacan's writings had used so copiously—Ragland-Sullivan concluded that Lacan had "reversed Saussure's theory."[73]

Since the object of my own book is not to debate the extent of Saussure's influence on Lacan, but to complete that marriage between the theories of Peirce and Durkheim by elaborating, in the next chapter, upon what Ragland-Sullivan had called "*je* codes," I must leave it up to my reader to verify for himself or herself just how much Lacan's three cognitive "categories" of the "Imaginary," the "Real," and the "Symbolic" —functioning as they did within that apparently Peircean framework of a triadic semiotic that Ragland-Sullivan had described as "Lacan's marriage of the concepts of subject, structure, and signifier"—had resembled Peirce's three cognitive categories (of Iconic Firstness, Indexical Secondness and Symbolic Thirdness, respectively). Having completed my exploration of Lacan's completion-by-reversal of G. H. Mead's model of the "social self," I must now, in the final section of this chapter, proceed to tie up those conceptual loose ends that my fitful sally into the psychoanalytical tradition of Freud—a sally that has uncovered the unexpected validation of Peirce's cognitive theory by Lacan's "Freudian" theorizing—has left: the connection of that concept of "internalization" common to both the Freudian and Durkheimian intellectual traditions, with Peircean pragmatics.[74]

Peircean Pragmatics and Durkheimian Internalization

Referring to Emile Durkheim's statement—within his posthumously published book *Moral Education*—that society "permeates us," his biographer, Steven Lukes, called the idea that "socially given norms and values become an integral and constitutive part of the individual personality" *internalization*. By the time, in 1973, that Lukes had published the first edition of his biography of Durkheim, the association that Talcott Parsons had made in 1952 in his essay "The Superego and the Theory of Social Systems" between this idea of Durkheim's about the "permeation" of the individual personality by society's normative culture and Sigmund Freud's psychoanalytical usage of the concept of "internalization" had become so firmly established in Anglophone sociologists' minds that the collection of essays put together as a book in 1995 by Anthony Giddens carries a single entry on the word *internalization* in its index. This single entry refers to the concept as used both by Durkheim—in three of his writings, *The Division of Labor*, *The Rules of Sociological Method*, and *Suicide*—and by Parsons in his post-1951 Durkheimian phase, writing about power. In the mind of Giddens—and, because of his extensive influence upon the minds of a whole generation of Western sociologists, in the minds of most social scientists in America today—it is upon that single concept of internalization common to "the 'normative functionalism' of Durkheim and Parsons" that the conceptual edifice of Durkheim's social realism—which Giddens excoriates for cognizing society as "external" constraint—stands.[75]

Since even as staunch a defender of Durkheim's social realism—against its Giddensian critique in the name of "unlimited agency" as well as the Giddensian tendency to comprehend Durkheim via Parsons—as Stjepan Mestrovic, does not deny the legitimacy of that assimilation of the Freudian theory of personality to Durkheim's social realism that Parsons made, it is to an American Freudian psychoanalyst interpretation of just what that sociological concept of "internalization"—as made by Parsons—entails that we must turn. As the Freudian psychoanalyst W. W. Meissner saw it, the sociological usage of the term *internalization*—as presented by Talcott Parsons and Edward Shils in their 1962 book, *Toward a General Theory of Action*—differentiated between two concepts used by Freudian psychoanalysts:

> Parsons and Shils distinguish imitation from identification on the grounds that imitation involves acquisition of specific behavioral patterns by copying from a social object without any particular attachment to the object beyond the mere process of acquisition. Identification, in contrast, involves acquisition of gen-

eralized patterns of orientation, including values, attitudes and beliefs, based on a motivated attachment to the object. Imitation thus serves as a mechanism for transfer of specific cultural elements, such as specialized knowledge or technical skills, while identification permits the transfer of more general aspects of the culture.[76]

As Lukes points out in his biography of Durkheim, it is definitely *not* imitation—the conceptual primacy of which Durkheim had tirelessly criticized in the social psychology of Gabriel Tarde—that Durkheim had in mind as the mechanism by which the individual personality "internalized" the moral culture of society. And—as if in pre-emptive agreement with Meissner's insistence in 1981 that "imitation clearly is not a kind of internalization, but is closely related to and often involved in identificatory processes"—Everett K. Wilson, the translator and editor of the English-language version of Durkheim's *Moral Education,* had already insisted in 1961 that it had been specifically the cognitive process of *identification* that Durkheim had seen as the core of how social norms permeated—and were internalized by—the individual.[77]

Having thus established that it is indeed what Freudians call "identification," and not Tarde's "imitation," that perdures in Durkheimian sociology's thematic of the individual's "internalization" of social norms, we may now focus specifically on how the concept of "identification" developed beyond Durkheim's lifetime. Ragland-Sullivan has helpfully traced Freud's development of this concept from 1914 to 1933 in four phases:

1. In his 1914 article, "On Narcissism: An Introduction," Freud had seen identification as occurring primarily with the mother.
2. In his 1921 article, "Group Psychology and the Analysis of the Ego," Freud had argued that the male child's identification was purely with his male parent as "identification is known to psychoanalysis as the earliest expression of an emotional tie with another person. . . . A little boy will exhibit a special interest in his father: he would like to grow like him and be like him."
3. In his 1923 article, "The Ego and the Id," Freud had seen the first identification occurring "with both parents."
4. In his 1933 book, *New Introductory Lectures,* Freud had compared identification with "oral-cannibalistic incorporation," reaffirming the "link to the mother in primary identification."

Ragland-Sullivan found this legacy of Freudian definitions of identification "confusing," with the confusion finally broken only by the clarity of Lacan's explication in 1949, with his presentation of his "mirror-stage theory" of the formation of the *moi* as the "unconscious subject of identifications" to the sixteenth International Congress of Psychoanalysis at Zurich.[78]

I have already presented to my readers Ragland-Sullivan's depiction of how the *je* part/aspect of the self, as theorized by Lacan, "translates" the unconscious imagery of the *moi*'s mirror-identifications with the parental care-giver into the "symbolic" realm of social rules and cultural conventions through language. I can now proceed with Ragland-Sullivan's further assertion about the "speaking *je*"— whose phraseology she had borrowed from "the Lacanian clinician James Glogowski"—that "after the literal (*je*) meaning of a statement has been completed, a second (*moi*) meaning or intentional pressure . . . remains in the listener's mind."[79]

It is this last Lacanian statement from Ragland-Sullivan that enables me to integrate, within this chapter's thematic of the social construction of the self, all those strands of the social scientific questions of meaning and power discussed in the last two chapters. What Ragland-Sullivan (following Glogowski) had characterized as the "literal (*je*) meaning of a statement" is precisely what, in chapter 1, I have identified as *semantic* meaning—that relationship between signs and their objects as Charles Morris had defined it in 1938, following Peirce's guidelines— whereas that "second (*moi*) meaning or intentional pressure" corresponds precisely to *pragmatic* meaning—that relationship between signs and their users that Morris had defined in 1938 and that I had, in my last two chapters, traced to its source in the *puissance* of social cooperation.[80]

Furthermore, as the sociologist-of-knowledge Karl Mannheim seemed to be aware when in his essay "Toward a Theory of Culture" he had followed Durkheim's usage of the term *institutions*, that Durkheimian term—corresponding in Ragland-Sullivan's Lacanian terms to those "rules and cultural conventions" of the *je* "subject of language"—belongs with the Peircean tradition's level of *semantics*. If, as Durkheim had stated in *The Rules of Sociological Method*, his project of sociology entailed the study of the "evolution" of such "institutionalized" semantic signifiers, such sociocultural evolution would be powered by that deeper process of the pragmatics of Ragland-Sullivan's "second (*moi*) meaning or intentional pressure": how the cooperative forms of a society create those "primary identifications" (*moi*) of its individual personalities would determine the institutional forms that such a society's linguistic interactions (of the "speaking *je*") structure and preserve.[81]

Since, as Mestrovic had averred in his critique of the sociology of Giddens, it is through Parsons's reading of Durkheim that contemporary sociologists are aware of Durkheim's formulations, I should, to ensure against misunderstanding of my equation of Peircean pragmatics with the Durkheimian theme of internalization, restate this equation by reference to Parsons's use of the term in his 1968 essay "Cooley and the Problem of Internalization," where Parsons had argued that

> the concept of internalization, which we have seen, is the same thing as the "incorporation of personality components in social systems," may be consid-

ered one of the three foci from which modern sociological theory emerged. The second focus, which concerns the cultural sphere, is usually referred to as the concept of institutionalization. . . . Institutionalization has to do above all with the values, norms and beliefs—in short, the normative structures—which form the content of the culture, but which also enter into social systems. The third focus comprises the core of sociological theory: the task of explaining the integration—or lack of integration—of cultural and social components in the structure of social systems as such.[82]

Of Parsons's "three foci" of "modern sociological theory," it is only the study of "institutionalization" with its focus upon the "content of the culture" that corresponds to the dimension of what Morris had in 1938 called *semantics*. The other two foci—internalization and social integration—dealing, as they do, with that "intentional pressure" that Ragland-Sullivan's Lacan had seen exerted by society's cooperative forms (such as the father-mother-me cooperative form of the family) upon the *moi* base of individual identity, correspond to that Peirce-Morris definition of *pragmatics* as the study of the relationship between (cultural) signs and their users.[83]

If in the next chapter I seem to turn my back upon the observational level of the individual's subjective semantics, to focus instead on theorizing about the pragmatic codes—what Ragland-Sullivan had called "*je* codes"—that underlie the social construction of that individual's personal identity, it is not out of any personal preference on my part for what the Weberian sociologist Dennis Wrong has called the "oversocialized conception of man," but rather because of my scientific realist methodology of moving to a theoretical depth beyond observation, in order to be better able to explain observed complexity. As the contemporary German sociologist Niklas Luhmann said about such scientific methodology of "levels":

> We can say that disorder at one level may be seen as order at another without confronting the paradox of saying that disorder is order. This expedient may be used whenever unavoidable.[84]

Such a need for the theoretical explication of the pragmatics of the social coding of semantic meaning had also been seen by that sociological theorist of globalization Roland Robertson when he maintained that

> one of the major lacunae in discussions of culture has been not merely the problem of the ways in which relationships between culture and social structure, on the one hand, and between culture and what is nowadays called agency, on the other, *vary* empirically, but also the issue of variation in the manner in which individuals and collectivities are constrained by deep meta-cultural codes to connect (or try to keep separate) culture and social structure and culture and action.[85]

My quest, within the next chapter of this book, for what Robertson had called "deep metacultural codes" will situate the pragmatics of globalization at the conceptual "height" of a sufficiently abstract level, so as to enable a synoptic view of global history without having to risk confusion in the surface details of the semantics of agency and institutionalization. And, according to Luhmann, the comprehension of history in such *longue duree*, requires just such abstraction:

> The prevailing opinion among historians is that the requirements of theory and concrete historical facts will never meet. In my view, however, it is a lack of good theory, not something intrinsic about sociology, which has prevented convincing sociological research on the nature of historical development. Sociologists simply are not familiar with historical facts. Nor are their theories very well attuned to the historical transformations of societies; their theoretical frameworks are too simple for that. Contemporary sociological theories are not, in this view, sufficiently abstract to allow the kind of complex research design that historical research demands.[86]

Having now, through the theoretical legacies of Mead and Lacan, theoretically "deconstructed" sociology's *semantics* of individual agency, it is to that "sufficiently abstract" theory of the Peircean *pragmatics* of globalization that I must turn.

Notes

1. Habermas, *The Theory of Communicative Action*, 2:1.

2. Habermas, *The Theory of Communicative Action*, 2:7.

3. Habermas, *The Theory of Communicative Action*, 2:3-4.

4. Kelly Oliver, *Subjectivity without Subjects: From Abject Fathers to Desiring Mothers* (Lanham, Md.: Rowman & Littlefield, 1998), 111.

5. Habermas, *The Philosophical Discourse of Modernity* (Cambridge, Mass.: MIT Press, 1987), 55-59.

6. Kusch, *Psychologism*, 257, cites Max Scheler's 1924 "Probleme einer Sociologie des Wissens," in Scheler's *Gesammelte Werke*, vol. 6 (Berne: Francke, 1980), 58. For Scheler's accusation against Durkheim of "sociologism," see Dennis Hume Wrong, *The Oversocialized Conception of Man* (New Brunswick, N.J.: Transaction, 1999). Adriaansens, *Talcott Parsons*, 164-75, contains detailed analyses by Martindale, Dahrendorf, and Mills of the criticism of the move by Parsons to Durkheim's "social realism" in his 1951 publication, *The Social System*.

7. Adriaansens, *Talcott Parsons*, 166.

8. Max Black, ed., *The Social Theories of Talcott Parsons: A Critical Examination* (Englewood Cliffs, N.J.: Prentice-Hall, 1961), 268; Stephen P. Savage, *The Theories of Talcott Parsons* (New York: St. Martin's Press, 1981), 90; Bruce Mayhew, "Structuralism vs. Individualism: Ideological and Other Obfuscations," *Social Forces* 59, no. 2 (December 1980) and no. 3 (March 1981); Stanislav Andreski, *Social Science as Sorcery* (London:

Deutsch, 1972); Roland Robertson and Bryan Turner, "Talcott Parsons and Modern Social Theory," *Theory, Culture, and Society* 5 (1989): 539.

9. Talcott Parsons, "Cooley and the Problem of Internalization," in *Cooley and Sociological Analysis*, ed. Albert J. Reiss, Jr. (Ann Arbor: University of Michigan Press, 1968), 56.

10. John Graves, *The Conceptual Foundations of Relativity Theory* (Cambridge, Mass.: MIT Press, 1971), 7. Mario Bunge, *The Philosophy of Physics* (Boston: Reidel, 1973), 85-86, also lists these same five points of "scientific" or "critical" realism.

11. Joseph W. Smith and Bryan Turner, "Constructing Social Theory and Constituting Society," *Theory, Culture, and Society* 3, no. 2 (1986): 127-28.

12. Graves, *The Conceptual Foundations*, 7-237.

13. Raziel Abelson, *Lawless Mind* (Philadelphia: Temple University Press, 1988), 11.

14. Jeremy Homes, *John Bowlby and Attachment Theory* (London: Routledge, 1993), 137, citing Donald W. Winnicott, *The Maturational Process and the Facilitating Environment* (London: Hogarth, 1965).

15. Peter L. Rudnytsky, *The Psychoanalytic Vocation: Rank, Winnicott, and the Legacy of Freud* (New Haven, Conn.: Yale University Press, 1991), 165 (italics in original), citing D. W. Winnicott, *Through Paediatrics to Psycho-Analysis* (New York: Basic Books, 1975), 99; Andre Green, *On Private Madness* (London: Hogarth Press, 1986), 50; D. A. Luepnitz, *The Family Interpreted: Feminist Theory in Clinical Practice* (New York: Basic Books, 1988), 194.

16. Rudnytsky, *The Psychoanalytic Vocation*, 165.

17. Mario Bunge, "Phenomenological Theories," in *The Critical Approach to Science and Philosophy*, ed. Mario Bunge (London: Collier-MacMillan, 1964), 234-54.

18. Peter Berger, *Invitation to Sociology* (Garden City, N.Y.: Doubleday, 1963), 1.

19. Mary Douglas, ed., *Rules and Meanings: The Anthropology of Everyday Knowledge* (Baltimore, Md.: Penguin, 1973), 15.

20. Marvin E. Olsen, *The Process of Social Organization* (New York: Holt, 1968), 25-26.

21. Levi-Strauss, *Tristes Tropiques*, 57-58.

22. Edwin R. Wallace, IV, *Freud and Anthropology: A History and Reappraisal* (New York: International Universities Press, 1983), 260 n. 1. Mestrovic (*Emile Durkheim and the Reformation of Sociology*, 98-99) goes further than Wallace, pointing out that not only Durkheim's *Elementary Forms*, but also his 1897 essay "Incest: the Nature and Origin of the Taboo," as well as Durkheim's "first preface to *L'Annee sociologique*" in 1897 and "subsequent issues" of this, "the only sociological journal at the time," had been cited by Freud in *Totem and Taboo*.

23. C. Fred Alford, *Melanie Klein and Critical Social Theory* (New Haven, Conn.: Yale University Press, 1989), 57-74. Alford refers for his definition of *methodological individualism* to May Brodbeck, "Methodological Individualisms: Definition and Reduction," in *The Philosophy of the Social Sciences*, ed. May Brodbeck (New York: MacMillan, 1968), 280-303.

24. Stephen A. Mitchell and Margaret Black, *Freud and Beyond: A History of Modern Psychoanalytical Thought* (New York: Basic Books, 1995), 91-113; Giddens, *Politics, Sociology, and Social Theory*, 130, 207, 235, 250, 257-58; Roy Schafer, *Aspects of Internalization* (New York: International Universities Press, 1968), 9, 30, 155, 159, 168, 228,

242; W. W. Meissner, *Internalization in Psychoanalysis* (New York: International Universities Press, 1981), 12.

25. Parsons, "Cooley and the Problem of Internalization," 65 (italics in original); Adriaansens, *Talcott Parsons*, 166; Schafer, *Aspects*, 9 n. 1, 30. In a critique of Cooley's theory of learning—which was to be echoed by the later accusation that Cooley's theory depicted humans as "oversocialized" passive conformists (Viktor Gekas and Michael L. Scwalbe, "Beyond the Looking-Glass Self: Social Structure and Efficacy-Based Self-Esteem," *Social Psychology Quarterly* 46 [1983]: 77-88)—Schafer had, in 1968, argued that "not everything that is learned, or not every aspect of what is learned, is taken over from the environment; one learns about oneself too."

26. Charles Horton Cooley, *Human Nature and the Social Order* (New York: Schocken, 1964 [1902]), 5, 182.

27. Cooley, *Human Nature*, 184.

28. Cooley, *Human Nature*, 184.

29. Charles Horton Cooley, *Social Organization* (New York: Schocken, 1962 [1909]), 5.

30. Cooley, *Social Organization*, 23 (italics added).

31. Parsons, *The Structure of Social Action,* 404; Parsons, *Sociological Theory and Modern Society*, 308; Grice, *Studies*, 26, 220.

32. Cooley, *Social Organization*, 121.

33. Charles Horton Cooley, *The Social Process* (Carbondale: Southern Illinois University Press, 1966 [1918]), 379.

34. Cooley, *The Social Process*, 39, 417.

35. Parsons, "Cooley," 66.

36. George Herbert Mead, "Introduction," in Cooley, *Human Nature*, xxx.

37. Parsons, "Cooley," 65.

38. Lewis Coser, *Masters of Sociological Thought: Ideas in Historical and Social Context* (San Diego, Calif.: Harcourt Brace Jovanovich, 1977), 329; Hans Joas, *G. H. Mead: A Contemporary Re-examination of His Thought* (Cambridge, Mass.: MIT Press, 1985); Ernst Tugendhat, *Self-Consciousness and Self-Determination* (Cambridge, Mass.: MIT Press, 1986), 219-62; Habermas, *The Theory*, 2:3-42.

39. Joas, *G. H. Mead*, 2.

40. George Herbert Mead, *Mind, Self, and Society: From the Standpoint of a Social Behaviorist*, ed. Charles Morris (Chicago: University of Chicago Press, 1934), 15; Charles Darwin, *The Expression of the Emotions in Man and Animals* (London: John Murray, 1872).

41. Mead, *Mind*, 74; Rescher, "The Ontology," 179 (italics added).

42. Mead, *Mind*, 75-76.

43. Mead, *Mind*, 79; Luhmann, "Modern Systems Theory," 178.

44. Mead, *Mind*, 154, 178.

45. Mead, *Mind*, 155.

46. Mead, *Mind*, 155.

47. Mead, *Mind*, 164.

48. Mead, *Mind*, 173.

49. Mead, *Mind*, 175.

50. Mead, *Mind*, 178.

51. Habermas, *The Theory*, 2:41.

52. Mead, *Mind*, 210 (italics in original).

53. Habermas, *The Theory*, 2:42.

54. Mead, *Mind*, 186, 273.

55. Anne Durand, "Lacan and Levi-Strauss," and Francoise Koehler, "Melanie Klein and Jacques Lacan," in *Reading Seminars I and II: Lacan's Return to Freud*, ed. Richard Feldstein, Bruce Fink, and Maire Jaanus (Albany: State University of New York Press, 1996), 98-108 and 111-17, respectively, present, to the nonspecialist in Lacan's theory, cogent summaries of the influences of psychoanalytic Object Relations thought and of Levi-Strauss's Structural Anthropology upon Lacan's thought.

56. Rita Kramer, *Maria Montessori: A Biography* (Reading, Mass.: Addison-Wesley, 1988), 59.

57. Lucien Malson, *Wolf Children and the Problem of Human Nature* (New York: Monthly Review Press, 1972), 83-84, 95.

58. Robertson, *Meaning*, 167; Smith and Turner, "Constructing Social Theory," 128.

59. Ellie Ragland-Sullivan, *Jacques Lacan and the Philosophy of Psychanalysis* (Urbana: University of Illinois Press, 1987), 25, 207, 317 n. 56, citing Lacan's student, Octave Mannoni, "Itard et son sauvage," in *Clefs pour l'imaginaire on l'Autre scene* (Paris: Editions du Seuil, 1969), 184-201.

60. Ragland-Sullivan, *Jacques Lacan*, 17. Rudnytsky (*The Psychoanalytical Vocation*, 71-83) rehashes all those charges of "linguistic bias" and a nonbiological neglect of the "environmental factors" impinging upon the organism made by anti-Lacan psychoanalysts within the American tradition of "ego psychology."

61. Ragland-Sullivan, *Jacques Lacan*, 315 n. 33.

62. Ragland-Sullivan, *Jacques Lacan*, x, 219, 318 nn. 62 and 64.

63. Judith Feher Gurewich, "The Lacanian Clinical Field: Series Overview," Maud Mannoni, in *Separation and Creativity: Refinding the Lost Language of Childhood* (New York: Other Press, 1999), xv-xvi.

64. Ragland-Sullivan, *Jacques Lacan*, ix-x.

65. Ragland-Sullivan, *Jacques Lacan*, 18.

66. Ragland-Sullivan, *Jacques Lacan*, 19-32.

67. Ragland-Sullivan, *Jacques Lacan*, 18 (italics in original).

68. Rudnytsky, *The Psychoanalytic Vocation*, 82-83.

69. Fredric Jameson, "Imaginary and Symbolic in Lacan: Marxism, Psychoanalytic Criticism, and the Problem of the Subject," *Yale French Studies* 55/56 (1977), 351.

70. Ragland-Sullivan, *Jacques Lacan*, 59; Mead, *Mind*, 210. Theodore Millon, "The Borderline Personality: A Psychosocial Epidemic," 200-203, provides the insight about the statistical correlation between the increase in the number of dyadic mother-child relationships in contemporary America's fatherless families and the corresponding increase in the number of juvenile cases of "borderline personality disorder" exhibiting poor impulse control.

71. Ragland-Sullivan, *Jacques Lacan*, xxi, 103; Habermas, *The Theory*, 2:41.

72. Rudnytsky, *The Psychoanalytic Vocation*, 82-83; Julia Kristeva, *Soleil noir: Depression et melancolie* (Paris: Gallimard, 1987); Ragland-Sullivan, *Jacques Lacan*, 103, 130-195, 258. In a process that I can only see as a "Freudian slip," occasioned by her ambivalent anxiety toward overtly identifying Lacan as a Peircean philosopher as I do—or else by her modesty in making assertions about Peirce in the face of the same absence of an organized book-form presentation of his writings that had also stymied Durkheim,

among others—Ragland-Sullivan ended her discussion of Lacan's use of the concepts of *metaphor* and *metonymy* (p. 258) by overtly alluding to Peirce's *icons*, but without ever mentioning the name Peirce in her book's index, thereby leaving out of her index one of the two founders of that theory of signs—the other being Saussure—that she discussed in her chapter 4, "The Relationship of Sense and Sign." In fairness to Ragland-Sullivan's lack of recognition of the Peircean roots of Lacan's theory of cognition, I should point out the complaint made by John Lechte, in his *Fifty Contemporary Thinkers: From Structuralism to Postmodernity* (London: Routledge, 1994), 145, that "although Peirce published more than ten thousand printed pages, he never published a book-length study—there is, in sum, no systematic and definitive Peircean document on the nature of signs; only successive re-workings which repeat as much as innovate."

73. Ragland-Sullivan, *Jacques Lacan*, 3, 159-62, 203-14, 258.

74. Ragland-Sullivan, *Jacques Lacan*, xxi, 203. Ragland-Sullivan narrated how "from 1946 onward Lacan developed distinctions among categories that he named the Imaginary, the Symbolic and the Real" (130). Later, in 1996, Ragland-Sullivan ("An Overview of the Real, with Examples from Seminar I," in Feldstein, Fink, and Jaanus, *Reading Seminars I and II*, 192-93) describes how in Lacan's "third period"—lasting from 1974 until his death in 1981—"he had gradually differentiated one order from the other" in his "tripartition of the symbolic, the imaginary and the real . . . those elementary categories without which we would be incapable of distinguishing anything within our experience." Despite this Lacanian preference for throwing Peirce's three categories out of Peirce's numbered order—by refusing to place Lacan's "Real," as Peirce's category of "Secondness," *between* the "Imaginary" and the "Symbolic"—and regardless of whether Lacan had fully developed his "tripartite" theory of cognition in his first phase of the 1950s or later, I still find it remarkable (or, to use a Freudian phrase, "uncanny") that one French psychoanalyst beginning from within the semiological tradition of Saussure had, within his lifetime, recapitulated the theoretical landmarks of *three* notable theorists within the tradition of American Pragmatism: Peirce's triadic phenomenology, Cooley's "looking glass" concept of the origin of the self, *and* Mead's "I/me" dynamics of the "social self"!

75. Giddens, *Politics, Sociology, and Social Theory*, 130, 207, 213; Lukes, *Emile Durkheim*, 131, citing Durkheim, *Moral Education*, 98. Whitney Pope, in his *Durkheim's Suicide: A Classic Analyzed* (Chicago: University of Chicago Press, 1976), 195, citing Durkheim, *Suicide*, 212, 258, 287, 320, 335, argues that Durkheim "employs a primitive notion of internalization but does not contain an adequate account of the social psychology of internalization."

76. Meissner, *Internalization in Psychoanalysis*, 12, citing T. Parsons and E. A. Shils, eds., *Toward a General Theory of Action* (New York: Harper & Row, 1962); Mestrovic, *Anthony Giddens*, 46; Mestrovic, *Emile Durkheim and the Reformation of Sociology*, 98-116.

77. Everett K. Wilson, editor's introduction to Durkheim's *Moral Education*, xi, xxiv; Meissner, *Internalization in Psychoanalysis*, 11; Lukes, *Emile Durkheim*, 305-13.

78. Ragland-Sullivan, *Jacques Lacan*, 17-18, 32-33, 42.

79. Ragland-Sullivan, *Jacques Lacan*, 59, 84.

80. Morris, *Foundations*, 21-43.

81. Karl Mannheim, *Structures of Thinking* (London: Routledge & Kegan Paul, 1982), 231; Durkheim, *The Rules*, 156.

82. Parsons, "Cooley," 58; Mestrovic, *Anthony Giddens*, 46-48.

83. Ragland-Sullivan, *Jacques Lacan*, 17-18, 59, 84.

84. Luhmann, "The Evolutionary Differentiation," 126.

85. Roland Robertson, "The Sociological Significance of Culture: Some General Considerations," *Theory, Culture, and Society* 6 (1988), 5 (italics in original).

86. Luhmann, "The Evolutionary Differentiation," 112.

My tendency over the years has, I think, been to be concerned less with equilibrium and more with the parent concept of system. Here, especially since the development of the "four-function paradigm"—about 1953—the defining of systems and subsystems, their relations and boundaries, has been a continual and increasingly important concern. . . . The problem of the conditions under which relationships among subsystems can be said to be in equilibrium or not is a further and independently complicated problem.
—Talcott Parsons, "Commentary," in *Institutions and
Social Exchange: The Sociologies of Talcott Parsons and
George C. Homans*, eds. Herman Turk and Richard L. Simpson.
(New York: Appleton-Century-Crofts, 1971), 382.

Some remarks on the evolution of subjectivity in the Western tradition from the medieval period to the present. . . . In contrast to the Occidental subject of scientific civilization, the medieval spiritual subject was hardly differentiated in consciousness from the hierarchical locus it occupied in a feudal and theocentric world order. Communal religious feeling provided the cement of social awareness, while outward, objective concentration on meeting the ritual obligations of this life precluded any sense of interiority.
—Ellie Ragland-Sullivan, "What Is I?" in *Jacques Lacan*, 7.

First there was the egotistical stage when man arbitrarily imagined perfection, now is the idistical stage when he observes it. Hereafter must be the more glorious tuistical stage when he shall be in communion with her. And this is exactly what, step by step, we are coming to.
—Charles S. Peirce, "The Place of Our Age in the History of
Civilization," in *Writings of Charles S. Peirce: A Chronological
Edition*, Volume I: 1857-1866, eds. Max H. Fisch et al.
(Bloomington: Indiana University Press, 1982), 113.

CHAPTER 4

Formal System: The Autopoietic Evolution of Pragmatic (Interpretant) Codes

"Who now reads Spencer?" had been the question—quoted from Crane Brinton's study of English political thought in the nineteenth century—that Talcott Parsons had used to introduce his 1937 book, *The Structure of Social Action*. "Talcott Parsons in his advancing years," came the ironic answer proposed by Ronald Fletcher in his 1974 essay, "Evolutionary and Developmental Sociology." The burden of Fletcher's message was that sociology's fragmentation into various "schools" or "types" stemmed from its ambivalence toward the idea of evolution. Evolution, argued Fletcher, was implicit in the formulation of social theory.

> The first point worth direct statement is that *no* sociologist has ever conceived a human society as a *"static"* system. Everyone from Comte to Radcliffe-Brown and beyond (i.e., in both sociology and anthropology), has thought of "statics" and "dynamics" as two aspects of sociological analysis, *not* two subject-matters.[1]

Anthropologist Margaret Mead might have agreed, when she said:

> My interest in evolution was reawakened in 1948, when I was asked to review *Touchstone for Ethics* (by Thomas Henry Huxley and Julian S. Huxley), and, while I was doing so, also took time to reread *The Origin of Species* (by Charles Darwin). . . . I went back to my notes on Franz Boas' lectures, and I found that in these lectures, so many of which were devoted to clearing away the stupid underbrush of nineteenth-century arguments based on ethnocentric superiority or insistence on identifying evolution as a particular form of

progress, a sufficient ground plan had been worked out for taking up the discussion of cultural evolution.[2]

The new introduction written by the distinguished philosopher of science Stephen Toulmin to the 1999 edition of Margaret Mead's 1957 Terry Lectures given at Yale University, *Continuities in Cultural Evolution*, points out that while in Mead's case, her collaboration with Gregory Bateson—whose father, William, had been one of the founders of twentieth-century biological genetics—had "put her in touch with the most lively and original circles of evolutionary biologists and psycholinguists in her time," it had been the transformation by the German *litterateur* Johann Gottfried Herder of "the Great Chain of Being" from a medieval idea of timeless essences "into an historical account of successive phases or cultures" that

> was to dominate nineteenth-century social philosophy via Hegel and Marx, to Durkheim and Weber. Even today sociologists and historians, writing about *social and cultural evolution* with the experience of Europe in mind, still think of History as tracing out a standard sequence—ancient, medieval, early modern, modern, and contemporary—in turn. But Herder's historical vision at once raised questions about Progress: Are the later phases in this sequence *improvements* on earlier ones? By what standards can Modernity (say) be considered *better than* Antiquity? In posing questions of this kind, Auguste Comte in France and Herbert Spencer in England launched academic sociology on a "progressivist" research program.[3]

Toulmin's question about the criteria for progress and direction in the conceptualization of cultural evolution may have been the reason that, in 1951— three years after the Boasian anthropologist Margaret Mead had "reawakened" her "interest in evolution"—Auguste Comte's early bifurcation of sociology into "statics" and "dynamics" had continued to dog the social theory of Talcott Parsons. In *The Social System* Parsons saw "the problem of the theory of change" as arising simply from a lack of knowledge: "A general theory of the processes of change of social systems is not possible in the present state of knowledge."[4]

In the third edition of *Sociological Theory: Its Nature and Growth* in 1967, Nicholas S. Timasheff pointed out that the insistence by Parsons in 1951 that the development of a full and systematic theory of social systems had necessarily to *precede* the formulation of any adequate theory of social change, had left such a strong imprint on his readers that to his critics Parsons had continued to be seen as the champion of a "static" anti-change theory of society *despite* his later writings on evolution. Thus in *The Evolution of Societies*, published in 1977 as a combined and edited version of two (1966 and 1971) of Parsons's more recent works, editor Jackson Toby had begun by acknowledging the seeming break that Parsons's seemingly sudden concern with evolution had presented to many of his readers:

Parsons' interest in societal evolution may have surprised some sociologists because it seems on first thought unrelated to his previous intellectual preoccupations. Actually it represents a return in a more sophisticated form to a problem that engaged him as a young man.[5]

That Toby had been technically correct in his sequential depiction of that Radcliffe-Brown-influenced static-synchronic functionalism of Parsons in *The Social System* of 1951 as a break between two diachronic-evolutionist phases in Parsons—as against the view of Parsons's critics, such as Ronald Fletcher, who had viewed Parsons post-1964 evolutionism as a late evolutionist irruption into his long-standing anti-evolutionism—can still be easily verified by reading a little further beyond that famous question about reading Spencer quoted by Parsons in 1937. For, referring to that British school of thought to which Herbert Spencer had claimed to belong, Parsons had said of that "positivistic-utilitarian tradition": "The thesis of this study will be that it is the victim of the vengeance of the jealous god, Evolution, in this case the evolution of scientific theory."[6]

What Parsons had been saying in those first three pages of his 1937 book on social action, was that Spencer's theory had—as Karl Popper would later put it—been "falsified." Popper's 1972 book *Objective Knowledge: An Evolutionary Approach* suggested that by the research testing procedures of science, an evolutionary struggle for survival had been unleashed on what he called the "Third World"—the realm of ideas, including scientific theories, which went extinct like biological organisms when they were falsified—and through a process of downward causation, this evolutionary process at the level of cultural artifacts then exerted deterministic pressures upon the "Second World" of subjective experiences, feelings, emotions, and consciousness and the "First World" of physical objects.[7]

"In a weak moment Parsons called himself a cultural determinist," said Toby of Parsons, and such a label could—despite the demurrals of Margaret Archer, who criticizes Parsons for "downward causation"—also be applied to Popper's 1972 Three Worlds epistemology. In his 1974 article "Evolutionary Epistemology," Donald Campbell proceeded to substitute a general model of evolutionary selection, which included both organic and cultural evolution within the same general principles of variation, selection, and evolutionary accumulation of selected variations, for Popper's downward causation from ideas to physical objects. Calling this "Campbell's Principle," W. H. Durham used it in 1991 to define his concept of "coevolution" between genes and culture.[8]

So Parsons's 1937 idea of the "evolution of scientific theories," which, according to him, had selected against Spencer's theory of evolution, had by the 1990s itself evolved, by using Campbell's Principle, into the science of memetics, which took its name from a chapter in Richard Dawkins's 1976 book *The Selfish Gene*, in which Dawkins introduced the concept of the *meme*, "a culturally transmitted unit of information analogous to the gene."[9]

We sociologists are indeed fortunate to be able to see in this very young science of memetics—barely emerging at the beginning of the twenty-first century—a perfect mirror of the struggles for conceptual definition that have gone
on for more than a century in the established social sciences, in the comprehension of cultural evolution. For, as Agner Fog argued in 1999:

> The paradigm of meme theory is only gradually crystallizing into a rigorous
> science. Most of the publications are in the popular science genre with no ex-
> act definitions or strict formalism. Memetics will probably continue to be a
> soft science. Heyes and Plotkin have used cognitive psychology and brain neu-
> rology to argue that information is being transformed while stored in human
> memory and may be altered under the influence of later events. This leads
> them to argue that memes cannot be distinct, faithful copies of particulate in-
> formation-bits, but blending and ever changing clusters of information.[10]

But *that* particular problem of the difficulty of defining "distinct, particulate information-bits" similar to cells or organismically self-contained units in biology, had already been pointed out by Auguste Comte in the middle of the nineteenth century: In volume 2 of his *Systeme de Politique Positive*—titled *Statique
Sociale*—Comte had already discussed, more than a hundred years before
Memetics, the problem of seeking such a biological analogue of discrete self-contained units in society, in that social "units," unlike biological organisms, tend to
lack clear material boundaries (such as animal skins) and are integrated only by
definitionally vague spiritual ties like language or religion![11]

The problem with *Memetics*, argues Fog, is that "the analogy with biology is
taken too far. . . . The products of cultural evolution or conceptual evolution cannot be systematized into distinct classes and it is impossible to make a strict evolutionary taxonomy of cultures."[12] Such a problem, says Stephen Toulmin, had
been acutely perceived by Margaret Mead in 1957 when she had attempted to address the problem of the definition of cultural "units" in her Terry Lectures:

> When she set out to define the "units" of cultural micro-evolution, for in-
> stance, these *units* were not just abstract theoretical notions. . . . She did not
> seek to develop a systematic classification of all cultural groups, or set out—
> like Balzac—to be the "Linnaeus" of Society or Culture. On the contrary, she
> knew that the bonds which unite members of any social "unit" have a political
> as well as a taxonomic point. Cultural and social groups are defined in terms
> of their shared ideals or ambitions: to accept this definition is implicitly to en-
> dorse their ambitions.[13]

And it is this problem—of having to preserve the biological connotation of
adaptive selection for fear of otherwise losing the meaning of "evolution" altogether, while taking care to avoid taking the analogy with biology too far in that

direction of "biologizing" the study of sociocultural evolution into artificially rigid, gene-like units—that we can see in the emergence in June 1964 of what Jackson Toby had called the "more sophisticated form" of evolutionism (as compared to his 1937, vaguely defined notion of the "evolution of scientific theory") of Talcott Parsons's essay "Evolutionary Universals in Society" in the *American Sociological Review*. Parsons's definition of "an evolutionary universal" clearly echoes the biological, Darwinian concept of adaptation:

> An evolutionary universal is a complex of structures and associated processes the development of which so increases the long-run adaptive capacity of living systems in a given class that only systems that develop the complex can attain higher levels of general adaptive capacity.[14]

But, as Nicholas Timasheff was to emphasize, even while echoing biological Darwinism with his concept of "general adaptive capacity," Parsons had been careful to clearly delineate the difference between his concept of *social* evolution from the Darwinian variety in biology:

> This formulation derives from the principles of natural selection, but in *social* evolution, Parsons stresses, "disadvantaged" systems are not necessarily "condemned to extinction."[15]

This lack of a determined process of "extinction" in Parsonsian social evolution follows by rigorous logic the insight of Auguste Comte earlier, and of the critics of memetics later, of the lack of a skin-like boundary to social units: if the units of social culture cannot be "distinct . . . particulate bits . . . but blending and ever changing clusters of information," it follows logically that they do not die or go extinct, all at once, as the discrete skin-enclosed biological units called organisms do, but form and re-form in myriads of kaleidoscopic formations.[16]

In that 1964 breakthrough to what Toby called his "more sophisticated form" of evolutionism, Parsons had displayed an array of "evolutionary universals" that included religion, language, social organization, and technology, supplemented in the modern era by the more evolved universals of bureaucracy, the money economy, and the growth of a general legal order. This cautious delineation of social evolution vis-à-vis the better-understood mechanisms of biological evolution was seen by Parsons as "tentative":

> Parsons notes the tentative nature of this depiction of evolutionary universals, especially with respect to the more recent period of human history. But his essay, and most notably the conception of the generalized adaptive capacity of social systems, is an important illustration of the current vogue of moderate evolutionism.[17]

All very well, Parsons's critic Ronald Fletcher would protest, but such a moderate evolutionist transcendence of social Darwinism had already been formulated earlier, before Parsons, with the evolutionary theory of the late nineteenth-century British liberal L. T. Hobhouse, whose book *Development and Purpose* had emphasized—in contrast to the blind, genetically adaptive struggle of biological organisms—the transforming and purposive teleology of mind and knowledge. According to Fletcher, Parsons had added absolutely nothing to Hobhouse's vision of a non-Darwinian process of social evolution.[18]

Such an absolutist claim, by Fletcher, to Hobhouse's priority in conceiving a non-Darwinist theory of social evolution is hard to substantiate: Darwin's contemporary T. H. Huxley had emphasized the difference between human ethics and animal struggle in that book titled *Touchstone for Ethics* that Margaret Mead was to read in 1948, and the founder of Pragmatism, C. S. Peirce, had in 1892 contrasted "the blind wasteful mechanisms of Darwinian natural selection "with the "agapistic evolution driven by purpose or love." And in 1999, without reference to either Hobhouse or Parsons—or Huxley or Peirce, for that matter—Agner Fog still finds arguments similar to those given by critics of excessive biologizing tendencies in the human sciences, from Huxley to Parsons, by those who find sociobiology and memetics taking the "analogy with biology" too far, thereby making their theories "vulnerable to criticism." Such critics of current memetics argue "that humans are intelligent and goal-seeking beings which are more influenced by logical, true, informative, problem-solving, economic, and well-organized ideas."[19]

Parsons had himself acknowledged, in his review of Hobhouse's *Sociology and Philosophy: A Centenary Collection of Essays and Articles*, having been influenced by Hobhouse's ideas through his teacher, Professor Ginsberg, at the London School of Economics: That influence had only been eclipsed, said Parsons, by the even greater impact that Hobhouse's two non-English contemporaries Max Weber and Emile Durkheim had had on him. In contrast to these latter two, Parsons had argued, what Hobhouse "seems to be missing is the analytically independent category of *cultural system*."[20]

Contrary to Fletcher, then, I can only see advantages in my crafting a Pragmaticist theory of cultural evolution, that will unite the insights of Durkheim's sociology with Peirce's philosophy—a project that Durkheim had himself begun in his 1913-14 lectures series "Pragmatism and Sociology"—of following the paper trail of Parsons's voluminous writings spanning four decades between 1937 and 1977.

System, Evolution, and the Habits of Knowledge

What the layman might recognize as "Murphy's Law"—the popular saying that "if anything can go wrong, it will"—was reputedly created by an engineer named

Murphy in the 1940s to characterize the degeneration of the content of communication, as it filtered downwards in a machine factory from the engineer's blueprint to the actual production floor, a corruption of the content of communication
that often led workers to screw in parts in a manner that had not been intended (or
often even foreseen—which accounts for the fatalistic phrasing of Murphy's
"Law") by the engineer in creating his blueprint. Such a corruptibility of the content of communication between social actors was also behind what Niklas Luhmann characterized as the "infinity problem" of the "double contingency" of
communicational perspectives, a problem that Luhmann had seen as having been
responsible for pushing Parsons away from his earlier Weberian individualism
toward the functional analysis of Durkheim's systemic vision of social interactions. But according to Charles Camic's analysis of Parsons's early essays, such
an approach toward Durkheim's thought by Parsons had emerged neither suddenly nor fully formed (like the birth of Athena from the head of Zeus) in Parsons's publication of *The Social System* in 1951 but had been already visible even
in the 1937 writing of Parsons's "Weberian" book, *The Structure of Social Action*,
where Parsons's *earlier* forecast of a "Marshall-Pareto-Weber 'convergence'" had
actually crystallized instead into "the first of several early variants of the Mar-
shall-Pareto-Durkheim-Weber convergence thesis."[21]

Camic attributes that growing appreciation by Parsons for Durkheim's scientific realism to "his encounter with Harvard's reigning authorities on the nature
and method of (natural) science, the philosopher Alfred North Whitehead and the
biochemist Lawrence J. Henderson. Prior to this point the philosophy of science
occupied little of Parsons's attention."[22]

Indeed, Whitehead's influence can be readily seen in Parsons's 1937 critique
of Weber's ideal types as "fictional" and his characterization of his own theory of
action as being within Whitehead's epistemological lineage of "analytical realism."[23] Of Max Weber's approach, Parsons had also said in 1937 that

> his "pluralism" tends, by hypostatization of ideal types, to break up, in a sense
> not inherent in analysis as such, the organic unity both of concrete historical
> individuals and of the historic process. In its reification phase it issues in what
> may be called a "mosaic" theory of culture and society, conceiving them to be
> made up of disparate atoms.[24]

But it had also been in that 1937 book on social action that Parsons had
charged Durkheim with having shifted his epistemological position from an earlier positivism in 1893 in *The Division of Labor* to a later idealism in 1912 in *The
Elementary Forms*—a charge that, according to Warren Schmaus, only betrays
Parsons's continuing incomprehension of Durkheim's realist methodology of science.[25] If Parsons had not really comprehended Durkheim's scientific realism in
1937, it is then not really surprising that, although he had cited Lawrence Henderson's book *Pareto's General Sociology* in his 1937 book (in his presentation of

Vilfredo Pareto's methodology), it would not be before 1970—i.e., after he had, in 1951, published his overtly "Durkheimian" book, *The Social System*—that Parsons would give evidence of having connected Henderson's interest in Pareto with his interest in the father of experimental medicine, Claude Bernard—who had, according to Schmaus, also extensively influenced Durkheim's view of scientific method[26]—to move up an "evolutionary step" conceptually, i.e., from having conceived of "system," as he had in 1937, in a "physico-chemical" manner, to his later focus on its biological connotations:

> Closely related to this was the conception of "system." . . . Henderson's own primary model, which he explicated at some length in *Pareto's General Sociology*, was the physico-chemical system. He related this, however, to biological systems. He was a great admirer of Claude Bernard and wrote a foreword to the English translation of the latter's *Experimental Medicine*. The central idea here was that of the "internal environment" and its stability. This connected closely with the idea of W. B. Cannon of homeostatic stabilization of physiological processes and also with the residues of my own exposure to biology.[27]

But by then Parsons had tied the concept of "system" to that of "function":

> I wish to argue that the concept function is central to the understanding of all living systems. . . . This proposition is based upon a dual consideration. First, as has been clear at least since the great contributions of Bernard and Cannon, a living system is one which maintains a pattern of organization and functioning which is both different from and in some respects *more stable* than its environment. Secondly, the maintenance of this specific and relatively stable pattern occurs not through total isolation or insulation from the environment but through continual processes of interchange with it. In this sense, all living systems are "open" systems.[28]

But the ensuing problem for later American sociological theory stemmed precisely from the fact that those two concepts, of "open system" and of "function," which Parsons had blithely connected, may not have been so mutually compatible. For, mathematically, as the systems theorist Mihajlo Mesarovic had already clarified in 1964, "closed systems" are *by definition* those that enable only "one-to-one relations" that "don't result in innovations," while "open systems" are all those that exclude such closed, one-to-one relations. And according to the mathematical geographer Peter Gould, while the mathematical definition of *function* is slightly broader than that of Mesarovic's *closed system*—in that it enables a graphic mapping of not only one independent (x) variable but also many such x-variables to one dependent (y) variable in the mathematical analysis of multiple regression—it still excludes the "many-to-many relations" of Mesarovic's "open systems," because:

when every X in a set is connected to a Y, and *only* one Y . . . we have what a mathematician calls a *function*, and that . . . is the sort of mechanical coupling that characterizes the world of physical things. Functions always take one, or perhaps many, Xs and connect them with just one Y. This is why a mathematician calls them a one-to-one, or a many-to-one *mapping*. . . . But even in the case of our quadratic, let alone more complicated functions, we saw that we could not "get back," because our Ys were not connected one-to-one (or many-to-one) with our Xs. A mathematician would say that going from Y to X we have a one-to-many *mapping*. . . . So a mapping is a much less constrained way of connecting things together than a function, and there is no reason why we cannot go all the way and have a many-to-many mapping. So we see that . . . all functions are mappings, but not *vice versa* . . . all functions are mappings are relations, but not *vice versa*.[29]

Once we comprehend this "many-to-many relation" (between variables in an open system) we realize, as Parsons did not, that the concept of "system"—defined by the mathematical systems theory of Mesarovic simply as "a relation among attributes of objects"—is really a *broader* concept than that of "function," and we can then more easily differentiate between the closed, nonevolutionary, one-to-one stability of relationships between variables within a salt crystal's form (for example) and the many-to-many, flexible evolution of variable relationships in social systems. But that concept of "function" had also been used by Durkheim in his *Rules of Sociological Method*, where he had explicitly separated it conceptually from the efficient cause of classical mechanics:

> *Therefore when one undertakes to explain a social phenomenon the efficient cause which produces it and the function it fulfils must be investigated separately.* We use the word 'function' in preference to 'end' or 'goal' precisely because social phenomena generally do not exist for the usefulness of the results they produce. We must determine whether there is a correspondence between the fact being considered and the general needs of the social organism, and in what this correspondence consists, without seeking to know whether it was intentional or not.[30]

Having proceeded from that definition of *function* to the assertion that "to the same effect there always corresponds the same cause,"[31] Durkheim too became the target of the accusation—made by Mike Gane in 1988—of having conceived of "function" as precisely such a one-to-one relationship between variables in a closed system:

> Function and functional interdependence is a second level logic which seems to involve some elements of teleology, specific to the phenomena of living systems. And every sociologist knows Durkheim's basic rule: the unique parity of one cause and one effect. Against Mill he argues that the same phenom-

enon cannot be the product of more than one cause or of different causes at different times. The relation is absolute and invariable.[32]

To Gane's charge against Durkheim—of having insisted that sociological method focus only upon one-to-one relationships between variables within social systems—Schmaus replies that Durkheim's "denial of a plurality of effects, like his denial of the plurality of causes, was a necessary consequence of his realism," a response that I find credible as I read Durkheim's assertion in *The Rules of Sociological Method* that "a relationship of causality can in fact only be established between two given facts. But this tendency . . . is not something that is given. It is only postulated as a mental construct according to the effects attributed to it."[33] As I regularly explain such scientific realism in my own homespun example to my students: Suppose they were to find themselves slipping and sliding, as they walked into my classroom, on a yellowish pool of liquid. They could—at the level of observation—suggest a many-to-many relationship between many observable causes of that pool of liquid being there (rain leakage, soda spillage, baby's urine, etc.) and the many different effects (such as slipping, sliding, or splashing) that this liquid-pool might have upon each student's behavior. Thus, we could have a many-to-many mapping of our observed (or potentially observable) variables: a list of many possible independent variables or (x's: leaking roof, soda-spilling, baby urinating, etc.), mapped against a similar list of many dependent variables or (y's: John slipped and fell, Mary slid but maintained her balance, Jim stamped his foot on the yellowish pool, splashing Tom, etc.). But at the ultimately explanatory level of scientific realist "theoretical entities" (which Durkheim, writing before the age of electron microscopes, would have called "mental constructs"), regardless of whether the yellow liquid had really been rain-water leaking through a dirty ceiling, or spilled soda or baby's urine, its unique property of fluidity (i.e., its "slipperiness/slidingness/splashiness" as compared with the non-slipperiness/slidingness/splashiness of solids) would ultimately be judged as the *single* effect of the *single* cause of its molecular structure. The two-level epistemology of scientific realism, thus permits the comprehension of those many-to-many variable relationships of J. S. Mill's observational empiricism to be explained by the deeper one-to-one relationships between "theoretical entities" (which scientific realists view as being "factual" in the sense that they are not fictions) of Durkheim's realist methodology.

Without such a comprehension of the philosophy of scientific realism, Parsonian functionalists did indeed deny social evolution by having their quest for such one-to-one functional relationships freeze their historical vision into a conservatism of closed systems. In studying the long-term historical identities of different nations, for example, the self-professed Parsonian functionalist Rainer Baum argued for the existence of the "evolutionary invariance" (as he called it), of "ex-toto cultural codes":

Nothing . . . asserts that these objects of invariance are secured against any kind of change from any kind of source. They may well change, but if they do, this will be essentially non-evolutionary change which may involve conquest or peaceful merger of nation states for example. The reason for stressing non-evolutionary change as the only likely one rests on the adequacy of these conceptions of authority and individualism for presently known forms of the complex organization on the one hand, and their function in maintaining societal identity on the other.[34]

In a coincidence fraught with historical irony, Baum's 1979 functionalist argument against the possibility of evolutionary change had sought support from "Max Weber's work on religion," at exactly the moment when the evolutionary dynamism of East Asian societies was about to falsify many Weberian assertions about Asian religions: faced with incontrovertible evidence of socioeconomic change in East Asia, Randall Collins, in his 1986 book *Weberian Sociological Theory*, was forced to admit that Weber's understanding of Asia, based "heavily on accounts by nineteenth century travelers and missionaries and other authorities . . . is in error."[35] From my own "privileged" observational viewpoint as a university student in India in the 1970s, I could easily see how such functionalist readings of one-to-one, invariant relationships into Weber's thematics of culture and society were really masking a Quine-like "meaning-variance" (in semantic meaning): Weber's book on *The Religion of India*, for example, had interpreted the Hindu doctrine of "dharma" (which prescribed the doing of one's duty regardless of the consequences) as upholding a caste system inimical to the rise of modern capitalism, an interpretation which had undoubtedly been true in Weber's day.[36] But since then, that same doctrine had been relatively easily detached by Mahatma Gandhi (in his public readings of the *Bhagavat Gita*) from its context of caste legitimation and used instead in contemporary India as the "functional equivalent" of Weber's Protestant Ethic, legitimating capitalist development by encouraging savings and investment! Such evolutionary change in Indian society by the semantic "meaning variance" of Hinduism's concept of "dharma," would have been missed by functionalists focusing upon invariant (closed system) one-to-one relations between religious formulations and social phenomena.

With even greater irony—given the charges by critics that functionalist theories of modernization projected Western models of modernization upon the rest of the world—such functionalist blindness to semantic meaning-variance over historical time risked incomprehension of even the processes of Western modernization themselves, as seen, for example in the semantic metamorphosis of that very master concept of Western (and Westernizing) modernity, "reason." As pointed out by Julia Douthwaite in her historical study of French literature,

In the fin-de-siecle epoch spanning the years 1680-1715, the period Paul Hazard has equated with the "crisis of the European conscience," a dramatic ideological shift reverses the connotations of reason. The term loses its association to *honnette* (aristocratic propriety and politeness), instead coming to imply a certain irreverence and philosophical curiosity. The *honnete homme* of seventeenth-century tradition practiced civilite and succeeded in the world by obeying the rigorous rules of *la bonne compagnie*. The early eighteenth century sees the *honnete homme* displaced by the *ecrivain-philosophe*, an inquisitive seeker of universal truth. . . . These changing meanings of reason reverse classicism's conservative deference to the master narratives of Catholicism and monarchy, preferring a more liberal, enlightened stance of spiritual skepticism, and social and religious tolerance.[37]

To his credit Parsons himself attempted to move—after his 1951 publication of *The Social System*—beyond such functionalist anti-evolutionist bias against sociocultural change by grafting a vision of societal evolution onto his established functionalist frame: this grafting of evolutionary theory upon the functionalist framework he had established in 1951 was carried through by stacking up his four "A-G-I-L" functional subsystems in what Jackson Toby called his "cybernetic hierarchy," with the lowest subsystem, "A"—the Adapting Economy—being the highest in energy and the lowest in information, followed in the order of descending energy levels and ascending information levels by "G," the Goal-Directing Polity; "I," the Integrating Community; and finally "L," the Latent pattern-maintaining cybernetic level of culture, which, according to Parsons, contained the highest degree of information and the lowest degree of energy of all four functional subsystems.[38]

At first glance, this Parsonsian model of a cybernetic hierarchy of subsystem levels—governed by inverse variations of energy and information—seems to fit the general systems' "theory of hierarchical, multilevel, systems" as presented by Mesarovic, the mathematical systems theorist, in the following rules:

1. A higher level unit is concerned with a larger portion or broader aspects of the overall systems behavior.
2. The decision period of a higher level unit is longer than that of lower units.
3. A higher level unit is concerned with the slower aspects of the overall systems behavior.
4. Descriptions and problems on higher levels are less structured, with more uncertainties, and more difficult to formalize quantitatively.[39]

Parsons would certainly have agreed with Mesarovic that the cultural subsystem, his cybernetic hierarchy's highest level, is concerned with broader aspects, slower in changing, and less prone to structurally precise or quantitative formalization than his lower, energy-richer levels of polity, economy, or personality-behavior.

But after such preliminary agreement, the divergence between the cybernetic-hierarchy models of Parsons and Mesarovic appears: Mesarovic's general system hierarchy fits biological evolution perfectly, because the *time-direction* of such organic evolution is recapitulated in its *ascending* levels from high-energy-plus-low-information unicellular organisms—which reproduce rapidly with lower cellular levels of genetic information—to slower reproducing, higher information-using primates.[40] If we were to apply this same logic of *time-direction* to Parsons's cybernetic hierarchy, we would only get the mistaken impression that the *earliest* stages of social evolution had been involved in purely economic, adaptive transactions, while the higher Parsonsian level of noneconomic cultural motivations had emerged later in history. But such a *reversed* historical sequence had been precisely what Durkheim had been arguing against in his polemics against the English utilitarians. Durkheim's theorization of the historical time-direction had really insisted upon the reverse picture: the earliest human societies, Durkheim had argued, had been permeated by the noneconomistic mentality of religion, whereas the crystallization of purely economic motives had been relatively recent. Parsons had simply not taken into account this problem of the *temporal* sequence of emergence of higher structural levels from lower ones—as Sigmund Freud had done[41]—but had contented himself instead with just defining the supposed mechanisms which propelled social evolution forward, such as "Adaptive Upgrading," "Differentiation," "Inclusion," and "Value Generalization."[42]

Parsons's functionalist followers have attempted to deploy his A-G-I-L schema to address the historical development of societies. But they too have failed to notice this problem of their theoretical models' lack of congruence between developing structure and historical sequence that the early Freud had—according to contemporary neurologist Oliver Sacks—so effectively mapped out between 1876 and 1896, by basing his (ego/id) personality structure upon the Darwinian evolutionary model of the human nervous system's hierarchical structure, developed in the early 1870s by the English neurologist Hughlings Jackson.[43] Rainer Baum, for example, has suggested that the correct historical sequence in a Parsonsian view of social development over long time periods would have Parsons's I and G subsystems—i.e., the subsystems of community integration and polity, respectively—emerging from an undifferentiated whole in premodern times, while Parsons's L and A subsystems—i.e., the cultural and economic subsystems, respectively—emerged as truly autonomous subsystems only with modernity. Richard Munch has contrasted the German and Anglo-American processes of modernization along Parsonsian evolutionary lines, by arguing that the former had been relatively unstable simply because it had lacked the "interpenetration" between the four (Parsonsian) subsystems that the latter had enjoyed.[44] But neither Baum—who actually had the two middle levels (the I and G subsystems) of the Parsonsian evolutionary hierarchy evolving before either the lowest level (the A subsystem) or the highest (the L subsystem)—nor Munch has been able to comprehend the theoretical elegance of that Jackson/Freud model of the structure of the human nervous system/personality, which, according to neurologist Sacks, had recapitulated in a spatial hierarchy, the time-sequence of Darwinian evolution: with the lowest level (Jackson's spinal cord/Freud's "id"—"pleasure principle") resembling functionally the earliest instances of the evolution of nervous structures (in lower animals which had evolved earlier than humans) and the highest level (Jackson's human neo-cortex/Freud's "ego"—"reality principle") having evolved last in evolutionary time. That such a Jackson/Freud model of congruence between the *upward* development of neural/psychic *structure* and the *temporally forward* (i.e., from past to future) flow of historical/evolutionary time is still considered scientifically valid at the beginning of the twenty-first century, can be gauged from the fact that scientific journalist John McCrone's summation of the state of brain research in 1999, titled *Going Inside: A Tour Round a Single Moment of Consciousness*, criticizes not the Jacksonian concept of the brain's evolutionarily driven hierarchical structure *per se* but only the expectations of a simple higher cortex-to-lower brainstem linear determinism that the nineteenth-century concept of neural hierarchy carried: the process of "neural Darwinism" studied by brain researcher Gerald Edelman, says McCrone, occurs in a far more complex situation of a "dynamical computation" involving mutuality of deterministic pressures between different structural subsystems in the brain, whose mathematical modeling resembles more the complexity of contemporary chaos theory than the linear determinism of nineteenth-century science.[45]

As if these two "strikes" against Parsonsian evolutionism—the mathematically incorrect comprehension of the concept of "function," and the lack of spatial-temporal congruence in his model of evolutionary hierarchy—were not sufficient to eliminate it as a serious conceptual competitor against the Peircean theory I am about to unveil, there was actually a "third strike" against it—one that I have already analyzed in depth in chapter 1, but to which I must now briefly return—in the amorphous definition of Parsons's master term, the concept of "culture." The concept has admittedly been subject to a wide spectrum of definitions, beginning, as Oxford Professor of English Literature Terry Eagleton has recently pointed out, from its Latin root *colere*, "which can mean anything from cultivating and inhabiting to worshipping and protecting," and ranging from Margaret Archer's view of its being "roughly coterminous with what Popper has called Third World Knowledge," to the Leftist cultural historian Raymond Williams's characterization of it as "a particular way of life, which expresses certain meaning and values in art and learning but also in institutions and ordinary behaviour."[46] Referring to the Popper-like triple division of the "object world" into "three classes of 'social,' 'physical,' and 'cultural' objects" by Talcott Parsons in *The Social System* in 1951, anthropologist Adam Kuper traces the influence of such a division by Parsons—with its consequent donation of the "cultural" realm to the discipline of anthropology, within the academic division of labor between the social sciences—upon that systematic tabulation and classification of "164 definitions of culture" by the two leading anthropologists of the day, Alfred Kroeber of Berkeley and Clyde Kluckhohn of Harvard, titled *Culture: A Critical Review of Concepts and Definitions*. In that exhaustive search—influenced by Parsons's 1951 publication of *The Social System* and itself published in 1952—for the definitive meaning of the concept of "culture," Kroeber and Kluckhohn concluded that there was "as of 1951 a wide recognition among philosophers, linguists, anthropologists, psychologists and sociologists that the existence of culture rests indispensably upon the development in early man of the faculty for symbolizing, generalizing, and imaginative substitution."[47]

While, as we have already seen in chapter 1, the pursuit of culture into linguistic semantics by the followers of the Husserl/Schutz variant of phenomenology and of some followers of Parsons risked descent into the relativistic confusion of an infinite multiplicity of perspectives, contemporary anthropologist Kuper too bemoans the slide by American anthropology—following Clifford Geertz's 1973 book, *The Interpretation of Cultures*, and the importation of European "cultural studies" into American anthropology—into "an extreme relativism and culturalism" to contend:

> It is a poor strategy to separate out a cultural sphere, and to treat it in its own terms. Parsons attempted a synthesis among culture theory, social theory, and psychology. He failed, however grandly, but unless we separate out the various processes that are lumped together under the heading of culture, and then look beyond the field of culture to other processes, we will not get far in understanding any of it.[48]

An attempt at such a separation between what Kuper calls the "processes lumped together under the heading of culture" was that conceptual separation by the contemporary Pragmatist philosopher Nicholas Rescher in 1977 of the "methods" by which we arrive at Popper's "Third World of Knowledge"—which Margaret Archer holds to be "roughly coterminous" with what Parsons understood as the "cultural system"—from the actual semantic contents of that knowledge system, which Rescher called "theses." While the semantic (contents) theses of knowledge, argued Rescher, showed no clear or definite process of evolution—since like all semantic contents they were subject to Quine's "meaning variance," and thereby to relativistic interpretations which often presaged their future return by mutations of meaning even after their supposed evolutionary extinction—the *methods* employed by science, seemed to exhibit a clear process of Darwinian evolution by survival of the fittest.[49]

Interestingly, although Rescher's 1977 book *Methodological Pragmatism* had criticized both William James and Charles S. Peirce for not having distinguished—within that specific domain of the evolution of science—between methods and theses, I find that, outside of that very specific domain of science, what Rescher had called "methods" of reaching knowledge can actually be comprehended within that larger Peircean optic of "habits": Any phenomenological "reflection" upon the methods we utilize in obtaining knowledge in our quotidian lives—from the way we each hold our telephones during our phone conversations to the idiosyncrasies of each person's habitual patterns of reading newspapers, watching television, or reading print—reveals either the habitual nature of such knowledge-gaining methods or the dependence of new methods upon previous habituation (as exhibited, for example, in the extreme difficulty experienced in that knowledge-acquiring method we know as "seeing" by anyone born blind who now is suddenly given sight by the recently developed surgical technology). As Christopher Hookway has pointed out, the concept of "habit" was so central to Peirce's "evolutionary cosmology" that Peirce really did not seem to care whether this concept was interpreted "materialistically" as a biological adaptation to the laws of physics or in the form of an "objective idealism" viewing the lawful behavior of the material universe as a form of "effete mind."[50]

As if anticipating that contrast offered by sociologist Randall Collins toward the end of the twentieth century between the "psychological approach" of William James and his "lightweight" status as a philosopher, James had proceeded to misinterpret Peirce's Pragmatic Maxim of meaning as a relativistic theory of truth—in those two books which had so misled Durkheim, *Pragmatism*, published in 1907, and *The Meaning of Truth*, published in 1909—*after* having proved himself utterly faithful to Peirce's original intentions when it had come to explicating the concept of "habit" in his 1890 publication of *The Principles of Psychology*: Beginning with that very Peircean assertion that "the laws of nature are nothing but the immutable habits which the different sorts of matter follow," James had pursued the concept of "habit" upwards in evolutionary direction from "dead matter" to organic life, where the increasing "plasticity" and "variability" of the operation of habit went from the relative fixity of animal instincts, to the greater variability of human reflexes, through the extensive plasticity of the neural pathways in the human brain's cortex, to those very "Durkheimian" concerns with habit as "the enormous fly-wheel of society, its most conservative agent" and the "maxims" of proper education so that in realizing "how soon they will become mere walking bundles of habits," young people "would give more heed to their conduct while in the plastic state."[51]

While, as compared to Jacques Lacan's 1949 theory of the "mirror stage," as we have seen in chapter 3, James may have had an exaggerated concept, shared with George Herbert Mead (and with C. H. Cooley), of the "plasticity" of young brains (Lacan pointed out that not only was the neonate's perceptual ability not the "buzzing confusion" that James had thought it but the completion of "primary identification" by the six-month-old infant already implants a definite structure of personality—a "habitual imagery," in Pragmatist terms—where James might have expected much greater plasticity), I found it curious—until I came across Charles Camic's 1986 essay "The Matter of Habit"—as to why contemporary sociologists seemed to have lost that Peirce-James vision of the evolutionary continuity from natural laws to social conventions of the growing plasticity of habit.

The thesis of Camic's essay, that contemporary American sociology's preference for what he calls the "reflective" model of human action—i.e., the Weberian concept of action as imbued with subjective meaning—over "habitual" action, stems from sociologists' institutional struggle to separate their subject-matter from psychology, is illustrated in his definition of a three-level "habit continuum" by his own unwillingness to read James in the original, citing James instead through the misreading of James's *Principles of Psychology* by a contemporary psychologist, Guy R. Lefrancois. That Camic, an American sociologist, only illustrated his own thesis about the separation of American sociology from psychology—a strict separation bordering on complete ignorance about each other's subject matter that I have previously characterized as the perfect illustration of what Durkheim had meant by the "anomic division of labor"—by not reading James's original writing but merely accepting in complete credulity Lefrancois's interpretation of what James had meant, is seen when Camic cites page 107 of James's *Principles of Psychology*, following Lefrancois' rendering of habit as "sequences of behaviors, usually simple, . . . that have become virtually automatic," illustrated by the "practice of putting on a left sock before a right one."[52] In the original, James actually defined only "a simple habit" such as "snuffling, for example, or of putting one's hands into one's pockets, or of biting one's nails" as "nothing but a reflex discharge" when compared with "the most complex habits"![53]

In reality Camic's "habit continuum" progressed along the same path to increasing complexity that James had followed, from that lowest level of what James had called "simple habits," to a "middle range" of complexity involving "habits of economic, political, religious, and domestic behavior; habits of obedience to rules and to rulers; habits of sacrifice, disinterestedness, and restraint; and so on"—an exposition of which prompted Camic to confess that "it is only Weber who explicitly conceives of habitual action as a pure type," i.e., as an extreme typification contrasting with Weber's equally extremely unrealistic typification of nonhabitual, "rational" action—to those "upper reaches of the habit continuum" where "habit is the durable and generalized disposition that suffuses a person's action throughout an entire domain of life" often denoted by the term *character*, but also "denoted by leaving the word in its Latin form, *habitus*," which "is a practice that both Durkheim and Weber followed, and it is a practice that Bourdieu has made a notable recent effort at long last to revive."[54]

What I find of inestimable importance in Camic's essay is his detailed tracing of Emile Durkheim's extensive usage of the concept of "habit"—a Durkheimian usage of the concept which establishes the main conceptual bridge I need between the undertheorized social evolutionism of Durkheim and the explicitly theorized general evolutionism of Peirce—in *all* of Durkheim's writings *except* for "Durkheim's frequent and fervent programmatic statements on the field of sociology itself."[55] What led to Durkheim's withdrawal from using the concept of "habit," according to Camic, was his belief, stated in 1895 in his conclusion to *The*

Rules of Sociological Method, that a science "lacks any justification for existing unless its subject matter is an order of facts which other sciences do not study."[56] Despite "his own testimony," said Camic, that "habits met the same criteria as the 'social facts' that were at the core of his sociology: that they were external to the individual in the sense that they were among the tendencies that 'education has impressed upon us,'" Durkheim retreated before "the aggressive 'new psychology' of the time," which had been busy annexing the concept of habit to its "organic and physical" view of human life. "Operating against this backdrop and determined to endow sociology with 'a subject peculiarly its own,'" said Camic, Durkheim abandoned the concept of "habit" to psychology in a manner that was to repeat itself later in America, when, faced with psychologist John Watson's behaviorist declaration in 1917 in his essay "Practical and Theoretical Problems in Instinct and Habits" that "man is the sum of his instincts and habits," W. I. Thomas "unequivocally reversed his once-positive stance toward physiology and likewise toward habit," substituting in its place—within his 1918 writing with Florian Znaniecki of *The Polish Peasant in Europe and America*—the concept of "attitude." Talcott Parsons's later "vigorous . . . polemicizing against behaviorism" was but a continuation, according to Camic, of that programmatic assertion made by Thomas in his 1918 reaction to Watson's annexation in 1917 of the concept of "habit" to his behaviorist psychology, that "the uniformity of behavior (that constitutes social life) is not a uniformity of organic habits but of consciously followed rules."[57]

Such a dichotomizing of a "psychophysical" concept of "automatic" habit against "reflective," conscious thought, as Camic has traced it in received sociological theory, contrasts—to sociology's detriment—with the integrated evolutionary vision of Pragmatist philosophy, as presented by John Dewey's realistic assertion in 1927 that "habits bind us to orderly and established ways of action because they generate ease, skill, and *interest* in things to which we have grown used. . . . Habit does not preclude the use of thought, but it determines the channels within which it operates."[58]

Of ultimate importance to my project here of reconnecting Durkheim's sociological tradition with those conceptual roots in Pragmatist philosophy that Durkheim had himself missed in his 1913-14 course of lectures on Pragmatism and sociology is Camic's location in his 1986 essay on "habit" of the precise historical turning point at which Durkheim had retreated from his earlier usage (and even later usage, despite his "programmatic" compunctions, in his 1912 writing of *The Elementary Forms* and his lectures on *Moral Education*) of the concept of "habit": in 1898, said Camic, Durkheim specifically cited the "psychophysical" connotations in Leon Dumont's 1876 conception of "*l'habitude*" in order to develop his specifically sociological—i.e., specifically non-psychological or *non*-psychophysical—theoretical methodology in the analysis of culture, in his essay "Individual and Collective Representations."[59]

Looking back in 1994 upon that 1898 formulation by Durkheim of the thematic of "collective representations"—with a better vantage point than Durkheim had had into the logic of scientific methodology, consequent upon the intervening debates between Karl Popper and the Logical Positivists about the epistemological implications of Relativistic physics—the philosopher of science Warren Schmaus had this to say:

> Durkheim's essay of 1898, however, left several problems unsolved. By his own admission he could provide no account of how collective representations give rise to other collective representations. . . . Nor did he shed much light even on the problem of how collective representations form from individual representations. . . . He argued merely that it would not be impossible for resemblance to be a cause of the association of ideas. . . . Three years later, in the preface to the second edition of *The Rules of Sociological Method*, Durkheim conceded that the laws of collective ideation were still unknown. He now said that the distinction between individual and collective representations does not necessarily rule out the possibility that the laws of collective ideation may "resemble" the laws of association of ideas. . . . Durkheim thus had no explanatory resources other than the so-called laws of the association of ideas, which did not themselves rest on a secure foundation. . . . Lacking a knowledge of the laws of collective ideation, it seems that at best Durkheim could explain only those collective representations that are formed from individual representations. Durkheim believed this kind of collective representation constitutes the collective consciousness of primitive societies, while the collective consciousness of more advanced societies also contains collective representations formed from other collective representations. He was thus unable to explain the formation of many of the collective representations that are characteristic of contemporary societies.[60]

Like Camic, Schmaus sees the root cause of Durkheim's conceptual difficulties lying in his anxiety to separate the scientific procedure of sociology from that of psychology in that he "could not use the principles the principles of associationist psychology to explain the formation . . . of collective representation without violating his own rules concerning sociological explanations," being driven thereby to "shift to a concern with primitive societies"—and, I might add, to that curiosity about Pragmatist philosophy that he displayed after that publication in 1912 of his celebrated study of "primitive" religion—"in order to solve the theoretical difficulties to which the concept of collective representations gave rise."[61]

Since Durkheim's day, the extensive studies of the history and philosophy of science occasioned by the post-Einstein debates about the nature of science (between Popper and the Logical Positivists, for example) have revealed Durkheim's apparently acute anxieties about the need to separate sociology's theoretical domain from that of psychology to have been, to say the least, exaggerated: by 1959, the scientific philosopher Mario Bunge was using the concept of "emergence" to explain the extensive usage by sciences situated at "higher epistemic levels" of explanatory theoretical entities from "lower" sciences. Without the use by chemistry, for example, of physics' theories of electron shells (to explain, for example, why carbon had a chemical valency of four compared to hydrogen's chemical valency of one) or the use by physiology of chemistry's theory of molecular interactions (to explain, for example, the acidic breakdown of ingested proteins in the digestive system), scientific research, argued Bunge, would simply come to a standstill. Such insightful progress, in the course of the twentieth century, into the logic of scientific argumentation may have been behind that unambiguous declaration by Claude Levi-Strauss in 1962 (in *The Savage Mind*)—in an apparent reversal of Durkheim's effort to separate social science from psychology—that "ethnology is first of all psychology."[62]

Not having been privy to the insights that post-Levi-Strauss French social thought has enjoyed—insights that have accrued from that 1949 presentation of the "mirror-stage theory" by Jacques Lacan (see chapter 3), as well as the "linguistic turn" in philosophy occasioned by the later Wittgenstein's arguments against the possibility of a "private language"[63]—Durkheim may now be forgiven his lack of clarity in seeing or phrasing that *direction* of scientific realist "emergence" that current French thought seems to have grown comfortable with (in all its Left Bank linguistic playfulness with the deconstructive "death of the subject") but may still trouble the stubbornly individualist conscience of American social science: that it is *not* individualist psychology which is the lower-level science from which sociology must explain the origin of "collective representations," but rather the other way around—that it is from the primordially cooperative processes of society, and its linguistic bank of collective representations, that psychology must strive to explain the emergence of the individual's character and its stock of individual representations.

It is such a post-Levi-Strauss level of intellectual comfort with the social-scientific incorporation of psychology that is displayed in the contemporary Francophone ethnology of Rene Devisch—professor of social anthropology at Leuven and Louvain—in *Se recreer femme* (expanded in English translation in 1993 as *Weaving the Threads of Life: The Khita Gyn-Eco-Logical Healing Cult among the Yaka*) as he proceeds to ethnologically interpret what Durkheim might have called a primitive culture, the "oral and nonliterate . . . Yaka society in the Southwest of Zaire," by conceptually assimilating Pierre Bourdieu's idea of *habitus*—itself a concept traced by Camic, as we have seen, to those "upper reaches of the habit continuum" that, as used by Durkheim and Weber, includes "the whole manner, turn, cast of the personality . . . even 'character'" of individuals within a particular culture[64]—to that definition of culture offered by British object-relations psychologist Donald Winnicott (in his most celebrated 1971 book, *Playing and Reality*) as the ultimate "transitional object," that "intermediate and potential space . . . between a given individual and relevant others, between, say, husband and wife, parent and child, the living and the dead, or between past and present."[65]

What really caught my attention about Devisch's ethnological theorizing about the oral culture of the Yaka, was that it, like the psychoanalytical theorizing of Lacan—whose uncanny resemblance, in having "three orders of cognition," to the three categories of Peirce's phenomenology of the cognitive process, I had indicated in chapter 3[66]—but without even a single mention of the semiology of Ferdinand de Saussure held in such esteem by Levi-Strauss, Lacan, and the French postmodernists, "re-invents the wheel" by adopting a three-step "semantic-praxiological approach" whose three "steps" turn out to be identical to that threefold division of Peirce's semiotics by Charles Morris in 1938, into syntactics, semantics and pragmatics, without giving any credit to Peirce, Morris, or any other Pragmatist philosophers (or even to linguistic philosophers such as J. L. Austin or H. Paul Grice, whose work in linguistic pragmatics I have been including here, as belonging within the broad tradition of Peirce's Pragmaticist approach to human knowledge and language).[67]

The magisterial analysis in 1999 by the Anglophone anthropologist Adam Kuper of the social scientific lineage of the concept of "culture" concluded by insisting that "to understand culture, we must first deconstruct it" by "the breaking up of culture into parts," so as to make "possible a *particulate* theory of culture; that is, a theory about the 'pieces' of culture, their composition and relations to other things."[68] But I have feared that my own vision of such deconstruction—having been already accomplished by Morris's threefold analytical breakdown in 1938 (in his *Foundations of the Theory of Signs*) of Peirce's Pragmaticist approach to the study of "meaning"—may not prove appetizing to social scientists reluctant to taste Morris's *philosophical* oeuvre (a reluctance to cross disciplinary boundaries within the current "anomic" division of intellectual labor in American academia possibly made worse by that historical happenstance that Peirce's lack of a book-length publication in contrast to William James's profusion of book-length misinterpretations of Peircean Pragmatism, which led Durkheim to condemn Pragmatism in 1913-14!). It therefore behooves me now to approach my final "consummation" of the marriage that I have been proposing between Durkheimian sociology and Peircean Pragmaticism by introducing my Morris-based program of (evolutionary) pragmatics via the recent ethnographic application of Morris's threefold division of Peircean semiotic by Devisch:

> As for the semantic-praxiological analysis of ritual production, I distinguish three partly overlapping steps. They do not constitute successive moments in the research or in the presentation, but offer distinct angles of approach. . . . There is first that of the internal structure of the ritual activity, namely the patterning of the devices into a ritual process. I situate myself, in terms of perspective, at the interior of the whole ritual process. To the extent that the process informs and links together a set of diverse activities that arise in connection with a death, therapy, or divinatory vocation, it is my task to highlight

the internal configuration. I thereby concentrate on the way in which an institutional set of activities is structured into a whole.[69]

There, in Devisch's explication of the first of three steps in his semantic-praxiological approach to ritual communication among the nonliterate Yaka, is recognizably what Morris called "syntactics," the study of the internal "relations of signs to one another in abstraction from the relations of signs or to objects or to interpreters." Amazingly, without ever mentioning Peirce or Morris, Devisch's first step has reproduced—from within the ethnographic study of what Durkheim would have seen as an "elementary form of the religious life"—a Morris-like semiotic approach to the "linguistic structure," or grammatical syntax of ritual communication![70]

"The second angle of analysis," says Devisch, "consists of discovering the lateral or connotative references which often occur—also in a latent fashion—in the production of the drama." By overtly mentioning the "latent references" in ritual practice that come about "by interweaving significant elements that evoke or stem . . . from various semantic structures and classifications,"[71] Devisch leaves us in no doubt that his second step corresponds precisely—although, apparently, unbeknownst to him—to that science of referential meaning that Morris, too, had called "semantics," dealing "with the relation of signs to their designata and so to the objects which they may or do denote," whose "rigorous development . . . presupposes" as a first step, "a relatively highly developed syntactics," with the "semantical rule for the use of a sentence" involving as lateral a "reference to the semantical rules of the component sign vehicles" as does Devisch's ritual drama, and whose "rules are only the verbal formulations of what in any concrete case of semiosis are habits of sign usage by actual users of signs."[72]

Finally, as if he had been waiting for precisely this cue from Morris's 1938 writing averring to the possibly conservative implications of semantic "habits of sign usage," Devisch's recent ethnographic study of Yaka ritual culture introduces us to the "third step" of his method of semantic-praxiological anthropological analysis by situating this third step in the context of a question about novelty in his subjects' behavior:

The third step consists in trying to find how a meaningful and empowering drama is brought about, involving the interactive fields of body, family, and life-world. In other terms, the dynamics, quasi intentionality, and efficacious or transformative nature of the ritual drama become the focus of attention. In order to discover how the healing drama differs from routine practice and mere reproduction, ritual may be studied in itself as a species and a creative totality. The central question might be put this way: how is a given ritual performance more than the nth reproduction of a model, or more than the sum of its parts?[73]

As if in a pre-emptive reply to Devisch's contemporary question, Morris had, in 1938, already addressed the possible stasis implied by the self-referential problem of language inherent in his own first two semiotic steps of syntactics and semantics. "'Rules of sign usage,'" Morris had argued, in ending his section on semantics, "like 'sign' itself, is a semiotical term and cannot be stated syntactically or semantically."[74] To comprehend how humans can creatively comprehend their "rules of sign usage" within their continuing usage of such signs, Morris had argued, one had to move beyond syntactics and semantics into a third science of meaning, "'pragmatics' . . . the science of the relation of signs to their interpreters":

> The term 'pragmatics' has obviously been coined with reference to the term 'pragmatism.' It is a plausible view that the permanent significance of pragmatism lies in the fact that it has directed attention more closely to the relation of signs to their users than had previously been done and has assessed more profoundly than ever before the relevance of this relation in understanding intellectual activities. The term 'pragamatics' helps to signalize the significance of the achievement of Peirce, James, Dewey, and Mead within the field of semiotic. At the same time, 'pragmatics' as a specifically semiotical term must receive its own formulation. . . . Since most, if not all, signs have as their interpreters living organisms, it is a sufficiently accurate characterization of pragmatics to say that it deals with the biotic aspects of semiosis, that is, with all the psychological, biological, and sociological phenomena which occur in the functioning of signs.[75]

Again as if in anticipation of situations such as my usage of Devisch's recent semantic-praxiological ethnography of the Yaka, Morris had ended his introduction to his 1938 section on the "pragmatical dimension of semiosis" with the assertion that "pragmatics, too, has its pure and descriptive aspects; the first arises out of the attempt to develop a language in which to talk about the pragmatical dimension of semiosis; the latter is concerned with the application of this language to specific cases."[76] While Devisch's ethnographic semantic-praxiological analysis of Yaka ritual culture was indeed an example of Morris's latter, or descriptive, application of pragmatics to a specific case, my own task in this book is with Morris's first aspect, to "attempt to develop a language" within sociological theory "in which to talk about the pragmatical dimension of" global-cultural signs.

In this attempt at a globally generalizable theoretical language comprehending that specific ethnographic application by Devisch, in his "third step" of "trying to find out how a meaningful and empowering drama is brought about" in human communication, I am helped, as I have stated before, by the insights of H. Paul Grice's linguistic pragmatics of meaning: "'A meant something by x,'" Grice had asserted, "is (roughly) equivalent to 'A intended the utterance of x to produce some effect in an audience by means of the recognition of this intention,'"[77] and for individual A to have expected such a "recognition of his intention" by her audience would imply some previous level of cooperation between A and her previous audiences, since, for A to even be competent in the use of her language—for as the later Wittgenstein (and the earlier Peirce of the "four denials" of 1868) had recognized, language, by definition, cannot be a "private" affair—there must have been some previous social group that had cooperated in A's attempts to communicate. In her 1995 book, *Meaning in Interaction: An Introduction to Pragmatics*, Jenny Thomas had offered a succinct summation of Grice's "Cooperative Principle" of meaning as this prescription: "Make your contribution such as is required, at the stage at which it occurs, by the accepted purpose or direction of the talk exchange in which you are engaged."[78]

As if he had been attempting to transport Grice's Cooperative Principle from its usual nesting place within the abstruse academic discussions of linguistic philosophers to the quotidian setting of normal sociality, historian R. G. Collingwood had, in 1942, offered us this simple example of the economy of communication within "the nature of the common task": "Watch two men moving a piano," Collingwood had urged. "At a certain moment one says 'lift,' and the other lifts."[79] We need hardly be reminded here of Hannah Arendt's definition of just such a "human ability not just to act but to act in concert," as social "power," nor of Charles Horton Cooley's perception of how the development of the "looking-glass" social self is comprehended by the developing human infant as the incorporation of such power, for self-feeling, noted Cooley, "appears to be associated chiefly with ideas of the exercise of power, of being a cause."[80]

Reinforcing this connection between Arendt's vision of the power of social cooperation and Cooley's phenomenological perception of one's individual self, the child-psychologist Joel Ryce-Menuhin has traced the etymological origin of the semantics of the very word *self* to the ancient perception of the Lacanian drama of "separation and belonging" in a social group:

> The base of Anglo-Saxon is *selbha*, which contains within its root the symbolic union of separation and of belonging. *Selbha* is compounded of the *se*, meaning away, separated, for, or by itself; and *bho* which refers to cohesive totality—compare Gothic *sibja*, old German *sippe* (kin, kinsfolk, totality of one's own people), English dialect *sib* (related by blood), Latin *sabini* (members of the clan), Indo-European *suebho* (belonging to one's own people, free). . . . The other important root is *poti*, or self in Ido-European languages. Thus Old Indian *pati* (lord or master), Greek *posis* (mighty), Old Latin *potic sum*, (I can), *potoir* (I seize upon).[81]

Strengthened in our resolve by such etymological evidence of the connection between one's personal empowerment (the feeling of self-efficacy) and the cooperative forms of social power, embedded within the very history of the semantics of self—the certainty that (to paraphrase the statement attributed a Roman Catholic saint, Philip Neri, about Divine Grace being the only thing that sep-arated him from the fate of a criminal on the way to execution) "there but for the grace of millennia of social cooperation, goes my self"—we may now return to that Lacanian problematic of Ragland-Sullivan's "*je* codes," the codes that govern the semantics of the "*je* who speaks," with whose conceptual possibility we had ended chapter 3.[82]

A *code*, as defined by T. Givon's *Mind, Code, and Context*, is simply a "sys-tem of signs," or, as in the more elaborate definition of the same concept by the functionalist sociologist Rainer Baum, a "code" is "a set of rules ordering the number of ways in which symbols can be combined into meaningful messages."[83] But if, as Charles Morris had pointed out in his 1938 book on signs, "syntactical and semantic rules are only verbal formulations within semiotic of what in any concrete case of semiosis are habits of sign usage by actual users of signs," then the analysis of such codes that construct and control such "habits of sign users"—as well as all those habits in "the upper reaches of the habit continuum" that form the *habitus*, as Camic saw it, of human "personality" or "character"[84]—must lie within that realm that Morris had designated as the purview of pragmat-ics, the study of "the relation of signs to their interpreters."[85]

Since that definition of pragmatics by Morris in 1938, we have seen the as-sertion by H. Paul Grice that for such signs to have any meaning at all, their inter-preters would have to have been in some relationship of cooperation, and the presentation by Jacques Lacan in 1949 of his "mirror stage theory," which re-quires the cooperation of parent and child to even produce that primordial sign—of the *moi* imagery of the perceiving self—for the language of the speaking *je* to even begin. The question of "pragmatic codes" then becomes a question about *what* forms of human cooperation produce *which* interpretant codes. Or, to return to that concrete setting of E. E. Evans-Pritchard's Azande which we examined in chapter 1: What kind of "code" of interpretation could have constrained the Azande to "foreshorten" the causal "chain of events" so as to define that "selec-tivity" and "social relevance" that Evans-Pritchard had seen operating in Azande imputations of death to personal witchcraft?[86]

In keeping with scientific realist methodology, we may expect that such "theoretical entities" as the pragmatic codes of social cooperation, operating at such a level of perceptual "depth" as to give birth (pre-linguistically) to one's very sense of self, must be "unconscious" in the Freudian/Lacanian, as well as Levi-Straussian, sense[87] and may be beyond our direct empirical observation, but should be deducible from the observation of the semantic meaning in communi-cation. Fortunately for our scientific realist deduction from *observed semantics* to *inferred pragmatics*, we have that observation by Charles Morris of the self-refer-ential limit of semantic meaning: "'Rules of sign usage' like 'sign' itself, is a semiotical term and cannot be stated syntactically or semantically," Morris had argued.[88] Just as Bertrand Russell's famous example of self-referential paradox—the case of Epimenides the Cretan asserting that all Cretans were liars (and thereby negating his own assertion)—had informed the concept of evolution by "self-referential autopoiesis"[89] of Francisco Varela in biology and Niklas Luhmann's sociological systems-theory,[90] so may that 1938 insight about the self-referential self-limitation of a semantic system guide our historical vision to those crucial *historical nodes* where accumulating semantic (i.e., institutional) contradictions in one form of social cooperation were relieved only by a (seemingly sudden) transition to another form. By focusing on such *transitions* between ways in which human habits of attention—what W. I. Thomas, according to Camic, would have called "attitudes"[91]—had been focused so as to constrain semantic meaning into predetermined channels of discourse, we may now map our globally evolutionary signification-codes.[92]

Modernization as Code-Transition from Filiation to Calibration

"*Ausgang des Menschen aus seiner Unmundigkeit*," the phrase used by Immanuel Kant in 1784 to characterize the *Aufklarung*, the Enlightenment of eighteenth-century Europe, is translated, in Gail Newman's 1997 study of the poet Novalis by the use of Donald Winnicott's object-relations psychology, as "the human being's exit from its state of minority."[93]

In *What's Left of Liberalism: An Interpretation and Defense of Justice as Fairness*, Jon Mandle translates the same line from Kant as "Enlightenment is man's emergence from his self-imposed immaturity," and follows Kant's argument further in proposing that "this immaturity is self-imposed when its cause lies not in lack of understanding," but rather, in the lack of "the freedom to use reason publicly in all matters."[94]

The theory of cultural evolution that I am about to unveil will actually view the historical process of social modernization ushered in by the European Enlightenment in the eighteenth century in that sense of Newman's translation of Kant's *unmundigkeit* as a *collective* state of "minority" or "childhood," from which humanity began *collectively* to emerge. But I have also included Mandle's 2000 version of the same phrase because his following of Kant's argument into that topos of "the freedom to use reason publicly in all matters" enables me to situate my own "non-Western" childhood experience into my theoretical argument about why the strictures of Anthony Giddens against what he characterizes as the "homology of society and personality"—an argument that he directs against that "homology" between social modernization and Jean Piaget's view of the decentering process of individual development in intelligence of the later Jurgen Habermas—should not stop my own carrying forward of the young C. S. Peirce's similar individual-society homology (in a three-stage model of social evolution analogous to the three steps of individual thinking, cited as an epigraph beginning this chapter) beyond that Piagetian homologizing of Habermasian evolutionism.[95]

The operative word that triggers my Lacanian/Peircean/Durkheimian awareness of how the "social fact" of language structures the existential parameters of
agential personality (and *not* the other way around as the structuration theory of
Giddens would insist that I include in my equation) is the Portuguese/African
word *muleque*: Having been born and raised, for the first seven years of my life,
in one of the poorest nations in the world, the East African nation of Mozambique, while it was still a Portuguese colony, I had been under the impression (as
had other members of my Portuguese-speaking community there) that *muleque*—
used generally to refer to men of all ages from preliterate tribal cultures on the
African mainland, whose poverty had led them to migrate into our island port
town in search of work, only to end up as badly abused domestic servants—had
meant simply "domestic servant."

Having then, at the age of seven, moved into an English-speaking school
environment in India—except for vacations spent with my maternal relatives in
Portuguese-speaking Goa where the word *muleque* did not seem to exist—I was
surprised to later discover the same word, spelled exactly as before, being used to
mean "little boy" in the Brazilian version of the Portuguese language. Puzzled as
to why the very same word had meant "domestic servant" in the Portuguese spoken in my native town (Mozambique Island) in colonial Mozambique and "little
boy" in Brazilian Portuguese, while the noncolonial residents of Lisbon (in Portugal) or the multiple-generation speakers of Portuguese in the Western Indian ter-
ritory of Goa seemed never to have heard of it, I was finally given the following
explanatory hypothesis by a Brazilian socio-linguist: that this word, like many
others in Brazilian Portuguese, had probably been transported into the Brazilian
language by African slaves, and that the reason that it had never been heard in
Goa—the former Portuguese colony on India's West coast where my maternal
relatives lived—was that, as in the similar case of the appellation "boy," applied
by white-slave owners to their adult black slaves in the American South—Portuguese settlers had, over the centuries, applied this similarly infantilizing appellation to the preliterate Africans of Mozambique's interior (whom they often en-
slaved or upon whom they imposed slave-like conditions), but *not* to the older
literate cultures that they had found in India.[96] My query about the semantics of
muleque had exposed me to a lesson that Giddens, as a resident of a modernized,
Western nation probably never had a chance to learn: that terrorized populations,
much like terrorized individual sufferers of traumatic stress, can literally appear
to their terrorizers to "regress" into an infantile manner. It is not only the appellation "boy," addressed to adult African-American men before the Civil Rights era,
but also the "Sambo" caricature of African-Americans popularized by Vaudeville
earlier in the last century that provides evidence, in a Western setting, of that phenomenon of the social infantilization of an entire social group that I had witnessed in colonial Mozambique.

Having thus "situated" my own conviction that there do indeed exist homologous attitudes between individuals and whole societies, I should also point out

that my childhood experience in the northern part of colonial Mozambique—a sufficiently terror-filled habitation close to the brush-fire guerrilla war for independence, which was then just beginning but whose looming presence was even then sufficiently strong to occasion those constant police roundups for interrogation (i.e., torture) of the "muleques" in our midst[97]—has colored my understanding, as a practicing sociologist in America now, of Louis Wirth's sociological definition of *minority*—a word that, beginning with the semantic connotation of "smaller number," had been transferred by Wirth, in 1945, to connotations of "differential and unequal treatment" as "objects of collective discrimination" by a "dominant group," but seems not to have yet arrived, within the institutional setting of American sociology, at that connotation I had found through my childhood experience in Northern Mozambique, of a literal infantilization-by-terror of the dominated population into a nonadult state of "minority"[98]—and of "nationalism"—whose true meaning as the collective emotion of a population attempting to emancipate itself, like Immanuel Kant's compatriots in 1784, from its dominated status as a "minority" (in that Kantian sense of people who have not attained the social maturity of the Enlightenment, which also assimilates to Wirth's connotations of people who "regard themselves as objects of collective discrimination," as Kant's fellow German-speakers so obviously did in 1784, and as the French and English nations had also earlier seen themselves as dominated, respectively, by a "Frankish-German" nobility and a "Norman Yoke" of conquering overlords, earlier), which even otherwise perceptive contemporary students of nationalism, such as Anthony D. Smith, fail to see.[99]

But having now disassociated myself from Giddens's proscription against the possibility of "the homology of society and personality" by asserting, based on my own "postcolonial" experience, that there seems to be a rather strong case for retaining that "general idea that the 'childhood of society' is like the childhood of the individual,"[100] that same "postcolonial" perspective from which I write also obliges me to *immediately* "put some distance" in my reader's mind— despite the fact that I will be returning to this topic of postmodernism in greater detail in the next section of this chapter—between my own usage here of words like *terror* and *pragmatics*, and the employment of the same terms by the postmodernist writer Jean-Francois Lyotard, in his very celebrated book, *The Postmodern Condition*[101]: from my postcolonial vantage point on global history, Lyotard's usage of *both* concepts, terror and pragmatics, appears truncated and artificially restricted to fit in a procrustean fashion the predetermined worldview of an ex-colonial center. Thus, to take each term in turn, Lyotard's apparent restriction of the connotations of terror to Stalinist (and, by implication, Jacobin) modernizing (and "totalizing") meta-narratives—though seemingly legitimate because of the undeniably real and painfully traumatic consequences of these ideologies—nevertheless risks eliding the longer-term terror of premodern history, which, precisely because of its incomparably longer duration has and will continue to have a proportionately greater impact on the process of global history. As the South American anthropologist Michael Taussig phrases it, it is the "terror as usual" view of "history as state of siege" in the writings of Walter Benjamin (influenced as Benjamin was by his sensitive reading of Biblical narrative and Paul Klee's artistic rendition of such terror)[102] that my reader should keep in mind as being closer to my own non-Eurocentric comprehension of historical terror than is Lyotardian "terror." Furthermore, Lyotard's ahistorical (and essentialist) juxtaposition of the "pragmatics of narrative knowledge" of a Cashinahua storyteller with the "pragmatics of scientific knowledge"[103]—without any attempt at all to map or to delineate the historical-temporal links by which such Cashinahua communication systems could conceivably *evolve* (or "change," if my reader prefers a term less laden with the historical accretion of negative connotations) to encompass and comprehend the pragmatics of scientific knowledge (or the other way around)—blatantly betrays the historical project of the founder of pragmatics, Charles S. Peirce, of situating such pragmatics *within* a wider evolutionism encompassing the developmental dynamics, or the future *possibilities* pregnant within any present entity, of human communities in historical time. To me, this double truncation by Lyotard of terms now in relatively common usage in academic debate, seems no accident: my reader may as well note that—despite my usage of Lacan's psychoanalytical theory within a framework of Peircean evolutionist "pragmatics"—my own references to the "terror" of history should not mask my suspicion of the "spin" given to such terms as *terror* or *pragmatism* by "postmodernist" writers, for I tend to agree with postcolonial writer Robert Young's assertion that "postmodernism can best be defined as European culture's awareness that it is no longer the unquestioned and dominant center of the world."[104]

Having thus clarified the referential boundaries "on all sides" of my own semantics here, I can now directly address that historical "beginning" of human cultural development, which Durkheim had outlined in chapter 7—dealing with the "origin" of "elementary beliefs"—of book 2 of *The Elementary Forms of the Religious Life*:

In the beginning, all the kingdoms are confounded with each other. Rocks have a sex; they have the power of begetting; the sun, moon and stars are men or women who feel and express human sentiments, while men, on the contrary, are thought of as animals or plants. This state of confusion is found at the basis of all mythologies; they can be classified in no definite group, for they participate at the same time in the most opposed groups. It is also readily admitted that they can go from one into another; and for a long time men believed that they were able to explain the origin of things by these transmutations.[105]

Durkheim's own explanation for what he referred to as this "anthropomorphic instinct," was that it was "religion that was the agent of this transfiguration;

it is religious beliefs that have substituted for the world, as it is perceived by the senses, another different one." As he described "the case of totemism":

> The fundamental thing in this religion is that the men of the clan and the different beings whose form the totemic emblems reproduce pass as being made of the same essence. Now when this belief was once admitted, the bridge between the different kingdoms was already built. The man was represented as a sort of plant; the plants and animals were thought of as the relatives of men, or rather, all these beings, so different for the senses, were thought of as participating in a single nature. So this remarkable aptitude for confusing things that seem to be obviously distinct comes from the fact that the first forces with which the human intellect peopled the world were elaborated by religion. Since these were made up of elements taken from the different kingdoms, men conceived a principle common to the most heterogeneous things, which thus became endowed with a sole and single essence.[106]

About this "remarkable aptitude" possessed by "primitive" people to cognitively collapse into each other the objective realms of inanimate objects, plants, animals, and human beings—which modern, scientific "objectivity" sees as *obviously* separate from each other—Durkheim confessed that although such cognitive confusion was "not peculiar to totemism," in that "there is no society where it is not active," it was nevertheless also "true that this logic is disconcerting for us."[107]

But it was left to another pioneer explorer in the human sciences, Sigmund Freud—who, in writing *Totem and Taboo* in 1913, cited Durkheim's 1912 *Elementary Forms*, as well as that 1897 essay by Durkheim in *L'Annee Sociologique*, "Incest: The Nature and Origin of the Taboo," which Stjepan Mestrovic says "was widely regarded as a kind of first draft for his *Elementary Forms*"[108]—to map the extent to which modern humans are *also* prone to this "disconcerting" logic of "primitives." Having already discovered, by the time he had written *The Interpretation of Dreams* in 1900, that in our quotidian dream-life we all seem to return to such totemic logic—in that our dreams regularly confuse separate realms of objects in those mysterious "transmutations" that Durkheim was to notice in 1912, in "primitive" thinking—Freud was to conclude in his 1915 essay "The Unconscious" that such a collapse of objective realms into each other, was the distinguishing feature of our unconscious mentation, and to conclude in his 1925 paper "On Negation" that our modern comprehension of reality itself depended on the proper functioning of the logic of negation. Writing in 1995 about the 1975 attempt by Argentine psychiatrist Ignacio Matte Blanco to systematize Freud's growing awareness—between his 1900 work on dreams and his 1925 paper on the logic of negation—into a logico-mathematical formulation of *The Unconscious as Infinite Sets*, British psychoanalyst Eric Rayner said:

Without negation there is no sense of external reality. For instance, Freud's (1925) paper on "Negation" pointed out the importance of negative judgements in the development of the sense of external reality. Matte Blanco comes to a similar conclusion but starts from different premises. For him the sense of external reality depends on the ideas of space and time. The location of external real objects is obviously important to any animal. All these—space, time and their offspring location—have been seen to be dependent upon a logical functioning of the mind which includes asymmetrical relations. These depend upon negation functions where a conceived relationship and its converse are not the same. In particular, when these are symmetrized, awareness of the "externalness" of reality can disappear.[109]

What Rayner had in mind in this discussion of the "asymmetrical relations" of the reality-comprehending logic of negation was the typical confusion of psychotic reasoning, as in, for example, the well-known schizophrenic tendency to what Aristotle had called a false syllogism: "I move; horses move; therefore I am a horse." In such a false syllogism, very apparent in victims of psychotic breakdown, the "asymmetry" between the concept of "moving" and its applicability to "horses" and "humans"—i.e., asymmetry in the sense that "all humans move" *cannot* be symmetrically reversed into the assertion that "all moving objects are human"—is collapsed in the breakdown of the wall of "negation" between the realm of "horses" and that of "humans": negation in the sense that the non-psychotic reasoning of adult human beings would quickly have proceeded from having noted the similarity in terms of "movement" between horses and humans to the *difference* (i.e., the *negation* of similarity) in other aspects of horses and humans. In an important sense, therefore, Durkheim's "primitives" engage in precisely such "psychotic" reasoning, for, as Durkheim noted, their "idea of force is of religious origin." So if Durkheim's famous thesis about the origin of such an idea in the "social forces" of religious ritual is correct, then the succeeding cognition of the "force" of the causal efficacy of natural objects could account for the "false syllogism" of their "primitive" mentality—"human society has force; lightning has force; therefore lightning is human society"![110]

As if in anticipation of my own anxiety that my comparison between the "logic" noted by Durkheim in "primitive" society to the thought processes of modern psychotics, may be misread as a blatant example of "politically incorrect" sensibility—a comparison, I might add, that in less sensitive times Freud had not hesitated to make in the subtitle he had chosen to pen in 1913 to his *Totem and Taboo*: "Resemblances between the psychic lives of savages and neurotics"!—Rayner reinforced the Freudian tradition's decidedly *nonpejorative* linkage of psychotic (or borderline psychotic, as in severe neurosis) thought with the thought processes of children by citing the work of Jean Piaget (specifically, *The Psychology of Intelligence and Play, Dreams, and Imitation in Childhood*) in support of his assertion that the "symmetrization" of conceptual relations so ap-

parent in psychotic thinking is really normal within the thinking processes of
modern children below the age of four years, which Piaget had labeled as a stage
of "ego-centrism." In the light of that criticism by Anthony Giddens (which I
have repeatedly cited) of the "thesis of the homology of society and personality,
which became an explicit supposition" in that equation in "Habermas's later writings," of the decentering social process of modernization with Piaget's notion of
the decentering of the individual ego,[111] it behooves me to reproduce in full here,
the citation by Rayner of Piaget's latter book:

> In a state of radical ego-centrism (as can be approximated to at times in the ut-
> terances of any small child) there is complete lack of differentiation between
> the ego and the external world. . . . The origin of the unconscious symbol is to
> be found in the suppression of the ego by complete absorption in, and identifi-
> cation with, the external world, it therefore constitutes merely a limiting case
> of assimilation of reality to the ego, i.e., of ludic symbolism.[112]

What Piaget—and, by extension, Habermas, in that "homology of society
and personality . . . in Habermas's later writings" that Giddens has excoriated—
called the cognitive stage of egocentrism had also been labeled by Peirce, in a
similarly homologous equation of social and individual cognitive processes the
"egotistical stage" of social evolution.[113]

That Peirce had *indeed* been indulging in precisely such homologizing "of
society and personality" that Giddens now condemns is made crystal clear by
philosopher Max Fisch (a recognized expert, specializing in the scholarly interpretation of Peirce's writings, designated as the general editor of the Chronological Edition of Peirce's writings) in his introduction to volume 1 of the *Writings of
Charles S. Peirce* (containing Peirce's writings of 1857-1866) when he specifically presents that 1863 periodization of social evolution by Peirce—into a past
"egotistical" stage, a present "idistical" stage, and a future "tuistical" stage—as a
direct derivation by Peirce, from his own earlier formulation, written in January
1959, of the cognitive-communicative process of individual linguistic behavior as
a process moving progressively from "I" (i.e., in Latin, the "*ego*-tistical" stage) to
"IT" (i.e., in Latin, the "*id*-istical" stage) to "THOU" (i.e. in Latin, "tu-istical"
stage). Furthermore, as if such direct etymological evidence of Peirce's intention
in creating a "homology of society and personality" (in Giddens's critical terminology) were not by itself sufficient, Fisch also compares Peirce's terminology
with Martin Buber's famous book *I and Thou,* a book which had itself been a
product of such a (non-Giddensian) society-personality "homology," by Buber's
own account: Buber had always openly admitted to having derived his *psychology*
of "I-Thou" relationships from Ferdinand Toennies's 1887 *sociological* conceptualization of a psychologically healthy past of premodern *gemeinschaft* relationships—focused upon personal *I-Thou* forms of communication—having been
displaced and superseded by a psychologically unhealthy present of modern

gesellschaft relationships—focusing upon impersonal *I-It* forms of encounter between individuals.[114]

Had Durkheim enjoyed the good fortune, as I now do, of reading "The Cambridge Conferences Lectures of 1898" by Charles Sanders Peirce, he might have noticed that in lecture seven of these 1898 lectures—dedicated specifically to the elucidation of his concept of "habit"—Peirce had specifically addressed that beginning of all cognitive habits in what he had termed the "association by resemblance," whereby "an idea which may be roughly compared to a composite photograph surges into vividness."[115] Peirce was later to call such a picture-like original idea emerging into human consciousness through such association by resemblance an *icon*, and the contemporary Peirce-influenced American sociologist Barry Schwartz has remained faithful to Peirce's definitional intention in his own presentation of the "iconic" sign as a signifier that "in some way resembles the signified, as a portrait represents a person."[116] Not only does Peirce's delineation in 1898 of such iconic "association by resemblance" explain that "confusion" between humans and the other objective "kingdoms" of animals, plants, rocks, and so on, noted by Durkheim in his 1912 study of "primitive religion"—in that, if Durkheim had been correct in his assertion that "the idea of force is of religious origin," then such an *icon* of force, formed by the perception of human collective force in religious ritual, would then carry over in subsequent perceptions of the *resemblances* of such force in nonhuman objects—but Peirce had himself, as Durkheim was later to do, focused upon the operation of such iconic thinking "by resemblance" in religion in his *Lecture Eight* in 1898, wherein, referring to religious people engaging in theological discourse, Peirce had said:

> They represent the ideas as springing into a preliminary stage of being by their own inherent firstness. But so springing up, they do not spring up isolated; for if they did, nothing could unite them. They spring up in reaction upon one another, and thus into a kind of existence. This reaction and this existence these persons call the mind of God. I really think there is no objection to this except that it is wrapped up in figures of speech, instead of having the explicitness that we desire in science. For all you know of "minds" is from the actions of animals with brains or ganglia like yourselves or at furthest like a cockroach. To apply such a word to *God* is precisely like the old pictures which show him like an aged man leaning over to look out from above a cloud. Considering the *vague intention* of it, as conceived by the *non-theological* artist, it cannot be called false, but rather ludicrously figurative.[117]

In his 1993 "essay in corporeal semiotics," the mathematical philosopher Brian Rotman sums up what Peirce had meant by *firstness*—the first of three steps or stages that Peirce had discovered in his phenomenological study of the process of human cognition—as "possibility, experience 'in itself.'"[118] If we keep in mind that assertion about the *external* focus of the human mind that Peirce had already made in 1868 in his first of four denials—asserting that "we have no power of introspection, but all knowledge of the internal world is derived by hypothetical reasoning from external facts"[119]—and then notice Durkheim's similar focus upon the *external* "thing" in his 1912 explanation of the totemic "representation" of the internal "collective force . . . felt" in religious ritual—"Men thus felt compelled," Durkheim had argued, "to represent the collective force, whose action they felt, in the form of the thing serving as flag to the group"[120]—it becomes obvious that whatever *convergence* Durkheim's thinking had been heading toward in 1912 had been *not* with general philosophical idealism, as Parsons had argued in 1937,[121] nor even with that merely sociological convergence with the thought of Marshall, Pareto, and Weber that Parsons's 1937 book had argued as its central thesis, but more specifically a convergence with what Christopher Hookway has broadly called the "objective idealism" and Nicholas Rescher has narrowed, more specifically, to the notion of "conceptual idealism" of Peirce's Pragmatism.[122]

In order then to fully comprehend that "beginning" of human cultural evolution, in which totemic association by resemblance had produced, according to Durkheim, a cognitive situation in which "all the kingdoms are confounded with each other,"[123] it is helpful to return to lecture three, "The Logic of Relatives," of Peirce's Cambridge Lectures of 1898, for Peirce's definition of the cognitive category of *Firstness*:

> It is the mode in which anything would be for itself, irrespective of anything else, so that it would not make any difference though nothing else existed, or ever had existed, or could exist. Now this mode of being can only be apprehended as a mode of feeling. For there is no mode of being which we can conceive as having no relation to the possibility of anything else. In the first place, the First must be without parts. For a part of an object is something other than the object itself. Remembering these points, you will perceive that any color, say *magenta*, has and is a positive mode of feeling, irrespective of every other.[124]

When Durkheim wrote in 1912 about how totemic religious practitioners "represent the collective force, whose action they felt,"[125] he could *not* have disagreed with the Peircean insight that "in the beginning" (a phrase which Durkheim had specifically used and which, more than coincidentally, bears the same connotation of Peirce's *Firstness*!)[126] of cultural evolution, there had only been the cognitive category of Peircean firstness, as a "mode of feeling" analogous to our seeing the color magenta. Since, as Peirce had explained, "the First must be without parts" for "a part of an object" must be "something other than the object itself," it is then no surprise at all that—unlike modern people who will almost automatically break down analytically their experience of "force" into its component experiences, thereby conceptually separating the "part" which is of human origin from another part which is of animal, plant, or inanimate origin—

Durkheim's "primitives" (now a politically incorrect word, which nevertheless also still maintains its etymological correctness in being a Latin cognate of the Peircean concept of "First") simply "felt" force, in that same simple, nonanalytical manner in which we "moderns" may still "feel" the color magenta (i.e., without having to immediately separate analytically into different categories all those possible objects that could have possibly been referred to by our general color word).

But the reason modern social scientists might feel, as Durkheim had indicated, that such primitive "logic is disconcerting for us" had *also* already been explained by Peirce in 1898, when he had argued that it was precisely because "Firstness is all that it is, for itself, irrespective of anything else," that

> when viewed *from without* (and therefore no longer in the original fullness of firstness) the firstnesses are all the different possible sense-qualities, embracing endless varieties of which we can all feel are but minute fragments. Each of these is just as simple as any other. It is impossible for a sense quality to be otherwise than absolutely simple. It is only complex to the eye of comparison, not in itself.[127]

But, having thus demonstrated the convergence around the concept of "association by resemblance" between the thinking of primitives (as studied by Durkheim in 1912) and the Pragmatist cognitive category of "firstness" (of individual cognitive process, as delineated by Peirce in 1898), I am still left with the problem of explaining the *precise mechanism* by which *all* the individuals in Durkheim's primitive society had been "constrained" to think by similar Peircean firstness. Or, to phrase my question in terms of that "thesis of the homology of society and personality" that Anthony Giddens has criticized in "Habermas's later writings," by what mechanism does that "childhood of society" presented in Durkheim's *Elementary Forms* "structurate" (to continue my usage of Giddens's terminology) its general cognitive norm of Peircean firstness into "the childhood of the individual" socialized in its totemic midst?[128]

As my reader can probably tell, this question about the *specific mechanism* of social-to-individual "structuration" now returns me to that question of Ellie Ragland-Sullivan's Lacanian "*je* codes" with whose enticing possibilities of formulation I ended chapter 3 on the social "empowerment" of the individual self. The enticement of Ragland-Sullivan's notion of such "*je* codes" lay in their promise of a dictionary-like translation of all the semantic meanings of the "speaking *je*" into their pragmatic equivalents in the social cooperation that had socialized the six-month-old infant's identificatory self-image (i.e., the Lacanian *moi*), with its "second meaning or intentional pressure."[129] Referring to this "brief discussion of Lacan's historical dimension" by Ragland-Sullivan, Teresa Brennan had lamented, in her 1993 book *History after Lacan*, that such a "historical dimension" implicit in Lacan's psychoanalytical theory of the individual's development of a sense of self had "not been developed" (by either Lacan himself, or by his exegetes such as Ellie Ragland-Sullivan). To then develop such a "historical dimension" implicit within Lacan's psychoanalytical theory, Brennan herself had focused upon that "time element" in the articulation between the *je* and *moi* aspects of the Lacanian personality, a "time element" that she accused Lacan of having left "obscure"—a Lacanian obscurity especially noted by Brennan as weighing heavily upon that Giddensian question of society-personality homology that concerns us here, about whether such temporal articulation between semantic *je* and pragmatic *moi* "operates on an individual or a social level"—to offer us her synthesis of the ideas of "Lacan, Freud, Klein, Marx, and Heidegger to an extent, also Derrida," within "the feminist context in which they were synthesized," in her own theory of "how the subject is founded in a hallucinatory fantasy" of its own "active agency" and "subjectivity," which is "projected" in paranoid fashion "onto the environment, apparently beginning with the mother."[130]

The problem that I find in any attempt to use Brennan's development of Lacan's "historical dimension" here—a problem that looms beyond the obvious opposition that her vision of the apparently *incurable* paranoid subject's "foundational fantasy" offers against Lacan's own *Peircean* insistence (contained within a passage from Lacan's *Ecrits* that Brennan herself cites!) about there invariably being a "way out" through "communication," from the paranoid tendencies of the subject's Imaginary *moi*[131]—is Brennan's own restriction of the applicability of her Lacanian theory of history to the specific locus of the "ego's spiral of aggression" in the modern "ego's era" of Western "colonization, urban and territorial expansion."[132]

In my own search then, for the specific mechanism operating in what Giddens calls the "homology of society and personality," in that collective employment of Peirce's category of *firstness* by Durkheim's "primitive" society, within the articulated personality dynamics between Lacanian *je* and *moi*—an articulation between aspects of the individual personality that does not *inevitably* result in what Brennan (borrowing from the Kleinian psychoanalyst Wilfred Bion) sees as the psychotic tendencies of the *moi*'s "attacks on linking" of the speaking *je*'s struggles for "insight"[133]—I can only fall back upon that reading of Lacan's personality dynamics within the tradition of Peirce's Pragmatism, for which I have already prepared the way by indicating (in my section on Lacan in chapter 3) the patently obvious theoretical convergence of Lacan's theory of the "three orders" of cognition with Peirce's triadic phenomenology of cognition.[134]

As I have indicated before, whereas it may be difficult to speak (without raising ambiguities in the reader's mind) about any unitary philosophical tradition of Peirce's Pragmatism—because Peirce had himself recoiled between 1902 and 1905, as Durkheim had been aware, from the "kidnapping" by the influential philosophical writings of William James of his Pragmatic Maxim of meaning to define his own relativistic theory of truth[135]—it is still possible to speak without any such ambiguity of an intact psychological tradition of Peirce's Pragmatism, because James's eminently influential 1890 textbook *The Principles of Psychol-*

ogy had faithfully preserved and transmitted Peirce's evolutionist definition of *habit* (as an organically adaptive echo of natural laws). It is therefore to that historical echo in the American institutionalization of sociology, of Durkheim's similar struggle to institutionalize sociology earlier in France, that Charles Camic had seen in W. I. Thomas's struggle with the incorporation by John Watson's behaviorism of the Pragmatist conception of "habit," that we may fortunately turn for our articulation between the Lacanian speaking *je* and imagistic *moi* self-identification.[136]

Keeping in mind then, that Lacan's *moi* is, by Lacan's own definition, unconscious (since for Lacan, the Freudian "unconscious" is defined by that prelinguistic imagery later excluded from linguistic consciousness by the growing infant's linguistic development), we may note that Thomas's 1927 exploration of the individual personality's unconscious part—an exploration of the personal "unconscious" that Thomas had undertaken nine years after his 1918 break, according to Camic, with Watsonian psychology's annexation of the Pragmatist concept of "habit"[137]—reveals the susceptibility of this personal unconscious, to the speaking voices of significant others (in G. H. Mead's terminology). For Thomas, within the personal "unconscious,"

> the verbalization of behavior, the voices of the living and the voices of the dead, the laws and the prophets, result in a body of collective habit—the "collective representations" of Durkheim and Levy-Bruhl and the "collective unconscious" of Jung. But for the individual it is a "lapsed consciousness," structuralized, shall we say, in the habit system, but not structuralized in the sense of organically inheritable, merely as a body of habit traditionally perpetuated.[138]

Lacan (whose therapeutic sessions had notoriously "turned out to be *shorter* than the prescribed forty-five to fifty minutes," according to Peter Rudnytsky, arousing "suspicions that the real purpose of his innovation was to serve the convenience of the analyst," but whose real motive, according to Steven Mitchell and Margaret Black had been "his central concern with the seductive dangers of compliance with the analyst's own ideals and values"[139]) could surely not have disagreed with that 1927 assessment by Thomas about the efficacy of "the voices of the living"—Lacan's own "seductive" analyst's voice, being among those then "living" voices—upon the unconscious imagery of his *moi*.

With that nonspeaking Lacanian *moi*—the "primary identification" of an individual formed by the time he or she is six months old—thus responding to the voices of the speaking *je*'s of all others within the same society, and in its responsiveness indicating to us the channel through which society could exert its normative impact upon even the most deeply "unconscious" part of the individual self, we are then left only with the question of how each individual's speaking *je* responds to its own *moi*, in order then to address society in its turn, with its (the Lacanian *je*'s) own semantics.

Again, it is W. I. Thomas who shows us the way out of Lacan's possibly confusing (postmodernist) rhetoric and into the relative clarity of Peircean Pragmatism. For, having defined his key concept of "attitude" in his 1918 book on *The Polish Peasant*—i.e., in that very definition of *attitude* that Charles Camic had seen as *decisive in sundering* American sociology from the concept of "habit" in the Pragmatist psychological tradition[140]—as "a process of individual consciousness which determines real or possible activity of the individual in the social world," and declared that "attitude is thus the individual counterpart of . . . social value," Thomas had proceeded to also identify, in a formulation of crucial importance to my project here, the manner in which psychology would study attitude differently from sociology:

> A psychological process is an attitude treated as an object in itself, isolated by a reflective act of attention. . . . An attitude is a psychological process treated as primarily manifested in its reference to the social world and taken first of all in connection with some social value. Individual psychology may later reestablish the connection between the psychological process and the objective reality which has been severed by reflection. . . . But it is the original (usually unconsciously occupied) standpoints which determine at once the subsequent methods of these two sciences. The psychological process remains always fundamentally a *state of somebody*; the attitude remains always fundamentally an attitude *toward something*.[141]

In having, sundered American sociology from psychology, as Camic accuses him of doing, Thomas may also, through the semantic formulations he had employed in his separation of the two sciences, help us decipher—in that notorious "elusiveness" which Mitchell and Black found in 1995 of the semantic formulations of Lacan's French attempt to *reunite* the two sciences upon the basis of human linguistic communication the key mechanisms behind the perceived homology between Durkheim's primitive society's collective thinking through association by resemblance and Peirce's First stage of individual cognition. For if, as we have just seen in Thomas's 1918 formulation, attitude is "a process of individual consciousness which determines real or possible activity"—which includes, one need hardly add, the activity of Lacan's "*je* who speaks"—"of the individual in the social world," and this attitude is a "reflective act of attention . . . *toward something*," then Giddens's possible question about the basis of my own "homology of society and personality" reduces to a simple question about the code by which any society—such as, for example, the primitive society studied by Durkheim in 1912—structures, through its cooperative process in socializing its young, the "habit system" of acts of attention in what Thomas had, in 1927, mapped as the "unconscious" and Lacan had, in 1949, delineated as the *moi* self-image of his mirror stage.[142]

To return then to that definition of the concept of a "code" in Talmy Givon's 1989 "Essays in Pragmatics" as a "system of signs," and then to notice the philosopher of science Mary Hesse's attempt to flesh out such a notion of "system" in her Durkheim-based "socializing" of epistemology by defining a "cognitive system" specifically as "a mental schema modeling some aspect of the world,"[143] we may then—having been helped by Thomas's formulations of 1918 and 1927, respectively—ask rather specifically, How was the "cognitive system" of Durkheim's 1912 primitive society structured *into* the personalities of its individual members as their individual habits of attention?

To be able to answer such a Thomasian question about what that "something" is in Thomas's 1918 definition of attitude as "a reflective act of attention . . . *toward something*" and how the cognitive code of a society can "structuralize"—as Thomas's 1927 essay "The Unconscious" phrased it—the "habit system" of its individual members in such a way that "unconsciously" those individuals return selectively (i.e., habitually) to focus mainly upon that "something" in their "reflective acts of attention," we must review, with Lacanian hindsight, that central thesis of Durkheim's *Elementary Forms*: the thesis stating that "the idea of force is of religious origin."[144]

The peculiarity of this Durkheimian thesis is that, when viewed through the hindsight of our knowledge of Lacan's theory of mirror-state identification, it reveals itself to be neither wholly true nor wholly false: It does not tell the whole truth, because Durkheim's adult primitives must obviously have once been children, and the male child, at least, as Freud pointed out in the last chapter—"Infantile Recurrence"—of his 1913 book *Totem and Taboo* (calling upon Charles Darwin's testimony, among that of various other, mostly social, scientists, in his refutation of Durkheim's thesis) has already had his experience of social "force," long before his adult participation in religious ritual, in "his fear of his father."[145]

In this debate between Freud's 1913 *Totem and Taboo* and Durkheim's 1912 *Elementary Forms* about the origins of the social "force" of taboo, the Freudian Lacan would, at first glance, seem to side with Freud against Durkheim by his very location of the "reality principle" learned by the child within that context that Ragland-Sullivan described as "the Law of the Name-of-the-Father, or the Oedipal Structure."[146] But, as we have already seen, Freud had, according to Ragland-Sullivan, changed his ideas about how the process of identification developed at least four times between his 1914 essay "On Narcissism" to his New *Introductory Essays* of 1933, where he finally "compared identification with the oral-cannibalistic incorporation of another person—reaffirming the oral pre-Oedipal link to the mother in primary identification."[147] If Freud's 1933 view of such pre-Oedipal primary identification with the mother is more correct than that Oedipal "fear of his father" presented in 1913 in *Totem and Taboo*[148]—and if there exists a single point of agreement between Jacques Lacan and all the British object-relations psychoanalysts from Melanie Klein to Donald Winnicott, it is that that 1933 view by Freud of the crucial importance for the child's cognitive and other development of the pre-Oedipal "primary identification" with the mother has greater empirical support from clinical observation than does that 1913 hypothetical linkage by Freud, of the later Oedipal "secondary identification" with the father to Darwin's theory of the "primal social state of man" (the Darwinian origin of that famous Freudian concept of the Primal Horde)[149]—then that 1933 Freudian conception of maternal "primary identification" transfers the age locus of Durkheim's problem of the "origin" of the "idea of force" even further back in age from Freud's 1913 location of its origin in the infant male's Oedipal struggle with his father: As the writings of Klein and Winnicott about the "Paranoid-Schizoid position" and the "ruthless" nature of the infant's desire to "kill the mother," respectively, even before it has achieved the age of six months, attest, all humans have already "known" the "idea of force" by the time they have reached Lacan's celebrated "mirror stage" at the age of six months. And in that extremely early cognition of "force" lies—paradoxically—the *truth* of Durkheim's thesis: For since, according to Lacan's theory of the mirror stage, any awareness that the six-month-old infant may have of the social "force" of its maternal caregiver's will is essentially preverbal, it is therefore rendered "unconscious" by the later development of its language. That "religious origin" of "the idea of force" that Durkheim had posited in 1912 in *The Elementary Forms* is true in that what Freud had labeled "infantile recurrence" in 1913 must essentially await the linguistic recognition of the infantile preverbal experience of parental force, in the adult (or adolescent) linguistically competent individual's participation in collective ritual. As the ex-Marxist French philosopher Simone Weil was to rediscover between December 1934—when she abandoned her postdoctoral academic status for her "experience of factory work . . . in heavy industry in the Paris region"—and "her presence at the Gregorian liturgy during Holy Week in 1938 in the Abbey of Solesmes," which completed her comprehension-through-participant-observation of proletarian religiosity, even in the modernity of the twentieth century the reality of force is, to paraphrase Durkheim, best recognized through religious ritual.[150]

Perhaps the most succinct expression of my post-Lacan line of argument here, that Durkheim's thesis in *The Elementary Forms* that "the idea of force is of religious origin" could be better rephrased as asserting that "the verbal re-cognition of force originates in collective ritual," is in that deployment by Fred Alford in his 1989 book *Melanie Klein and Critical Social Theory* of the homology between Winnicott's conception of the maternal function of "holding" the infant and the Durkheimian social group's function of "containing" the adult individual's anxieties (an argument that Alford proffered explicitly against the "methodological individualism" of Max Weber's type). As Alford, explained:

> Winnicott has developed the concept of "holding" or what I will sometimes call containment, especially when referring to the group. . . . Originally the

term referred to the first stage of the infant's development, in which the infant and mother are symbiotic. At this stage, as Klein points out, the infant's deepest fear is of disintegration, the fragmentation of his poorly integrated ego. Holding contains this potential for fragmentation, not merely by the act of providing security (the paradigm of holding is, of course, the physical act of cradling) but also by providing a medium through which the infant can express his needs and receive a satisfying, calming response. In the absence of holding, the infant will seek to "hold itself," withdrawing from any stimuli that might overwhelm his nascent ego. Here is the breeding ground for severe emotional disorder. . . . Group culture is a form of holding, of containment, in Winnicott's sense. This is not merely an analogy. If an analytic session can be a form of holding, so too can a group experience, such as the president's State of the Union Address. . . . Like the analyst's interpretation, cultural explanations give anxiety a name, a locus, and a meaning, all of which help distinguish anxiety from the self experiencing the anxiety. This mitigates the anxiety, rendering it less overwhelming, less prone to disintegrate the self, and hence more manageable. . . . It is this view of the group as holding and interpreting its members' anxieties that connects individual and group psychology.[151]

And it was this Winnicottian view presented by Alford, of the individual's social matrix as literally—as in that Latin derivation of the word "matrix" from *mater*—a maternal entity "cradling" the terror-filled anxieties of Durkheim's primitives within the amply "containing" function of its collective ritual, that led me to name the possible "interpretant" (in that Peircean sense discussed in the introduction to this book) code[152] that "structuralized . . . the habit system" (in W. I. Thomas's phrasing) of their conscious individual "attitudes"—their "reflective acts of attention . . . *toward something*" (again according to Thomas's phrasing)— toward those quasi-parental "spirits and gods" (that Durkheim had discussed in his last chapter of book 2, on the origins of totemic beliefs, in *The Elementary Forms* in 1912, and Peirce had discussed in lecture eight of his 1898 lectures as resulting from the association by resemblance of *Firstness*)[153] as the code of *filiation*: the code which structures the semantic, verbalized cognition of the preverbal human experience of having once "belonged," as a child, to a parental caregiver, whose "force" of will had been (however slowly, within those first six months after birth) originally experienced—"in the beginning"—as "external" to oneself.

The functioning of this socially cooperative, communicative code of *filiation*—a concept of the functioning of a pragmatic code that constructs the effectiveness of communication by first structuring every communication-receiver's habits of attention along those very lines that Anthony Giddens has criticized as "the general idea that the 'childhood of society' is like the childhood of the individual"[154]—had already been explained by the Peirce-influenced sociologist

Barry Schwartz in 1981, when he had pointed out the "metaphoricality" of those socio-cognitive categories, that, beginning with the 1901 essay by Emile Durkheim and Marcel Mauss, "Some Primitive Forms of Classification," and continuing with Durkheim's *Elementary Forms* in 1912, had marked the attempts at formulating a sociology of knowledge by Durkheim's "French School" of sociological thought all the way to the structural anthropology of Claude Levi-Strauss. As Schwartz had pointed out, that association by resemblance noted by almost every social-scientific study of preliterate societies by thinkers of Durkheim's French School, assimilates to those signs of *Firstness* that Peirce had classified as "icons"—which had included images, as well as diagrams and metaphors—and it is the functioning of such *iconic* communication in preliterate society that cognitively converts that experience that pediatrician Rene Spitz had noted of the child's constant looking up at the parent—a looking up that begins, as Dr. Spitz had noted, with that "first visual percept in life to be crystallized out from the various kinds of light blurs . . . the human face"[155]—through what Schwartz characterized as a "parallel in language," to that infantilized social connotation of the "child-like" adult "dependent" upon socially dominant others:

> To be "dependent" means to be "hanging down." But from what? Thass-Thienemann has shown that in at least several archaic languages it is the nursing child who is said to be "hanging down from its mother's breast." And even today the overly dependent child is described as one who too zealously "hangs on" to his parent. Similarly, adults who are dependent on some superior for their well-being are said to be "hangers-on." They get along by clinging to someone bigger than themselves.[156]

"Durkheim overemphasized social constraints on primitive thought," Schwartz argued, by not locating, as he was now trying to do, his conception of the "sacred" within the semiotic system of communicative and cognitive signification:

> The derivation of "revere" is from the Latin: the prefix re (again) is joined to *vereri* (to fear). The word "respect" is also derived from Latin: the same prefix (*re*) is connected to the root *spect* (to look or see). The sacred (revered and awe-inspiring) object may thus be said to be *consistently* and *conspicuously* awe-inspiring. In this sense, the entailments of sacredness are embodied in the very words we use to define it.[157]

Or, as a famous example from classical literature not cited by Schwartz demonstrates, the *pietas* which the Roman poet Virgil's hero, Aeneas, had directed in the *Aeneid* specifically toward his own father, was later in the Middle Ages directed by Christian society toward God the Father in such an exclusive manner as to change the meaning of the word *piety* itself—through that linguistic translation that Schwartz calls "vertical classification"—from its individual-to-individual "verticality" in Virgil's son-to-father "piety" to the purely social-religious connotations of later Christian piety.

Indeed, this metaphorical transfer of meaning from the infant's experience of personal dependence into the "self-description" of social organization—a linguistic homology between personality and society that Schwartz called "vertical classification" but that I, in my respect for the possibility that egalitarian hunter-gatherers may have lacked such "verticality" in their stratification, have preferred to neutrally label as the communicative "interpretant" code of *filiation*—was historically so ubiquitous until modernization (which, as we have seen, Immanuel Kant, arguing in 1784, had seemed to release humanity from its state of "immaturity" or "minority") that the political sociologist Peter Manicas suggested in 1988 it be considered as the single, universal mechanism of "legitimation" in premodern polity:

> "King" relates etymologically to "kin" and "kindred," and kings had been thought of as head of a "nation," or a "people," whereas as the word "king" suggests, the basis for the unity of the group was a fictive progenitor of a common identity defined in terms of local language and inherited custom. Similarly, grounded in the root metaphor of "a family," customary rights could be sufficient for the distribution of authority. These ideas continued to have a strong hold, even well past the seventeenth century when they were challenged by the new ideas that we associate with the "contract theory" of Hobbes and Locke.[158]

That suggestion by Manicas of "the root metaphor of 'a family'" had originally tempted me to name my social code of Peircean *firstness* as "familism." However, I changed the name to "*filiation*," not only because I had been influenced, as I indicated earlier, by Fred Alford's critique of Weberian methodological individualism by using Melanie Klein-to-Donald Winnicott object relations psychology, but also because the continuing changes in family structure in Western society might have risked confusion as to what type of "family" my socio-cognitive adaptation of Peirce's *first* cognitive step of thinking by "similarity" or "resemblance" refer: since, in whatever type of family, the experience of "*filiation*" continues to enjoy a universal meaning (of a dependent childhood in infancy), this latter word grounds that Peircean concept of "similarity" in the same sense of Manicas's "root metaphor"—socio-political dependence is conceptualized (or "legitimated," in that Weberian terminology employed by Manicas) as "similar" to childhood dependence on adult care-givers. Any semantic search through the premodern historical experience of humanity—across the global range of human social arrangements—should reveal the "familistic" connotations of the interpretant code of *filiation*: from the "Pope" (i.e. "Papa" meaning "father") of Roman Catholicism, to the Imperial "Son of Heaven" in premodern

China, whose portraiture as physically bigger than his subjects vividly displays the iconic representation of what Schwartz called "vertical classification."[159] the interpretant code of *filiation* had enabled that historical increase in social inequality that Gerhard Lenski had seen in humanity's socio-technical development from hunter-gatherer to agricultural subsistence-forms, by "legitimating" such increasing inequality by its semantics of "filial" dependence.[160]

In a deft reminder of how my Peirce-Durkheim-later Parsons theoretical "lineage" in the conceptualization of social power—as outlined in chapter 2's extended argument against that "domination-plus-legitimation" theme that both the Pluralism of Robert Dahl and the Elitism of C. Wright Mills, had inherited from Max Weber's socio-historical formulations—differs from the Weberian theorization of "legitimation" by Manicas, Schwartz had focused upon that very target of Parsons's 1960 theoretical polemic about the nature of social power, Mills: "The structuralist approach to the sociology of knowledge," said Schwartz, "invites us to put aside C. Wright Mills's notion of language as a mediator of mind and society in favor of a language of mediators."[161] So, to remind my reader of the similar difference between my Peircean code of "*filiation*" and the Weberian thematics of "legitimation" by Manicas: unlike that Weberian vision of prelinguistic, fully formed subjects (or agents) having their historical subjectivity "legitimated" by the "root metaphor of 'the family,'" Peircean pragmatics would see instead how the "metaphoricality" of linguistic communication in the premodern "interpretant" of *filiation* constructs and forms/shapes subjectivity to such an extent that premodern subjects may have often been "unconscious" about how such a code operated to "constrain" their actions—and their very habits of attention—within the "piety" (or loyalty) that the code demanded from them toward the "sacred" bodies of their social superiors.

But the problem with such a deep-structural approach to the "unconscious" construction of the historical actor's subjectivity by communication is that—unlike that easy clarity displayed by the Weberian individualist conceptual optic of Manicas in his seeing the possible historical ending of the "root metaphor of 'the family'" in the emergence of the competing "legitimation" paradigm of the conception of society as "contract" by Thomas Hobbes and John Locke—such Durkheimian (and Peircean) collectivist deep-structuralism, appears to falter in its attempt to comprehend the cognitive structures of modernity: Talking about modern class stratification, for example, Schwartz betrayed his obvious puzzlement about the status (within modernity) of his linguistically metaphorical concept of "vertical classification," by confessing:

> In most modern societies, all of which (according to the *Ethnographic Atlas* definition) have elaborate systems of class stratification, body inclination forms are hardly perceptible. The traditional bow, for example, shows up as a slight nod or leaning forward of the head. . . . Many observers of developing countries have been told, in response to questions concerning the propriety of

profound abasements, that "we no longer do that sort of thing." Several of the university students interviewed in connection with the survey on synonyms . . . made the same point. On the other hand, while gestural abasements have become less pronounced with the breakdown of traditional society, we have seen that linguistic metaphors remain as vivid as ever. This raises the question of whether the linguistic form is to be understood as a "survival" of more primitive conceptions, or whether it is the more basic and resistant and the last to give way to changing conditions.[162]

Since Schwartz had only used Peirce's concept of the "iconic" sign of *first-ness*—without proceeding to analyze or utilize either Peircean *secondness* or *thirdness*—in his own theorizing about (premodern) vertical classification, he had been poorly equipped to explore modernity, which I believe can only be comprehended as the communicative reign of Peirce's second or "indexical" signs, literally functioning in modernity as the Dow-Jones or NASDAQ economic index, as well as other economic and scientific "indicators," much as religious icons dominated premodernity.

But furthermore, by having refused to follow, as I have done, Charles Morris's disciplinary breakdown of Peircean semiotic into that triple disciplinary distinction of syntax, semantics and pragmatics, Schwartz incapacitated the acuity of his own theoretical vision in following up his very relevant question about the possible *survival* of premodern "linguistic form" within modernity. Such an evolutionary survival is visible, as I will show, not at the level of purely semantic meaning, but "nested" within the deeper, "unconscious" structures of a *hierarchy* of pragmatic codes.

What Schwartz's refusal to "go all the way"—as I do—with Peircean Pragmatics leaves him doing is lamenting, with that other Durkheimian structuralist, Mary Douglas, the paucity of guidance given us by Durkheim into the cognitive structures of modernity. As Schwartz implicitly agrees, in citing Douglas, "Instead of showing us the social structuring of our minds, he showed us the minds of feathered Indians and painted aborigines."[163]

That paucity of Durkheimian formulation lamented by Douglas and Schwartz about the cognitive process of cultural evolution into modernity now also constrains my own path into this major historical transition point between two pragmatic codes—from the premodern Peircean *firstness* of iconic thinking by resemblance (to filiated persons) to modern Peircean *secondness* of indexical thinking by contiguity (to calibrated objects)—to the furrow plowed by Max Weber's celebrated historical question: Why did such a modernizing transition occur first in Europe and not in the much older civilizations of China or India?

In order to address the much debated "Weber Thesis" of *The Protestant Ethic*—so as to theoretically metabolize its specifically cognitive themes into my Peircean evolutionism—I must situate within my evolutionary time frame that all-important cognitive-communicative human achievement, the development of literacy, without which Weber's Reforming Protestant agents would not even have been capable of counterposing their post-Gutenberg printed Biblical texts against the authority of Papal Catholic *filiation*.

Though we may not yet have agreement—as is clear, for example, in Wayne Senner's 1989 presentation of the historical debates about *The Origins of Writing*—about the precise origination of the literary skill,[164] we do know that, within that historical process of (a Darwinian struggle for) adaptation of human bodies to environmental constraints (for cultural evolution does not suspend the biological need for food and shelter any more than it suspends physical gravity), increasing human populations pressed for inclusion within spatially broader territorial cultural units. Those processes of coercive inclusion within ever-larger political units—coercive processes comprehended within Hegelian (or Hegelian-Marxist) theories as instances of the "master-slave dialectic" and reformulated here (in a more realistic fashion, I believe) within my own Peircean (i.e., non-Hegelian) view of history as a resigned acceptance by defeated and terrorized populations, of more inclusive (and more abstract) *filiation* interpretant-codes—strained those "face-to-face" communicative relationships of original hunter-gatherer tribal *filiation*. Without the skills of literacy—mastered by political elites, at least—premodern communication over those increasingly greater spatial distances would just not have been possible.

Regardless then, of the precise historical origination of literary skill, we may now gauge the pragmatic consequences of literacy upon human cognitive habits by combining the insights of anthropologists such as Jack Goody with those of communications-theorists such as Walter Ong—as Alfred Burns does in his description of the Grice-like Cooperative Principle operating between writer and reader, when distance forces the written letter to substitute for oral speech:

> The hearer is no longer face-to-face with the speaker. The Reader cannot ask the writer to clarify his meaning, nor can the writer expect any feedback telling him whether he has been understood. Therefore much greater precision in expression becomes imperative; definition of terms and causal connections must be stated. Written communication has to follow certain mutually agreed-on rules of logic and organization.[165]

That new cooperative principle of written communication developed, in David Olson's similar synthesis of Goody's anthropology with Ong's communication theory and with the socio-linguistic theory of M. A. K. Halliday (which I cited in chapter 1), into new habits of attention—attention to objects rather than, as had hitherto been the case, to parental or child-like people within the earlier (i.e., the first, in Peirce's terminology) interpretant code of *filiation*—producing that "identification of objectivity with a text" by the later European Middle Ages, which developed, with the Protestant Reformation's emphasis on reading Biblical Scripture, into the scientific objectivity of reading the "Book of Nature." As Olson summarizes this lengthy historical development of the human mastery of the skill of literacy into the modern attitude of objectivity, "Objectivity is just reading the Book of Nature according to the evidence available to the senses," and social cooperation in such reading of the Book of Nature produces that accumulation of texts that the philosopher of science Karl Popper had, in 1972, called "World Three" of "objective knowledge." Or, as Victor Hugo had comprehended such a historical movement occasioned by the diffusion of literacy in his 1831 novel, *Notre Dame de Paris*, the cognitive attitude of objectivism bred by a book-oriented cultural sensibility would "kill" the filiative subjectivism of traditional religion represented by the church edifice of Notre Dame in Paris: "This will kill that. . . . The printing-press will kill the Church. . . . All civilizations begin in theocracy and end in democracy."[166]

What we find, in other words, by such a tracing of the historical process of the (literary) transfer of communicative attention away from subjectively significant, parental (or filial), persons to the objective world—a pragmatic transfer of attention, as Peirce had seen it in 1863, from the *ego*tistical needs of the "I," to the *id*-istical demands of the "IT"[167]—is the precise cognate, in terms of Peircean cognitive evolution, of that transition from personal-to-impersonal relations formulated by the German tradition of the narrative of modernization, common to Karl Marx, Ferdinand Toennies, Max Weber, and Georg Simmel. Indeed, in a remarkable echo of Charles Peirce's 1863 characterization of the historical "now" as an "idistical stage"—a socio-cognitive stage focusing on the objective "it" (*id* in Latin), superseding the earlier cognitive focus on the subjectivity of the "I" (*ego* in Latin)—Simmel wrote at the beginning of the twentieth century, in his essay "The Metropolis and Modern Life," that "the development of modern culture is characterized by the preponderance of what one may call the 'objective spirit' over the 'subjective spirit.'"[168]

Such a focus on the historical transfer of the cognizing subject's habits of attention—from the subjective to the objective realms—enabled by the development of literacy, now renders a well-formulated answer to that question pondered by the semiotically inclined sociologist Barry Schwartz, which I had highlighted earlier: the question about the cognitive locus of the evolutionary "survival" within modernity, of premodernity's "linguistic form" and its pragmatics of "bodily inclination" and "gestural abasement."[169] As Benedict Anderson's theorization of nationalism as an "imagined community" enabled by post-Gutenberg "print capitalism," (and the discussion by literary critics of the "textual *filiation*" of writing)[170] attests, literacy does not destroy the premodern communicative pragmatics of *filiation* but only displaces it to a social equivalent of the Lacan's cognitive order of the "imaginary"—a socially unconscious cognitive region in the Lacanian sense of having its imagery exert emotional charge upon, while being relatively inaccessible to, quotidian linguistic analysis, as in the aura of sacrality attendant upon the rituals of "civil religion"[171]—as the premodern extended family (extended, I should emphasize, not only in that conventional "sociological" sense of two or more adult generations, of grandparents, grandchildren, aunts, uncles, and so forth, sharing a common household economy but also, through the cognitive-interpretant code of *filiation*, extended politically and metaphysically by the worldview of what the philosopher Arthur Lovejoy had called "the Great Chain of Being"[172]) begins its historical breakdown toward the individualism of the "nuclear" two-parent and "post-nuclear" single-parent families. *Filiation* is progressively displaced in modernity, from the premodern reality of the family extending in a "great chain" across space and time, into Anderson's "imagined community" of the "fatherland" (Latin *patria*, from which we derive the word *patriotism*), whose common language "filiates" the reader into an imagined "republic of letters."

Having thus situated the cognitive evolution of the modern attitude of "objectivity" within the historical development of the written text, I may now return to Weber's famous question of historical geography, by more precisely rephrasing it as. Why did modernity emerge in that historical latecomer to social literacy, Western Europe, rather than within the much-older literate populations of China or India?

We know Weber's answer—that it had been the pursuit of not only profit but "forever *renewed* profit,"[173] a pursuit encouraged by Protestant, and more specifically Calvinist, Christianity—that had occasioned (by "elective affinity") such a rise of capitalist modernity in Europe. We may also be aware of the attempt by Weber's critics to shift the historical locus of the rise of capitalism to pre-Reformation Europe. The historian Hugh Trevor-Roper, for example, pointed to the pre-Reformation power of Northern Italy's Renaissance-era bankers, and their ideological tilt—not to that Bible-centered reading of the later Protestant reformers, but to the writings of the philosophical Humanists—to argue that the non-Protestant Humanist Erasmus had as much right to be seen as the ideological precursor of modern capitalism, as had the Protestant Reformer John Calvin. The legal historian Howard Berman has, likewise, focused upon Weber's theme of modernity's "legal-rational" culture to argue that such modern legal-rationality had been created not by Protestant Reformers but by the Roman Catholic Pope Gregory's founding of a specifically modern legal school—employing the methodology of modern scientific induction—in Bologna in the eleventh century.[174]

But such a theoretical tug-of-war—between Weber's focus on historical Calvinism as the cultural locus for the origin of modern capitalism's procedural rationalism, and the attempts by Weber's critics, Trevor-Roper and Berman, to shift that cultural locus southward to an earlier time period in the intellectual effervescence of pre-Reformation Northern Italy—was resolved by William Bouwsma's recent conceptualization of "the two faces of Humanism," one face of which was Calvin's "Augustinian Humanism." In a formulation which supports David Olson's conception of the "two books" which fascinated the Reformation-era mind, the book of Biblical Scripture and the Book of Nature,[175]—Bouwsma traced such a conceptual separation of these "two books"—i.e., the separation of the (scientific) reading of the Book of Nature from the (religious) reading of the Bible's Scripture—to Calvin's interpretation of Saint Augustine's conceptual separation (in his reaction to the Sack of Rome) of a "Heavenly city" from its "Earthly" counterpart. This "Augustinian Humanism," contrasted by Bouwsma with that better known "Stoic Humanism" of Erasmus, had Calvin declaring in his *Institutes*—that founding document of "Calvinism," as we have historically known it—that "there is one understanding of earthly things; another of heavenly ones," with the former including within its cognitive purview, "government, domestic economy, all the mechanical skills and the liberal arts," and the latter, left to religious hermeneutics, "the knowledge of God and of his will, and the rule by which we conform our lives to it."[176]

In Bouwsma's view, such a conceptual separation of "earthly things" from "heavenly ones" by Augustinian Humanism also "promoted that secularization of the cosmos implicit in the Copernican revolution" because "Galileo relied heavily on Augustine to support his argument that the proper concern of religion is how one goes to heaven, not how heaven goes," as did also—according to Bouwsma—Machiavelli's "secularizing" vision of society.[177] If we keep in mind that such a "secularizing" vision of Augustinian Humanism's separation of the cognitive realm of an objectively lawful universe from its premodern entanglement with the personal whimsy of Divine will, developed historically—via Newton's physics—into both the natural science of Laplace's assertion (to Napoleon) of a clockwork universe without that "unnecessary hypothesis" of Divine creation and (via the writings of Montesquieu) the social (political) science of James Madison's mechanistic view of the Constitution of American Society (running by its own "clockwork" of "checks and balances"), what we have in such cognitive modernization is the achievement by a cultural-communicative network of interactive humanity of the social equivalent of psychologist Jean Piaget's genetic epistemological notion of "object permanence," whereby modernizing society, like Piaget's two-year-old infant, achieves a stable view of an "objective world"—i.e., an external world with its own objective lawfulness, independent of "parental" ("Divine") will—what Louis Althusser had elsewhere described as a "process without a subject."[178]

That Weber viewed capitalistic modernity as such an objective "process without a subject" is evident from his repeated emphasis on the procedural nature of modern legal-rationality—with this modern respect for the objective legal procedure contrasting with the judicial focus on the subjective conditions of the litigants' personal qualities in the substantive value-rationality of premodern Solomonic or Qadi law. Furthermore, Weber's sharp juxtaposition of the "Protestant Ethic"—as personified by the Puritan Richard Baxter's preaching of "asceticism"—holding that "waste of time . . . is the deadliest of sins," with Benjamin Franklin's celebrated later equation, "time is money,"[179] certainly suggests that the conventional focus by sociologists, upon his discussion of the practical consequences of Calvinist beliefs such as predestination and work-as-a-calling (vocation), risks ignoring the specific cognitive-evolutionary import of Weber's "Protestant Ethic" thesis: that Calvinism translated (evolved) historically into the social cognition that time—like money—can be quantified and therefore accumulated (i.e., it is not to be "wasted").

Such a reading of Weber's Protestant Ethic thesis as a history of the socio-cognitive discovery of the quantifiability of time certainly meshes well with the studies of the contemporary historian Jacques Le Goff, in his "Merchant's Time and Church's Time in the Middle Ages" and "Labor Time in the 'Crisis' of the Fourteenth Century: From Medieval Time to Modern Time": the technology of timekeeping and clockmaking in the Middle Ages had been most developed within the monasteries, as monastic asceticism demanded accurate time measurement for its liturgical rituals. With this asceticism that monks such as Martin Luther exported from their hitherto monastic vocations into the Reformation's external world of work-as-a-calling, went also their ascetic quantification of labor-time. Indeed it is this quasi-obsession with *measurement* and *quantification* of *all* reality, temporal as well as spatial, that the contemporary historian Alfred Crosby, in his 1997 book *The Measure of Reality*, sees as the proximate cause—the real distinguishing mark of Western civilization between the years 1250 and 1600 of the Christian Era—of Western modernization.[180]

Crosby's historical focus on the Western drive to measure and quantify reality in a period beginning with the year 1250—i.e., before the Protestant Reformation—is in keeping with the efforts of other historians already mentioned such as Hugh Trevor-Roper, Harold Berman, and William Bouwsma to trace the cultural-cognitive roots of modernity farther back in time from the period of the Protestant Reformation so favored by those "Weberian" sociological theorists of modernization obsessed in finding "equivalents of the Protestant Ethic" *globally*. Indeed, if we are to take Bouwsma's formulation about Calvin's Augustinian Humanism seriously, the roots of Protestantism's modernizing mentality itself lie not in the restricted time period of the European Reformation, but in Augustinian antiquity. It is indeed to such a pre-Reformation finding of modern "perspectival" art—that equivalent, in the painter's mind, of Newton's three-dimensional physical space—that the art historian and philosopher Jean Gebser referred when he stated that "although already shaped in the Mediterranean world of late antiquity, the perspectival world began to find expression about 1250 A.D. in Christian Europe."[181] We have here, around 1250 in Europe, a converging "take-off" point, between the general processes of measurement/quantification studied by Crosby and the specifically artistic representation of spatial perspective studied by Gebser—a specific historical point of take-off in cognitive modernization in Christian Europe that does not preclude a more general historical view of the pre-Christian cognitive achievement in antiquity upon whose base it occurred.

That cognitive take-off in the Christian Europe of 1250 toward modernity's cognition of the external world's "object permanence"—i.e., the perceptual and conceptual "depth" of perspective of a "lawful" objective cosmos existing in the relative stability of quantifiable space and time, independently of personal (or divine) subjective whims (or willfulness)—was later to culminate not only in that modern legal-rationality studied by Weber but also in that literary-cultural form that cognitively encompasses the self-consciousness of such social objectivity: the modern novel, which Wolfgang Iser has characterized as "a system of perspectives."[182] As if—to use that favored term of Goethe and of Weber—in "elective affinity" with the "depth perception" of modern law, science and visual art, whose objective "depth" is cognized by the triangulation of several individual (subjective) perspectives (in law through adversarial courtroom advocacy, in science through adversarial falsification, and in art through the mimicry of binocular vision i.e., the "adversarial" perspectives of two eyes), the modern literary novel, which, according to Harry Levin, began with Cervantes's binocular presentation of the different perspectives of Don Quixote and Sancho Panza,[183] also attempted to present to its reader the perspectival depth of its cognized object (situation) through the multiple perspectives of its several characters.

My attempt here to incorporate the historical theme of Weber's *Protestant Ethic* within a more general cognitive-evolutionary theory, encompassing modernity's switch of attention from subjectivity to objectivity—across the range of cognitive-cultural activity in economics, politics, science, and the arts—might appear strange to contemporary "Weberian" sociologists, accustomed, as they well might be, to Modernization Theory's self-limitation to the global "equivalents" of Calvinist textual exegesis. But such an effort at a truly global view of human cognitive evolution might have been warmly welcomed by Weber himself, who, in ending his *Protestant Ethic* book described it as "this purely historical discussion" requiring "the next task" of showing

the significance of ascetic rationalism. . . . Then its relations to humanistic rationalism, its ideals of life and cultural influence; further to the development of philosophical and scientific empiricism, to technical development and to spiritual ideals would have to be analyzed. Then its historical development from the medieval beginnings of worldly asceticism to its dissolution into pure utilitarianism would have to be traced out through all the areas of ascetic religion. Only then could the quantitative cultural significance of ascetic Protestantism in its relation to the other plastic elements of modern culture be estimated.[184]

Thanks to Weber's own felicitous historical juxtaposition of the Puritan Richard Baxter's preaching against the "waste of time" with Benjamin Franklin's later assertion that "time is money"—a juxtaposition that enables an implicit thesis in *The Protestant Ethic* about modernity being the (monetary) quantification of time—and the more explicit statement of such a cognitive-evolutionary thesis by Weber's friendly intellectual collaborator, Georg Simmel, that (mathematical) "logic is the money of the mind,"[185] I can now proceed to what Weber called "the next task" of incorporating the historical insight of *The Protestant Ethic* within a more general theory of socio-cognitive evolution, by introducing my conception of modernity as Peircean secondness via that specific historical occurrence of the Calvinist legitimation of the monetary measurement of time, *The Idea of Usury*, by Benjamin Nelson.

Nelson's 1949 study of the development of socio-political attitudes to usury—from pre-Christian Jewish proscriptions against the lending of money with (usurious) interest to Jewish "tribal brothers," to the Roman Catholic geographical/demographical extension of such nonusurious "brotherhood" across Christendom, to the collapse of such a Christian attempt at the "universalization of tribal brotherhood" with Calvin's lifting of the ban on such financial-banking lending-at-interest practices to now recognized "universal others" (a cognitive switch of attention by Calvin, from the attention-to-subjective persons of pre-modern *filiation*, to the modern *calibration* of time's monetary objectivity)—was felicitously subtitled "From Tribal Brotherhood to Universal Otherhood."[186]

I regard Nelson's characterization of our post-Calvinist modernity as a situation of "universal otherhood" as particularly felicitous, because Peirce had, in defining *Secondness* in his 1898 Harvard lectures, also connected it conceptually to such a concept of "other-hood." "A *Secondness*," Peirce had stated, "may be defined as a modification of the being of one subject, which modification is *ipso facto* a mode of being of quite a distinct subject, or, more accurately, secondness is that in each of two absolutely severed and remote subjects which pair it with the other."[187]

Attempting to explicate Peirce's difficult phraseology in his 1966 book on *Peirce's Theory of Signs*, John Fitzgerald had further teased out such Nelson-like nuances of "otherhood" in Peirce's definition of *secondness*: "Secondness is something which retains its numerical identity even though acquiring various and even contrary qualities. Secondness is not, then, purely opposition to others, but is also the intrinsic feature by means of which an individual is able to retain its identity in the face of others."[188]

To further grasp the full implications of what Brian Rotman in 1993 was to characterize simply as the "brute actuality" of Peircean secondness,[189] I invite my reader to try the simple thought experiment of substituting the phrase "the lending of money at interest" for the word *secondness* in Fitzgerald's two-sentence explication above, to see how those themes of its "acquiring various and even contrary qualities" (as in modern capitalism's contrary qualities of promoting material well-being while risking personal alienation) and the modern individual's struggle "to maintain its identity in the face of others" (those modern others who may quantify one's identity purely in terms of one's monetary "worth") to see how well this Peircean theme of alienating secondness assimilates to Nelson's Weberian vision of modernity as "universal otherhood."[190]

If we remember that Peirce's definition of *secondness* in 1898 as the second of three stages of cognition had emerged from his 1861 perception of communication as a three-stage process proceeding from its first stage in the subjective consciousness of an "I" toward its final terminus in the communication receiver's "THOU," through a second-stage of grappling with the otherness of an "IT,"[191] we can locate the cognitive source of modernity's grappling with this "second" social-evolutionary stage of the recognition of objective "otherness," in René Descartes's philosophical sundering of the objective realm of quantitative material "extension" from the subjective realm of qualitative ideal "freedom"—a Cartesian bifurcation of the unified medieval worldview against which Peirce had protested by beginning his own Pragmatist philosophy by pitching four denials against Descartes in 1868.[192]

Indeed, it is Cartesian geometry's depiction of extensionless "points" joined by measurable lines that is the best graphic representation of Max Weber's characterization of modern human relations at the end of *The Protestant Ethic*—as that celebrated "nullity" of "specialists without spirit and sensualists without heart." Having emptied themselves of all those "filial" attributes of premodern social relations—in which human actors had related to each other as "substantive" actors holding definite positions in a Schwartzian "vertical classification"—to become those universally definable formal "citizens" standing before the procedural machinery of modern law and enjoying purely formal equality and freedom, these empty "geometrical points" relate to each other only through those quantifiable "geometrical lines" containing their quantifiable skills, qualifications, and financial worth.

To recapitulate: human society had begun in the "face-to-face" code of "*filiation*" of hunter-gatherer "tribal brotherhood" (to echo Benjamin Nelson here)—a code of *filiation* that, in enabling the cognition of social dependence as a metaphorical analogue to the dependent child's "looking up" to the parent's face, also projected such human faces onto its cognized cosmos as religious deities.[193] It later "stretched" such *filiation* by attempting to incorporate ever greater numbers of people within such social systems of *filiation* (in that process of increasing population "volume" that Durkheim had in 1893 seen as causally necessitating, when accompanied "at the same time and in the same proportion" by the interactively "intimate contact" of social "density," a "greater division of labor"[194])—as in Nelson's example of the Roman Catholic attempt to stretch the Jewish tribal proscription of usurious lending between Jewish "brothers" into a similar "brotherhood" of all Christians—by a cognitive "upwards-abstraction" of such icons. For example, the Jews and Greeks of the "Axial Era" of 600 B.C. had already abstracted their iconic deities "upwards" (as compared to those earthbound totemic animals studied by Durkheim in 1912 in "primitive" religiosity)—the Jews to the spatial height of Mount Sinai and the Greeks to Mount Olympus.

As if such mountain-height "vertical classification" of Sinaitic and Olympian religion had not been sufficient, the further incorporation of both Greeks and Jews into the larger social-communicative unit of the Roman Empire had involved a farther abstraction upwards (by Pauline Christianity) of such iconic *filiation* into a "Father in Heaven" that made Christians (in that famous Pauline phrase) "neither Greek nor Jew." The cognitive limits to such iconic abstraction are visible, to the social historian, in those cyclical movements in medieval history between the centralizing thrust of authoritative verbalizations of dogmatic "orthodox" belief and the usually emotive and imagistic counterpull of the "heterodoxy" of popular or folk religiosity. Such cycles between verbal orthodoxy and imagistic heterodoxy were also visible in those cyclical processes of struggle between orthodox *jnana* philosophizing of literate Hindu thinkers (such as the Vedanta of Shankara) and the *bhakta* emotive cults of popular Hinduism, or between the abstract philosophizing of the Mandarins and the colorful imagistic practices of folk belief in China.

Such central-versus-local cognitive tensions were inherent to the "overstretch" of fitting "too many people" within a code of *filiation*—attuning its habits of attention by the infant's looking up toward the human face of its caregiving parent—that had originally evolved within that strictly "face-to-face" primary-group environment of hunter-gatherer society. This cyclical stretching of each communicatively interactive social unit between the poles of upwards abstraction and downwards concretion, resulting in those cyclical "rise and fall" processes of various such civilizations through history, might have continued indefinitely in the scattered human habitations around the globe, had not a new code of *calibration*—that quantifying, measuring cognitive reach of the objectivity of modernity—emerged in Western Europe by the eighteenth century.

Europe's achievement of Peircean *secondness* in modernity's pragmatic (interpretant) code of *calibration* enabled a previously impossible global reach of communicative interaction, because, by switching attention from substantive personhood to procedural and quantifiable objectivity, this new code enabled—as Georg Simmel had grasped so well—objective interactions with "strangers" within a material environment of ever-greater control of the objective world through its quantitative cognition (the "book of nature," as Galileo had seen, was written in the mathematical language of quantity).

Modernity's *calibration* code diffused slowly from its modernizing ("bourgeois") elites to the majority of the members of its first national communicative units—as comprehended, for example, in those "class codes" theorized by Basil Bernstein in his studies of differential educational achievement in Britain (the "elaborated code" of the professional class's mentality of objective *calibration*, contrasted with the "restricted codes" of proletarian lagging in *filiation*) and similar studies in the United States by Melvin Kohn of the educational ill effects of the working-class valuation of conformist (i.e., filiative) behavior when contrasted with middle-class individualism in taste and judgement (i.e., calibrative behavior)[195]—and in some national communicative units the historical evolution from *filiation* to *calibration* even suffered sudden regressions (akin to individual psychosis occasioned by environmental stress), as Nazi Germany and Stalinist Russia suddenly proliferated icons instead of evolving ever-more-elaborate systems of indices (signs defined by Peirce as operating in the cognitive stage of *secondness* to "point" or indicate the relations of spatial contiguity between objective others).[196]

But the ultimate "Weberian" historical question remains why such a transition—through the achievement of a cognitive vision of the world as "object-permanent"[197]—to the modern social cognition of (Peircean) secondness occurred first in Europe rather than in the older civilizations of Asia. Why, in other words, did the Buddhist emphasis on the lawfulness of the world stop short of discovering any empirical instance of such lawfulness in the nonhuman, natural world, such as the Law of the Flotation of Bodies, discovered in the third century B.C. by the Greek Archimedes of Syracuse?

It is perhaps no accident that, coming to the study of sociology from a prior background in the history and philosophy of science as I did, my awareness that Archimedes' Law of Flotation is the first known "scientific law" (relating to the empirically known external world) emerging in all of (thus far known) human history led me to focus very sharply on Joseph Needham's comparison of the relative accessibility to deepwater (ocean) navigation between Europe and China. In fact, in contrasting the relatively small coastline-to-land area ratio of China to Europe's comparatively larger ratio (of length of coastline/land area), Needham had boldly asserted that

> had the environmental conditions been reversed as between Euro-America and China, all else would have been reversed too—all the great names in the heroic age of science, Galileo, Malpighi, Versalius, Harvey, Boyle, would have been Chinese and not Western names.[198]

This bold assertion led me immediately to realize that—whereas it had been the South Indian kingdoms that had been known historically for their prowess in deep-water navigation (and their consequent cultural influence upon Indo-China)—the North Indian Indo-Gangetic Plain, within which Buddhist formulations about universal lawfulness had been forged, had enjoyed even fewer experiences with deep water navigation than the Chinese (whose pre-Portuguese-incursion navigational mastery of the Indian Ocean has been duly noted by World-System theorist Janet Abu-Lughod)[199] with such Asian experience with deep-water navigation being, in its totality, ridiculously small when compared with Hellenic navigational experience between their island city-states and along the Ionian coast of Asia Minor: in fact, the pragmatic *consequences* of such Greek-Asian differences in deep-water navigation upon their respective cultural constructions-of-meaning can be readily gauged from the contrast between the numerous references to such navigation in the two principal Greek epics, Homer's *Iliad* and *Odyssey*, against the complete landwards orientation—such as Krishna's chariot-ride and Rama's need of the monkey-god Hanuman's aid in crossing over to the island of Lanka—in the two equivalent Indian epics of the *Mahabharata* and the *Ramayana*. Should not a theory of global

pragmatics, aiming at a non-Eurocentric comparative-historical science of how the
Grice-an cooperation of different communicating human-groups differentially constructed their cultural patterns of meaning, take due account of the repeated coinci-
dences—in the Ancient Greece of Archimedes, the Italian cities of Galileo (and
Christopher Columbus), and the English Royal Society environment of Isaac Newton—of extensive cooperative efforts at ever-greater prowess ("power-to," *puissance*) at deep-water navigation?

Should not, in other words, the global approach to Weber's Protestant Ethic
thesis ask not, as Robert Bellah was still doing between 1956 and 1970, what the
"analogy in Asia" is to the uniqueness of the Protestant Reformation as a cul-
tural-historical event, but rather, what the cooperative experiences of Hellenic,
Hellenistic, and Greco-Roman audiences were that selected into the "Christian
Canon"—out of a range of "apocryphal" gospel-narratives, as we know today,
about the meaning of the life of Jesus—the writings of Luke, for example, so influential (as in the Christmas story) upon popular Christianity (and so obviously
beholden in narrative form, as for example, in his narrative in *The Acts of the
Apostles* of Paul's journey toward Rome, to Homer's Odyssey) so that the "rationalism of world-mastery" begun in the time of Archimedes was culturally preserved for further development in the later navigational efforts of Genoa, the
Netherlands, and England?[200]

What Max Weber had known merely as "Christianity" was later shown, by
the intense scholarly focus on the *Gospel of Thomas*—provoked by the unexpected bonanza of ancient manuscripts discovered at the Dead Sea and at Nag
Hammadi, long after Weber's death—to have been merely a product of Hellenistic
(or Greco-Roman) selectivity about which of the several accounts of the life and
works of Jesus of Nazareth should enter into the (Greek) Orthodox and (Roman)
Catholic official canons. The Asian (Syriac) followers of Thomas—the "doubting
Thomas" of the Hellenistic John's Gospel narrative—had apparently been less interested than the Hellenists in accounts of the "miraculous" control allegedly exhibited by Jesus, and such "Asian" cognitive selectivity is reflected in the portrait
of Jesus by Thomas as a Buddha-like "teacher of wisdom," preaching a rather
Buddhist control of self, rather than a Greek-Archimedean control of nature.[201]

When viewed from this perspective of our contemporaneous wealth of information on the history and development of different cultural traditions, Weber's
comparative analysis of religion—based, as it was, on a relatively restricted
knowledge base—seems obviously "dated." Not only was his understanding of
Christianity—deprived as it had been of non-canonical textual sources, such as
the *Gospel of Thomas*—severely limited but so was his knowledge of non-Christ-
ian Asian religions. We have already seen the 1986 complaint by the "Weberian
sociologist" Randall Collins that Weber's knowledge of Chinese Confucianism,
Taoism, and Buddhism—drawing, as it had done, "heavily on accounts by nineteenth century travelers and missionaries"—had been "in error." In 1995, Helmut
Loiskandl began his essay "Religion, Ethics, and Economic Interaction in Japan"

by blaming Weber's mistaken "expectation that the inner-worldly asceticism" which he had found in early Calvinism "might have had a counterpart in Confucianism," for Robert Bellah's later overvaluation of the "rational ethics" of Confucianism—at the expense of Buddhist and Shinto influences—in what Bellah had called "Tokugawa Religion." And, in his 1992 "Critique of Weber's Islam," Bryan Turner had declared that Weber's imputation of a warrior "feudal ethic" to the nascent Islamic society of the Prophet Muhammad's Mecca—a society that, according to Turner, had been "primarily urban, commercial and literate"—had been simply "factually wrong."[202]

In contrast to such growing uneasiness—emerging from within the increasing global awareness of academics in the last two decades of the twentieth century (i.e., after Japanese automobile production had so dramatically overtaken its Western rivals)—with the Eurocentric error implicit in Weber's (and, more broadly, "Weberian" sociology of religion such as Bellah's) efforts to locate the impelling social force of modern "rationalism" within (religio-cultural) semantics, Joseph Needham's 1969 tracing of the source of the difference in Chinese/Western historical journeys toward such modern scientific "rationalism" to the difference in their geographies seems to fare much better. The 1985 critique of Needham's thesis by the Chinese scholar Wen-Yuan Qian—a critique which Qian titled *The Great Inertia* in obvious contrast to Needham's *The Grand Titration*—for example, limits itself to faulting Needham for overestimating the objectivity of traditional Chinese science when compared to modern Western science. But if Needham had really overestimated the "rationalism" of traditional Chinese science, that error only adds to, rather than subtracts from, the relevance of his "geographical" thesis. A simple glance at a global map would suggest that the substantial difference between the lengths of the Chinese and European coastlines, when seen in proportion to their respective land areas—the two ratios suggesting, then, substantial differences in the probabilities of their respective navigational social (pragmatic-cooperative) historical experiences—would also yield that sizable difference between their respective developmental paths in science that Qian upholds but that Needham—with his non-Chinese tendency to romanticize Chinese history and culture—had underestimated.[203]

Needham's 1969 *Grand Titration* comparative-historical study of Chinese and European cultural development was not the first to focus on the causal efficacy of Europe's uniquely long coastline upon its cultural development: Ludwig Dehio's 1959 study *Germany and World Politics in the Twentieth Century* had situated German expansionism as just the latest historical attempt—in a series of such attempts that had begun with the Hapsburg Emperor Charles V and had been continued by Napoleon Bonaparte—to centralize European polity within a Chinese-type unified empire, with all such efforts at Chinese-like political centralization being defeated historically, according to Dehio, by the very non-Chinese geography of Europe's extended coastline (which allowed a naval power, like Britain, to successfully frustrate both Napoleon's and Hitler's land-based drives to

geopolitical centralization). We know—from, among others, the Weberian sociological tradition's prolific historical studies in this area—that such a weakness in
centralizing political authority in Europe enabled the growth of the autonomous
power of the town-and-city-based moneyed bourgeoisie: Not only did the splin-
tered European monarchies fail to control the ambitions of merchant money-cap-
ital in the way that the unified Chinese Imperial bureaucracy could, but the arms
races fueled by the constant wars between feuding European monarchs—the
"pursuit of power" as the historian William H. McNeill labeled this European
phenomenon in 1982—actually rendered these monarchs hostage to the financial
power of their banking houses. We know, too, that navigational efforts over ever-
longer distances—with the Genoese interest in outflanking their Venetian commercial rivals financially (and intellectually) stimulating Portuguese efforts to
round the coast of Africa, which in turn stimulated the Genoese Christopher
Columbus's "discovery" of America on behalf of Spain, in turn bringing the non-
Mediterranean nations of England and the Netherlands into Atlantic ocean navigation—depended on the financial innovations of large-scale commercial banking and the formation of joint-stock corporations of limited liability. With
Simmel's dictum that "logic is the money of the mind," and the reported entry by
Columbus in his ship's logbook asserting his belief that navigation is the greatest
stimulant to society's intellectual development, is it too much to hypothesize,
against the now-obvious limitations of the "Weber thesis" for a truly global, non-
Eurocentric social history, the causal efficacy of navigational pragmatics—the
Gricean meaning-developing cooperative form historically determined by the political decentralization occasioned by Europe's unique coastline—in the cultural
breakthrough to modern scientific rationalism?[204]

The implicit Eurocentrism of the Weberian sociological tradition's focus on
comparative religious semantics is contained within (and possibly, thereby
masked by) a larger current of more-explicit Eurocentric views propounded by
Western observers of the non-Western world that Edward Said famously casti-
gated in 1978 as Orientalism.[205] Said's attack on the supposed "objectivity" of
Western Orientalists, was followed in 1987 by Martin Bernal's controversial
Black Athena, exposing "the Afroasiatic roots" of Classical Greek civilization,
and in 1989 by Samir Amin's book *Eurocentrism*. Both these latter books, according to Andre Gunder Frank and Barry K. Gills, "argue that ancient Greece
was less the beginning of 'western' than the continuation of 'eastern' civilization
and culture."[206]

While cautioning against the "misuse of Bernal's work by some of his new
'Afrocentrist' interpreters," and the similar misuse of "'poly-centrism' . . . by
multiculturalist counterattacks on Eurocentric culture," Gunder Frank and Gills
offered their own model of a historically long-range unitive "5,000-year world
system" as "a powerful antidote" against Eurocentrism. "Our world system," they
argued,

not only reinforces the Amin and Bernal ideological critique of Eurocentrism, but carries it much further still. We offer an analytical framework, within which to perceive the "interaction with these larger structures" by Greek, Roman, and other "civilizations" in "classical" times. Thus, our perspective offers a powerful antidote to the Eurocentric classical historians, who imposed their bias upon studies of the ancient world by privileging the role of Graeco-Roman civilization in the story of world history. The contributions of nonwestern, and particularly "oriental" societies were systematically denigrated or dismissed as unimportant. Most importantly, Eurocentric classicism distorted the real political and economic position of the "West", i.e., the Graeco-Romans, in the ancient world as a whole. Yet we know that Hellas began its ascendance after a preparatory period of so-called "orientalizing," i.e., emulating and integrating with the more advanced and prosperous centers of civilization and commerce in the "East." . . . Culturalism and the assumption of Western superiority has distorted analyses of the true historical position and relations of the west European and west Asian (Middle Eastern) regions. A world system framework clarifies that for most of world history, including ancient "classical" history, Europe was ever "marginal" and west Asia ever "central."[207]

Of this 1993 attempt by Gunder Frank and Gills to overcome the historically entrenched Eurocentrism of earlier Western historical and social sciences, by insisting upon the unitive vision of this "5,000-year world system," Janet Abu-Lughod—the 1989 proponent of "the World System A.D. 1250-1350" preceding the European expansion which created Immanuel Wallerstein's later "Modern World System"[208]—comments:

Gunder Frank is correct to speak of one long march, rather than a set of equal cycles. . . . [But] the fact is that the axis of Central Asia, Anatolia, northern India, and the Levant-Egypt—an axis of central importance in earlier times which was scarcely destroyed by the seventeenth century—never again occupied the center-stage of the world-system. I urge study of not only the continuities at the subsystem level, but also the discontinuities most evident at the large scale.[209]

Max Weber's sociology of comparative religion was, of course, the most celebrated attempt by a "classical" sociological theorist to explain this most salient of all historical "discontinuities" alluded to by Abu-Lughod: that Europe, which, according to Gunder Frank, had been "ever marginal" to the centrality of West Asia—to the point where, according to Gunder Frank, Imperial Rome had "itself played a largely parasitic role" upon the culturally and economically advanced East[210]—had suddenly "taken off" culturally, between the Humanism of Renaissance Italy, which had "resurrected" the cultural formulations of Ancient Greece and Rome, and the French Enlightenment (a period that had included within its historical span the Protestant Reformation upon whose semantic formulations Weber had so famously focused), toward that "center-stage of the world system" hitherto occupied, according to Abu-Lughod, by that non-European "axis" stretching from Egypt to Central Asia. That historical discontinuity is what *must* be explained by a truly *global* sociological theory removed from the semantic Eurocentrism of conventional Weberianism.

Informed as I am by my appreciation of Joseph Needham's successful overcoming, in his 1969 *Grand Titration* comparison of Western and Chinese cultural (scientific) developmental paths, of the "Weberian" temptation to explain pragmatic action by semantic meaning (a causal privileging of semantic meaning by Weber that I believe is what Gunder Frank had meant by "culturalism and the assumption of Western superiority"[211]) by focusing instead upon the geographical structuring of pragmatic, meaning-constituting, cooperative interactions, I see Gunder Frank's anticulturalist anti-Eurocentric vision tilting into the *opposite* error of ignoring the uniqueness of European—and even more specifically Hellenic—geography. For even a cursory look at a map of Greece from the Ionian to the Aegean seas—and more specifically that island-studded area of the Aegean, north of Crete, roughly between the 23rd degree of longitude just west of Athens and the 29th degree of longitude just east of the island of Rhodes (six degrees of longitude that include the salients of Asia Minor's irregularly extended eastern coastline)—reveals a unique, navigationally rich setting for what Gunder Frank calls Greece's "preparatory period of so-called 'orientalizing,' i.e. emulating and integrating with the more advanced and prosperous centers of civilization and commerce in the 'East.'"

What such a historically unique process of cultural diffusion from the land-oriented cultural formulations of West Asia (and Egypt) to the navigationally minded Hellenes—a historically unique process of cultural diffusion, I must emphasize, because the only grouping geographically similar to the relatively small islands of Hellenic linguistic communication in the Eastern Mediterranean seems to be in the Pacific Ocean, too distant for cultural diffusion from the Afro-Asiatic "centers" of historical civilization, although on the other hand, in contrast to the relatively self-contained Hellenic (linguistic) communication system, other Ancient navigators, such as the Phoenicians, Chinese, or South Indians, must have had their navigational cultural formulations overwhelmed by the preponderant weight of existing nonnavigational formulations from their hinterland linguistic-communicational systems—implied, can be seen from the fact that whereas the number mysticism of the Greek Pythagoras, whose famous theorem about the ratio of the hypotenuse to the sides of right-angled triangles had reportedly borrowed from previous Afro-Asiatic empirical observations of land-surveying, is clearly echoed at the Eastern edge of the West Asian silk route by the philosophical speculations of the Indian mathematicians Aryabhata, Brahmagupta, and Bhaskara,[212] the empirically discovered ratio of the "Law of Flotation of Bodies"—the first-ever known empirical law of science, of fundamental pragmatic consequence (i.e., "functional") to a navigationally dependent Hellenic society—simply has no Afro-Asiatic equivalent (known to history) at all!

Am I then proposing the causal factor of navigation-inducing geography as the global-pragmatic alternative to the Eurocentric semantics of the Weberian Protestant Ethic hypothesis. Indeed, I most certainly am. As I hope I have demonstrated, the proximate causal efficacy of John Calvin's semantic formulations can be easily incorporated within my broader global pragmatics. While I readily admit that my limited academic expertise cannot even begin to test or confirm the immense historical range—from the Hellenic and Hellenistic navigational environment that first cognized water itself as rational, to the navigational social environment of Galileo Galilei that incorporated such Hellenic rationalism into the formulation of modern scientific method,[213] to the Anglo-Saxon navigational environment (from Isaac Newton to the invention of the measuring instruments of geographical longitude) that institutionalized such scientific method and broadened its vision of universal lawfulness (the world as "object-permanence") of James Madison's mechanistic "checks and balances" yielding a government "of laws and not of men"—I am also aware that, according to the current post-Popper philosophy of science of Imre Lakatos, the function of theoretical argument, like my argument in this book, is to develop hypotheses to be tested in new "research programmes."[214]

It is toward the formation of such Lakatosian "research programmes" in a truly global sociology that I will now lay out my final reason why I believe that what Weber had seen as the "rationalism of world mastery" could only have emerged within a culture—Hellenic-to-Western European—that repeatedly found itself grappling with problems of navigation. "Water in all its forms," Carl Gustav Jung had noted, "sea, lake, river, spring—is one of the commonest typifications of the unconscious." The drive to the conscious, "rational" mastery of the environment, thought Jung, is often "confronted" by the irrationality of the "avenging deluge" of the unconscious.[215] Of all these forms of water—sea, lake, river and spring—that are symbolic "typifications" of unconscious irrationality, Jung unequivocally declared in *The Archetypes and the Collective Unconscious*, "the sea is the favorite symbol for the unconscious."[216]

While in my admittedly limited global-historical awareness, I am conscious of non-Hellenic cultural formulations exhibiting positive attitudes toward three of Jung's four specified forms of water-symbolism—the lake, as in the Chinese Chan (Zen in Japanese) injunction to still the mind by meditation like the still waters of a reflecting lake (pool); the river, as in the traditional Hindu imagery of the river's (atman-soul's) journey to the sea; and the spring, as in Taoism's image of spring water's natural tendency to settle at the lowest level—it seems to me that non-Hellenic attitudes to the sea are typified by that negative imagery that Mircea Eliade's study of "water symbolism," a global-comparative study of religious symbolism influenced (according to Eliade) by Jung and Karl Kerenyi's *Introduction to a Science of Mythology*,[217]—found in "the Babylonian creation story . . . of a watery chaos . . . *Tiamat* was the salty and bitter sea inhabited by monsters."[218]

In significant contrast to such a non-Hellenic view of the "bitter sea inhabited by monsters"—a negative view of the sea that in the Judaic Exodus even has Moses "parting" the Red Sea, i.e., converting the sea into a nonnavigational path of dry land!—the "monsters" of Homer's Hellenic *Odyssey*, such as the deadly Sirens whose songs would lure mariners to their deaths or the one-eyed Cyclops who devoured Ulysses' mariners, seem all to threaten from dry land,[219] as they also do in the Hellenistic narratives of the *canonical* Christian gospels, where Christ's absolute command of navigable water—as in his miracles of walking on the water, or stilling a storm while in a boat, or even His ability to multiply the non-monstrous fruits (fish) of the sea—fades into apparent impotence before the monstrous authorities of Jerusalem. According to A. N. Wilson, the narrative of the Apostle Paul's missionary journeys, in *The Acts of the Apostles*, mimics the structure of Homer's *Odyssey*:[220] the Christianity upon whose semantic formulations Weber's "Protestant Ethic" thesis had focused, had faithfully preserved—for later development—the unique Greek translation of Pythagorean ratio—a philosophical ratio-nality, that, as we have seen, may have been common to other nonnavigational societies such as Bhaskara's India—into a navigational environment. Thales of Miletus had begun the history of Western philosophy by the historically unique assertion that water was the basic substance from which the world had been formed. By the time of Archimedes' Law of Flotation—which gives us the precise ratio of the apparent (virtual) loss of weight of a floating body to the weight of the water it has displaced—water—that "typification," according to Jung, of the "avenging deluge" of unconscious ir-ratio-nality—had itself yielded to the ratio-nality of Pythagoras, and thereby prepared the way for that "rationalism" of eighteenth-century Western modernity's vision of the inherent ratio—the lawfulness—of the whole world.

Ironically, given the tendency that we have seen of contemporary Western sociology to turn to Weber because of the supposed paucity of Durkheim's theorization of cultural modernity, my turn to Jung's psychology of the "collective unconscious" in order to dissolve within a global pragmatics the residual Eurocentrism of Weberian cultural comparisons, returns us to Durkheim, for, as the Jungian psychologist Ira Progoff has explained:

> Jung is most indebted to the sociological concepts of Emile Durkheim and Lucien Levy-Bruhl. Like Durkheim, Jung postulates society as a primary human datum, and he agrees that the individual must be understood in terms of the social situation in which he lives. He also takes over Durkheim's basic conception of the "collective representations." By this is meant the basic beliefs and assumptions about the nature of things, the world, and the conduct of life held in common by members of the group, imposed on them by the pressures of the group, and transmitted from generation to generation.[221]

Before moving on then, in the next section of this chapter, to focus upon the globalizing transition of humanity from Peircean *secondness* to *thirdness*, it behooves me to encapsulate this section's modernizing transition from the (Peircean) *first* pragmatic (interpretant) code of (pre-modern) *filiation* to the *second* pragmatic code of *calibration*, in the relatively more familiar terminology of Durkheim: The increasing population "volume" that Durkheim had seen in 1893, as one of two population variables causing an increasing division of labor—accompanied by the subjective perception, in my own cognivist/phenomenological description in this section, of "too many persons"—is a necessary but not sufficient condition for transition to modernity. For that *second* Durkheimian population variable—the "density" of "fairly intimate contact"[222]—to occur in any stable and stably permanent process (i.e., a process that because of its stability does not suddenly implode, as Germany did for example, into that orgy of filiative icons) to occur, a society needs that sufficient condition of a cognitive change about those "basic beliefs and assumptions about the nature of things, the world, and the conduct of life" which I have (following Piaget) here called "object permanence," the vision of the whole world as a lawful process, to be thereafter faithfully "transmitted," as Progoff says about the Durkheim-Jung realm of "collective representations," "from generation to generation."[223]

Globalization and "Postmodernity"

Consider the following statement written by an urbane and sophisticated European intellectual in the first half-decade of the twentieth century:

> Money economy and the dominance of the intellect are intrinsically connected. They share a matter of fact attitude in dealing with men and things; and in this attitude a formal justice is often coupled with an inconsiderate hardness. The intellectually sophisticated person is indifferent to all genuine individuality. . . . Money is concerned only with what is common to all; it asks for the exchange value, it reduces all quality and individuality to the question: How much? All intimate emotional relations between persons are founded in this individuality, whereas in rational relations man is reckoned like a number, like an element which is in itself indifferent.[224]

This statement was written by the sociologist Georg Simmel, in his essay on "The Metropolis and Social Life." In connecting money, that ultimate index (in Peirce's definition of the signs of cognitive *secondness*) of modern life, with the intellectuality of modern life, which reckons "man . . . like a number," Simmel was only describing the reality of what I—in adapting Peirce's cognitive category of secondness to comprehend the metacultural code of modernity—have called the pragmatic (interpretant) code of *calibration*.

The historical irony in the fact that Simmel published this essay containing such a perfect description of how the modern code of *calibration* focuses the individual's habits of attention upon quantifiable objects (to such a point as to also objectify one's fellow humans in society) around 1905 was that with Albert Einstein working within the same period on his Special Theory of Relativity, the cognitive journey of humanity was about to reach the point of discovering the limits of modern *calibration*. With the sequel to that Special Theory already blossoming in Einstein's mind into his later General Theory of Relativity, literate humanity would soon learn that that primordial "substance" which John Calvin's legitimation of the usurious use of Simmel's "index"—money—of intellectuality had sought to calibrate and quantify—i.e., time itself—had lost that "inconsiderate hardness" that Simmel had seen as required for quantification: Einstein's Theory of Relativity had revealed the hitherto unexpected pliability of time!

More blows to modernity's expectations of what I can best describe only as "universal commensurability"—reflected in Simmel's assertion that "money is concerned only with what is common to all"—soon followed. In 1927 Werner Heisenberg formulated his famous "Uncertainty Principle" of quantum mechanics, setting limits to the calibrated measurement of physical micro-reality just as Einstein had set the speed of light as such a *calibration* limit at the macro-level of physical reality. In 1934, that ultimate "anti-Descartes" Kurt Godel delivered his Princeton Lectures "On Undecidable Propositions of Formal Mathematics Systems." If Rene Descartes had inaugurated modern philosophy by demonstrating, with his "Cartesian" geometry, the *calibration*al measurability of what his critic, Blaise Pascal, had called the "infinite spaces," then Godel, by his *counterproposal* about the *calibration*al limits of Descartes's measuring instrument—i.e. the cognitive methodology of mathematics, itself—had cognitively ushered in a "post-modern" vision.

That "Godelian" year of 1934 is—like the earlier historical conjuncture, around 1905, between Simmel's declaration of an "intrinsic" connection between money and the calibrating intellect, and Einstein's revelation of the slippery pliability of time (which Calvinist modernity had sought to calibrate with interest-bearing money!)—significant because of a certain coincidence in intellectual history. In her first chapter, "Defining the Post-Modern," of her 1991 book *The Post-Modern and the Post-Industrial*, Margaret Rose points out how, despite the fact that after World War II historian Arnold Toynbee had consistently dated the "post-modern" period of Western history "from 1875 on. . . . It should be noted that when that period is mentioned in volume I (of [Arnold] Toynbee's *A Study of History*) of 1934 . . . the term 'Post-Modern' is not used." Since, according to Rose, we can only know for certain that it had been by 1939 that Toynbee had been aware of the possibility of there being a "post-modern" age—because "Toynbee had used it in volume V of his *A Study of History* of 1939 to describe the age inaugurated by the war of 1914-18"—I can *only surmise* that between 1934 (when Toynbee's publication of volume 1 of his multiple-volume *A Study of*

History had occurred) and 1939 (when his first published usage of the term *post-modern* had become visible), the erudite and intellectually curious Toynbee must have become aware of the widely discussed implications of Godel's 1934 Princeton Lectures on mathematical "undecidability."[225]

In *Modernism as a Philosophical Problem*, Robert Pippin's search for "the original coinage of the notion of postmodernity" also led him back to Toynbee's use of the term "after the Second World War." Toynbee's usage of the term—which Rose had seen as Toynbee's marking of the end of the two and three-quarter centuries of the "ascendancy" of the monetarily rational Western "bourgeoisie" (i.e., that very class of which Simmel had been such an eminent representative, spokesperson, and social analyst)[226]—is seen by Pippin to describe "an era of irrationalism and anxiety and lost hope." Since that apparently original coinage by Toynbee around the time of World War II, Pippin sees the widespread interest in postmodernism as having generated

> a diversity of issues worthy of the postmodernist ethos itself: heterogeneous, fragmented, resistant to general discussion. The postmodern label, now used so widely and casually as to be virtually meaningless, has become in the minds of many representative of various, quite diverse enterprises—deconstruction, hermeneutics, Foucauldean genealogy, post-structuralism, Lacanean psychoanalysis, or the work of often very different people, from Harold Bloom to Jean Baudrillard. And it has certainly attracted various polemical counters.[227]

It is precisely because of this threat to textual comprehensibility posed by the "heterogeneous" usage of the term *postmodern*—a term that Pippin sees as "now used so widely and casually as to be virtually meaningless"—that, by defining modernity as the generalized cognitive attitude (pragmatic code) of *calibration* (i.e., measurability), helps me now to focus on the possibility of a period of postmodernity as that period "post" (after) Kurt Godel's famous proof of the "incompleteness" of—i.e., the "incommensurability" built into—arithmetic. Even though we may have no direct historical evidence that the inventor of the term *postmodern*, Toynbee, had himself meant to refer, by its usage, to Godel's "undecidability" theorem, Jean-Francois Lyotard's seminal later book, *The Postmodern Condition*, referred twice to "Godel's theorem" as "a veritable paradigm" of "the striking feature of postmodern knowledge": the acceptance "that all formal systems have internal limitations," and the fragmentation of knowledge, therefore, into "language games."[228]

Recent critiques of postmodernist theory—such as, for example, the 1998 essay by Chris Carleton, titled "Relativity, Uncertainty, and Imaginary Time: The Pseudoscientific Basis of Postmodernist Literary Theory"[229]—also appear to accept my periodization of a postmodernist sensibility as dawning with Einstein's Relativity Theory and Heisenberg's Uncertainty Principle casting doubt upon modernity's expectations of universal *calibration*. In 1959 *The Sociological Imagination* of C. Wright Mills had connected such fears of looming "incommensurability" with the historiography of Toynbee and of Oswald Spengler, by excoriating them as "well-known examples" of theories of history that distort it "into a trans-historical strait-jacket into which the materials of human history are forced and out of which issue prophetic views (usually gloomy ones) of the future." Although Mills had agreed that "we are at the ending of what is called The Modern Age," he had compared the apprehension with which Western academics seemed to be viewing the dawn of "a post-modern period" to that earlier transition in which "Antiquity was followed by several centuries of Oriental ascendancy, which Westerners provincially call The Dark Ages."[230]

But that 1959 charge of "provincialism" by Mills against Toynbee seems unjustified, for, according to the postcolonialist writer Robert Young's 1990 book *White Mythologies*, Toynbee had himself written "against a current Late Modern Western convention of identifying a parvenue and provincial Western Society's history with 'History,' writ large sans phrase," a Western historiographical convention which Toynbee had roundly condemned as "the preposterous off-spring of a distorting egocentric illusion to which the children of a Western civilization had succumbed like the children of all other known civilizations and known primitive societies." The purpose that Toynbee had had in mind when he had coined the term *postmodern* in *A Study of History*, was, according to Young:

> To describe the new age of Western history which, according to Toynbee, began in the 1870s with the simultaneous globalization of Western culture and the re-empowerment of non-Western states. If this new period brought with it a phase of Spenglerian pessimism after the long years of Victorian optimism, Toynbee did not himself assume that the West was in decline as such, but rather that paradoxically the globalization of Western civilization was being accompanied by a self-consciousness of its own cultural relativization, a process to which Toynbee's own equally totalizing and relativizing history was designed to contribute.[231]

That decade of the 1870s to which Toynbee had shifted the starting point of his postmodern age (according to Rose), after World War II—to having first located it, in his 1939 publication of volume 5 of *A Study of History*, in that 1914-18 period of World War I—had been marked by the modernizing Meiji Revolution in Japan. As a British historian (and son of that other Arnold Toynbee, the historian who had pioneered the historiography of the origins of the Industrial Revolution in Britain) Toynbee had to have been impressed by the efficiency with which Japan had, in 1942, divested Britain of its entire Asian empire east of India. What Young refers to as "the re-empowerment of non-Western states" weighing so heavily on Toynbee's post-World War II mind, as he shifted his periodization of the postmodern era backward in time to coincide with the beginning of Japanese modernization, had been typified specifically by the efficacy demonstrated by Japan in "re-empowering" itself by rapidly absorbing the West's technological rationality without surrendering its cultural identity.

Pondering then, in 1998, the obviously contrasting example of the rapid absorption by a triply expansive Western culture (of market capitalism, parliamentary democracy, and Christian religiosity) of the preliterate Baruya culture of New Guinea—a preliterate culture whose first contact with Western intruders into their isolated mountain habitation (with a total population of eighteen hundred people) had been only in 1951—the French anthropologist Maurice Godelier differs from Toynbee's earlier assessment by concluding that "Westernization will spread" because, although "the tiny society of the Baruya is as nothing alongside Japan . . . there are hundreds of such societies." In fact, despite the preservation by Japan and other East Asian societies of their religious and cultural identity, Godelier insists that "Westernization no longer is just the expansion of the West, since . . . it has also become a product of the East, of Japan and the four or five 'little dragons.'"[232]

Godelier, we may remember, had been the author of *Rationality and Irrationality in Economics*, a book first appearing in English translation in 1972, which he had written under the influence of Louis Althusser's Structural Marxism. Having pondered the question "Can Marx survive the collapse of Communism or 'Real Socialism'?" after the disappearance of the Soviet Union in 1991, Godelier still betrayed his lingering Marxist anxiety about assumptions of inherent compatibility between capitalism and political democracy by pointedly reminding his readers, in his 1998 essay on the Baruya of New Guinea, that "as late as 1906, Max Weber wondered whether there was any necessary link between capitalism and democracy."[233] Godelier's complete identification of "globalization" with "Westernization" appears to fit well within that tradition of Western Marxism—that began with Marx's own apparent exultation about the triumphs of Western colonialism (in India and in Algeria)—that seemed to welcome every victory of Western colonialism over the supposed stasis of "Oriental Despotism."

It is against such a backdrop of ready conflation between any possibly emerging truly global culture and the mere global imitation of Western ways—a contrast between two possibilities that Zygmunt Bauman characterized in 1995 as the "proud project" and "Herculean mission" of universality in a "history-by-design," versus the mere globality of "meek acquiescence" (to "feed on McDonald's hamburgers and watch the latest made-for-TV docudrama"!)[234]—that we may comprehend the reception accorded to Roland Robertson's 1992 book *Globalization*, about which David Slater says that it

> does indicate contra Giddens that the present concern with globalization cannot be comprehensively considered simply as an outcome of the Western

"project" of modernity. For Robertson there has been a heightening of civilization, societal ethnic, regional and individual self-consciousness that makes globalization and Westernization a problematic duo.[235]

While Slater has obviously misread the particular page he cites of Robertson's book—by interpolating the term *Western* where Robertson had merely faulted Anthony Giddens for his "simple proposition that globalization is a 'consequence of modernity'"[236]—his error nevertheless underscores the point made by Robertson elsewhere in his book, that the tendency of Giddens "to think of 'time-space distantiation' as a product of relatively free-floating and ahistorical 'structuration'" could mislead his readers, habituated as they may be to the historical imagery of Western colonialism's crushing of non-Western cultures, to re-embed such Giddensian abstraction into that more concrete imagery of globalization as a historical process of Westernization. For, Robertson argued, while Giddens

> may claim that globalization does not involve the crushing of non-Western cultures he does not seem to realize that such a statement requires him to theorize the issue of "other cultures." His suggestion that there is no Other in a globalized world apparently absolves him from undertaking such a task. He fails to understand that it is only in a (minimally) globalized world that a problem of "the Other" could have arisen. What he apparently doesn't see is that a view of the world as marked by unicity can coexist with a view of the world as a place of others (leaving on one side the question of extraterrestrial others)—indeed that such recognition is central to the mapping of the global circumstance.[237]

Robertson's own attempt "to theorize the issue of 'other cultures'" involved a return to that "other" society which, as we have seen, had been the stimulus to Toynbee's post-World War II transfer of the originating point of his postmodern era from that 1914-18 historical location that he had earlier, in 1939, assigned to it, to that 1870s coincidence with Japan's Meiji Revolution. To "theorize 'other cultures'" Robertson appears to have rephrased that paradox that Robert Young had seen preoccupying Toynbee—the paradox that "the globalization of Western civilization was being accompanied by a self-consciousness of its own cultural relativization"[238]—as an "interpenetration" between "relativism and worldism" in a "massive, twofold process involving *the interpenetration of the universalization of particularism and the particularization of universalism.*"[239]

From Japan—that "other" society studied by both Toynbee and Robertson (as "other" to Western culture)—Robertson borrowed the word "*dochakuka,* roughly meaning 'global localization'" to translate into his own term "*glocalize,*" in order to bring the "global . . . macroscopic aspect of contemporary life . . . into conjunction with the local . . . microscopic side of life in the late twentieth century," with this term which had been "developed in particular reference to marketing issues, as Japan became more concerned with and successful in the global economy." In focusing thus upon Japanese marketing culture, Robertson argued against the Marxist tradition's economic determinism (or, as Althusser's "structural" Marxism might have phrased it, "determination in the last instance") that

> the consumerist global capitalism of our time is wrapped into the increasingly thematized particular-universal relationship in terms of the connection between globewide, universalistic supply and particularistic demand. The contemporary *market* thus involves the increasing *interpenetration* of culture and economy: which is not the same as arguing, as Jameson tends to do, that the production of culture is *directed* by the 'logic' of 'late' capitalism. More specifically, the contemporary capitalist creation of consumers frequently involves the tailoring of products to increasingly specialized regional, societal, ethnic, class and gender markets—so-called 'micro-marketing.'[240]

The response by the Marxist Fredric Jameson to this critique by Robertson of his view of postmodernism as "the cultural logic of late capitalism" was to dismiss Robertson's central concept of "globality"—which Robertson had defined generally as "the circumstance of extensive awareness of the world as a whole, including the species aspect of the latter," and more specifically "in the immediate context as consciousness of the (problem of) the world as a single place"[241]—as "a utopian vision."[242]

But it is precisely at this point of contention between "culturalists" like Robertson and self-styled "Marxists" like Jameson—who, according to Robert Young, has complained about "frequently" having "the feeling that I am one of the few Marxists left"[243]—that the need, nay, the indispensability of a "Peircean" framework to comprehend "globalization" and "postmodernity" can be clearly seen. For Robertson is not alone in his "culturalist" critique of Jameson's Marxist comprehension of postmodernism as the logic of "late capitalism": Young too, in his own "postcolonial" critique, argues, "contrary" to Jameson's "more overreaching definition," that "postmodernism itself could be said to mark not just the cultural effects of a new stage of 'late' capitalism, but the sense of loss of European history and culture as History and Culture, the loss of their unquestioned place at the center of the world," with this "loss of Eurocentrism" resulting in "orientalism's dialectical reversal: a state of dis-orientation."[244]

While pointing out that "Marxism, as Jameson confesses, continues to endorse global capitalism—on the grounds that it is the necessary preparation for global socialism"—i.e., that same historical tendency, which I have earlier criticized, of Western Marxism to view the overwhelming of other cultures by the West as somehow inevitable—Young also points to Terry Eagleton's characterization of Jameson as "a shamelessly unreconstructed Hegelian" with the prescription "always historicize."[245] Against the postmodernist "dis-orientation" (Young's term) of Lyotard's ahistorical juxtaposition—which I have criticized earlier—of

Cashinahua "pragmatics of narrative knowledge" with the "pragmatics of scientific knowledge,"[246]Jameson's "Hegelian" Marxism, like Peirce's Pragmaticism, insists on viewing any present phenomenon within the range of its historical possibilities, and this "historicist" convergence between the two is more than merely coincidental, for, as we have seen before, Peirce had unequivocally declared that "the truth is that pragmaticism is closely allied to the Hegelian absolute idealism, from which, however, it is sundered by its vigorous denial that the third category (which Hegel degrades to a mere stage of thinking) suffices to make the world."[247]

Peirce's Pragmaticism and Marxism share, moreover, that similar commitment to comprehending future possibilities embedded within present (and past) realities through the two-level epistemology of scientific realism. For, as Levi-Strauss had seen in 1955 (in writing *Tristes Tropiques*), Marxism, like psychoanalysis and geology, attempts to grasp reality at two levels simultaneously, in that epistemic strategy that the realist philosopher of physics Mario Bunge would define as being of fundamental importance to the scientific realist task of predictive comprehension—the epistemic level of observed phenomena being predictively explained by a deeper level of unobserved theoretical entities.[248]

But the historical error—as seen from the vantage point of Peircean Pragmaticism—made by Karl Marx and later Marxists was to conflate the epistemic levels of scientific theoretical entities and observational variables with the (economic) "base" and (cultural) "superstructure," respectively. As I explained in chapter 3, *both* the "culture" and the "economy" of any society are merely observational variables of institutionalized *semantic* meaning, *both* "surface" variables whose variance is determined by the "deeper" (i.e. often unobserved and potentially unobservable, because present adult behavior is not always easily traceable as the effect of past childhood socialization) pragmatics of intergenerational cooperation. The result of this Marxist conflation of scientific realism's two epistemic levels with the "base-superstucture" dichotomy—a historical error of Marxist theory which Jameson has now, according to Young, "reformulated as 'allegorical'"[249]—has been the serious predictive error in overestimating the capacity of socialist revolution to create a "new man" (an overestimation of the capacity of political indoctrination to overcome the conservative influence of the existing forms of intergenerational cooperation in socialization) or the admittedly embarrassing prediction by Christopher Chase-Dunn in 1989 (the year the Berlin Wall came down), pointed out by Robertson, about the "widening space" made available for future "experiments with socialism." But while Jameson's "reformulation" of the Marxist "base-superstructure" relation as allegorical fudges the issue, Robertson commits the opposite mistake of merely describing the observed "increasing interpenetration of culture and economy" without attempting to theoretically *explain why* such an observed phenomenon is occurring. Apparently preoccupied by the embarrassment suffered by Marxist attempts at prediction, Robertson seems to have forgotten Karl Popper's lesson that science progresses by such falsification: Just because Marxist predictions were falsified, social science should not have to abandon—as Robertson seems to imply by offering us his purely descriptive theory of globalization—its quest for better explanatory-predictive theories.[250]

As I have pointed out earlier, Robertson, in his 1988 essay "The Sociological Significance of Culture,"[251] indicated the possibility of going beyond (*meta* in Greek) the observational level of cultural semantics, into theorizing the pragmatics of "deep metacultural codes" that determine the surface meaning of observed semantics. The main weakness, then, which I see in Robertson's subsequent theorization in 1992 of the "contingencies" of globalization is that while correctly observing that "economic matters . . . are considerably subject to cultural contingencies and cultural coding,"[252] Robertson had still made no attempt to elucidate the nature and functioning of such cultural—or *meta*-cultural—"coding." Having therefore "stepped into the breach" left by Robertson by having already delineated the pragmatic "deep metacultural codes" (which Robertson had suggested in 1988)—of *filiation* and *calibration*, respectively—that governed the transition to modernity, I must now complete this process of the "pragmaticizing" of Robertson's cultural vision, plugging the holes in his 1992 theorization of globalization by delineating the third Peircean interpretant code which could govern a Toynbeean postmodernity.

In proceeding to that Peircean *thirdness* of a "post"-modernity, it behooves me to begin by addressing that confusion of "a diversity of issues . . . heterogeneous, fragmented, resistant to general discussion," that has rendered "the post-modernist label . . . to be virtually meaningless"—a Lacanean *meconnaissance* (misrecognition) between communicating speakers, I should note, that is normal in periods of transition. As the mathematical philosopher Brian Rotman observed, William Shakespeare, that expert observer of human frailty who had himself lived through the transition from tradition and modernity, immortalized the scene of such inter-code miscommunication by writing it into his major tragedy, *King Lear*: When Lear demands from his daughter Cordelia that she quantify her love, and then punishes her for her incapacity to do so, the resulting tragedy ending in the death of both miscommunicants is really the result of Lear speaking in the code of *calibration*—the objective quantification of "love"—and Cordelia responding in the code of *filiation*, where the loyalty of the daughter to her father is absolute and therefore nonquantifiable. Each code is like Ferdinand de Saussure's linguistic *langue*, enjoying absolute dominion over every communicative act of *parole*. The difference between Peirce's and Saussure's semiotics then re-emerges into view with Peirce's system able to comprehend that diachronic evolutionary transition between codes, which Saussure's single synchronic *langue* fails to comprehend.[253]

That such *meconnaissance* in the evolutionary transition between interpretant codes could also occur—with a tragedy of larger magnitude—in the cognitive communication of groups much larger than Shakespeare's father-daughter pair in King Lear, was grasped by Niklas Luhmann when he attributed the Terror of the French Revolution—the same Terror that led to Jean-Francois Lyotard's postmodernist proscription of metanarrative *Grand Recits*—to the Jacobin misrecognition of the emerging code of *calibration* within the familistic semantics of the previous code of *filiation*. That "rhetoric of humanity," argued Luhmann,

> leads to the guillotine as the most humane and fastest way of killing people without spilling too much of their blood. . . . It seems that the semantics of happy, personal, harmonious interaction as opposed to cool, reckless, impersonal, capitalistic, bureaucratic society was and is particularly likely to give expression to the reality shock modern society receives by its own realization. What was intended as progress and immaculate growth, as wealthy and enlightened humanity, emerged as a functionally differentiated system with all its risks, inabilities, insecurities, and contradictions.[254]

I happened to witness this phenomenon that Luhmann characterized as the "reality shock society receives by its own realization,"—thankfully on a much smaller scale than did the people who lived through the French, Russian, or Cambodian revolutions—when in a 1988 conference with Brazilian students at the University of São Paulo, dealing with the topic of their experience of four years of democratization, I was introduced to student accounts of psychological depression many of them had experienced upon discovering, after years of struggle against military repression by entire families looking forward to the coming day of harmonious human brotherhood, that the procedural mechanics of modern democracy had less to with the hopes of "fraternity" (conceived by the premodern code of *filiation*) than with "deadening mechanical boredom" (that reality of modern *calibration* that Simmel had comprehended so well in 1905). Joseph Schumpeter's equation in 1942, of the calibrated political exchange of votes for promises (of future performance by political candidates for elected office) and the calibrated economic exchanges between buyers and sellers in the market, showed a better conceptual grasp of the nature of modernity's interpretant code than did Marx's attempt to circumvent this code of *calibration* by his icon of perfect *filiation* within that perfect human family taking "from each according to his ability" and giving "to each according to his need."[255]

Having clarified those empirically related points, I am now ready to begin completion of my attempt to satisfy Luhmann's demand that sociological theories move from that "too simple" level in which they have long persevered, to that Peirce-like level of theoretical formulation which is "sufficiently abstract to allow the kind of complex research design that historical research demands."[256] To traverse the experiential fog of an ongoing or future transition to global postmodernity, we need that "sufficient abstraction" (in Luhmannian terms) that first looks back to the previous transition *to* modernity, to "abstract" from the blinding maelstrom of historical events the formal conditions that made transition possible. As we have seen in the previous section, the transition from premodern *filiation* to modern *calibration* had involved just two formal conditions. The first was the necessary condition of the phenomenological perception (on the part of the *filiation* code's subjects) of "too many people." The second, the sufficient condition for the successful transition out of the resulting historical cycles of abstracting orthodoxy and concretizing heterodoxy, was the social-cognitive achievement of a vision of the "world as object permanence," a cognitive construction first fully achieved in eighteenth-century Euro-America. What are the formal equivalents of those two conditions for transition that can now help us navigate through the theoretical fog surrounding the—often misrecognized—issues debated around the terms *globalization* and *postmodernity*?

A simple analysis of the two formal conditions that governed the *earlier* transition *to* modernity reveals their conceptual relationship with their respective transition-termini: The "necessary condition" had to do with the nature of the cultural signs of *filiation*—icons of human or human-like personalities. The population volume in perceived situations of "too many people" was bound to overwhelm such a system and stretch it into unstable abstraction. The "sufficient condition" of "object permanence" similarly had to do with the "objective" nature of the habitual focus of attention required by the (modern) pragmatic code of the transition-terminus: if there is no "permanence" to be perceived in that objective realm such a lack will obviously fail to hold the attention of the individual subjectivities in this code.

We look then through similar formal reasoning for the "necessary condition" of the next transition, i.e., the condition which will "stretch" modernity's *calibration* code to its breaking point. Since the *filiation* code of pre-modernity had focused cognitive attention on (parental) people and that attention had been "stretched" to the breaking point by "too many people," one may now formally expect a morphologically comparable phenomenological perception of "too many objects" to stretch the "object-ive" cognitive attention span of modern *calibration* to its breaking point—and that is precisely what seems to be happening. From Georg Simmel's observation in his essay "The Metropolis and the Mental Life," written at the beginning of the twentieth century, of "a frightful disproportion in growth" between "the immense culture which for the last hundred years has been embodied in things and in knowledge," as compared to "the cultural progress of the individual during the same period,"[257] to Walter Benjamin's concern about "the work of art in an age of mechanical reproduction," and from Jean-Paul Sartre's description of Roquentin's *Nausea* to Jean Baudrillard's "hyper-reality of simulacra" and Jean-Francois Lyotard's observations about the apparent fracturing of language itself (into "language games") under the weight of "too many objects," from the credential inflation that Randall Collins sees in the American competition for ever-accumulating academic qualifications to the anorexia and bulimia provoked by the unending stream of junk-food commercials, there seems to be an exponential proliferation of those "objective" signs by which modernity calibrates its objectified subjects.

At the level of popular culture this view of the ending of modernity is extensively described by Robert Lane in his recent book, *The Loss of Happiness in Market Democracies*.[258] To summarize Lane's detailed descriptions through my formal-pragmatic reading: "Too many consumer objects to choose from" forcibly turn attention away from that objective realm prescribed by modernity's code—those Weberian-instrumental-rational *calibrations* of measurable means to unquestioned ends—back to those "Who am I?" "What is the meaning of my life?" questions (identity questions which contemporary Weberians often confuse with mere "lifestyle" options) forbidden by modernity (Like many other *meconnaissances* Johann Wolfgang von Goethe's definition of modernity as *bildung* self-cultivation erred in not seeing the self-repressing nature of modernity's objective-*calibration* attention-structuring[259]).

The immediate reaction to such a ("return of the repressed") yearning for a communal discourse about personal identity is to regress toward past discourses of *filiation* still buried within the collective unconscious "Imaginary," i.e., that localistic "fundamentalism" that Robertson sees as having been "institutionalized" by Woodrow Wilson's post-World War I "norm of national self-determination" into that "universalisalization of the particular" pole of his bipolar theory of globalization's "central dynamic."[260] The problem with such localistic regressions is that they are unsustainable for any length of time, as different regressive entities—from hippie communes to survivalist militias to Iranian Ayatollahs—soon discover: the objective world is now too densely interconnected to allow a permanently stable regression into the subjective. The very surfeit of "too many objects"—from plastic garbage to toxic chemicals to discarded information packages haunting the cyberspaces of our electronic ether—presses increasingly upon our planetary environment (and ultimately leak back into our bodies in unexpected ways), and there simply is no local solution to our planetary environmental degradation: in an ironic reversal of that catchy old slogan ("Think globally, Act locally"), those who "think locally" for too long find themselves sooner or later having to "act globally" (often in terroristic ways).

Where then lies our collective "way home"?[261]

Nowhere, for there is no "way home," according to contemporary postmodernist thinkers. Despite his evident nostalgia for the "narrative knowledge" of preliterate Cashinahua tribal culture—a nostalgia that, from Marx's formulations about "primitive communism" to the Marxism of the early Levi-Strauss's *Tristes Tropiques*, had expressed its yearning for humanity's lost tribal "home" in the "grand narrative" of a future possibility of return to (a technologically advanced) "communism"—Lyotard had famously declared that "in contemporary society and culture—postindustrial society, postmodern culture— . . . the grand narrative has lost its credibility, regardless of what mode of unification it uses, regardless of whether it is a speculative narrative or a narrative of emancipation."[262]

As if echoing Lyotard's connection of the postmodernist loss of credibility in "grand narrative" to the fact that "now Godel has effectively established the existence in the arithmetic system of a proposition that is neither demonstrable nor refutable within that system," Richard Rorty's American version of postmodernism also limits its cognitive reach to a "liberal ironism" which believes that there is "no noncircular theoretical backup for the belief that cruelty is horrible," nor for any other such moral belief, because

> anybody who thinks that there are well-grounded theoretical answers to this sort of question—algorithms for resolving moral dilemmas of this sort—is still, in his heart, a theologian or a metaphysician. He believes in an order beyond time and change which both determines the point of human existence and establishes a hierarchy of responsibilities. . . . A historicist and nominalist culture of the sort I envisage would settle for narratives which connect the present with the past, on the one hand, and with utopian futures, on the other. More important, it would regard the realization of utopias, and the envisaging of still further utopias, as an endless process."[263]

The historical irony is that current postmodernist thought has reacted to Kurt Godel's discovery of the proneness of *calibration*al mathematics to the "undecidability" problem of linguistic self-reference—i.e., the problem of deciding, for example, if the sentence "All Cretans are liars," uttered by Epimenides the Cretan, is true or false—by, on the one hand, Lyotard's assertion that "the grand narrative has lost its credibility," and on the other, Rorty's assertion that the loss of such "noncircular theoretical backup" calls for the "endless" proliferation of such narratives![264]

The further historical irony is that despite Rorty's expressed fear that "ironist intellectuals" such as himself "are far outnumbered (even in the lucky, rich, literate democracies) by . . . nonintellectuals (who) are still committed either to some form of Enlightenment rationalism," it is that very majority of "nonintellectuals" who—judging from viewer ratings on large audiences for Western television's escapist programming—"would regard the realization of utopias, and the envisaging of still further utopias as an endless process"![265] The large viewer audience that so-called reality TV such as CBS's "Survivor" seems to have attracted, for example, would seem to bear out Daniel Bell's 1976 warning that "the post-modernist temper demands that what was previously played out in fantasy and imagination must be acted out in life as well."[266]

I have, in my analysis of semantic meaning's referential nature earlier in this book, pointed out the pragmatist philosopher Nicholas Rescher's warning of the inherent fragility of such linguistic meaning's referential link to reality in that, according to Rescher, "the link to reality is broken when we move from universals to particulars and from their features to the things themselves," a situation of innate linguistic referential fragility now made worse, according to that other philosophical student of current problems of meaning, Hilary Putnam, by an exploding division of linguistic labor within which even the same word, such as "gold," may connote very different experiential consequences to the different specialists—such as goldsmiths, chemists, etc.—handling it. Now with the "endless" proliferation of "too many objects," pushing endless media-manipulations of prospective consumers of such objects by that endless procession of images that the postmodernist Jean Baudrillard has generally labeled "simulacra," it is no surprise to find Baudrillard—whom Rex Butler has credited with a last-ditch "defence of the real"—now situating the earlier analyses by Walter Benjamin and Marshall McLuhan of the technological reproduction of imagery, as having occurred at those historical "limits of reproduction and simulation, at the point where referential reason disappears."[267]

The crucial question for global sociology's comprehension of our current historical problem of postmodernity is whether human language—which Martin Heidegger called the "house of Being"—could be really losing, under the pressure of "too many objects" and their televised fantasy-images, its referential link to reality. While, as we have seen, Lyotard's reply was that our linguistic mirror of reality had fractured, in the "postmodern condition," into a multiplicity of "language games," and Baudrillard's response was that the proliferation of "simulacra" in our current "hyper-reality" had broken the referential link of language to reality around the time when Benjamin and McLuhan had first examined their reality content, it is the "deconstuctionist" philosophy of a third French postmodernist thinker, Jacques Derrida—who, according to Richard Rorty, "wants to undercut Heidegger as Heidegger undercut Nietzsche," despite the fact that "his project is continuous with Heidegger's in that he, too, wants to find words which get us 'beyond' metaphysics"[268]—that is widely seen as posing the biggest challenge to the traditional (and modern) belief in the referential efficacy, the semantic linkage to extralinguistic reality, of language. As Rescher wrote in 1998:

> Deconstructionism is a theory regarding the interpretation of texts that denies any prospect of objectivity in this domain. Initially projected with regard to literary texts, the enthusiasm of its more ambitious exponents soon led them to expand the theory's application to texts in general—historical, biographical, philosophical, what have you. . . . At the core of this doctrinal stance lies a view of textual plasticity—that as the enterprise of text interpretation proceeds, it brings an ever increasing range of viable and more or less equivalent alternative interpretations. . . . On this basis, the partisans of deconstructionism condemn with the dismissive epithet of *textualism* the view that a given text has a meaning in such a stable and objective way as to favor one particular interpretation over the rest. They insist that there is no room for objectivity here: interpretation is a matter of to each his own.[269]

As we have seen, that other philosophical critic of deconstructionism, Christopher Norris, has proposed an "aerodynamic test" for such "anti-realism": Would a deconstructionist flying at 3,000 feet in an airplane really deny the view of the aerodynamic text upon whose reading that airplane had been built, that, as Rescher put it here, that "given text has a meaning in such a stable and objective way as to favor one particular interpretation"—i.e., that it will continue to fly, rather than fall out of the sky—"over the rest"?[270]

Rescher saw the two crucial deconstructionist theses of "plasticity"—the deconstructionist belief that "every text has multiple interpretations"—and "equivalency"—the deconstructionist assertion that "every interpretation is as good as any other"—as following upon the prior thesis of what Rescher called "omnitextuality," that insisted that "any proposed interpretation of a text must itself take the form of simply another text." In the "hermeneutical sphere" of deconstructionism, argued Rescher, "there is no way of exiting from the textual domain."[271]

But, it had been Charles S. Peirce—as we briefly glimpsed at the beginning of this book—who, long before those whom Rescher in 1998 viewed as the "more ambitious exponents" of Derrida's "deconstructionism," had stated:

> The meaning of a representation can be nothing but a representation. In fact, it is nothing but a representation itself conceived as stripped of irrelevant clothing. But this clothing never can be completely stripped off; it is only changed for something more diaphanous. So there is an infinite regression here. Finally, the interpretant is nothing but another representation to which the torch of truth is handed along; and as representation, it has its interpretant again. Lo, another infinite series.[272]

In comprehending such "omni-representationality"—to paraphrase Rescher's 1998 characterization of the first thesis of deconstructionism as "omnitextuality"—Peirce had *not* followed the deconstructionist argument into its second and third "theses" of asserting the "plasticity" and "equivalency" of representations/texts,[273] but had instead used the language of "limits" of the Newton-Leibniz mathematical calculus (dealing with the "limit" condition of an infinite series) to argue that "an endless series of representations, each representing the one behind it, may be conceived to have an absolute object at its limit."[274]

What Peirce had grasped and deconstructionism "overlooks, to its decisive detriment," according to the contemporary Peirce scholar and philosophical pragmatist Rescher, "is the crucial matter of *context*":

> The process of *deconstruction*—of interpretatively dissolving any and every text into a plurality of supposedly merit-equivalent constructions—can and should be offset by the process of *reconstruction*, which calls for viewing texts within their larger contexts. After all, texts inevitably have a setting— historical, cultural, authorial—on which their actual meaning is critically dependent. And this contextual setting projects beyond the textual realm itself in

comprising both processes (know-how) and products (artifacts) relating to human action in relevant regards. In particular, it encompasses both noncommunicative practices (behavioral) and communicative practices, including the processes, and methods in relation to text-contemporaneous styles of life, the products of noncommunicative processes and practices (material involvements), and the relevant social traditions. To the extent that we do not understand the ways and means of a people's mode of living—what they are concerned to do and to produce—we will have great difficulty in understanding their texts. In sum, texts have a wider functional context. . . . To see texts and the libraries that warehouse them as context-disconnectedly self-sufficient is akin to contemplating the molehills without the mole.[275]

What then is "the mole"—i.e., the social context—behind "the molehills" of contemporary Western (and especially French) postmodernist textual production? In his 1987 book *Culture, Identity, and Politics*, political anthropologist Ernest Gellner had proposed his "Rubber Cage thesis," in modification of Daniel Bell's earlier "Weberian" agonizing, in his 1976 book *The Cultural Contradictions of Capitalism*, over the decline of "the traditional bourgeois organization of life—its rationality and sobriety," which, Bell had lamented, "now has few defenders in the culture." Gellner's Rubber Cage thesis, proposed "as an alternative to the Iron Cage thesis (whose applicability to the emergence of industrial society I do not wish to dispute," was "meant to apply to a later or fully developed stage of industrialism," where the decline in the traditional manufacturing sector of heavy industry, manifested itself in a cultural attitude of "disenchantment with (Weberian) disenchantment." "The activities requiring Cartesian thought are diminishing (both as a proportion of the population and as a proportion of the time of individuals," Gellner had argued, "whilst the activities calling only for easy, intuitive, near-self-evident responses are increasing."[276]

But, what Gellner had characterized as "a later or fully developed stage of industrialism" is still limited, at the beginning of the twenty-first century, to a tiny fraction of the human race, perched around the North Atlantic and East Asia: a year after Lyotard's French-language publication of *The Postmodern Condition* in 1979, the American journalist Alvin Toffler had published *The Third Wave*, which described the technological revolution of electronics—the technology which, according to that sociological expert on technological organization, Jon Shepard, underlies the flood of media images and electronic information that constitutes postmodernism as "a generic term"[277]—then just breaking over the United States, as a "third wave" of technological innovation, following the previous two "waves" of the industrial and agricultural revolutions, then still in progress or still just breaking over other parts of the world.[278] To use that "aerodynamic test case for anti-realism" by Christopher Norris, again, while Derrida's deconstructionist disciples were hopping over the Atlantic Ocean, denying "any prospect of objectivity" (according to Rescher) in textual interpretation,[279] the very same companies that had built the airplanes in which these deconstructionists flew—and built

them to the "objective" specifications of aerodynamic texts—were also technologically reproducing dozens of other similar airplanes that were "shrinking" the
world into greater communicative "density." Postmodernism then, as Robert
Young proposed, can truly "best be defined as European culture's awareness that
it is no longer the unquestioned and dominant center of the world."[280]

But postmodernity, as an objective condition of society, may yet be more
than this mere fragmentation of language—or of linguistically represented reality—described by Western postmodernist literary writers. In offering us "a sociological theory of postmodernity," sociologist Zygmunt Bauman proposed that

> the term *postmodernity* renders accurately the defining traits of the social con-
> dition that emerged throughout the affluent countries of Europe and of Euro-
> pean descent in the course of the twentieth century, and took its present shape
> in the second half of that century. . . . Postmodernity may be conceived of as
> modernity conscious of its true nature—*modernity for itself.* The most con-
> spicuous features of the postmodern condition: institutionalized pluralism, va-
> riety, contingency and ambivalence—have been all turned out by modern so-
> ciety in ever increasing volumes; yet they were seen as signs of failure rather
> than success, as evidence of the unsufficiency of efforts so far, at a time when
> the institutions of modernity, faithfully replicated by the modern mentality,
> struggled for *universality, homogeneity, monotony, and clarity.*[281]

I invite my reader to compare for himself or herself Bauman's introduction
of postmodernity, as the consciousness of "failure . . . of the unsufficiency of efforts so far" of the institutions of "the modern mentality" to achieve those exaggerated goals of "*universality, homogeneity, monotony, and clarity,*" with Peirce's
similar introduction of his concept of cognitive *thirdness*, as emerging through
the failure of the "exaggerated language" of cognitive *secondness*:

> All exaggerated language, "supreme," "utter," "matchless," "root and branch,"
> is the furniture of minds which think of seconds and forget thirds. Action is
> second, but conduct is third. Law as an active force is second, but order and
> legislation are third. Sympathy, flesh and blood, that by which I feel my neigh-
> bor's feelings, is third.[282]

I especially urge my reader to notice that Peirce's last sentence in the passage that I just cited—"Sympathy, flesh and blood, that by which I feel my neigh-
bor's feelings, is third" (as contrasted with the immediately preceding sentence
asserting that "law as an active force is second")—prefigures the postmodern
"morality of the human face" of Emmanuel Levinas, which has elsewhere so fascinated Bauman, in the latter's essay "Morality Begins at Home; or, Can There Be
a Levinasian Macro-ethics?"[283] Bauman's "sociological theory of modernity"
continued, defining *postmodernity* by reference to *modernity*:

The postmodern condition can be therefore described, on the one hand, as modernity emancipated from false consciousness; on the other, as a new type of social condition marked by the institutionalization of the characteristics which modernity—in its designs and managerial practices—set about to eliminate and, failing that, to conceal.[284]

If we were to sum up in one word "the characteristics which," according to Bauman, "modernity . . . set about to eliminate and, failing that, to conceal," the answer stares us in the face with that word which the mathematical semiotician Brian Rotman finds permeating Peirce's conception of *Thirdness*: *habit*. Peirce had defined the sign of *Thirdness*, the "symbol," as "the general name or description which signifies its object by means of an association of ideas or habitual connection between the name and the character signified." "Such signs," Peirce added, "are always abstract and general, because habits are general rules to which the organism has become subjected."[285] We may therefore now use that "exaggerated language" which Peirce had seen as "the furniture of minds which think of seconds but forget thirds" to sum up what "the modern mentality," according to Bauman, had "set about to eliminate": the solipsistic modern *ego* cogito of Cartesian rationality, had declared itself "supreme" and "matchless" in attempting the "utter," "root and branch" elimination—as we saw outlined for us in that March 1986 essay "The Matter of Habit" in the *American Journal of Sociology* by Charles Camic—the "habitual" nature of premodern custom.[286]

When Bauman defined postmodernity "as modernity conscious of its true nature," that "true nature" consisted, according to Peirce, of the "habits . . . to which the (human) organism has become subjected" through millennia of history, habits which resurfaced in the form of that "institutionalized pluralism, variety, contingency and ambivalence" that Bauman had seen as "the most conspicuous features of the postmodern condition" and which modernity's "designs and managerial practices" failed "to eliminate." Postmodernity is then simply, as Bauman recognized it, the continuation of a "modernity emancipated from false consciousness"—a false consciousness which had simply lacked moderation in dealing with the habitual nature of human beings. As Peirce had phrased it: "Continuity represents Thirdness almost to perfection. Every process comes under that head. Moderation is a kind of Thirdness."[287]

That this dawning of the consciousness of the failure of what Bauman saw as the "designs and managerial practices" of "the modern mentality" to impose "*universality, homogeneity, monotony, and clarity*"[288] should have resulted originally in what anthropologist Arjun Appadurai saw as an explosive plethora of "imagined worlds . . . ethnoscapes, mediascapes, technoscapes, financescapes and ideoscapes" moving in "a deterritorialized context" of "global cultural flow"—a "flow" which, according to Appadurai, could only be comprehended through the new "polythetic" language of mathematical fractal and chaos theory[289]—is not surprising, given the coincidence of the dawning of the postmodern consciousness in the West, with that release of the colonized "Third World," not only from the repressive pressures of those demands by modern "rationality" for Bauman's "universality, homogeneity, monotony and clarity" but also from the doubly repressive imposition of such demands upon them by their erstwhile colonial masters. What needs to be "handled with care" by sociologists not especially trained in mathematics is the word *chaos*, which, as exposed to popular view by James Gleick's 1987 book *Chaos: Making a New Science*, did not mean, as Webster's dictionary would have it, "a state of utter confusion," or disorder, for, as Gleick blithely informed us in that successful popularization of this new mathematics, "physiologists found a surprising order in the chaos that develops in the human heart."[290]

Gleick's graphic displays of the "Lorenz Attractor" of chaos theory should have reminded readers of Karl Popper's 1972 essay "Of Clouds and Clocks," where Popper had used his talent at crafting visual images to explain his otherwise possibly difficult physico-mathematical concepts to a general audience. In explaining the difference between Peirce's philosophy of science and the mechanistic determinism of Peirce's contemporaries within the scientific community (of Peirce's day), Popper's image of a clock had accurately comprehended the prevailing meaning of scientific determinism from Descartes to Laplace—the linear determinism of a near-perfect transfer of momentum (i.e., except for friction's loss of energy) between the levers and gears of mechanical clocks. In that clockwork determinism, perfect predictability was assumed. In fact, even in today's quartz crystal clocks that may work without mechanistic levers and gears, less-than-perfect predictability would render a clock or watch useless! Peirce's "determinism" on the other hand, according to Popper, had been that of "clouds" rather than "clocks"—mapping a range of future possibilities, rather than aiming to predict with perfect "clockwork" accuracy. Given that chaos theory emerged from weather prediction, Popper's 1972 characterization of Peirce as the scientist of "clouds," and not of "clocks," had been prescient: the chaos and fractal theories discussed by Gleick and Appadurai as new "polythetic" languages are just some of the new mathematical languages discussed by Ben Goertzel's 1997 book *From Complexity to Creativity*, a book which, overtly recognizing the contribution to such conceptualization of "complexity" made by the *Collected Papers* of Charles Peirce, aims most of all to fashion a contemlanguage of mathematical complexity in the evolutionary process that has so far culminated (as far as we know at the present moment) in the complexity of the human brain.[291]

Goertzel's assertion at the beginning of this book that "complexity science is young enough"[292] helps place Lyotard's earlier assessment in 1979, that "the postmodern would be that which, in the modern, puts forward the unpresentable in presentation itself" (thereby fracturing the linguistic vehicle of that presentation into "language games"),[293] within its proper historical context: for such a Lyotard-ian putting forward of "the unpresentable in presentation itself," had occurred before the world had become familiar with the term *postmodern* in the visual medium of painting as an art form, and such a *visual* example serves well to convey my intended "deconstruction" of Lyotard's "postmodern condition." Consider, then, this assessment from 1948 of the meaning of the Cubist paintings of Georges Bracques and Pablo Picasso—exemplified by Picasso's well-known 1913 painting "The Woman of Arles"—by the art critic Thomas Herzog. In attempting to explain how a flesh-and-blood "woman of Arles" could end up being represented by Picasso as that well-known juxtaposition of a series of angled planes, Herzog had begun with this quasi-Lyotardian sentence about the problem of presenting the "unpresentable": "It seeks to present the infinitude of space itself." But as he proceeded with his analysis of Cubist painting-technique, Herzog in fact showed us the way to think *beyond* Lyotard's postmodern "report on knowledge" as fractured "language games":

> The cubistic forms, corners, surfaces, and lines, glimpsed in ever-new constellations by the shifting viewpoints, are conjoined in such a way that an illusion of a dynamic process occurring in endless space is created. Here too, the intent is recognizable: anyone wishing to portray the infinitude of space must also paint time as the fourth dimension. He must show how each act of seeing superimposes a spatial figure, glimpsed now in this way, now in that, over the respective previous spatial figure. The aim is to make palpable a kind of spatio-temporal process out of the wealth of intersecting and complementary spatial components.[294]

What Herzog's analysis of Cubist painting demonstrates is a twist to that Godel paradox of self-reference that had bedeviled Lyotard:[295] Rather than arriving involuntarily at a problem of undecidability because of the linguistic system's self-reference, the Cubist Picasso had instead, in painting "The Woman of Arles" in 1913, voluntarily decided to use self-reference to broaden his knowledge of the object beyond what it might otherwise have been. The painting of "time as the fourth dimension" that Herzog saw in Cubist painting was after, all, not objective or universal time, but the painter's own subjective time line as he "glimpsed" the object "now in this way, now in that" (in Herzog's words); in Cubist painting, the painter, in effect, also paints his own act of painting!

It should be noted that this "turn to the subject" is not new in the history of Western thought. From the Socratic attempt to "know thyself," to Rene Descartes's "I think, therefore I am," to Immanuel Kant's "Copernican Revolution" in epistemology, Western philosophy has repeatedly committed "self-reference," as it "turned to the subject" as a way out of the problems experienced at the relevant point in time, when faced with the "undecidability" problem in objective cognition. What is new in the postmodern repetition of such a "reverse Godel procedure" (i.e., turn deliberately to self-reference as a way *out* of undecidability), is that, unlike past philosophy's turn to a "non-physical" subject (as neither Socrates' *nous*, nor Descartes's *cogito*, nor Kant's *transcendental ego* can be calibrated on a weighing machine), physics has now committed "self-reference" by turning to the physical subject in order to transcend the "undecidability" of its objective knowledge. Gleick's 1987 book *Chaos* had begun by reporting Stephen Hawking's 1980 lecture, titled "Is the End in Sight for Theoretical Physics?" The question that Hawking was asking was answered by the Peircean philosopher Nicholas Rescher in his 1989 book *Cognitive Economy*: Borrowing from Karl Marx's concept of the "falling rate of profit" of the capitalist economy, Rescher argued that the scientific enterprise might also be governed by such a "falling rate" of scientific discovery.[296]

Rescher's economistic limits on the rate of scientific discovery have now been visible for some time in physics, both at its micro-level, where the discovery of new subatomic particles require ever-more-expensive supercolliders, and at its macro-level, where cosmological discovery needs ever-more-expensive telescopes. It is in this economistically constrained context of discovery that Hawking—and his colleague, Roger Penrose, after him—adopted his (weak) version of the "anthropic principle," which deduces some properties of the objective universe, such as some "cosmological constants," from the fact that we humans exist.[297]

Hawking's scientific usage of the anthropic principle coheres conceptually with Peirce's usage of the concept of "habit" for *both* the level of association of ideas *and* for physical law: whether biological habituation is an evolutionarily driven effect of the lawfulness of our physical environment, or (as Christopher Hookway presents this Peircean equation between psycho-biological habituation and physical law) matter is "effete mind," the point is that, after pre-modernity's primary focus upon human subjectivity and modernity's focus upon the realm of the "objective," Peirce had been one of the first, and the physicists using the cosmological anthropic principle some of the latest, to use a postmodern subject-object equation.[298]

A similar subject-object equation has emerged around the concept of the "hologram." Originally a result of the physicist Dennis Gabor's invention of a special kind of photography, the hologram is concisely explained by neuro-psychologist Zoltan Torey in the glossary to his 1999 book, *The Crucible of Consciousness*:

> The photographic record of an object (image) in unrecognizable patterns of stripes and whorls which, when illuminated by coherent (laser) light, organizes the light into a three-dimensional representation of the original object. Any portion of the record can be used to reconstruct the image, though portions of diminishing size decrease its clarity.[299]

In his 1980 book, *Wholeness and the Implicate Order*, the concept of the hologram was adopted by the quantum physicist David Bohm as a hypothesis to explain the universe as a whole, because, as is again concisely explained by neuro-psychologist Torey, of the strange circumstance that while the probabilistic outcome of large-sacle (summated) quantum occurrences is extremely stable, that of the individual occurrences is not. This effect is quite inexplicable in causal terms and makes one wonder . . . whether this unvarying constraint is not in fact a significant residual characteristic of the singularity [the "Big Bang" which began our universe], a characteristic that is preserved on the quantum plane holographically as it were and finds expression in quantum behavior now that the singularity is dispersed into its expanded form, the cosmos.[300]

In the meanwhile, because American psychologist Karl Lashley had discovered, in learning experiments with maze-running rats, that "he could remove up to ninety per cent of their cortex without significant deterioration in their power to thread their way through the maze,"[301] later neurophysiologists such as Karl Pribram adopted the model of the hologram to explain brain structure.[302]

Since I am here not so much interested in the question of ultimate reality as I am in indicating the state of our postmodern knowledge that presents quite a different picture from Lyotard's fractured language games, I will leave aside the fascinating question—which has haunted, among others, physicist Penrose[303]— about whether mental processes are in any way related to (or identical with) quantum-physical processes. What I will focus on instead are the implications that G. R. Taylor drew in his book *The Natural History of the Mind*, which had been first published, ironically, in 1979, the very same year that Lyotard's *The Postmodern Condition* had first been published in its original French:

> Memory is distributed, as Lashley's butchery of rats made plain. And here the holographic parallel is the best clue we have. We can be pretty sure that memory is not recorded in a simple tape-recorder-like way, but consists of *a vast tapestry or pattern in which smaller and smaller patterns are nested*, in a way slightly reminiscent of some of Escher's unique etchings. (The hologram, of course, is only a parallel: more accurately, there is a Fourier transform.)[304]

"A vast tapestry or pattern in which smaller and smaller patterns are nested": having earlier described Niklas Luhmann's theoretical conception of "levels" of system-functioning, "levels" which enable the scientist to "say that disorder at one level" could be "order at another without confronting the paradox of saying that disorder is order,"[305] I now arrive at the point where I discover that the human brain may function in this way, too—and it may be no coincidence since Luhmann built his theory on the *biological* model of Francisco Varela and Humberto Maturana. Not only does this postmodern recapitulation of Arthur Lovejoy's Medieval "Great Chain of Being" adapt to Godel's paradoxes—by having upper levels of organization take over when lower ones have been incapacitated by self-referential paradox—but also, since consumer demand is likely to exert selective pressures toward more user-friendly computers, the individual brain is also likely to emerge as the model for a "social brain" built out of electricity-conducting wire but connecting individual human communicators together. Borrowing the term *conceptual coherence* from Goertzel's young "complexity science" and applying it to that Peircean thirdness of postmodernity, I can predict, in the Peircean sense of a "limiting condition," that, from the apparently fragmented state of knowledge with the current near-demise of modernity's second code of *calibration* in developed nations—the necessary condition for transition—it is toward that equilibrium state (sufficient condition) of "symbolic coherence" (the social antonym of Leon Festinger's "cognitive dissonance" concept) that postmodern society will move as it globalizes, i.e., as all human social groupings proceed, in Peirce's terms, from each situation of local knowledge, through an "endless series of representations . . . to have an absolute object," *globality*—that "species aspect" of humanity as a whole that Robertson had intimated[306]—"at its limit."[307]

This possibility, that the current process of the third of three Peircean cognitive steps, the interpretant code of *globalization*—the working through the "cognitive dissonance" by each human grouping, of the "endless series of representations" of oneself, one's others, and the nonhuman world unleashed by the globalizing networks of electronic media and financial capital—leads not to that desirable "absolute object at its limit" of Robertson's hope for a "globality . . . including the species aspect" of humanity but to mutually assured destruction, is also there. Peirce's theory, as Popper reminded us, is not a clockwork determinism, but a cloud of possibilities: Like those butterfly-like "attractors" of chaos theory, Peircean evolutionism yields no future certainty but only a range of possibility.[308]

To better focus, then, upon this range or map of globalizing possibilities at the beginning of the twenty-first century, I will look back—in a parting glance—at Roland Robertson's "thesis" about the globalization process in the late twentieth century. "My own argument," Robertson had argued,

> involves the attempt to preserve direct attention *both* to particularity and difference *and* to universality and homogeneity. It rests largely on the thesis that we are, in the late twentieth century, witnesses to—and participants in—a massive, twofold process involving the *interpenetration of the universalization of particularism and the particularization of universalism.*[309]

Farther along, Robertson explained that "in my perspective globalization in what I call its primary sense is a relatively autonomous process. Its central *dynamic* involves the twofold process of the particularization of the universal and the universalization of the particular."[310] Of the former aspect of the twofold process, Robertson's sole example was "the rise of movements . . . searching for the meaning of the world as a whole," and of the latter—the "universalization of the particular"—Robertson focused upon the periods after World War I, with Woodrow Wilson's proclamation of the norm of national self-determination, and after World War II, with the beginnings, growing into the 1960s, of Third World independence—with these foci functioning within an overall definition of this second aspect of the "twofold process" of globalization as "the global universality of the search for the particular, for increasingly fine-grained modes of identity presentation" which included "fundamentalism."[311]

The robustness of generalizing "grand theory" in science is, of course, its comprehensive range. Had Newton's gravitational theory, for example, explained the planetary movements in the solar system but failed to account for falling apples on earth, it would have failed in its theoretical mission. Since globalization is possibly the largest social process that has yet occurred (or is occurring), the question of the comprehensive applicability of Robertson's theoretical categories immediately arises. In 1994, for example, Charles Taylor placed before us a certain type of the "universalization of the particular" which is worth examining under the optic of Robertson's general theory of globalization: "The charge leveled," said Taylor,

> by the most radical forms of the politics of difference is that "blind" liberalisms are themselves the reflection of particular cultures. And the worrying thought is that this bias might not just be a contingent weakness of all hitherto proposed theories, that the very idea of such a liberalism may be a kind of pragmatic contradiction, a particular masquerading as the universal.[312]

As if she had been "waiting in the wings" to furnish Taylor with an example of precisely "such a liberalism" which "may be a kind of pragmatic contradiction, a particular masquerading as the universal," Jyotsna Singh offered us in 1996 this historical account:

> By all accounts it would be fair to consider William Jones a liberal, and a humanist, albeit with an intensely romanticizing imagination. . . . Jones' interest in Indian culture was accompanied by an abiding concern for the Indian natives. . . . Yet these (characteristics) are countered by (and contained within) the pervasive ideological assumption about the British rulers' role as interpreters, translators, and mediators of Indian culture, language, and laws in the face of the Hindus' inability to carry out these tasks.[313]

What makes the fit between this historical account by Singh of the specific case of William Jones, "a liberal" albeit a British colonial "ruler," and Taylor's earlier theoretical speculation about the possibility of "such a liberalism" being "a kind of pragmatic contradiction, a particular masquerading as the universal," of special relevance as an objective test case for Robertson's globalization theory, is that, despite the appearance from the matching phraseology of Singh's having provided that case of Jones-the-liberal-cum-colonial ruler to specifically bolster Taylor's theoretical position, there is no evidence at all within this particular book by Singh—not even a single mention of this particular Taylor anywhere in this book—to suggest that Singh had even been aware of Taylor's 1994 essay "The Politics of Recognition."

What Singh's historical example of Jones, the famous Orientalist, does— fitting so well, as it does, within Taylor's felicitous phrasing of the possibility of "a particular masquerading as the universal," itself a perfect counter-possibility to Robertson's surprisingly blithe elision of the period of colonialism as the master example of the "Universalization of (the colonial master's) particularism"!—is to provide me with the perfect case with which to demonstrate the scientific superiority of a Peircean approach to globalization over Robertson's theory.

Even Taylor's labeling of "such a liberalism" as a "kind of pragmatic contradiction" proves felicitous, for the problem here is precisely the contradiction between two pragmatic codes. Singh's wording about "the pervasive ideological assumption about the British rulers' role as interpreters, translators, and mediators of Indian culture, language, and laws in the face of the Hindus' inability to carry out these tasks," is precisely what I have earlier called the process of "infantilization" of the Hindus by their "liberal" colonial masters into the premodern pragmatic code of *filiation*: Only parental figures "assume," on behalf of their infant children, the latter's "inability to carry out" the "tasks" of speaking for themselves in their own language! In contrast—i.e., in what Taylor called a "pragmatic contradiction"—to this overwhelming all-encompassing environment of Briton-to-Hindu filiative relations is the pretense to liberalism on the part of the orientalist Jones: I say pretense not because I doubt in any way what Singh has herself pointed out, that "he was a typical product of the eighteenth-century Enlightenment, a rationalist and universalist who sought 'to explain cultural unity through common origins,'"[314] but simply because he must have been aware, accomplished scholar that he was, that as Immanuel Kant was to phrase it in 1784 (ten years before Jones's death in 1794) Enlightenment involved a collective effort by society—not just by isolated individuals—to emerge from the state of their "minority" into the openness of free processes of *calibration* between mutually independent, formal citizens.

With Jones having died, according to Singh, in 1794,[315] Roland Robertson's historical wait for the American President Woodrow Wilson to formally open the gate to what Robertson believes is meant by "the universalization of particularism" simply masks the historical reality of colonialism having quintessentially been the enforced "universalization" of the colonial master's "particularism." It helps to "translate" these terms about "particular" and "universal" into their Peircean cognitive equivalents, simply because the *cognitive* equivalents enjoy greater currency in psychiatric literature, and may therefore give a more accurate "flavor" of the historical damage inflicted upon the personality-socialization pragmatics of the colonized culture, the trauma to its "social self" inflicted by the extended historical period of colonialism.

The Peircean-cognitive equivalent of "particularism"—that frank enjoyment of one's master-ful subjective "bias"—is "subjectivism," while the similarly cognitive equivalent to "universalism"—with its attempt as de-anthromorphizing self-restraint in the interests of duly objective procedures (or, as legal theorists might want it phrased, "objective due process")—is "objectivism." With British colonialism in India officially dating from the Battle of Plassey in 1757, that meant, especially for today's "Westernized Indian" self, often a descendant of a coastal region brought to heel early by the seafaring colonialists, at least 190 years of being forced to live the lie of the colonial master's subjectivity—from his Milton and Shakespeare, to his tastes for gin-and-tonics and polo, to his glorification of the signing of the Magna Carta as the fount of all historical freedom, to his Christmas and Guy Fawkes day, on his year numbered according to his Christian era—pretending to be the objectivity of human reason (or the Weber-Schluchter "rationalism of world mastery"). The crucial question for Robertson's "Globality" as "the circumstance of extensive awareness of the world as a whole, including the species aspect of the latter"[316]—a question that Robertson did not pose and cannot therefore be expected to readily answer—is: How long after having lived 190 years of the "solitude" of an "objectivity" that one had all along suspected to be the master's subjective fraud—and after how many self-hating "fundamentalisms" one fell into simply to counter the "colonial-master-within"—will it still take the "postcolonial" subject to be ready to embrace that "species aspect" of her global selfhood?

Conclusion, 2000 C.E.: Globality as "Semantic Regionalization"?

We can expect, from the apparently contradictory paths taken by two neighboring nations in the Middle East, Turkey and Iran—neither of which had been, strictly speaking, a colony of the West—that answering broad historical questions like the one with which I had ended the previous section of this chapter may be a risky business. But, given the growing gap between the *speed* with which economic and media influences are globalizing and the correspondingly slow pace of mutual cultural understanding between people of different global regions, even a failed effort in working on the global-cultural equivalent of Mendeleyev's Periodic Table of chemical elements is still worthwhile, if its falsification encourages others to take up the challenge of thinking globally when it comes to a multicultural geography.

Besides, even test-case reading of the latest materials available to me on the Turkish and Iranian revolutions—Andrew Mango's *Attaturk* and Hamid Dabashi's *Theology of Discontent*—convinced me that the supposedly opposite directions of their revolutionary ideologies had really been similar in being both genuine nationalist attempts to—in the "Peircean" terminology I have developed in the last three sections of this chapter—shirk off "minority" filiative status that they had both found irksome, in Turkey's case against Arab-Persian cultural tutelage (with the Westernizing trends of Kemal Attaturk greatly exaggerated to mask his rather extreme Turkish self-regard, as Mango shows),[317] and in Iran's case—usually taken to be a bitterly anti-Western revolution—again, the surprisingly vast Western, secular influence on Ali Shariati, the second most influential original propagandist of the Islamic Revolution (after Khomeini himself).[318]

My success so far in manipulating the machinery of Peirce's cognitive evolutionism to comprehend world history should not blind my reader to the fact that Peirce's "triadomania"—his tendency to see time as moving in three steps—was shared by others such as Jacques Lacan, whose "three cognitive stages" of the Imaginary, the Real, and the Symbolic I have analyzed elsewhere to show its isomorphism with Peirce's three-stage model of cognitive evolution. According to psychological therapists Maggie Phillips and Claire Frederick, Catholic theologian Teilhard de Chardin's book *On Happiness* had proposed a similar three-stage model of emotional development, from "centration" in childhood to "de-centration" in young adulthood, to "super-centration" in one's mature years.[319] In his anthropological study of Tibetan culture, Stan Mumford discovered a convergence between the medieval Buddhist monk Atisa's (982-1055) three-step model of spiritual development (similar to Kierkegaard's three stages, it seemed to me) and the Russian literary theorist Mikhail Bakhtin's idea of three "sociocultural periods" or "chronotopes" as laid out in Bakhtin's *The Dialogic Imagination*. As Mumford acknowledges, Bakhtin had admitted to having been influenced by Martin Buber's concept of the "I-Thou" dialogue, which, as we have seen, Max Fisch, the editor of Peirce's chronological edition of his collected works had found similar to Peirce's. All these similarities are no mere coincidence because they all appear to be based on the same notion as Peirce's, that all communication proceeds from an "I," through an "IT," to a "THOU."[320]

While Peirce's three-stage model of communication—based as it is, like other similar three-stage models on matching the time intervals to the I-It-Thou direction of communication itself—seemed the logical model upon which to base a long-historical-range model of global cultural evolution, given my sense that Robertson's globalization terminus of "globality" as "the extended awareness of the world as a whole, including the species aspect of the latter,"[321] seemed like the perfect description of the possible terminus of a *generalized* Peircean communication process from all possible "I"s-through/about all possible "IT"s to all possible "THOU's," Peirce's pragmaticist tradition—as defined by Charles Morris in 1938 as a three-science model of syntactics, semantics, and pragmatics—had also that other theoretical advantage of enabling a semantic meaning-to-pragmatic meaning two-level observational variables-to-theoretical entities scientific realist epistemic structure.

Further, in enabling a two-speed structure between levels, as all such two-level scientific realist structures do—as for example, in chemistry, the observed interactions at the molecular level move/change much faster than do the internal atomic structures of the theorized subatomic particles (thus chemistry can continue its observations without having to worry about the nuclear decay of the "two protons + two neutrons" nucleus of helium atoms decaying with the similar speed of chemical interactions into the single-proton nucleus of hydrogen)—such an "observed semantics/theorized pragmatics" dual scientific-realist approach to cultural meaning, enabled me first to map out, as I have done so far, the *longue duree* direction of historical development, before being now forced to surface to that shallower obscrvational level of semantic meaning.

Such "surfacing" from the deep level of pragmatic meaning is forced upon me at this stage by the fact that the colonial history of the last two centuries has possibly, as I indicated at the end of the previous section, created a radically uneven global situation, where some of the ex-colonial powers may be readying themselves for rapid transition to the postmodern globalization interpretant code of cultural meaning, while their ex-colonies may be still struggling with legacies of colonial *filiation*, still finding their "sea legs" in the modernizing code of *calibration* as the cultural wave of globalization washes all around their shores. Such "interference" patterns between pragmatic codes moving at deeper levels of the "ocean of meaning" are best gauged by their effects on the readily observable ripple effects at the shallower level of semantic meaning.

In the Peirce-Morris pragmaticist tradition, semantics is understood to be a wholly different scientific specialty from pragmatics. Having spent the bulk of this book's space on mapping out my pragmatic field, and recognizing that this transition to semantics could have been a separate book in itself, I hope nevertheless to provide some closure about the situation at this turn-of-the-millennium by very briefly mapping the semantic global situation as it stands in 2000 C.E. In this endeavor I will be basically assuming the thesis of "postimperialism" of David G. Becker and Richard L. Sklar,[322] which states that, especially now that the Cold War is over, political-economic conflicts between nation-states have assumed a back row to the political-economic interplay between the economic might of transnational corporations—who accounted for more than one-third of total world output around 1999, according to Becker and Sklar—and the political power-sharing coalitions between different socio-economic classes, relating to each other both within and across nations. Given Roland Robertson's perception of a current global business phenomenon of "globalization," which "more specifically . . . frequently involves the tailoring of products to increasingly specialized regional, societal, ethnic, class and gender markets—so-called 'micro-marketing,'"[323] it may well be to the communicative meaning structured within such national or regional coalitions of mutually *cooperating* consumer-groups that we must look to understand the future of Becker and Sklar's "postimperialist" transnational corporations.

In my attempt to "visualize," then, those broad coalitions of consumers—especially among those consumer groups that I, as a college teacher, seem to know best: college-age students—that seem to form across nations (and maintain, often into old age, in this age of televised nostalgia binges, their loyalties to themes and symbols of their college-age youth) I was led to posit the formation in 2000 C.E. of globally spread semantic regions. Recognizing again that such a theory's development might require longer—possibly book-length—treatment, I can nevertheless offer this brief narrative as my future nucleus in developing a Peircean semantics of globalization: The question in semantic geographical formation, it seems to me, is to ask what happened to the cultural (meaning) formations of that old world system outlined by Janet Abu-Lughod in her 1989 book *Before European Hegemony: The World System A.D. 1250-1350.* Since we still have cultural texts from that epoch, I assume that those cultural forms may still be around even if buried in some social-Lacanean unconscious/imaginary realm.[324]

Accepting then the undeniable truth of Abu-Lughod's assertion that "the fall of the East precedes the rise of the West,"[325] as well as the thesis put forward by Eduardo Galeano's *Open Veins of Latin America* that "without five centuries of the pillage" of the American continent, the gold and silver bullion needed for the capitalist monetization of European economies would simply not have been available,"[326] I can proceed to focus sharply on those three subsystems—the European, the Mideast Heartland, and Asia—of Abu-Lughod's thirteenth-century world system, to trace processes that transpired as the opening of Atlantic navigation shifted the centers of trade, finance, scientific, and general cultural development northwestward from the northern Italian cities toward northwestern Europe.

The cultural-semantic consequence of the process that led to what Abu-Lughod calls "European hegemony" emerged to my surprise, the more I pondered it, into a four-region semantic global map—with Galeano's South Atlantic now forcibly incorporated, as a fourth semantic subsystem into a cultural world system that also now contained, in somewhat modified form, the three previous subsystems of Abu-Lughod's thirteenth-century world system—which resembled nothing more than it did a direct spatial imposition upon a global map, of Talcott Parsons's A-G-I-L four functional subsystems.[327] I will therefore proceed to outline the four semantic regional nuclei, which I see forming. Like all human arrangements, these four regions are not exactly congruent with the four spatial quadrants formed by superimposing Parsons's A-G-I-L grid on a global map. I will also develop some testing possibilities for this Parsonsian semantic system.[328]

A. North Atlantic Region: "Adaptive" Function/"Economistic" Semantics

"Beginning with Hobbes, Macpherson argued," says Joseph Carens, "one finds a tradition of political theory in which ownership is constitutive of individuality, freedom and equality."[329] That common Anglo-American tradition of political theory, dating from Thomas Hobbes and John Locke, which C. B.

Macpherson labeled "possessive individualism," has perdured through Ronald Reagan in America and Margaret Thatcher in England, to the beginning of the twenty-first century, despite movements that had arisen in the 1960s in both nations to challenge its cultural hegemony.

What the semantic institutionalization of such possessive individualism in the English-speaking North Atlantic did—in citizens' habits of thought, feeling, and action—was to produce an adaptive upgrading, in Parsons' terminology, of the northwest corner of Abu-Lughod's world system: it created a *milieu interieur*. According to the French physiologist Claude Bernard, "A complex organism should be looked upon as an assemblage of simple organisms that live in the liquid of the *milieu interieur*."[330] What Karl Marx had called the alienation of land and the alienation of labor of this modern capitalist system was also, from the system's perspective, the development of a more "complex organism" where the environment instead of being outside the system, now circulated in symbolic form within it.

But such an adaptive upgrading did not immediately benefit the whole world system because money's *calibration* code was encased within a "social unconscious" of persisting *filiation*. Only slowly opening up to incorporate first other Protestants, then other people of European descent, this North Atlantic subsystem finally incorporated people of non-European descent, according to Michael Omi and Howard Winant, only in the 1960s, after first having destroyed and metabolized the North American native cultures.[331] The evidence for the strong and lengthy persistence of old ethnocentric habits of *filiation* is given by Jay Fliegelman's 1982 book on the trauma displayed in historical semantics between 1750 and 1800 in North America, in breaking filial ties with England.[332]

I should note that I suspect the semantic habits of possessive individualism have sunk such deep roots in the U.S. population that even the cultural left is captured. Virtue, like all else in the United States, is to be possessed—either you have it or you don't—which explains the brittle nature of attitudes toward "political correctness" in Anglo-America.

G. Confucian Asia: "Goal-Directing" Function/"Political" Semantics

When Alvin Gouldner predicted, around 1980, that Russia might give up the communist system while China would continue it because the former was part of European culture unlike the latter, I dismissed this prediction as coming from Gouldner's Eurocentric view of the world.[333] Once Gouldner's culture-based prediction had proved itself accurate, I paid closer attention to the arguments, such as those of Eamonn Fingleton, that it was the Confucian emphasis on "respect for superiors and conformity to society's wishes" that made possible Japan's political culture of recruiting the very best crop of graduating students every year to work in the all-powerful Ministry of Finance, so as to have this ministry dictate, according to Fingleton, every aspect of Japan's economic life.[334]

Speaking of the Confucian nations of East Asia, Fingleton reminds us that "above all, these nations share a history of struggle against Western colonization." Actually, given the powerful combination of possessive individualism and xenophobia in English-speaking culture, it is not surprising to find the defensive use of the state against "perfidious Albion," beginning first with France and moving steadily eastward. In fact the weakening of state interventionism with Ludwig Erhard's policies of economic liberalization occurred only after West Germany's integration with the rest of industrial Western Europe within the North Atlantic Treaty Organization. With NATO's move east to Poland's eastern frontier—a move welcomed by its population, suggesting possibly a permanent popular commitment on the part of even Eastern Europeans now to possessive individualism—and the Russian state limping toward an uncertain future, it is only the Confucian-culture nations in East Asia that still represent a commitment to strong government.

Despite the "Asian flu," Fingleton remained bullish on Japan's economy in a 1999 interview with Think-Tank's Ben Wattenberg, titled "Whatever Happened to Japan Inc.?", arguing that the trade figures were good, Japan's debt was to Japanese lenders, not foreigners, and the promised "Big Bang" of financial liberalization would be really a "small bang" with little change in traditional government control of the Japanese economy. With China still faithful, since Deng-Xiao Ping, to "learning from Japan," one may expect a solid East Asian Confucian Bloc to continue its semantic emphasis on the government's goal-directing function.

I. Indian Ocean Rim: "Integrative" Function/"Communal" Semantics

In *The Oceanic Feeling: The Origins of Religious Sentiment in Ancient India*, the psychoanalyst Jeffrey M. Masson mentions a medieval Buddhist conference in Tibet, which scholars from India as well as China attended. The records show, says Masson, that whereas the Chinese contingent readily expressed their feelings of homesickness, the Indians would not speak about their feelings. While Masson uses this example to make a psychoanalytic point about Indians' traditional fear of expressing emotion, I was struck more by the similar fear that my American students often show in undergraduate classes of saying something "wrong," especially if it is socially or "politically" incorrect. Talking about expatriate "tribes" of foreign workers in the West today, Richard Sklar says of expatriates from the Indian subcontinent, that "its diversity is far greater than that of the Chinese" as it "includes Hindus, Muslims, Sikhs, Buddhists, and Jains as well as Hindi, Dravidian, Bengali, Gujarati, Marathi, and many other language groups."[335] This greater ethno-linguistic diversity, which has long existed South and West of the Himalayas, could possibly account for the different historical direction taken by this latter region's institutionalized semantics from the historically authoritarian statism of Confucian Asia.

Arguing against Rene Dumont's ideological orientation to India's caste system, Declan Quigley finds the "common structure underlying caste systems . . . in constraints given by kinship on the one hand and kingship on the other, both of which are set against a particular material backdrop which allows a territorially limited kind of centralization to develop."[336] In the midst of diversity and poor political centralization, in other words—both conditions being the opposite of the Chinese experience—India's caste system had been a desperate attempt to maintain a wider community beyond kinship. And India's problems of *building community* in the absence of common ethnicity language and often weak political systems were probably common all along the silk route to the West, all the way to Palestine: a clash of Semitic and Iranian language groups in a region open on three sides to invasion, and finally subject even from the fourth side on the south, to the coming of European imperialists.

It is against this background of a desperate quest to conceive of a wider community transcending the weakness of royal dynasties and ethnic-linguistic disunity, that I see both the "Axial Age" universalistic religious leaders *and* the regional triumph of Islam. For, with its uncompromising concern with the *umma*, the community, and equally uncompromising insistence on the monotheistic *tawhid*, symbol of such communal unity, which contemporary Islamic thinkers from the Egyptian Qutb to the Iranian Shariati did not fail to emphasize, Islam brought a relatively integrated community—which stretched all the way to Mozambique (i.e., "Mausam Beg")—to a hitherto fractured region. As Narasingha Prosad Sil emphasizes in *Swami Vivekananda: A Reassessment*, Vivekananda, the Ramakrishna Mission organizer, had consistently demanded that India develop a Hindu soul within a Muslim body, since modern Hinduism is inseparable from Islamic influences. In a region which has hungered the longest, historically, for an ecumenical communitarianism transcending monarch and tribe, even the political fundamentalisms of two nuclear powers, India and Pakistan sharing a long common border, can only remind locals of their centuries-old hunger for that community beyond the bureaucratic overreach of the state.[337]

L. South Atlantic: "Latent Pattern Maintenance" Function/"Cultural Literary" Semantics

A quota system is to be introduced on fiction set in South America. . . . Ah the propinquity of cheap life and expensive principles, of religion and banditry, of surprising honour and random cruelty. . . . Ah, the fredonna tree whose roots

Formal System 261

grow at the tips of its branches, and whose fibres assist the hunchback to impregnate by telepathy the haughty wife of the hacienda owner.[338]

This quotation from British novelist Julian Barnes parodies that style of "magic realism" during the "boom" of the 1960s and 1970s when Latin American literature suddenly caught the fascination of the world. In his "Five Hundred Years of Latin American Literature," Gustavo A. Alfaro attempts to explain in a few sentences what "the most influential" of the authors of that boom, Gabriel Garcia Marquez, was narrating in that most influential of his novels, *A Hundred Years of Solitude*. This novel, says Alfaro,

> chronicles Latin America's first hundred years of independence by tracing several generations of a family in a remote Caribbean town. On a larger scale it refers to Latin American history since the arrival of Columbus, and with its biblical overtones, it suggests the story of mankind, from the creation to the Apocalypse.[339]

Wendy Faris lists five primary characteristics which characterize such "magical realist" fiction:

1. The text has an "irreducible element" of magic, something we cannot explain according to the laws of the universe as we know them. . . .
2. Descriptions pay great attention to realistic detail, the "realist" part of "magical realism."
3. The reader may hesitate (at one point or another) between two contradictory understandings of events—and hence experiences some unsettling doubts.
4. We experience the closeness or near-merging of two realms, two worlds. Fluid boundaries between the worlds of the living and the dead are traced only to be crossed in *One Hundred Years of Solitude*.
5. These fictions question received ideas about time, space, and identity.[340]

In *The Spirit of Carnival*, David Danow suggests that "magical realism's most far-reaching origin is perhaps rooted in the remembrance of childhood."[341] Perhaps. But that passing between realms and questioning ideas about time, space and identity resemble more the hallucinatory world of the abused or neglected child, suffering from multiple personality disorder, or, as it is now called, dissociative identity disorder.[342]

The possibility of social trauma as the cause of such a proliferation of "magical" narratives in Latin America is suggested by the equally rapid spread of this genre of literature to West Africa.[343] In the construction of the modern world system, Europe's expansion would appear to have weighed most on the Americas and upon the coast of West Africa. In contrast to the proliferation of authors in this genre in South America and in West Africa, Salman Rushdie stood out among Asia's large Islamic community as a possibly lone practitioner of the "magical realist" literary art, and even then, the fact that members of his religious community might express strong preferences for the preservation of the community over Rushdie's right to write and speak freely (as, for example, in the rather vociferous support given by significant numbers of Britain's immigrant Muslim community to Ayatollah Khomeini's *fatwa* sentencing Rushdie to death) only highlights this stark difference between the community-preserving institutionalized preferences originating around the Indian Ocean region, and the carnivalesque "magical realism" of the South Atlantic region.

On the other hand, the source book on dissociative identity disorder that I have consulted for better understanding of the "trance"-like states described in Latin American and West African literature, does also outline all the possible similarities between shamanism and dissociative identity disorder, such as trance states, hypnotic anesthesia, symbolic dreams, ritual dismemberment, possession by the souls of ancestors or helping spirits, out-of-body experiences, transformation of identity, or even "structured, meaningful hallucinations."[344]

Perhaps in consciously practising this ancient skill of "structured meaningful hallucination" through magical realist literature, these Southern Atlantic cultural producers are maintaining "latent patterns" of healing, for global humanity's present and future use in treating the wounds of social trauma inflicted upon it by the ongoing violence of the very process of globalization.

Empirically Testable Global A-G-I-L Connections

Of the "four major focal points of the dominant globalization process since the sixteenth century" seen by Roland Robertson—"nationally constituted societies, the international system of societies, individuals, and humankind":[345]

1. I expect that the dominant discourse between the North Atlantic and the Confucians will be about the nature and function of nation-states. Right now the use of nation-state apparatuses is especially different between the individualist West and the "respectful" Confucian societies.
2. The international system should be the major topic of conversation between Confucians and Indian Ocean Rim dwellers. With the two most populous nations of India and China straddling this divide, any international system dealing with, say, global air pollution will have to be discussed between these heavily populated nations.
3. The question of the nature of individuality can only increase as a discussion topic between the possessive individualist mentality of the North Atlantic and the Carnivalesque culture of the South Atlantic.

4. Finally, Frantz Fanon-like questions about the true nature of humanity should be increasingly heard debated between the carnivalesque cultures of the South Atlantic and the communal cultures of the Indian Ocean Rim.

Out of such extended conversations should emerge a clearer picture of the further process of globalization, globality, and of ourselves as a biologically unique (human) species.

Notes

1. Ronald Fletcher, "Evolutionary and Developmental Approaches," in *Approaches to Sociology*, ed. John Rex (London: Routledge & Kegan Paul, 1974), 41 (italics in original).

2. Margaret Mead, *Continuities in Cultural Evolution* (New Brunswick, N.J.: Transaction Publishers, 1999), xxv-xxvi.

3. Stephen Toulmin, "Introduction to the Transaction Edition," in Mead, *Continuities*, xiv-xv (italics in original).

4. Parsons, *The Social System*, 486.

5. Jackson Toby, "Parsons' Theory of Societal Evolution," in Talcott Parsons, *The Evolution of Societies* (Englewood Cliffs, N.J.: Prentice Hall, 1977), 1; Nicholas S. Timasheff, *Sociological Theory: Its Nature and Growth*, 3rd ed. (New York: Random House, 1967), 287.

6. Parsons, *The Structure of Social Action*, 3.

7. Popper, *Objective Knowledge*, 112-17, 155-56.

8. Donald Campbell, "Evolutionary Epistemology," in *The Philosophy of Karl Popper*, vol. 1, ed. P. A. Schilpp (La Salle, Ill.: Open Court Publishing, 1974): 413-63; W. H. Durham, *Coevolution: Genes, Culture, and Human Diversity* (Stanford, Calif.: Stanford University Press, 1991); Toby, "Parsons' Theory," 8. Margaret S. Archer, in her *Culture and Agency* (New York: Cambridge University Press, 1988), 33-45, 104-5, accuses Parsons and Levi-Strauss of "downwards conflation," while absolving Popper from all being a "conflationist." Susan Blackmore, in *The Meme Machine* (Oxford: Oxford University Press, 1999), 28-29, uses the expression "downward causation" to characterize Popper's theory of "Three Worlds"—which Archer (*Culture and Agency*, 104-6) defends—to contrast it negatively with Campbell's "Evolutionary Epistemology."

9. Agner Fog, *Cultural Selection* (Boston: Kluwer Academic Publishers, 1999), 41; Blackmore, *The Meme Machine*, 17, 18, 35, 53-66; Richard Dawkins, *The Selfish Gene* (Oxford: Oxford University Press, 1976).

10. Fog, *Cultural Selection*, 43, citing C. M. Heyes and H. C. Plotkin, "Replicators and Interactors in Cultural Evolution," in *What the Philosophy of Biology Is*, ed. Michael Ruse (Boston: Kluwer, 1989), 139-62.

11. *Systeme de politique positive; ou, Traite de sociologies instituant la religion de l'humanite*, vol. 2: *Statique Sociale*, 4th ed. (Paris: Cres, 1912), 194.

12. Fog, *Cultural Evolution*, 43.

13. Toulmin, "Introduction," xviii.

14. Talcott Parsons, "Evolutionary Universals in Society," in *American Sociological Review* 29, no. 3 (June 1964): 340-41.

15. Timasheff, *Sociological Theory*, 287.

16. Comte, *Statique Sociale*, 194; Fog, *Cultural Evolution*, 43.

17. Timasheff, *Sociological Theory*, 287.

18. Fletcher, "Evolutionary and Developmental Approaches," 58-63.

19. Fog, *Cultural Selection*, 43; Hookway, *Peirce*, 380; Thomas H. Huxley and Julian S. Huxley, *Touchstone for Ethics* (New York: Harper, 1947).

20. Talcott Parsons, *Social Systems and the Evolution of Action Theory* (New York: The Free Press, 1977), 77-81 (italics in original).

21. Charles Camic, ed., *The Early Essays/Talcott Parsons* (Chicago: University of Chicago Press, 1991), xlvii; Luhmann, "Generalized Media," 508.

22. Camic, *The Early Essays*, xxxiii.

23. Parsons, *The Structure of Social Action*, 589-93, 753-57.

24. Parsons, *The Structure of Social Action*, 607.

25. Parsons, *The Structure of Social Action*, 410, 420-27; Schmaus, *Durkheim's Philosophy*, 12-20.

26. Schmaus, *Durkheim's Philosophy*, 107.

27. Talcott Parsons, "On Building Social System Theory: A Personal History," reprinted from *Daedalus* (Fall 1970) in Parsons, *Social Systems and the Evolution of Action Theory*, 27-28.

28. Talcott Parsons, "Some Problems of General Theory in Sociology," in *Theoretical Sociology: Perspectives and Developments*, ed. J. C. McKinney and E. A. Tiryakin (New York: Appleton-Century-Crofts, 1970), 29 (italics in original).

29. Peter Gould, "Languages and Frameworks: Where the Structure Comes From," in *The Geographer at Work*, ed. Peter Gould (London: Routledge & Kegan Paul, 1985), 308-9 (italics in original); Mihajlo D. Mesarovic, "Foundations of a General Systems Theory," in *Views on General Systems Theory: Proceeding of the Second Systems Symposium at Case Institute of Technology*, ed. Mihajlo D. Mesarovic (New York: John Wiley and Sons, 1964), 1.

30. Emile Durkheim, *The Rules of Sociological Method*, 123 (italics in original).

31. Durkheim, *The Rules*, 150.

32. Mike Gane, *On Durkheim's Rules of Sociological Method* (London: Routledge, 1988), 164.

33. Durkheim, *The Rules*, 139; Schmaus, *Durkheim's Philosophy*, 75.

34. Rainer Baum, "Authority and Identity: A Case for Evolutionary Invariance," in *Identity and Authority*, ed. Roland Robertson and Burkart Holzner (New York: St. Martin's Press, 1979), 118.

35. Randall Collins, *Weberian Sociological Theory* (Cambridge: Cambridge University Press, 1986), 59.

36. Max Weber, *The Religion of India: The Sociology of Hinduism and Buddhism* (Glencoe, Ill.: Free Press, 1958), 117-18.

37. Julia A. Douthwaite, *Exotic Women: Literary Heroines and Cultural Strategies in Ancien Regime France* (Philadelphia: University of Pennsylvania Press, 1992), 87 (italics in original). Lionel Trilling, *Sincerity and Authenticity* (Cambridge, Mass.: Harvard University Press, 1972), had traced—through the reading of the popular eighteenth-century novel *Rameau's Nephew*—a similar semantic shift in the connotation of "truth," from

artless *sin-cera* ("without wax") to a more urbanized "authenticity" akin to Goffman's notion of "civil inattention."

38. Jackson Toby, "Parsons' Theory, 10-21.

39. Mihajlo D. Mesarovic, "Theory of Hierarchical, Multilevel, Systems," in *Theory of Hierarchical Multilevel Systems*, ed. Mihajlo D. Mesarovic, D. Macko, and Y. Takahara (New York: Academic Press, 1970), 54-55.

40. Stephen Jay Gould, *Wonderful Life: The Burgess Shale and the Nature of History* (New York: Norton, 1989), argues against the evaluative imputation of a direction to evolution, without denying the fact that there was a temporal direction in the emergence of multicellular complexity in organisms, in that unicellular organisms emerged temporally before multicellular ones.

41. Oliver Sacks, "The Other Road: Freud as Neurologist," in *Freud: Conflict and Culture*, ed. Michael S. Roth (New York: Alfred A. Knopf, 1998), 224-32, explains how the English neurologist Hughlings Jackson's development in the 1870s of "a hierarchic view of the nervous system," recapitulating in ascending order from the spinal chord to the neo-cortex the temporal order of Darwinian evolution, had survived in Freud's "assumption that our psychic mechanism has come into being by a process of stratification," despite Freud's disagreement with Jackson's support for the theory of brain localization of psychic events.

42. Parsons, *The Evolution of Societies*, 279-320; Talcott Parsons, *Societies* (Englewood Cliffs, N.J.: Prentice-Hall, 1966), 7-29. Stephen K. Sanderson, *Social Transformations: A General Theory of Historical Development* (Lanham, Md.: Rowman & Littlefield, 1999), 1-10, 11-15, 166-68, shares with Parsons, a focus upon the adaptive and differentiating processes of social evolution. However, in following Immanuel Wallerstein's attempt to synthesize Marx's materialism with Weber's individualism, Sanderson's "evolutionary materialism"—unlike the later Parsons's Durkheimian collectivism—risks, in my view, collapsing into either a Darwinian noncultural evolutionism or meaninglessness. In addressing, for example, the declining demographic fertility of nations that were the earliest in having achieved modernization (what Sanderson calls "the capitalist revolution"), Sanderson does not even address the conceptual dilemma faced by his materialist individualism: Whose individual "adaptedness" is increased when high-status individuals in advanced capitalist nations wait too long today to conceive children biologically, and then adopt children from overpopulated precapitalist nations—the biological parents from those poorer nations (as Darwinian sociobiology would have it) or the adoptive parents whose resulting ignorance of their adopted children's genetic information actually places them at a financial/emotional risk—in these days of genetic medicine, when compared to low-status teen mothers within their own advanced capitalist societies (who should at least find compatible bone-marrow donors from within the group of their own biological relatives, in case their children contract cancer)? It is Sanderson's refusal to even address such conceptual lacunae within his Marx-Weber/ materialist-individualist theory of social evolution, that leads me to believe that such a non-Durkheimian, non-Peircean theory of social evolution really turns the clock back from that—admittedly imperfect—formulation of social evolution that Parsons had reached in his later, Durkheimian, theorization.

43. Sacks, "The Other Road," 221-24.

44. Rainer Baum, "The System of Solidarities," *Indian Journal of Social Research* 16, nos. 1 and 2 (April, August 1975), republished in *Essays on the Sociology of Parsons: A Felicitation Volume*, ed. G. C. Hallen (Meerut, India: Indian Journal of Social Research,

1975), 316; Richard Munch, *Understanding Modernity: Toward a New Perspective Going beyond Durkheim and Weber* (London: Routledge, 1988), 12-280.

45. John McCrone, *Going Inside: A Tour of a Single Moment of Consciousness* (London: Faber and Faber, 1999), 40-119, 166-78, 268-76.

46. Raymond Williams, *The Long Revolution* (New York: Columbia University Press, 1961), cited in Hal Colebatch, *Blair's Britain* (London: Claridge Press, 1999), 7; Archer, *Culture and Agency*, 104; Terry Eagleton, *The Idea of Culture* (Oxford: Blackwell Publishers, 2000), 2.

47. Kuper, *Culture*, 52-57, citing Parsons, *The Social System*, 4-15, and A. L. Kroeber and Clyde Kluckhohn, *Culture: A Critical Review of Concepts and Definitions* (Cambridge, Mass.: Peabody Museum, 1952), 153.

48. Kuper, *Culture*, 206, 229-45, 247.

49. Rescher, *Methodological Pragmatism*, 70; Archer, *Culture and Agency*, 104.

50. Hookway, *Peirce*, 262-78.

51. William James, *Principles of Psychology*, vol. 1 (New York: Henry Holt & Co., 1927 [1890]), 104-27.

52. Charles Camic, "The Matter of Habit," *American Journal of Sociology* 91, no. 5 (March 1986), 1040-45.

53. James, *Principles*, 107-8; Camic, "The Matter," 1045, citing Guy R. Lefrancois, *Psychology*, 2d ed. (Belmont, Calif.: Wadsworth, 1983), 393.

54. Camic, "The Matter," 1045-46; Roger Chartier, *On the Edge of the Cliff*, 115, 143, 181 n. 16, 186 n. 16. Chartier, the contemporary French cultural historian, traces Pierre Bourdieu's usage of the concept of "habitus" to Norbert Elias's definition of the concept as "second nature" in *The Civilizing Process* (p. 447). While throwing light on the "proximate" source of Bourdieu's famous concept of "habitus," Chartier does not really contradict Camic, since Elias had been very familiar with the writings of both Durkheim and Weber.

55. Camic, "The Matter," 1050-55.

56. Durkheim, *The Rules*, 162.

57. Camic, "The Matter," 1056, 1068, 1072-73.

58. John Dewey, *The Public and its Problems* (Chicago: Swallow Press, 1927), 159-60 (italics in original).

59. Camic, "The Matter," 1056, citing Emile Durkheim, "Individual and Collective Representations" (1898), in *Sociology and Philosophy*, ed. D. F. Pocock (New York: Free Press, 1974), 5; Leon Dumont, "De l'habitude," *Revue Philosophique* 1 (1876): 321-36.

60. Schmaus, *Durkheim's Philosophy*, 182-83.

61. Schmaus, *Durkheim's Philosophy*, 183.

62. Henaff, *Claude Levi-Strauss*, 111, citing Levi-Strauss, *The Savage Mind*, 131; Bunge, *Metascientific Queries*, 109.

63. Ragland-Sullivan, *Jacques Lacan*, 17-18. Schmaus (*Durkheim's Philosophy*, 253) sees Durkheim's problem of "collective representations" as embedded within his pre-linguistic-turn philosophical separation of human thought—within which collective representations inhere—from language. This is an unrealistic separation which, as I pointed out in the introduction, Hookway (*Peirce*, 19-23) sees Peirce as already having overcome as early as 1868 in the third of his four denials, stating that "we have no power of thinking without signs."

64. Camic, "The Matter," 1046.

65. Rene Devisch, *Weaving the Threads of Life: The Khita Gyn-Eco-Logical Healing Cult among the Yaka* (Chicago: University of Chicago Press, 1993), 1, 48-49, citing Donald Winnicott, *Playing and Reality* (London: Tavistock, 1971). Maud Mannoni (*Separation and Creativity*, 4, 62-63, 79-82) overtly identifies Winnicott's concept of "playing" in "potential space" with Lacan's *jouissance*, the process by which the developing child—or the psychoanalytic patient—is supposed to bridge the "imaginary" and "symbolic" realms.

66. See Ragland-Sullivan, *Jacques Lacan*, 59, 130-95, or Ellie Ragland, "An Overview of the Real: With Examples from Seminar I," in Feldstein, Fink, and Jaanus, *Reading Seminars I and II*, 192-209, for excellent analyses of Lacan's "three orders" of cognition.

67. Devisch (*Weaving*, 38-46) does acknowledge that his approach is "selectively in line with some of the perspectives taken" in Merleau-Ponty's phenomenology, Levi-Strauss's structuralism, Julia Kristeva's structuralist semiotics, the poststructuralist praxeology of Pierre Bourdieu and Jean Comaroff, and the 1991 "processual performance study of Bruce Kapferer." Since his index only lists Kapferer's 1983 book, *A Celebration of Demons*, I am not at all sure from which source Devisch might possibly have imbibed Peircean Pragamaticist methodology—albeit unknowingly—although from Levi-Strauss, whose *Structural Anthropology* and *The Savage Mind* he cites, he must surely have gotten an introduction to Saussure's semiological approach, and from Kristeva's version of structuralist semiotics, a sufficiently close proximity to Lacan's three orders of cognition to have made that cognitive leap into Peirce-Morris semiotics on his own.

68. Kuper, *Culture*, 245-46 (italics in original).

69. Devisch, *Weaving*, 40.

70. Morris, *Foundations*, 13-21.

71. Devisch, *Weaving*, 41.

72. Morris, *Foundations*, 21-29.

73. Devisch, *Weaving*, 42.

74. Morris, *Foundations*, 29.

75. Morris, *Foundations*, 29-30.

76. Morris, *Foundations*, 30.

77. Grice, "Meaning," 220.

78. Thomas, *Meaning in Interaction*, 61-62.

79. R. G. Collingwood, *The New Leviathan: Man, Society, Civilization, and Barbarism* (Oxford: Clarendon Press, 1942), 153-54.

80. Cooley, *Human Nature*, 145; Arendt, *On Violence*, 44.

81. Joel Ryce-Menuhin, *The Self in Early Childhood* (London: Free Association Books, 1988), 4-5.

82. Ragland-Sullivan, *Jacques Lacan*, xxi.

83. Rainer Baum, "On Societal Media Dynamics," in *Explorations in General Theory in Social Science*, ed. Jan Loubser et al. (New York: Free Press, 1976), 599; T. Givon, *Mind, Code, and Context: Essays in Pragmatics* (Hillsdale, N.J.: Lawrence Erlbaum Assoc., 1989), 70.

84. Camic, "The Matter," 1046.

85. Morris, *Foundations*, 29-30.

86. Evans-Pritchard, *Witchcraft*, 25.

87. Ragland-Sullivan, *Jacques Lacan*, 17-18; Henaff, *Levi-Strauss*, 94-119.

88. Morris, *Foundations*, 29.

89. Arthur Battram in his *Navigating Complexity: An Essential Guide to Complexity Theory in Business and Management* (London: Industrial Society, 1998), 37-233, explains— in simple language accessible to the average business manager who is not necessarily an expert on mathematical logic or theoretical biology—the concept of "autopoiesis," from the work of two Chilean biologists, Humberto Maturana and Francisco Varela, *The Tree of Knowledge: The Biological Roots of Human Understanding* (Boston: Shambala Publications, 1987), as "the self-preserving tendency of all organisms—as an 'inward urge' to retreat to the core of the identity; the 'me' as opposed to everything that is 'not me'. . . . 'self-making'—the process by which living creatures constantly recreate and maintain their own identity," a process "characterized by their continual self-production." The Peircean interpretant codes that I delineate in this chapter instantiate what Battram calls "the autopoietic nature of communication," with each successive code's tendency to maintain, repair, and reproduce itself, until its "self-referential crisis" brought about by the accumulation of socio-cognitive learning provokes a mutational evolutionary transition to its successor interpretant code. While Battram's handy 1998 "guide to complexity theory in business" should enable access to my usage of the Maturana-Varela biological concept of "autopoiesis" to a wider reading public, I urge my readers who may be more familiar with the debates in sociological theory of the last three decades to consult Niklas Luhmann, "The Autopoiesis of Social Systems," in *Sociocybernetic Paradoxes: Observation, Control, and Evolution of Self-Steering Systems*, ed. Felix Geyer and Johannes van der Zouwen (Beverly Hills, Calif.: Sage, 1986) or Niklas Luhmann, *Essays on Self-Reference* (New York: Columbia University Press, 1990). See also the definition of a *reflexive* approach to sociology by Alvin Gouldner, *The Coming Crisis of Western Sociology* (New York: Avon, 1970), 493, as knowledge of the world that is also "a knowledge of our own experience with it and our relation to it" to theoretically situate my adaptation of Peirce's triadic *phenomenology* in this chapter on the autopoietic evolution of pragmatic codes of meaning-interpretation.

90. Francisco Varela, *Principles of Biological Autonomy* (New York: North Holland Press, 1979), 99-109, cited Bertrand Russell's *Introduction to Mathematical Philosophy* (London: Allen & Unwin, 1919), for Russell's paradox of self-reference; G. Spencer-Brown's algebraic *Laws of Form* (New York: Julian Press, 1972); Hegel's dialectics; and that same book that had influenced Talcott Parsons, Lawrence J. Henderson's *The Fitness of the Environment: An Inquiry into the Biological Significance of the Properties of Matter* (Boston: Beacon Press, 1913), 1, to argue that unless one defined adaptation in the rigorously mathematical-logical fashion he was adopting from Russell and Spencer-Brown, it was subject, as Henderson had predicted, to the imprecision of definition about whether the organism had "adapted to the environment" or whether it had really been "a case of fitness of the environment for life, in the most general sense." Luhmann ("The Autopoiesis of Social Systems," 192) cited Varela's work in support of his own call for the adoption of such a view of autopoietic evolution in social systems.

91. Camic, "The Matter," 1072.

92. Battram (*Navigating Complexity*, 231-32) sums up the presentation of the concept of self-referential "auto-poiesis" (a neologism meaning "self-production" in its original Greek) in Maturana and Varela, *The Tree of Knowledge,* in a few simple statements, such as "An organism has an internal model of its world," "This internal model of the world determines (the organism's) response, not the input," and "We resist change, and

when forced to change, we respond in such a way as to maintain our unbroken sense of self." If we substitute the term *pragmatic interpretant code* for Battram's "internal model" and *society* for "organism," Battram's propositions here perfectly describe the Peircean model of socio-cultural evolution that I am about to delineate.

93. Gail A. Newman, *Locating the Romantic Subject: Novalis with Winnicott* (Detroit: Wayne State University Press, 1997), 14, citing Immanuel Kant, *"Was ist Aufklarung?"* (Stuttgart: Reclam, 1974), 9.

94. Jon Mandle, *What's Left of Liberalism? An Interpretation and Defense of Justice as Fairness* (Lanham, Md.: Lexington Books, 2000), 285, citing Immanuel Kant, "An Answer to the Question: What Is Enlightenment?" in *Perpetual Peace and Other Essays* (Indianapolis, Ind.: Hackett, 1983), 41-42.

95. Giddens, *Politics, Sociology, and Social Theory*, 257-58. In his attack on the homologies between the "childhood of society" and that of individuals, Giddens says that "the views of Levi-Bruhl seem to me today to be less compelling than those of Levy-Strauss." But Levi-Strauss's concept of a social (collective) "unconscious," as seen, for example by Henaff, *Claude Levi-Strauss*, 94-119, or by Rossi, *The Unconscious in Culture*, 137-39, takes such homologizing to the extreme of theoretically eliminating even the possibility of Giddens's "knowledgeable" agents.

96. A Brazilian graduate student at my university has just pointed out, in a personal communication, that whereas in the more southern regions around São Paulo and Rio de Janeiro in Brazil—which is where I had made my original inquiries about the origins of the Brazilian-Portuguese word *muleque*—the word *muleque* does indeed carry only the connotation of "boy" in the Northeastern regions where she comes from, and where the bulk of African forced immigration had occurred, the word has the added connotation of "irresponsible boy." Far from negating my thesis of "social infantilization-through-terror," this serendipitous communication from a northeastern Brazilian only reinforces it. As in the analogous situation in the United States, where it had been in the heartland of slavery in the deep South where the appellation "boy" had carried its most negative connotations—associated as it had been, with the negative stereotypes of "laziness" and "disposition to sexual aggressiveness" applied, in America, to African-American men—so too in Brazil, the closer one apparently gets to its heartland of slavery (in the Brazilian Northeast, around the state of Bahia), the clearer do the negative connotations of "social infantilization"—of not only perceiving of slave men as "boys," but of also imputing to them the natural "irresponsibility" of very small infants—become.

97. For an "objective" view—i.e., one not colored by my personal experience—of the brutal effectiveness of the methods used by the Portuguese dictator Salazar's secret police (the PIDE) in Mozambique during that period of my childhood there immediately preceding the emergence of a cohesive Mozambican Liberation Front (FRELIMO), see Malyn Newitt, *A History of Mozambique* (London: Hurst & Company, 1995), 517-19.

98. Louis Wirth, "The Problem of Minority Groups," in *The Science of Man in the World Crisis*, ed. Ralph Linton (New York: Columbia University Press, 1945), 347.

99. Anthony D. Smith, *Nationalism and Modernism* (London: Routledge, 1998). Smith's dichotomizing between Primordialists and Perennialists on the one hand (with whose views his own vision of deep-rooted "ethnies" seems to lie) and modernists with whose "construction-for-modern-ends" views of nationhood he's clearly uncomfortable leaves the evolutionist view that I outline in this chapter literally falling between two stools. While the pragmatic code of *"filiation"* that I am about to outline makes what

Smith calls the "psychology of ethnic af*filiation*" (p. 165-69) a "perfect fit" within my theory, I also see nationalism itself as a specifically modern variant of that complex of attitudes that Louis Wirth's 1945 definition of "minority" emphasized. In my view, all nationalisms, including those relatively older English, French, or German forms that crystallized between the seventeenth and nineteenth centuries began as people's self-perceptions as Wirthian minorities—from the English variant which had sought a mythical state of "Anglo-Saxon" freedom, supposedly existent before the Norman conquest of 1066, to "*la nation*" of the French revolution crystallizing in the call of Abbe Sieyes for the Frankish nobility to return to their original habitations in "the forests of Franconia," to that Kantian philosopher Fichte's "addresses to the German nation" rallying for their liberation from Napoleon's yoke. While Smith makes scattered references to Georg Simmel's suggestions that nationalism, like most of human culture, can only be understood in its historical emergence out of conflict, he does not see, as I do, the Simmelian roots of the conception of "minority" by Wirth (who was a close associate of Simmel's student, Robert Park).

100. Giddens, *Politics, Sociology, and Social Theory*, 257-58.

101. Jean-Francois Lyotard, *The Postmodern Condition: A Report on Knowledge* (Minneapolis: University of Minnesota Press, 1984), x, xxiv, 9-10, 18-28, 46, 53, 63-66, 81.

102. Michael Taussig, "Terror as Usual: Walter Benjamin's Theory of History as State of Siege," in *The Nervous System*, ed. Michael Taussig (New York: Routledge, 1992), 11-35; Walter Benjamin, "Theses on the Philosophy of History," in *Illuminations*, ed. Hannah Arendt (New York: Schocken Books, 1969), 257-58. Benjamin's famous passage about "a Klee painting named 'Angelus Novus,'" where he sees the angel being propelled "irresistibly . . . into the future, to which his back is turned, while the pile of debris before him grows skyward," portrays with an almost Biblical sensibility the terror before the "storm" which propels Klee's Angel—backwards into the future—through the progress of historical time. As Freud said, the hysteric suffers from incurable "reminiscences," something with which we, as a society, are now more than familiar, having been saturated with news-media portrayals of the intrusive "flashback" memories of the innumerable victims of post-traumatic stress disorder. In that sense of having its gaze "fixated" upon past horror, Benjamin's famous depiction of Klee's backward-looking angel as the real muse of history, comprehends—far more accurately than does Lyotard's "postmodernist" fixation upon that single Jacobin-to-Stalinist period of modern history—the terror-soaked nature of the whole historical experience of humanity.

103. Lyotard, *The Postmodern Condition,* 18-27.

104. Young, *White Mythologies*, 19.

105. Durkheim, *The Elementary Forms*, 235.

106. Durkheim, *The Elementary Forms*, 235-36.

107. Durkheim, *The Elementary Forms*, 1, 235-37.

108. Sigmund Freud, *Totem and Taboo: Resemblances between the Psychic Lives of Savages and Neurotics* (New York: Vintage Books, 1946), 147, 161 n. 51; Mestrovic, *Emile Durkheim and the Reformation of Sociology*, 98.

109. Eric Rayner, *Unconscious Logic: An Introduction to Matte Blanco's Bi-Logic and Its Uses* (London: Routledge, 1995), 45-46. What neither Rayner nor Blanco—both psychoanalytical practitioners of individual therapy—emphasize is the social development of the cognition of space and time (and location), a concept that is crucial to my Peircean conceptualization of socio-cognitive evolution. Thus, Durkheim's preliterate "primitives" could hardly have been expected to have conceived space in terms of Eu-

clid's geometry and the Cartesian three-dimensional space that Kant's Enlightenment-era society assumed to have been the only variety possible (as the Berlin-based, twentieth-century logical positivist philosopher Hans Reichenbach, in fact, severely criticized as the most unacceptable aspect of Kant's philosophy in this age of Relativistic physics) can no longer now claim to be *the* apodictic account of "reality," after Einstein-Minkowski's formulation of a Riemannian geometry of "space-time," or the 10-to-26 multiple-dimensionality of string theory's space in contemporary theoretical physics.

110. See Schmaus, *Durkheim's Philosophy*, 216-24, for a concise exposition of the philosophical implications drawn by Durkheim for the logical "category of causality," and "the concept of the soul," in totemism's derivation of its "idea of force" from religious ritual. Given this very obvious contrast drawn by Durkheim (*Elementary Forms*, 234-37) between this "very curious trait of human mentality" in totemistic thinking, whose "logic is disconcerting to us," and those "us" who find such a "primitive" mentality "disconcerting," I am not at all surprised by Dominique Merllie's revelation in 1998 ("Did Lucien Levy-Bruhl," 29-38) that Levy-Bruhl was surprised and outraged by the later insistence by Durkheim and his sociological followers that Levy-Bruhl's conception of a "primitive mentality" different from our own could in any way be traced to Durkheim's own formulations. In fairness to the Durkheimian anxiety to separate their master's statements from Levy-Bruhl's assertion of a distinct primitive mentality, I should point out that Durkheim, as usual, had "hedged his bets"—and correctly so, as I will point out further in this chapter, in my delineation of a "Peircean" approach to this whole problem of a "primitive mentality"—by his careful statement asserting about this "curious trait of human mentality" in the "primitive" confounding of "all the kingdoms . . . with each other," that it had, "even though more marked formerly than to-day . . . not yet disappeared."

111. Giddens, *Politics, Sociology, and Social Theory*, 257.

112. Jean Piaget, *Play, Dreams and Imitation in Childhood* (London: Routledge, 1951), 199, cited in Rayner, *Unconscious Logic*, 140-41, which also cites Jean Piaget, *The Psychology of Intelligence* (London: Routledge, 1950), 121-27, to focus upon how Piaget had emphasized that the "egocentrism" of the below-the-age-of-four toddler constrains it to survive—and develop in intelligence—by imitation. Piaget's description of the process of imitation shows it to connote the extreme variant of that process of pre-Enlightenment social "immaturity" that Kant's 1784 essay "What Is Enlightenment"—cited at the start of this section—had described as a lack of resolve to use the faculty of human reason and understanding "without guidance from another." Since this same statement by Kant has also been cited by Michel Foucault in *The Foucault Reader*, ed. Paul Rabinow (New York: Pantheon Books, 1984), 38, it helps focus on the principal difference between that attitudes of Habermas and Foucault toward the Enlightenment. While Habermas would agree with Foucault about the possibility of a great number of people in Western society being still within a state of what Kant would have called "immaturity" or "minority" (and what Piaget's American disciple Lawrence Kohlberg would call the stage of "formal operations," which a large number of his American test subjects showed they had not reached) two centuries after the Enlightenment, he Habermas argues that it is therefore imperative to proceed with the emancipatory project of the Enlightenment, whereas Foucault grew skeptical, after the student uprising of 1968 in Paris, of Kant's Enlightenment project—of that full Kantian "freedom to use reason publicly in all matters"—even being possible.

113. In his oration delivered at the reunion of the Cambridge High School Association on Thursday evening, November 12, 1863 (whose relevant excerpt I have cited as my

Chapter 4

third epigraph at the beginning of this current chapter dealing with a Peircean theory of so-cio-cognitive evolution).

114. Max Fisch, introduction to *Writings of Charles S. Peirce*, 1: xxviii-xxix; Ferdi-nand Toennies, *Community and Society* (East Lansing: Michigan State University Press, 1957 [1887]).

115. Charles Sanders Peirce, *Reasoning and the Logic of Things: The Cambridge Conferences Lectures of 1898* (Cambridge, Mass.: Harvard University Press, 1992), 234.

116. Barry Schwartz, *Vertical Classification: A Study in Structuralism and the Soci-ology of Knowledge* (Chicago: University of Chicago Press, 1981), 124, citing Peirce, *Col-lected Papers*, 2: 156-73.

117. Peirce, *Reasoning*, 259-60 (italics in original); Durkheim, *The Elementary Forms*, 204.

118. Brian Rotman, *Ad Infinitum—the Ghost in Turing's Machine: Taking God out of Mathematics and Putting the Body Back In: An Essay in Corporeal Semiotics* (Stanford, Calif.: Stanford University Press, 1993), 32.

119. Hookway, *Peirce*, 23, citing Peirce, *Collected Papers*, 5.265.

120. Durkheim, *The Elementary Forms*, 236.

121. Parsons, *The Structure of Social Action*, 61, 67, 304-7, 410, 420-27, 438.

122. Hookway, *Peirce*, 262-88. Nonphilosophically specialized readers wondering how the "objective idealism" that Hookway saw in Peirce's Pragmatism may differ from what Parsons in 1937 had called "idealism" in Durkheim's later work, should see the dis-section of philosophical idealism into *eight* possible variants, by the contemporary Prag-matist philosopher Nicholas Rescher in *A System of Pragmatic Idealism*, 1:305-10. Of the eight varieties of philosophical idealism that Rescher dissects, the *only* variant that Peirce's Pragmatism can be accused of resembling is the one which Rescher refers to as "concep-tual idealism," which—unlike that general idealism which Parsons had in 1937 accused Durkheim of espousing in his 1912 writing, which could fit into any of the *other* seven categories dissected by Rescher—does *not* negate scientific realism, because, as Rescher explained, Peirce's conceptual idealism only "holds that whatever is real is in principle knowable, and that knowledge involves conceptualization."

123. Durkheim, *The Elementary Forms*, 235.

124. Peirce, *Reasoning*, 147.

125. Durkheim, *The Elementary Forms*, 236.

126. Durkheim, *The Elementary Forms*, 235.

127. Peirce, *Reasoning*, 147 (italics in original).

128. Giddens, *Politics, Sociology, and Social Theory*, 257-58.

120. Ragland-Sullivan, *Jacques Lacan*, xxi-84.

130. Teresa Brennan, *History after Lacan* (London: Routledge, 1993), 7 n. 6, 11, 21-22, 34-36.

131. Brennan, *History*, 31-32, citing Lacan, *Ecrits: A Selection* (London: Tavistock, 1953), 30-113. It seems to me that Brennan, like several other postmodernist and feminist readers of Lacan, is overly fond of dwelling upon the darker, violent, and paranoid impli-cations of Lacan's theory of personality.

132. Brennan, *History*, 73-74.

133. Brennan, *History*, 35, citing Wilfred Bion, *Learning from Experience* (London: W. Heinemann Medical Books, 1962).

134. See Ragland-Sullivan, *Jacques Lacan*, 59, 130-95; Giddens, *Politics, Sociology, and Social Theory*, 257.

135. Durkheim, *Pragmatism*, 6.

136. Camic, "The Matter," 1056, 1072.

137. Camic, "The Matter," 1072.

138. W. I. Thomas, "The Unconscious: Configurations of the Personality" reprinted—from *The Unconscious: A Symposium*, ed. Charles Manning Child et al. (New York: Knopf, 1927), 143-63—in *W. I. Thomas on Social Organization and Social Personality: Selected papers*, ed. Morris Janowitz (Chicago: University of Chicago Press, 1966), 146-47.

139. Rudnytsky, *The Psychoanalytical Vocation*, 73; Mitchell and Black, *Freud and Beyond*, 201.

140. Camic, "The Matter," 1072.

141. W. I. Thomas and Florian Znaniecki, *The Polish Peasant in Europe and America*, vol. 1: *Primary-Group Organization* (Boston: Gorham Press, 1918), 22-23 (italics in original).

142. Camic, "The Matter," 1072; Thomas, "The Unconscious," 147 (italics in original); Giddens, *Politics, Sociology, and Social Theory*, 257; Mitchell and Black, *Freud and Beyond*, 201.

143. Mary Hesse, "Socializing Epistemology," in *Construction and Constraint: The Shaping of Scientific Rationality*, ed. Ernan McMullin (Notre Dame, Ind.: University of Notre Dame Press, 1988), 110; Givon, *Mind, Code*, 70.

144. Durkheim, *The Elementary Forms*, 204.

145. Freud, *Totem and Taboo*, 162-67.

146. Ragland-Sullivan, *Jacques Lacan*, 34.

147. Ragland-Sullivan, *Jacques Lacan*, 32-33.

148. Freud, *Totem and Taboo*, 167.

149. Freud, *Totem and Taboo*, 162-67.

150. Athanasios Moulakis, *Simone Weil and the Politics of Self-Denial* (Columbia: University of Missouri Press, 1998), 136-44; Mitchell and Black, *Freud and Beyond*, 85-134, 193-203; Ragland-Sullivan, *Jacques Lacan*, 16-67; Durkheim, *The Elementary Forms*, 204.

151. Alford, *Melanie Klein*, 57, 63-64, 74.

152. See Peirce, *Pragmatism as a Principle and Method of Right Thinking: The 1903 Harvard Lectures on Pragmatism* (Albany: State University of New York Press, 1997), 216. In lecture five of these seven Harvard lectures given in 1903, Peirce says, "I call a representamen which is determined by another representamen an *interpretant* of the latter" (Peirce's italics). Since I have already fully discussed my usage of Peirce's concept of *interpretant* in the introduction to this book, I need just briefly remind my reader here that I will be using this notion of "interpretant" to "determine" the functioning of a whole code, or system of signs. For example, in the code of *filiation* that I will outline below, it is the sign (or the "representamen," as Peirce had defined his concept of sign) of having once been a parent's child that determines the habits of attention (to parent-figures in society) in the cognition and communication of Durkheim's "primitives" (as described by Durkheim in *The Elementary Forms*). A useful way for my contemporary sociological reader to comprehend what I mean by that master sign, which by focusing communicative actors' atten-

tion upon itself, "determines" the particular "interpretant code" of those actors' society, has been suggested by Schwartz, *Vertical Classification*, 95. In citing the statement by George Herbert Mead asserting that "collective representations do not exist for the individual other than in the form of the 'generalized other,'" Schwartz in effect reminded me that how the "generalized other" is conceived by a society at any time in history will determine which "interpretant code" is dominant at that moment in history in the significance of that society's communication. In that code of "*filiation*" which I outline here as the pragmatic code governing the significations of preliterate societies, the Meadian "generalized other" is conceived along that axis of what Schwartz called "vertical stratification" between parent and child.

153. Peirce, *Reasoning*, 259-60; Durkheim, *The Elementary Forms*, 293-94; Thomas, "The Unconscious," 147; Thomas and Znaniecki, *The Polish Peasant*, 22-23.

154. Giddens, *Politics, Society, and Social Theory*, 257-58.

155. Rene Spitz, *The First Year of Life* (New York: International Universities Press, 1965), 81, cited in Schwartz, *Vertical Classification*, 103.

156. Schwartz, *Vertical Classification*, 212 n. 2, 216 n. 2, citing, respectively, Theodore Thass-Thienemann, *The Interpretation of Language*, vol. 1, *Understanding the Symbolic Meaning of Language* (New York: Jason Aronson, 1973), 39-42, and Peirce, *Collected Papers*, 2:157.

157. Schwartz, *Vertical Classification*, 24, 211 n. 1 (italics in original). David Bloor, "Durkheim and Mauss Revisited: Classification and the Sociology of Knowledge," in *Society and Knowledge: Contemporary Perspectives on the Sociology of Knowledge*, ed. Nico Stehr and Volker Meja (New Brunswick, N.J.: Transaction Books, 1984), 51-52—whose "strong programme in the sociology of knowledge" seems to be in agreement with Schwartz's other assertion that Durkheim had attributed "to modern conceptions more integrity and autonomy than they deserve"—also accuses Durkheim's sociology of knowledge, in both his 1901 writing with Mauss of "Primitive Classification" and his own 1912 writing of *The Elementary Forms of the Religious Life*, of having given "no systematic account" of the cognitive mechanism by which "they said the classification of things reproduces the classification of men."

158. Peter T. Manicas, "The Legitimation of the Modern State: A Historical and Structural Account," in *State Formation and Political Legitimacy*, ed. R. Cohen and J. D. Toland (New Brunswick, N.J.: Transaction Books, 1988), 177.

159. Julia Ching, *Mysticism and Kingship in China: The Heart of Chinese Wisdom* (Cambridge: Cambridge University Press, 1997), provides a very informative introduction, for the nonspecialist in Chinese history, to the historical relationship between Chinese philosophy's cognitive formulations and Chinese "kingship."

160. Gerhard E. Lenski, Patrick Nolan, and Jean Lenski, *Human Societies*. 7th ed. (New York: McGraw-Hill, 1995). Since Stephen K. Sanderson's 1999 book, *Social Transformations*, is dedicated to Gerhard Lenski (among others), I need remind my reader here that my Peircean evolutionist pragmatics encompasses Lenski's evolutionary themes without being purely "materialistic" in Sanderson's sense.

161. Schwartz, *Vertical Classification*, 27.

162. Schwartz, *Vertical Classification*, 213 n. 7.

163. Mary Douglas, *Implicit Meanings* (London: Routledge and Kegan Paul, 1975), xx, cited in Schwartz, *Vertical Classification*, 9.

164. Wayne M. Senner, "Theories and Myths on the Origins of Writing: A Historical Overview," in *The Origins of Writing,* ed. Wayne M. Senner (Lincoln: University of Nebraska Press, 1989), 1-26.

165. Alfred Burns, *The Power of the Written Word: The Role of Literacy in the History of Western Civilization* (New York: Peter Lang, 1989), 296.

166. Olson, *The World on Paper,* 60, 171, 195; Andre Maurois, *Olympio: The Life of Victor Hugo* (New York: Harper, 1956), 147-48, quoting from Victor Hugo's 1831 novel, *Notre Dame de Paris.*

167. Peirce, "The Place of Our Age," in *Writings of Charles S. Peirce,* 1:113.

168. Georg Simmel, "The Metropolis and Mental Life," in *The Sociology of Georg Simmel,* ed. Kurt H. Wolff (New York: Free Press, 1950), 421.

169. Schwartz, *Vertical Classification,* 213 n. 7

170. Benedict R. Anderson, *Imagined Communities: Reflections on the Origin and Spread of Nationalism* (London: Verso, 1983); Christine Van Boheemen-Saaf, "Derrida and *Filiation*" in *Joyce, Derrida, Lacan, and the Trauma of History: Reading, Narrative, and Postcolonialism* (Cambridge: Cambridge University Press, 1999), 181-84; D. C. Teel, "Excessive Children: Textual *Filiation* and the Command of the Other," in *Dissent and Marginality: Essays on the Borders of Literature and Religion,* ed. Kiyoshi Tsuchiya (London: MacMillan, 1997), 126-50; Harold Bloom, "Prologue: It Was a Great Marvel That They Were in the Father without Knowing Him," in *The Anxiety of Influence: A Theory of Poetry* (New York: Oxford University Press, 1973), 3.

171. Robert N. Bellah and Phillip E. Hammond, *Varieties of Civil Religion* (San Francisco: Harper & Row, 1980), captures my sense of a Lacanian "social unconscious"— with contemporary nationalism borrowing religious imagery to confer the emotional aura of traditional *filiation* upon modern linguistic transactions of *calibration*—better than does the overtly Lacanian Marxism of Fredric Jameson, *The Political Unconscious: Narrative as a Socially Symbolic Act* (Ithaca, N.Y.: Cornell University Press, 1981).

172. Arthur O. Lovejoy, *The Great Chain of Being: A Study of the History of an Idea* (Cambridge, Mass.: Harvard University Press, 1936).

173. Max Weber, *The Protestant Ethic and the Spirit of Capitalism* (New York: Scribner, 1958), 17 (italics in original). Weber's full statement in his introduction to this celebrated book is "But capitalism is identical with the pursuit of profit, and forever *renewed* profit, by means of continuous, rational, capitalistic enterprise."

174. H. R. Trevor-Roper, *Religion, the Reformation and Social Change, and Other Essays* (London: MacMillan, 1967), ix-x, 4-28; Harold J. Berman, *Law and Revolution: The Formation of the Western Legal Tradition* (Cambridge, Mass.: Harvard University Press, 1983), 103-31.

175. Olson, *The World on Paper,* 171.

176. William J. Bouwsma, "The Two Faces of Humanism: Stoicism and Augustinianism in Renaissance Thought," in *A Usable Past: Essays in European Cultural History* (Berkeley: University of California Press, 1990), 53, citing John Calvin, *Institutes,* II. ii. 13; IV. vi. 10.

177. Bouwsma, "The Two Faces," 52.

178. Jean Piaget, *The Origin of Intelligence in the Child* (London: Routledge & Kegan Paul, 1936). Louis Althusser, *For Marx* (New York: Pantheon Books, 1969), praised Hegel for having been the first thinker to conceive of history as a "process without

a subject," praise which, I think, should rightfully go to the framers of the American Constitution, who, in fashioning a "government of laws, and not of men," were, in effect, defining the American polity as a "process without a subject."

179. Weber, *Protestant Ethic*, 48, 157-58.

180. Alfred W. Crosby, *The Measure of Reality: Quantification and Western Society, 1250-1600* (Cambridge: Cambridge University Press, 1997).

181. Jean Gebser, *The Ever-Present Origin* (London: Ohio University Press, 1985), 11.

182. Wolfgang Iser, *The Act of Reading: A Theory of Aesthetic Response* (Baltimore, Md.: Johns Hopkins University Press, 1978), 35.

183. Harry Levin, *The Gates of Horn: A Study of Five French Realists* (New York: Oxford University Press, 1963).

184. Weber, *Protestant Ethic*, 182-83.

185. Weber, *Protestant Ethic*, 157-58; Georg Simmel, *The Philosophy of Money* (New York: Routledge, 1990).

186. Benjamin Nelson, *The Idea of Usury: From Tribal Brotherhood to Universal Otherhood* (Princeton, N.J.: Princeton University Press, 1949).

187. Peirce, *Reasoning*, 147.

188. John J. Fitzgerald, *Peirce's Theory of Signs as Foundation for Pragmatism* (The Hague: Mouton, 1966), 31.

189. Rotman, *Ad Infinitum*, 32.

190. Nelson, *The Idea of Usury*.

191. Charles S. Peirce, "I, IT, and THOU: A Book Giving Instruction in Some of the Elements of Thought," in *Writings of Charles S. Peirce*, 1: 45-46.

192. See Hookway, *Peirce*, 19-23.

193. Weston La Barre, *Shadow of Childhood*, 7-9, 18-22, 102-48, pushes this homology between the "childhood of society" and the individual's personal childhood to its logical limits by borrowing—from Steven Jay Gould, *Ontogeny and Phylogeny* (Cambridge, Mass.: Harvard University Press, 1977), 183-375—the idea of "neoteny," of a human as being really a "fetalized ape" whose "retardation as a life-history strategy for longer learning and socialization . . . clearly characterized human evolution" and which La Barre sees as responsible for all those social phenomena of religion and politics that I comprehend within my code of "*filiation*." With theoretical intentions similar to mine, the psychologist Kevin Fateux in his *The Recovery of Self: Regression and Redemption in Religious Experience* (Mahwah, N.J.: Paulist Press, 1994), has also comprehended religious experience as being a "regression" to childhood experience.

194. Emile Durkheim, *The Division of Labor in Society* (New York: Free Press, 1984), 204-5. Having completed the first of three parts by discussing the "function" of the division of labor, Durkheim had, in chapter 2 of book 2, focused upon the processes of increasing population "volume and density" as "causes" of a proportionate increase in the division of labor.

195. Basil Bernstein, *Class, Codes, and Control*, 3 vols. (London: Routledge & Kegan Paul, 1971-75); Melvin L. Kohn, *Class and Conformity: A Study in Values* (Chicago: University of Chicago Press, 1977).

196. Peirce, *Reasoning*, 235; Fitzgerald, *Peirce's Theory of Signs*, 45-56, 60, citing Peirce, *Collected Papers*, 1.369, 2.288, "the second is the *index* which . . . forces the attention to the particular object intended without describing it," and "some indices are more or

less detailed directions for what the hearer is to do in order to place himself in direct experiential or other connection with the thing meant," as, for example, the Notices to Mariners issued by the Coast Survey, "giving the latitude and longitude, four or five bearings of prominent objects, etc." so as to indicate the *"there"* spatial location of "a rock, or shoal, or buoy, or lightship. Although there will be other elements in such direction, yet in the main they are indices."

197. Roland Robertson (*Meaning and Change*, 128-29) deserves the credit for analytically separating out "the inner-worldly/other-worldly dimension" in Weber's sociology of religion (and giving it "analytic precedence") from its usual embedment, in conventional readings of Weber, within the other Weberian distinction of "asceticism/mysticism." This "reconstruction of Weber's Stance" by Robertson certainly facilitated my own reading of the "inner-worldly" vision of Calvin as a cognitive breakthrough to seeing the objective world independently of personal (divine) whimsy on a par with the cognitive achievement of "object-permanence" by Piaget's two-year-old infant.

198. Joseph Needham, *The Grand Titration: Science and Society in East and West* (Toronto: University of Toronto Press, 1969), 152. Needham's argument on the previous two pages (150-51) boils down to the tracing of Galileo Galilei's scientific achievement—which Needham takes as the decisive overtaking by Europe of China's scientific development (which had reached, according to Needham, a level equivalent to Leonardo da Vinci's atheoretical prowess in technology)—as being the theoretical unification of the tradesman/artisan's method of logical induction, with the scholar's method of logical deduction. These two hitherto separate and mutually antagonistic classes of artisans and scholars had been brought together in Galileo's Northern Italy, by the social intensity of its navigational effort.

199. Janet Abu-Lughod, "Discontinuities and Persistence: One World System or a Succession of Systems?" in *The World-System: Five Hundred Years or Five Thousand?* ed. Andre Gunder Frank and Barry K, Gills (London: Routledge, 1993), 288.

200. Robert Bellah, *Beyond Belief: Essays on Religion in a Post-Traditional World* (New York: Harper and Row, 1970), 20-36, 54-63. It should be noted that Bellah's two essays from which I cited themes here—"Religious Evolution" and "Reflections on the Protestant Ethic Analogy in India," respectively—are both traced in Bellah's footnotes to lectures and presentations going all the way back, in the case of the former essay, to 1956. Wolfgang Schlucter, *The Rise of Western Rationalism: Max Weber's Developmental History* (Berkeley: University of California Press, 1981) repeatedly refers to the "rationalism" that Weber saw as unique to Western history as the "rationalism of world-mastery." Inasmuch as the Western quest for the world's ratio led beyond Pythagoras—with Archimedes—outward into the empirical world, unlike the inward Buddhist quest for such ratio within the human mind, I believe Schlucter is correct. As a reader of different religious texts I am impressed, not only by St. Luke's account of St. Paul's "Odyssey" across the Eastern Mediterranean toward Rome but also by the sheer abundance of miracle accounts of Jesus involving water and its abundant riches (turning into wine, multiplying fishes)—and even more specifically, miraculous forms of navigation, such as calming stormy seas and walking on water—in contrast to the paucity of such water-related accounts either in the Hindu *Baghavat-Gita* or the Islamic *Koran* or *Hadith*. In contrast to the Christian canonical texts' reflection of their Hellenistic authors' reception of Jesus as master of the waters—a feeling of "being at home" on water going all the way back to the ecstatic Greek shouts of *"Thalassa,"* reported by historians, upon Alexander's sighting of the Persian Gulf—the Mosaic

narrative's accounts of the parting of the Red Sea and of striking water from rock seem to reflect a desert people's determination to stick to dry land at all costs.

201. Richard Valantasis, *The Gospel of Thomas* (New York: Routledge, 1997), 29-196, serves as an excellent up-to-date introduction to the manuscript sources of our current knowledge of this noncanonical gospel. Gregory J. Riley, *Resurrection Reconsidered: Thomas and John in Controversy* (Minneapolis, Minn.: Fortress Press, 1995), 7-126, presents, in detailed socio-historical analysis, the Eastern Mediterranean conflict—over the correct interpretation of the life and death of Jesus—between the Evangelist John's Hellenistic followers and the Asiatic disciples of Thomas that apparently resulted in "the periscope of Doubting Thomas" in the John 20:24-29.

202. Bryan S. Turner, *Max Weber: From History to Modernity* (London: Routledge, 1992), 51; Helmut Loiskandl, "Religion, Ethics, and Economic Interaction in Japan: Some Arguments in a Continuing Discussion," in *Religion and the Transformations of Capitalism: Comparative Approaches*, ed. Richard H. Roberts (London: Routledge, 1995), 63; Collins, *Weberian Sociological Theory*, 59.

203. Wen-yuan Qian, *The Great Inertia: Scientific Stagnation in Traditional China* (London: Croom Helm, 1985).

204. William Hardy McNeill, *The Pursuit of Power: Technology, Armed Force, and Society since A.D. 1000* (Chicago: University of Chicago Press, 1982); Ludwig Dehio, *Germany and World Politics in the Twentieth Century* (New York: Knopf, 1959).

205. Edward W. Said, *Orientalism* (New York: Pantheon Books, 1978).

206. Gunder Frank and Gills, *The World System*, 21, citing Martin Bernal, *Black Athena: The Afroasiatic Roots of Classical Civilization* (New Brunswick, N.J.: Rutgers University Press, 1987), and Samir Amin, *Eurocentrism* (London: Zed, 1989).

207. Gunder Frank and Gills, *The World System*, 21-22.

208. Immanuel M. Wallerstein, *The Modern World System*, 3 vols. (New York: Academic Press, 1974-1989); Janet L. Abu-Lughod, *Before European Hegemony: The World System A.D. 1250-1350* (New York: Oxford University Press, 1989).

209. Abu-Lughod, "Discontinuities," 289.

210. Gunder Frank and Gills, *World System*, 22.

211. Gunder Frank and Gills, *World System*, 21.

212. V. S. Varadarajan, *Algebra in Ancient and Modern Times* (Providence, R.I.: American Mathematical Society, 1998), 11-32, presents a lucid introduction to the mathematical thinking of the ancient Indians Aryabhata, Brahamagupta, and Bhaskara, in the context of "Pythagoras and the Pythagorean triplets." Bhascara-carya, *Lilavati* trans. Colebrooke (Allahabad, India: Kitab Mahal, 1967), contains Bhaskara's "Pythagorean" speculations about the number-ratios of the universe.

213. I owe to my University of Cincinnati colleague, Bulgarian-born historian Dr. Elizaveta Todorova, my awareness that Galileo's city of Pisa had been itself a center of navigational enterprise, like the Genoa of Christopher Columbus and of the financial and intellectual backers of the Portuguese Prince Henry the Navigator's navigational discoveries, which had been sharply etched into my consciousness earlier. Dr. Todorova also reminded me of Plato's famous characterization of Greek civilization as merely "frogs around a (Mediterranean) pond."

214. Imre Lakatos, *The Methodology of Scientific Research Programmes* (Cambridge: Cambridge University Press, 1978)

215. C. G. Jung, *Mysterium Coniunctionis: An Inquiry into the Separation and Synthesis of Psychic Opposites in Alchemy*, vol. 14 of his *Collected Works* (New York: Pantheon Books, 1963).

216. C. G. Jung, *The Archetypes and the Collective Unconscious*, 2d ed. (Princeton, N.J.: Princeton University Press, 1969), 177-78.

217. Mircea Eliade, *Patterns in Comparative Religion* (New York: New American Library, 1974), 374 n. 6, 422 n. 2, 436, citing C. G. Jung and K. Kerenyi, *Introduction to a Science of Mythology* (London: Routledge & Kegan Paul, 1951).

218. Eliade, *Patterns*, 191.

219. Balachandra Rajan, in *Under Western Eyes: India from Milton to Macaulay* (London: Duke University Press, 1999), 32, 43-44, writes about the Portuguese poet Luis Vaz de Camoes's *The Lusiads*—an epic celebration of Vasco da Gama's 1498 voyage to India, written in imitation of Virgil's *Aeneid*—that although "Camoes assiduously courts comparison with Virgil by making more than eighty allusions to the *Aeneid*," *The Lusiads* is nevertheless "Homeric rather than Virgilian," because "it invites reading as a work of imperialist innocence" and "is only marginally given to the self-examination that in Virgil undercuts victory with some of the sadness of things." It may just be the rare "privilege" that I enjoyed in being included within one of the last cohorts of schoolchildren in independent India to undergo a typical British colonial education—which mandated, rather fortuitously, the reading of Macaulay-like British historians writing about the colonial period of the British Raj immediately after reading Homer's *Odyssey* (in preparation for the high school O-level examinations)—that suggested, to my schoolboy mind, the extensive narrative similarities between the British colonial historians' accounts of the horrors of "the Black Hole of Calcutta" (and other Indian atrocities committed against British colonial families from the Battle of Plassey to the "Great Indian Mutiny of 1857"), and the Cyclops episode in Homer's *Odyssey*. Postcolonial writers have also noted the similarities between Ulysses' struggle with the Sirens' song and the typical colonialist fear of "going native," as portrayed, say, in E. M. Forster's *A Passage to India*. In the fact that British colonialists preferred to build their great cities—like Bombay, Calcutta, and Madras—within easy reach of their offshore ships (for easy escape in case of native "mutiny") lies readily visible evidence of the straight historical path from the navigational ethos of Homer's *Odyssey* to "Rule Brittania, Rule the Seas. . . ."

220. A. N. Wilson, *Paul: The Mind of the Apostle* (New York: W. W. Norton, 1997).

221. Ira Progoff, *Jung's Psychology and Its Social Meaning: An Introductory Statement of C. G. Jung's Psychological Theories and a First Interpretation of Their Significance for the Social Sciences* (New York: Julian Press, 1969), 167-68.

222. Durkheim, *The Division of Labor*, 204-5.

223. Progoff, *Jung's Psychology*, 168.

224. Georg Simmel, "The Metropolis and Mental Life," in *The Sociology of Georg Simmel*, ed. Kurt H. Wolff (New York: Free Press, 1950), 411.

225. Margaret A. Rose, *The Post-Modern and the Post-Industrial: A Critical Analysis* (Cambridge: Cambridge University Press, 1991), 9; Kurt Godel, *On Undecidable Propositions in Formal Mathematics Systems: Notes on Lectures by Kurt Godel, February-May 1934* (Princeton, N.J.: Institute for Advanced Study, 1934); William C. Price and Seymour S. Chissick, eds., *The Uncertainty Principle and Foundations of Quantum Mechanics: A Fifty Years' Survey* (New York: Wiley, 1977). Price and Chissick describe their

book as "a tribute to Professor Werner Heisenberg to commemorate the fiftieth anniversary of the formulation of quantum mechanics."

226. Rose, *The Post-Modern*, 9-10, citing vol. 8 of Arnold Toynbee's *A Study of History* (London: Oxford University Press, 1934-61). Young, *White Mythologies*, 180 n. 53, cites Charles Jencks, *What Is Post-Modernism?* (London: Academy Editions, 1986), 3, as also having given credit to Toynbee for his "early use of the term 'postmodern.'"

227. Robert B. Pippin, *Modernism as a Philosophical Problem: On the Dissatisfactions of European High Culture*, 2d ed. (Oxford: Blackwell, 1999), 168-70.

228. Lyotard, *The Postmodern Condition*, 42-43, 54-55, 58. Lyotard also focused, as I do, upon Pierre Laplace's perfectly deterministic physics as the ultimate exemplar of the zenith of modernity's expectations of total, universal *calibration*.

229. Chris Carleton, "Relativity, Uncertainty and Imaginary Time," in *The Silent Word: Textual Meaning and the Unwritten*, ed. Robert J. C. Young, Ban Kah Choon, and Robbie B. H. Goh (River Edge, N.J.: World Scientific, 1998) 71-79.

230. C. Wright Mills, *The Sociological Imagination* (New York: Oxford University Press, 1959), 22-23, 165-66.

231. Young, *White Mythologies*, 19, citing Toynbee, *A Study of History*, 9: 410.

232. Maurice Godelier, "Is the West the Universal Model for Humanity? The Baruya of New Guinea between Change and Decay," in *Terror and Consensus: Vicissitudes of French Thought*, ed. Jean-Joseph Goux and Philip R. Wood (Stanford, Calif.: Stanford University Press, 1998), 173-93.

233. Godelier, "Is the West," 174; Maurice Godelier, "Can Marx Survive the Collapse of Communism or 'Real Socialism'?" in *Post-Marxism and the Middle East*, ed. Faleh A. Jabar (London: Saqi Books, 1997), 41-66; Maurice Godelier, *Rationality and Irrationality in Economics* (London: New Left Books, 1972).

234. Zygmunt Bauman, *Life in Fragments* (Oxford: Blackwell, 1995), 24.

235. David Slater, "Other Contexts of the Global: A Critical Geopolitics of North-South Relations," in *Globalization: Theory and Practice*, ed. Eleonore Kofman and Gillian Youngs (New York: Pinter, 1996), 278-79, citing Roland Robertson, *Globalization: Social Theory and Culture* (London: Sage, 1992), 27.

236. Robertson, *Globalization*, 27, citing Anthony Giddens, *The Consequences of Modernity* (Stanford, Calif.: Stanford University Press, 1990).

237. Robertson, *Globalization*, 13-14, 144-45.

238. Young, *White Mythologies*, 19. Robertson, *Globalization*, 162 n. 1, asserted that Toynbee's "work, however controversial, has been an important stimulus to civilization analysis and world history," and contrasted that Toynbean oeuvre with Spengler's German *kulturpessimismus* in that "Toynbee rejected Spengler's denial of *communication between different civilizations*. Toynbee insisted on seeing world history in terms of the *mixing* of ideas and/or people; Spengler considered such mixing to be a sign of *degeneration*. . . . This inattention to 'mixing' and to inter-civilizational matters has been a common characteristic of much of German social theory to this day" (Robertson's italics).

239. Robertson, *Globalization*, 99-100 (italics in original).

240. Robertson, *Globalization*, 100, 173 (italics in original), citing Fredric Jameson, "Postmodernism; or, The Cultural Logic of Late Capitalism," *New Left Review* 146 (1984).

241. Robertson, *Globalization*, 78, 132.

242. Jameson, preface to *The Cultures of Globalization*, xi-xii.

243. Young, *White Mythologies*, 91, citing Fredric Jameson, "Cognitive Mapping," in *Marxism and the Interpretation of Culture*, ed. Cary Nelson and Lawrence Grossberg (London: Macmillan, 1988), 347.

244. Young, *White Mythologies*, 20, 117.

245. Young, *White Mythologies*, 91-92, 117, citing Jameson, *The Political Unconscious*, 102, and Terry Eagleton, "The Idealism of American Criticism," *New Left Review* 127 (1981), 60.

246. Lyotard, *Postmodern Condition*, 18-27.

247. Peirce, *Collected Papers*, 5.436.

248. Bunge, *Metascientific Queries*, 109; Levi-Strauss, *Tristes Tropiques* (New York: Atheneum, 1974), 57.

249. Young, *White Mythologies*, 92.

250. Robertson, *Globalization*, 100-101.

251. Robertson, "The Sociological Significance," 5.

252. Robertson, *Globalization*, 4.

253. Brian Rotman, *Signifying Nothing: The Semiotics of Zero* (London: MacMillan, 1987), 78-86.

254. Luhmann, "The Evolutionary Differentiation," 123-25.

255. Joseph A. Schumpeter, *Capitalism, Socialism, and Democracy* (New York: Harper, 1942). I should clarify that while I see market exchange as operating under the signification code of *calibration*, I see the inheritance of property as an evolutionary "survival" from premodern *filiation* to be progressively abolished—in a democratic process of Pragmatic social learning—in order to live more fully within *calibration*. The Marxian error in the twentieth century has been to summarily abolish the premodern *filiation* within inherited property and discover too late that what they had really abolished had been the free exchanges of modern *calibration*, instead, thereby regressing to that psychotic variant of *filiation* to the Stalinist "big brother"!

256. Luhmann, "The Evolutionary Differentiation," 112.

257. Simmel, "Metropolis," 421. Franco Moretti, *Modern Epic: The World-System from Goethe to Garcia Marquez* (London: Verso, 1996), 123-67, traces the shattering impact on the "stream of consciousness" of individual subjectivity, of that "intensification of nervous stimulation" that Simmel had seen the explosive growth of the objective world causing, a century ago.

258. Robert E. Lane, *The Loss of Happiness in Market Democracies* (New Haven, Conn.: Yale University Press, 2000), 36-192, 319-37. What Lane seems unwilling to accept is that "the way home" out of *calibration*'s unhappiness can only be found through the long-term construction of a new cognitive-communicative interpretant code, and not through political action by individuals blinded by the constraints of the old codes of *filiation* and *calibration*.

259. Jos de Mul, *Romantic Desire in (Post)Modern Art and Philosophy* (Albany: State University of New York Press, 1999), 64-65, has a brief but accurate portrayal of J. W. von Goethe's role in "the ambivalence of romantic desire."

260. Robertson, *Globalization*, 177-78.

261. Lane, *The Loss*, 319-37.

262. Lyotard, *Postmodern Condition*, 18-21, 37. In contrast to Lyotard, Levi-Strauss (*Tristes Tropiques*, 412) had said: "The final step, which cannot be achieved without all the others, validates them all retroactively. In its own way and on its own level, each one

corresponds to a truth. Between the Marxist critique which frees man from his initial bondage—by teaching him that the apparent meaning of his condition evaporates as soon as he agrees to see things in a wider context—and the Buddhist critique which completes his liberation, there is neither opposition nor contradiction."

263. Richard Rorty, introduction to *Contingency, Irony, and Solidarity* (New York: Cambridge University Press, 1989), xv-xvi; Lyotard, *Postmodern Condition*, 42-43.

264. Rorty, *Contingency*, xv-xvi; Lyotard, *Postmodern Condition*, 37; Godel, *On Undecidable Propositions*.

265. Rorty, *Contingency*, xv-xvi.

266. Daniel Bell, *The Cultural Contradictions of Capitalism* (New York: Basic Books, 1976), 53-54.

267. Baudrillard, *Simulations*, 102, cited in Rex Butler, *Jean Baudrillard: The Defence of the Real* (London: Sage, 1999), 48; Rescher, "The Ontology of the Possible," 179; Putnam, *Meaning and the Moral Sciences*.

268. Rorty, *Contingency*, 123.

269. Rescher, *Communicative Pragmatism*, 197 (italics in original).

270. Norris, *Against Relativism*, 248-65.

271. Rescher, *Communicative Pragmatism*, 198.

272. Peirce, *Collected Papers*, 1.339.

273. Rescher, *Communicative Pragmatism*, 198.

274. Peirce, *Collected Papers*, 1.339.

275. Rescher, *Communicative Pragmatism*, 199-200.

276. Ernest Gellner, *Culture, Identity, and Politics*, 154-55, citing Bell, *Contradictions*, 53-54.

277. Jon M. Shepard, *Sociology* 7th ed. (Belmont, Calif.: Wadsworth, 1999), 516.

278. Alvin Toffler, *The Third Wave* (New York: Morrow, 1980).

279. Rescher, *Communicative Pragmatism*, 197; Norris, *Against Relativism*, 248-65.

280. Young, *White Mythologies*, 19.

281. Zygmunt Bauman, *Intimations of Postmodernity* (London: Routledge, 1992), 187-88 (italics in original).

282. Peirce, *Collected Works*, 1.337.

283. Zygmunt Bauman, "Morality Begins at Home; or, Can There Be a Levinasian Macro-Ethics?" in *Closeness: An Ethics*, ed. Harald Jodalen and Arne Johan Vetlesen (Oslo: Scandinavian University Press, 1997), 218-45. For similar thoughts on Levinas by Bauman, see also Zygmunt Bauman, *Postmodernity and Its Discontents* (New York: New York University Press, 1997), 46-71, and *Mortality, Immortality, and Other Life Strategies* (Stanford, Calif.: Stanford University Press, 1992), 161-200.

284. Bauman, *Intimations*, 188.

285. Peirce, *Collected Papers*, 1.369; Fitzgerald, *Peirce's Theory of Signs*, 62-63, citing Peirce, *Collected Papers*, 3.360; Rotman, *Ad Infinitum*, 32.

286. Camic, "The Matter," 1040-45; Peirce, *Collected Papers*, 1.337; Bauman, *Intimations*, 188.

287. Peirce, *Collected Papers*, 1.337; Bauman, *Intimations*, 187-88.

288. Bauman, *Intimations*, 188.

289. Arjun Appadurai, "Disjuncture and Difference in the Global Cultural Economy," *Public Culture* 2, no. 2 (Spring 1990): 6-21.

290. James Gleick, *Chaos: Making a New Science* (New York: Viking, 1987), 4-6.

291. Gleick, *Chaos*, 29, 114; Popper, *Objective Knowledge*, 206-55; Ben Goertzel, *From Complexity: Explorations in Evolutionary, Autopoietic, and Cognitive Dynamics* (New York: Plenum Press, 1997), xv-xxvi, 371.

292. Goertzel, *From Complexity*, xv.

293. Lyotard, *Postmodern Condition*, 9, 81.

294. Thomas Herzog, *Einfuhrung in die moderne Kunst* (Zurich: Classen, 1948), 148, 152, cited by Jean Gebser, *Ever-Present Origin*, 476-77.

295. Lyotard, *Postmodern Condition*, 42-43, 55.

296. Nicholas Rescher, *Cognitive Economy: The Economic Dimension of the Theory of Knowledge* (Pittsburgh, Pa.: University of Pittsburgh Press, 1989); Gleick, *Chaos*, 6-7.

297. Roger Penrose, *The Emperor's New Mind: Concerning Computers, Minds, and the Laws of Physics* (Oxford: Oxford University Press, 1989), discusses Hawking's version of the "anthropic principle." John D. Barrow and Frank J. Tipler, *The Anthropic Cosmological Principle* (Oxford: Oxford University Press, 1996), presents and discusses this principle more generally.

298. Hookway, *Peirce*, 262-88.

299. Zoltan Torey, *The Crucible of Consciousness: A Personal Exploration of the Conscious Mind* (Oxford: Oxford University Press, 1999), 263.

300. Torey, *Crucible*, 230.

301. Gordon Rattray Taylor, *The Natural History of the Mind* (New York: E. P. Dutton, 1979), 49.

302. Karl H. Pribram, *Brain and Perception: Holonomy and Structure in Figural Processing* (Hillsdale, N.J.: Lawrence Erlbaum Associates, 1991).

303. Roger Penrose, *Shadows of the Mind: A Search for the Missing Science of Consciousness* (Oxford: Oxford University Press, 1994).

304. Taylor, *Natural History*, 250 (italics added).

305. Luhmann, "Evolutionary Differentiation," 126.

306. Robertson, *Globalization*, 78.

307. Peirce, *Collected Papers*, 1.338.

308. Gleick, *Chaos*, 29, 114; Popper, *Objective Knowledge*, 206-55; Robertson, *Globalization*, 78; Peirce, *Collected Papers*, 1.338.

309. Robertson, *Globalization*, 100 (italics in original).

310. Robertson, *Globalization*, 177-78.

311. Robertson, *Globalization*, 178.

312. Charles Taylor, "The Politics of Recognition," in *Multiculturalism*, ed. Charles Taylor (Princeton, N.J.: Princeton University Press, 1994), 44.

313. Jyotsna G. Singh, *Colonial Narratives, Cultural Dialogues: "Discoveries" of India in the Language of Colonialism* (London: Routledge, 1996), 68-69, cited by Richard King, *Postcolonial Theory, India, and "the Mystic East"* (London: Routledge, 1999), 131.

314. Singh, *Colonial Narratives*, 66.

315. Singh, *Colonial Narratives*, 66.

316. Robertson, *Globalization*, 78.

317. Andrew Mango, *Attaturk* (New York: Overlook Press, 1999), 492-511, shows the supposed "Westernizer" Attaturk propounding rather surprising theories about the supremacy of Turkish history and language.

318. Hamid Dabashi, *Theology of Discontent*, 102-46.

319. Maggie Phillips and Claire Frederick, *Healing the Divided Self: Clinical and Ericksonian Hypnotherapy for Post-Traumatic and Dissociative Conditions* (New York: Norton, 1995), 310-28, citing Pierre Teilhard de Chardin, *On Happiness* (London: Collins, 1966).

320. Stan Royal Mumford, *Himalayan Dialogue: Tibetan Lamas and Gurung Shamans in Nepal* (London: University of Wisconsin Press, 1989), 16-27, citing Mikhail Bakhtin, *The Dialogic Imagination* (Austin: University of Texas Press, 1981), 16-27; Stan Mumford, "Tibetan Identity Layers in the Nepal Himalayas" in *Selves in Time and Place: Identities, Experience, and History in Nepal*, ed. Debra Skinner, Alfred Pach III, and Dorothy Holland (Lanham, Md.: Rowman & Littlefield, 1998), 176-77.

321. Robertson, *Globalization*, 78.

322. David G. Becker, Richard L. Sklar, Jeff Frieden, and Sayre P. Schatz, eds. *Postimperialism: International Capitalism and Development in the Late Twentieth Century* (London: Lynne Rienner, 1987); David G. Becker and Richard L. Sklar, eds., *Postimperialism and World Politics* (London: Praeger, 1999), 1-13.

323. Robertson, *Globalization*, 100, 173-74.

324. Abu-Lughod, *Before European Hegemony*.

325. Abu-Lughod, *Discontinuities and Persistence*, 288.

326. Eduardo H. Galeano, *Open Veins of Latin America: Five Centuries of the Pillage of a Continent* (New York: Monthly Review Press, 1973).

327. I give full credit to Roland Robertson for having suggested to me—in a private communication during the summer of 1988—that a modern global cultural system might resemble a superimposed Parsonsian A-G-I-L grid stuck onto a global map. At that time— with the Soviet Union on the verge of collapse—I had dismissed this idea of a Parsonsian world system, but more information about the Japanese Ministry of Finance, among other regional details about the Southern Hemisphere, together with my growing awareness of a needed semantic component to a Peircean theory of evolutionary globalization, now has me borrowing Robertson's original hypothesis, with some modifications.

328. Lest my reader seem surprised that I should end this book on Peirce with a Parsonsian cultural world system, I remind my reader that in chapter 3, I explained why the social world of institutions belonged to the semantic study of meaning, rather than to pragmatics.

329. Joseph H. Carens, "Possessive Individualism and Democratic Theory: Macpherson's Legacy," in *Democracy and Possessive Individualism: The Intellectual Legacy of C. B. Macpherson*, ed. Joseph H. Carens (Albany: State University of New York, 1993).

330. P. Q. Hirst, *Durkheim, Bernard, and Epistemology* (London: Routledge & Kegan Paul, 1975), 64.

331. Michael Omi and Harry Winant, *Racial Formation in the United States: From the 1960s to the 1990s* (New York: Routledge, 1994).

332. Jay Fliegelman, *Prodigals and Pilgrims: The American Revolution against Patriarchal Authority, 1750-1800* (Cambridge: Cambridge University Press, 1982).

333. Alvin W. Gouldner, *The Two Marxisms: Contradictions and Anomalies in the Development of Theory* (New York: Seabury Press, 1980).

334. Eamonn Fingleton, *Blindside: Why Japan Is Still on Track to Overtake the U.S. by the Year 2000* (Boston: Houghton Mifflin, 1995), 128-69, 310.

335. Richard S. Sklar, "Postimperialism: Concepts and Implications," in Becker and Sklar, *Postimperialism and World Politics*, 23; Jeffrey Moussaieff Masson, *The Oceanic Feeling: The Origins of Religious Sentiment in Ancient India* (Boston: Reidel, 1980).

336. Declan Quigley, "Is a Theory of Caste Still Possible?" in *Contextualizing Caste*, ed. Mary Searle-Chatterjee and Ursula Sharma (Oxford: Blackwell, 1994), 42.

337. Narasingha Prosad Sil, *Swami Vivekananda: A Reassessment* (Selinsgrove, Pa.: Susquehanna University Press, 1997); Roxanne L. Euben, *Enemy in the Mirror: Islamic Fundamentalism and the Limits of Modern Rationalism* (Princeton, N.J.: Princeton University Press, 1997), 56-92; Elizabeth Sirriyeh, *Sufis and Anti-Sufis: The Defence, Rethinking, and Rejection of Sufism in the Modern World* (Richmond, England: Curzon, 1999), 164-72.

338. Julian Barnes, *Flaubert's Parrot* (New York: McGraw-Hill, 1984), 104.

339. Gustavo A. Alfaro, "Five Hundred Years of Latin American Literature," in *Latin America: An Interdisciplinary Approach*, ed. Julio Lopez-Arias and Gladys M. Varona-Lacey (New York: Peter Lang, 1999), 192.

340. Wendy B. Faris, "Scheherazade's Children: Magical Realism and Postmodern Fiction," in Lois Parkinson Zamora and Wendy B. Faris, eds., *Magical Realism: Theory, History, Community* (Durham, N.C.: Duke University Press, 1995), 163–190.

341. Danow, *Magical Realism and the Grotesque* (Lexington: University of Kentucky Press, 1995), 70.

342. Colin A. Ross, *Dissociative Identity Disorder: Diagnosis, Clinical Features, and Treatment of Multiple Personality Disorder* (New York: John Wiley & Sons, 1997), 64.

343. Brenda Cooper, *Magical Realism in West African Fiction: Seeing with a Third Eye* (London: Routledge, 1998).

344. Ross, *Dissociative Identity Disorder*, 10-13.

345. Robertson, *Globalization*, 175.

INDEX

ABOUT THE AUTHOR

Blasco José Sobrinho is assistant professor of sociology at the University of Cincinnati. Building upon this book's Pragmatist critique of Jacques Lacan's psychoanalysis, he is currently exploring the applicability of Charles S. Peirce's sociocognitive homology to Heinz Kohut's self-psychology so as to map the history of Western Orientalism through Kohut's "grandiose self/idealized other" polarity. Dr. Sobrinho pulls inspiration for his research from a wide range of disciplines, including the history and philosophy of science, theology and religion, and social psychology.